Folklore Genres

Publications of the American Folklore Society
Bibliographical and Special Series
General Editor, Wm. Hugh Jansen
VOLUME 26   1976

Folklore Genres

Edited by Dan Ben-Amos

University of Texas Press   Austin & London

Library of Congress Cataloging in Publication Data
Main entry under title:

Folklore genres.

(Publications of the American Folklore Society, bibliographical and special
series; v. 26)
Originally published in Genre, 1969 and 1971.
Includes index.
CONTENTS: Literary and linguistic analysis of folklore genres: Utley, F. L.
Oral genres as a bridge to written literature. Lüthi, M. Aspects of the Märchen
and the legend. Bynum, D. E. [etc.]
  1. Folk-lore—Theory, methods, etc.—Addresses, essays, lectures. 2. Folk-
lore—Classification—Addresses, essays, lectures. I. Ben-Amos, Dan. II. Genre.
III. Series: American Folklore Society. Bibliographical and special series; v. 26.
GR40.F64   398   75-17698
ISBN 0-292-72415-2

Contents

Part Three. The Classification of Folklore Genres

Acknowledgments

The essays that comprise this symposium were originally published in *Genre* 2, nos. 2–3 (1969): 91–301, and 4, no. 3 (1971): 281–304. They are reprinted here with minor editorial changes, by permission of the University of Illinois Press and the Faculty-Student Association of the State University College of Arts and Sciences, Plattsburgh, New York. I would like to thank the editors of *Genre*, Donald E. Billiar, Edward F. Heuston, and Robert L. Vales, for their receptivity to the idea of the symposium and for their assistance in the preparation of these essays for original publication. Earlier, Francis Lee Utley had urged them to deal with the subject in their journal, and, as soon as he learned of my proposed symposium, he offered his full support and contributed an essay to the present collection. Hence, we were particularly saddened by his death in 1974. Last, but not least, I wish also to thank William Hugh Jansen, without whose encouragement and help the symposium would not have been published in its present form.

Introduction

DAN BEN-AMOS

Like other literary genres, symposia have their own distinctive features, proprieties, and purposes; they adhere to clear conventions—
of which this Introduction is one—and generate distinct expectations.
They have characteristics that distinguish them from related genres
and "archaic" patterns that set models for each individual symposium.
The main attribute of this genre is unity within diversity: the essays
examine a single subject from different theoretical perspectives or,
conversely, apply a single theory to a variety of subjects. Often the
articles are explorative not conclusive in nature. As a meeting place
of ideas symposia often generate new thoughts rather than provide a
contemplative overview of past achievements and discarded theories.
The sense of immediacy with which such essays vibrate actually
hinders them from exhausting a subject. After all the ink has dried
and the typewriters have been silenced, there still remain many relevant questions that are merely alluded to, hardly elucidated. Other
problems are not mentioned at all, and not necessarily because they
lack import.

Certainly, the present symposium has most of the shortcomings that
characterize the genre; we trust that it has also retained some of the
merits. The contributors, in discussing the concept of genre in folklore—the unifying thread of the symposium—draw upon either recent field research or new directions in folklore, literary criticism,
linguistics, and anthropology. The variety of subjects and methods
underscores both the diversity of oral literary experience and the current interdisciplinary fervor in folklore scholarship. This heterogenei-
ty, it is hoped, will not generate a sense of futility but will encourage
debate about folklore genres, their heuristic value, and their significance as cultural constraints of communication.

The Position of the Concept of Genre
in Folklore Scholarship

The concept of genre has attained a central position in folklore, per-
meating instruction, publication, and research in the field. University
courses are organized around such subjects as the folktale, the ballad,
and the oral epic. Folklorists, in fact, were among those who pio-
neered "Type" courses within the academic curriculum in the United
States. Francis J. Child's lectures on "The English and Scottish Popular Ballad," offered at Harvard during 1894–1895 and once again in
1895–1896, constituted one of the early genre-oriented courses in
American universities. After Child's death, George L. Kittredge presented the course every odd year from 1897 on. On the West Coast,
another of Child's students, William M. Hart, introduced similarly
designed courses on the ballad, the epic, and the gest at the University
of California, Berkeley, during 1903–1904. The folk story received
somewhat limited attention; among the major universities only Columbia included a course by that title, offered by G. P. Krapp at Teachers
College during 1902–1903.[1] In later years, after Type-oriented courses
had declined in literature programs, their position was sustained and
even strengthened in folklore studies. A survey of the growth of folklore courses in American universities conducted by Richard M. Dorson
in 1948 indicates that "beyond the survey level, some sentiment exists
for Type courses, as 'The Popular Ballad' or 'The Folktale,' while
several advanced programs recognize area and regional unities, such
as 'Folklore of Southeastern Pennsylvania,' 'Southwestern Hispanic
Folklore,' and 'Folk Culture of the Baltic States.' "[2] Actually, genres
have served as the principle of organization even for lectures on regional or ethnic folklore. For example, Alfred L. Schoemaker describes
his course on "Pennsylvania Folk Literature in Standard German" in
the catalog of Franklin and Marshall College as follows: "A study of
popular ballads, folk songs, spirituals, proverbs and riddles, and of
popular literature as disseminated by Pennsylvania-printed German
broadsides, pamphlets, almanacs, books and newspapers."[3] At present,
as folklore courses have multiplied and several degree-conferring
programs have been established, genre-oriented classes have retained
a respectable position in the university curriculum. Of all the schools
that report teaching folklore, 33 percent list courses on ballad and

folksong and 13 percent on the folktale. These two topics are the second and fourth in popularity, trailing respectively only general introduction to the field (55%), and surveys of American folklore (30%).[4]

Perhaps genres have functioned to systematize publications even more than curricula. As any cursory glance at folklore journals and bibliographies reveals, genre principles are the basis of most text collections, anthologies, and indexes. A volume of folktales rarely includes ballads or proverbs, and a book of riddles seldom contains texts of legends. Like the biblical wool and linen that do not mingle (Deuteronomy 22:11), prose and poetry are kept apart in publications of oral literature. Even ethnic and regional surveys designed to present a body of folklore in its entirety use generic standards as principles of organization. The chapter headings, for example, of Y. M. Sokolov, *Russian Folklore* (New York: Macmillan, 1950), read like a list of Russian folklore genres: "Wedding Ceremonials and Chants," "Funeral Ceremonies and Laments," "Laments for Recruits or Departing Soldiers," "Divinations and Charms," "Proverbs and Riddles," "The *Byliny*," "Historical Songs," "Religious Verses," "Tales," "Folk Drama," "Lyric Songs," and so forth.[5] More recently, Ruth Finnegan, in *Oral Literature in Africa* (Oxford: Clarendon, 1970), has adhered to a similar system of presentation; she divides all of African oral literature into three parts: Poetry, Prose, and Some Special Forms. The chapter headings reflect the particular genres that prevail in Africa: "Panegyric," "Elegiac Poetry," "Religious Poetry," "Special Purpose Poetry—War, Hunting, and Work," "Lyric," "Topical and Political Songs," "Children's Song and Rhymes," "Prose Narratives," "Proverbs," "Riddles," "Oratory, Formal Speaking, and Other Stylized Forms," "Drum Language and Literature," "Drama." Perhaps the exception that stresses the rule is Richard M. Dorson's *American Folklore* (Chicago: University of Chicago Press, 1959), which traces the emergence of oral tradition in the New World, historically and regionally, not generically, from Colonial New England to modern life in big cities and on campuses.

The genre orientation in folklore publication is a direct continuation of the first stage of research—the very act of collecting. Whenever folklore expeditions enter new territories they espy genres of oral traditions and often concentrate on a single species at a time. The three types of collecting projects that Kenneth S. Goldstein describes in his *A Guide for Field Workers in Folklore* (Hatboro, Pa.: Folklore Associates, 1964), "Survey Projects," "Depth Projects," and "Local Projects," vary in intensity, not in basic approach. All concentrate on kinds of folklore, only the scope and the nature of the group varies.

Moreover, not only are collecting projects or literary analyses based upon the concept of genre but also those anthropological and psychological studies of folklore that seek to discover the dynamics of culture. For example, Jerome R. Mintz's description of Hasidic culture as reflected in oral tradition relies almost exclusively on a single genre, the legend, omitting the proverbs and songs with which Hasidic folklore abounds.[6] Similarly, Roger Abrahams's attempt "to show how much insight can be obtained into the life of a group through the analysis of its folklore"[7] hinges basically upon three specific forms—the dozens, the toast, and the joke—spoken by the black peoples of South Philadelphia whose culture he describes. The idea of genre in general and these respective forms in particular have served both Mintz and Abrahams as frameworks for field research and cultural study; they have utilized genre as a methodological paradigm that enabled them to formulate problems and to propose solutions.

The Concept of Genre in Folklore

Undoubtedly, this brief survey demonstrating the dominant role the concept of genre has had in the instruction, research, and publication of folklore is for many a truism, a rehash of the familiar. It points to facts and ideas we all take for granted and hardly pause to contemplate; they accompany the student from the moment he chances upon an introductory textbook until he hands in, with a sigh of relief, his doctoral dissertation. Given the extent to which the concept of genre figures in folklore studies, it is doubly startling to realize that, as Alan Dundes has stated, "thus far in the illustrious history of the discipline, not so much as one genre has been completely defined."[8] Such a critical statement reflects not only the development of folklore from an avocation to a science requiring rigor and clarity in the definition of terms, but it also indicates the continuous changes in theoretical perspectives that pervade folklore. After all, the adequacy of generic descriptions depends entirely on the theoretical view they are designed to satisfy.

Initially terms for folklore genres were words in a language, devoid of any theoretical significance. They were the words for speaking about speech and for conceiving of categories of tradition. Terms like *myth*, *tale*, *legend*, *proverb*, or *riddle*, had meanings in English—and their correlates in other languages—long before they acquired new connotations from evolutionary, functional, and structural theories. With the consolidation of folklore studies into a discipline and a method, proponents of various theoretical persuasions defined these terms of genres, enumerated their attributes, and formulated their structures from their respective perspectives. Each claimed to have revealed, once and for all, the real nature of the particular genres; each thought to have removed the words from the context of "natural language," in which ambiguities, ambivalences, historical changes, and multiplicity of meanings appear to reign, and to have successfully considered them terms in the language of science, whose meanings are clear and specific referents.

The failure of folklore in this respect is common knowledge and hardly a surprise. Unfortunately, the learned dialogues have not achieved their set goals; the qualities of genres have rarely become definitive and the descriptions of terms have seldom reached a wide consensus. As might have been expected, natural and scientific languages have not easily meshed. Words like *myth*, *legend*, and *tale* have retained their previous connotations even when redefined as terms for classes, and thus the blurred boundaries which exist in reality have affected the analytical categories of formal models. Consequently, some folklorists either have called for a complete overhaul of genre terms and their definitions or have offered an even more radical solution to the problem by suggesting exclusion of the concept of genre from folklore research, at least for a while. For example, Robert Georges has examined a hypothetical synthesis of legend definitions and finds it illogical, inconsistent, and hence dismissable.[9] He insists that before any research on this genre continues there is a need to have "a new concept of legend upon which we can build with assurance and integrity."[10] In another vein, Alan Dundes has argued that the

concept of genre in general impedes folklore research because it pre-
vents scholars from examining the folk ideas that underlie and per-
meate verbal expressions. It has become too narrow and too shallow
as an explanatory principle for the dynamics of tradition. Dundes
points out that there is a wide domain in folklore that does not fit
into the constraints of any existing categorization system and consequently has not been and will not be fully explored as long as the
genre research paradigm prevails.[11]

How then has a concept so dominant in folklore research and instruction reached this critical point, at which its dismissal is seriously
considered? Apparently at least a partial reason for this situation can
be found in the fact that folklorists have worked at cross-purposes.
While arguing for the merits of one definition or another, they have
neglected to clarify whether they subscribe to the same concept of
genre. A brief examination of the various definitional debates about
folklore forms reveals that the crux of the dispute lies not in differences of opinions about what a proverb, a legend, or a ballad is, but
in the diverse conceptions of the general category to which all these
forms belong; that is, at variance are not the principles for describing
single forms but the general ideas of what kind of a category genre is.

Comparative literature, another discipline in which the concept of
genre functions significantly, is in a similar state of quandary. Elias
Schwartz notes that "critics have tended to steer clear of the topic [of
genre]."[12] An example of such strategy of avoidance is Paul Hernadi's *Beyond Genre: New Directions in Literary Classification* (Ithaca:
Cornell University Press, 1972). This book is, among other things, a
comprehensive survey of major theories of genre, as developed by
modern critics and theoreticians of literature. But nowhere is the nature of the concept they use for their poetics examined. Claudio Guillén is more specific about his intent. He examines systems of poetics
from historical perspectives and deliberately avoids facing "the problems posed by the concept of genre itself."[13]

Yet it is these problems, rather than their surface manifestations,
which are responsible for the incongruities, discrepancies, and divergencies between the various models for genre distinctions. The choice
of features for defining genres is secondary to the ideas about what
folklore forms really are. In folklore scholarship these differences in
views do not necessarily parallel historically recognized trends in folk-

lore such as the historic-geographic, the anthropological, the psychological, the structural, and the contextual.[14] Quite often folklorists of conflicting persuasions subscribe to the same concept of genre in oral tradition, and, conversely, within any given school there may be competing views of the nature of distinctions of genres in folklore.

In the course of time students of folklore have attributed to the term *genre*, its correlates, and the particular forms subsumed under it at least four distinct meanings: (*a*) classificatory categories, (*b*) permanent form, (*c*) evolving form, and (*d*) form of discourse. Each concept serves a specific research purpose but would not be applicable to other analytical problems. Once the limited capacities of each concept are recognized, the respective notions of genre can continue to function in folklore scholarship and provide a framework for suitable projects.

Genres as Classificatory Categories

During the late nineteenth century and first half of the twentieth century, the formulation of a classification system in folklore was considered a prerequisite for any progress in scientific research. Such a strategy had pragmatic and logical foundations, as well as precedents in other disciplines. A coherent classification system introduces principles of order into an apparent chaotic mass of information by establishing features, forms, and subjects as criteria for organization and by revealing patterns in multitudes of detail and individual cases. The eighteenth-century Swedish botanist Carolus Linnaeus (1707–1778) provided a model. His classification revolutionized the biological sciences, and, by inference, students of folklore projected that a folklore classification system would have the same effect on research into traditional life and literature.[15] Stith Thompson, Carl W. von Sydow, and Vladímir Propp, to name but three prominent twentieth-century scholars, regard the construction of an adequate classification system as the initial step in research, preceding any other analytical endeavor.[16] All have realized that, ideally, any classification system should correspond to the actual traditional forms; otherwise it would be devoid of any practical use. The major categories for systematic classification of folklore, therefore, have first been the recognized European genres such as tales, legends, ballads, proverbs, and riddles.

Theoretically the different genres of folklore could have been ideal categories for such an organization scheme. Goethe's analogy between forms in nature and genres in poetry would have yielded support to such a system.[17] But in fact neither assumption proved true. Classification systems did not have the same effect in folklore that they had in natural sciences, and genres played but a secondary role in their formation. Whereas Linnaeus discovered the order inherent in nature, folklorists constructed models of ideal order and imposed them upon the reality of tradition.

Apparently, Propp and von Sydow realized this fault in the major typology of narratives that the Finnish school in folklore research produced, Aarne and Thompson's, *The Types of the Folktale* (2d ed., Folklore Fellows Communications, no. 184; Helsinki: Suomalainen Tiedeakatemia, 1961). They challenged this system, seeking better correspondence between the abstract categories of animal, ordinary, humorous, and formula tales and the actual formal differences between tales of each kind. Respectively, each of them proposed morphological attributes and number of characters as the distinctive features of prose-narrative genres. However, in doing so, they either ignored or missed the basic purpose and premise underlying the classificatory endeavors of most of the historic-geographic scholars. The purpose of the Finnish folklorists and their colleagues in other countries was not the discovery of regularities and patterns but the design of a system that would facilitate the historical reconstruction of tales and motifs and the tracing of their geographical distribution. They searched for themes, not forms, in their quest for the transformations of narratives and episodes over different historical periods and in remote lands. In pursuit of that goal they disregarded both the kinds of folklore and the cultures of peoples. Often they deliberately ignored the boundaries between genres of folklore. For example, Walter Anderson, whose monograph *Kaiser und Abt* (Folklore Fellows Communications, no. 42; Helsinki: Suomalainen Tiedeakatemia, 1923) was hailed as a classic example of this kind of scholarship,[18] drew freely upon Talmudic riddles, Islamic exempla, English ballads, and Jewish European jokes as equally valid sources for the reconstruction of the original form of the tale. He could consider this procedure a legitimate scientific method only because his ultimate goal was the formulation of the *Ur*-form of the narrative sequence.

In fact the fundamental historic-geographic metaphor of tale diffusion, "like ripples in a pond," enforces the neglect of genre distinctions. They are insignificant in light of the major research aim of the historic-geographic method. Because "the same tale in different lands takes on varying forms and is variously received by hearers and readers"[19] and because themes and motifs are transmitted "from one Märchen to another and then migrated farther in a new form until they have entered a new union and then move on a new path,"[20] there is neither sense nor purpose to the delineation of the actual distinctive features of forms of folklore.

Consequently, the notion of genre played a secondary role in the classificatory effort of folklore scholarship. Never defined as a conceptual category, it was either taken for granted or became a criterion for subdivisions of folk narratives. Except for Stith Thompson's *Motif-Index of Folk-Literature* (6 vols.; Bloomington: Indiana University Press, 1955–1958), which is comprehensive in design, and except for the motif-indexes modeled after his work, all other indexes, as well as anthologies and collections of folklore, use a genre framework for classification. Within each volume, terms for genres designate chapters and subdivisions. For example, *The Types of the Folktale* is organized in terms of "animal tales," "ordinary folk-tales," "jokes and anecdotes," "formula tales," and "unclassified tales." Save for the last, each of these groups is apparently a prose-narrative genre. However, it is the last division, "unclassified," that reveals the concept of genre underlying this and similar works. The terms for genres designate classificatory categories. They form a storage and retrieval system, which facilitates the archival filing of texts and their usage in research. Historical research in folklore has been content oriented and has used available terms of folklore forms to identify similarities and variations in the content of narratives, for example, without regard for the cultural perception or conception of genres nor for their intrinsic literary qualities.

Recently Lauri Honko spelled out the concept of genre that was assumed in the historic-geographic research method.[21] He attempts to offer us a string to guide us in the labyrinth of genre definitions and to provide direction for the future, but in fact he elucidates the past. He borrows a concept from Max Weber and an approach to literature from Benedetto Croce and applies them to folklore scholarship. In the process he comes to treat genres as if they were merely technical terms, instruments of research that have, at most, notational, but not conceptual value. Honko sets up his categories to serve technical use; they are neither aimed at a theoretical purpose nor derived from a cohesive theoretical system or from a cultural world view. In order to formulate a single genre he employs such concepts as contents, form, style, structure, function, frequency, distribution, age, and origin, which are drawn from different, often conflicting, theoretical systems. Honko proposes to regard genres as "ideal types" and not as real entities. Each text constitutes a particular constellation of relations between stylistic structural, thematic, functional, and historical factors which only approximate an ideal system. The relationship between single texts, recorded in tradition, and the ideal type—the classificatory category—needs to be defined anew in each case. While Honko, no doubt, provides a broader base for classification of folklore forms than that espoused by the historic-geographic method, he maintains their concept of genre. It is basically a category for classification. Honko's suggestion to consider functional, structural, and other attributes of a genre indeed increases the number of factors that need to be accounted for in the formulation of a classificatory category, but the combination of criteria does not amount to a new systemic theory. Rather it is merely a restatement, albeit refined, of a concept that has been employed in practice until now. In the conduct of historic-geographic inquiry genres have been regarded as ideal types in archives and museums; there they have been instruments for storage and retrieval of information. These "ideal types" of folklore forms exist in filing cabinets and in analytical dialogues of scholars; in culture itself, according to Honko, there is only a multitude of texts, each of which embodies a unique constellation of relations between these elements.

The concept of genre as a classificatory category is not limited to the historic-geographic method and other past scholarship. Modern scholars incorporate it into their formulations of genres and utilize the notion in discussing the systematization of performance and literary analysis, as, for example, Roger Abrahams and Wolfgang Kosack have done. These two scholars consider genres as classificatory categories that relate to each other in addition to the individual texts. They order genres along a scale between polar opposites of "total interpersonal involvement" and "total removal," as in Abrahams's scheme, or between rhythmic and prosaic text on the one hand and religious and suspense narration on the other, as in Kosack's model. Each genre has a position in relation to all other forms within these frameworks of polarities. At the same time each individual text approximates one of these classificatory categories, and as the resemblance to one of these ideal types decreases, it increases in relation to the next category along these scales.[22]

Correctly, Honko contends that the recognition of folklore genres as "ideal types" and the formulation of a system of categories on that basis would have a positive effect on folklore scholarship. First this development would eliminate the perennial debates, often futile, about the definitions of folklore forms and would offer clear measures for the recognition and classification of similar expressions in tradition. Consequently scholarly communication would improve considerably. Then the progress possible in genre studies, Honko concludes, will be mainly technical, consisting of an increase in the efficiency of genre divisions as a system for storage and retrieval of information.

Though terminological consensus is highly desirable, the fact is that even within the ranks of the historic-geographic school dissenting voices have been raised. Some scholars who shared the same interest in research did not consistently maintain the concept of genre as a classificatory category but changed their notion of genres as they shifted their scholarly concerns. For example, Carl W. von Sydow, in spite of his ardent criticism of the Aarne-Thompson classification system,[23] has actually conceived of genres in the same way as most folklorists who traced the history and the geographical distribution of themes. He has coined new terms—the *memorate*, the *fabulate* and the *chimerate*—each having certain distinctive features,[24] but, like Honko after him, he has maintained the same concept of genre while improving the system of classification. However, when von Sydow formulates principles of narrative migrations, he shifts gears and concepts completely. Symptomatically, he adopts the term *oicotype* from botany, where it "denotes a hereditary plant-variant adapted to a certain *milieu* (seashore, mountain-land, etc.) through natural selection amongst hereditarily dissimilar entities of the same species."[25] The analogy to oral tradition seems simple enough: "a country is often made up of several different cultural districts, with comparatively slight contact with one another. Such districts will then also vary in their folk-tales: partly in that to a certain extent they have different repertoires, partly in that tales of the same main type will form special types, *oicotypes*, in different districts."[26] In agreement with this train of thought, von Sydow extends the idea of special geographically bound, internationally diffused tales to the concept of genre in folklore. He regards each genre as language bound and each linguistic family as having its own dominant form, which originated and has persisted historically within its specific confines. The *Märchen* is thus an Indo-European genre *par excellence*; other languages have their own genres that dominate their repertoire. The novella is, for example, a Semitic genre, and the fable Hellenistic. In cases of dissemination into new languages, genres become muddled, garbled, and misunderstood; the best preserve for a specific folklore form is its home-growth ground, the indigenous culture and language in which it originated and has flourished.[27] Such a theory is no longer based on the assumption that genres are analytical conceptual categories, ideal types, but it implies a notion that they are forms that have a historic and linguistic reality in cultures and societies.

Genres as Permanent Forms

While von Sydow is still wavering between two concepts of genre, the evolutionary, functional, and structural studies in folklore consistently maintain the notion that genres are real cultural entities, existing in the oral traditions of the world, constituting the backbone of folklore. They are, to use Kenneth Burke's term, the permanent forms that underlie both changing historical emphases and differing cultural views and usages.[28] They have an independent literary integrity, which withstands social variations and technological developments.

Evolutionary Approaches. The evolutionary emphasis in nineteenth-century anthropology and folklore was on ideas and mental capabilities, not on literary forms. In the views of Edward B. Tylor, Andrew Lang, James G. Frazer, and George Laurence Gomme, man progressed toward rationality and evolved from magical through religious to scientific thought. But throughout man's evolutionary phases his folklore forms remained constant. The proverb of Tylor's animistic man does not differ in kind from the proverb of the rational man, only its position in culture and society changes. In fact folklore genres stand in reverse order to the evolutionary phases. As a permanent form a genre continues its existence in a changing society, but while the culture progresses upward its position in society, and in the hierarchy of genres, is downgraded. Folklore forms that were central in the cultures of early evolutionary phases remained identical in form in later stages of progress but began to occupy peripheral positions. Tylor is very specific in that regard.

> The proverb has not changed its character in the course of history; but has retained from first to last a precisely definite type. The proverbial sayings recorded among the higher nations of the world are to be reckoned by tens of thousands, and have a large and well-known literature of their own. But though the range of existence of proverbs extends into the highest levels of civilization, this is scarcely true of their development. At the level of European culture in the middle ages, they have indeed a vast importance in popular education, but their period of actual growth seems already at an end. Cervantes raised a proverb-monger's craft to a pitch it never surpassed; but it must not be forgotten that the incomparable Sancho's wares were mostly heirlooms; for proverbs were even then sinking to remnants of an earlier condition of society. As such, they survive among ourselves, who go on using much the same relics of ancestral wisdom as came out of the squire's inexhaustible budget, old saws not to be lightly altered or made anew in our changed modern times.[29]

Thus, according to Tylor, proverbs are a constant factor in an otherwise changing society; they are the permanent forms, the invariable element, which survives progress yet loses significance as man advances in knowledge. Other evolutionists viewed the relationship between genres and cultural advances somewhat differently. For example, for Alice B. Gomme, who shared her husband's theoretical direction, evolution acted, in regard to folklore genres, like a centrifugal force, pushing themes from culturally central genres to the marginal forms. With the evolution of man comes a different distribution of subjects and forms. The subject of a central ritual of human sacrifice which is the focus of social actions at one stage becomes the theme of a nursery rhyme and children's game in later years.

> London Bridge is broken down
> Dance over the Lady lea
> London Bridge is broken down
> With a gay lady (la-dee).[30]

The concept of genre as a permanent form in changing cultural situations was not confined to nineteenth-century British anthropologists and folklorists. In fact, earlier the Grimm Brothers formulated a similar concept of genre, although they described and interpreted change in historical, not evolutionary, terms. Cultural contacts and religious conflicts affected the relations between form and content in oral tradition. Under the impact of Christianity the themes of European pagan myths broke down into fairy stories, proverbs, riddles, and verbal images and manifested themselves in peasant customs and dialect expressions. The metaphor "broken-down myth," commonly applied to their theory,[31] encapsulates their notion of genre change. They conceive of paganic myths as narratives and as statements of belief that were crushed under the impact of Christianity in Europe and became crystalized in other forms. Jacob Grimm's *Teutonic Mythology* (trans. James Stevens Stallybrass; London: George Bell and Sons, 1883–1888) abounds with such examples. Their own statement makes their idea even clearer:

> Common to all fairy tales are the remnants of a faith which goes back to the most ancient times and which is expressed in the figurative conception of supersensual things. This mythic element is like little pieces of a splintered jewel that lie on the ground covered over by grass and flowers and only to be discovered by very sharp eyes. The meaning of the mystical element is long since lost, but it is still felt and gives the fairy tales their content while at the same time satisfying the natural pleasure in the miraculous; they are never just ornamental play of idle imagination.[32]

In other words, historical circumstances, rather than evolution, change the distribution of themes among the forms of folklore. Each genre has distinct attributes and capabilities, but under differing historical and cultural circumstances the same subject would appear in other genres that correspond to these changes. Myth, for example, requires the attitude of belief, but in its absence the same theme would be transformed into a fairy tale.

Their theories still have currency in modern scholarship and even serve as a basis for a classification system of genres. Without necessarily alluding to his illustrious predecessors, C. Scott Littleton has proposed "a two-dimensional scheme for the classification of narratives."[33] He suggests that, in the course of progress and historical developments, European societies change their attitude to their narrative themes in oral tradition along the axes of the factual and fabulous and of the sacred and secular. Accordingly he recognizes five genres in European tradition: (1) myth, (2) legend (or saga), (3) folktale (or *Märchen*), (4) history, and (5) sacred history. These differ from each other in their relations to truth and belief. With the increase of rationality in European civilizations, Littleton assumes there was a constant reevaluation of narrative themes, a changing of their positions along these axes. Each position, however, locates a definite genre of oral tradition. As the cultural attitudes toward a theme change and an increase or decrease of either factual or fabulous occurs, there is a shift in the position of the theme along these axes. Thus, according to this view, genres are permanent and their respective places along the axes of truth and religiosity are constant; only their themes may vary.

Functional Approaches. The functional theory in anthropology and folklore adds a dynamic aspect to genres as permanent forms of expression. They do not exist in culture merely as constant verbal forms but also play an active role in social affairs. Bronislaw Malinowski, who reacts against the survivalistic premise in cultural evolutionism, does so without digressing from the Tylorian conception of forms of oral tradition. In fact, from his point of view the reality of genres acquired even greater concreteness; they became culturally effective forms. He considers genres within his general functional theory of culture and reifies them as effective acting entities. His functional theory is an explanation of the biological, social, and cultural survival of the group. In reaction to cultural evolutionary theory in anthropology, he changes the focus of inquiry from the explanation of surviving relics in modern life to the survival of a group as a whole. Every single element in culture, including folklore genres, is a contributing factor to the maintenance and continuity of social groups.[34] Accordingly, myth "expresses, enhances, and codifies belief; it safeguards and enforces morality; it vouches for the efficiency of ritual and contains practical rules for the guidance of man. Myth is thus a vital ingredient of human civilization; it is not an idle tale, but a hard-worked active force; it is not an intellectual explanation or artistic imagery, but a pragmatic charter of primitive faith and moral wisdom."[35] Legends satisfy social ambition by glorifying the ancestry of the narrator, and tales amuse. Genres, therefore, are means to an end which instrumentally satisfies social and spiritual needs. They are concrete cultural isolates of an organized system of purposeful activities and are conceived of contextually in relation to the culture as a coherent whole.

The actual function a genre fulfills is subject to observation and interpretation. Also, the actual social unit which folklore forms serve may fluctuate in size from an individual person to a splinter group, to a tribe, and to a nation. On the basis of such consideration, Edmund Leach and Raymond Firth reversed the interpretation of the function of myth and conceived of it, among other things, as a manipulative and divisive rather than as a cohesive and integrative force.[36] But differing interpretations notwithstanding, all these conceptions of genres view them as effective forms in society, having distinct rhetorical properties that enable them to fulfill their functions and providing a system of checks and balances for sociocultural interactions.

In agreement with the general thesis of Malinowski, Thomas Williams analyzes the riddles of the Dusun, a North Borneo people. At the same time he avoids attributing a single function to a form, which Malinowski implies in his description of myth, legends and tales. Williams considers the riddle as having validating, explanatory, and magical functions. They serve as a conceptualizing mechanism and "as one of several integrative forces in maintenance of social structure," as well as an instrument for "reducing interpersonal aggression through canalization of levels of tension and potential conflict into an acceptable form of physically harmless and generally less disruptive social behavior."[37] From this perspective, genres function in rhetorical contexts, social conversations, personal interactions, and even in individual attempts to cope with conflicting forces.

In a similar vein, Roger Abrahams combines functional analysis with a rhetorical theory of folklore and extends Kenneth Burke's idea that proverbs "name typical recurrent situations"[38] to include superstitions as well. Abrahams suggests that the former functions as support in interpersonal conflicts, whereas the latter operates within the context of extrapersonal, natural and supernatural, confrontations.[39]

Originally Malinowski assumed that functions were universal and hence essential to human society. Accordingly, a functional system of genres should have had universal applicability and constituted a classification scheme of categories for storage and retrieval of information from world-wide oral traditions. It was, thus, only logical for William Bascom to formulate a classification system for the forms of folklore that would be based primarily on functional criteria.[40] But he soon found that, although attitudes such as belief, disbelief, and amusement might be indeed universal, their application to subject matter is culturally specific. Ethnic genres fulfilling these functions constitute only a relative system, one bound by ethnic cognition, performance, and language. Aware of the difficulties involved, Bascom nevertheless attempts to synchronize the native and the analytical categorization of prose narratives.

> Myth, legend, and folktale are not proposed as universally recognized categories, but as analytical concepts which can be meaningfully applied cross culturally even when other systems of "native categories" are locally recognized. They derive from the tripartite classification employed by students of European folklore, and presumably reflect the "native categories" of the "folk" of Europe; but they are easily reducible to the dual classification recognized in those societies which, as we shall see, group myths and legends into a single category ("myth-legend"), distinct from folktales which are fictional.[41]

Actually the discrepancy between the native categories and analytical concepts is not the only difficulty that Bascom faces. More crucial are the differing concepts of genre upon which the ethnic-particular and the cross-cultural systems are based. If forms such as myth, legend, and folktale are analytical concepts, then they are ideal types which each tale only approximates. But ideal types cannot be subject to the attitude of belief and cannot have a cultural context of narration—only individual tales can. If, in spite of that predicament, Bascom applies the criteria of time, place, and belief to genres and proceeds to construct a classification system on that basis, he must consider them as permanent forms and classificatory categories at the same time. However, while each of these two concepts of genres has its own logical validity, the irreconcilable differences between them do not allow for their combination without bending ethnographic information or sacrificing consistency.

The Structural-Morphological Approach. Structural-morphological analyses of folklore forms avoided vacillating between concepts of genre and consistently assumed the existence of genres in oral tradition. Such a premise has been the only justification for the structural-morphological analyses of riddles, proverbs, tales, and legends. Had these types of folklore been merely conceptual classificatory categories there would have been no reason to define their formal features. Structuralism would have amounted to a chess game one plays with oneself. The ultimate purpose of structural studies in folklore is the discovery of the distinctive features of each genre, their relations within the respective forms, and their capacity to differentiate genres within the totality of oral tradition. Whether these attributes are universal and common to respective genres in all cultures or whether they are particular and are part of the cultural system of communication is still a controversial point. Alan Dundes, for example, has made the boldest statements in regard to the universal existence of genres. Not only does he assume genres to be permanent forms of oral tradition, but he also insists upon the methodological priority of structural analysis in the scientific inquiry of folklore. He states, "the primary need of folklore *as a science* is descriptive structural analyses of all the genres of folklore."[42] Together with Robert Georges he claims that "an immediate aim of structural analysis in folklore is to define the genres of folklore. Once these genres have been defined in terms of internal morphological characteristics, one will be better able to proceed to the interesting problems of the function of folkloristic forms in particular cultures."[43]

Georges and Dundes thus assume the universality of folklore genres, and the universality of their structural-formal features. Myth, legend, tale, riddles, proverbs, and songs are subject to variation and change on the thematic and stylistic levels; their structural features are assumed to be universal. The attributes of those genres as found in a particular culture would be considered by them a surface structure based upon universal principles of genre differentiations. Any historical changes and cultural modifications in forms of folklore are just variations on basic structures that are permanently rooted in human thought, imagination, and expression. Or to employ another metaphor, folklore genres are like solid vessels: they have their own structures and each society may fill them with its own appropriate cultural, historical, and symbolic substance.[44]

Genres as Evolving Forms (History-of-Civilization Approach)

The difference between the concepts of genre as permanent and as evolving forms is fundamental, in spite of the apparent similarities. Folklorists who take either of these positions employ the same vocabulary. In particular there is an apparent similarity between the structural-morphological and the history-of-civilization approaches. In both cases terms such as *form, gestalt, relations,* and *pattern* frequently appear. But the resemblance ends there. The premise of the structural-morphological approach is that at the basis of each text and genre there is a fundamental "deep" structure, expressed in the relations between the narrative components of a particular story. This structure has not a historical but a cognitive primacy in the formation of folklore. In contrast, the idea that genres are *evolving forms* is based on the premise that at the roots of each genre there is a distinct *field of meaning*. Folklore and literary types are historical variations evolving from simple to complex forms of the respective fields of meanings manifested in human and verbal expressions.

Further distinction should be made between evolutionalism in literary criticism and in folklore. Ferdinand Brunetière, the champion of the former, believes "in the reality of genres as if they were biological species. He constantly parallels the history of genres with the history of human beings . . . in his genre histories [he] even uses the analogy of the struggle for existence to describe the rivalry of genres and argues that some genres are transmuted into other genres."[45] In folklore such ideas have not played a part. André Jolles, who has developed the thesis of evolution of genres from simple (primary) to complex forms, avoids such Darwinian concepts as "the survival of the fittest" and "natural selection," even though he continues to entertain the notion of the transmutability of oral genres into literary kinds.

André Jolles bases his theory of the formation and transformation of genres on three fundamental ideas:

1. Language has an inherent ability to transform words into forms, under precise conditions. This process is a fundamental mental activity (*Geistesbeschäftigung*).
2. Words crystalize into forms centering around distinct fields of meanings (*Bedeutungsfeld*).[46]
3. The genre is transformed into a new, often more complex, type which corresponds in meaning to the earlier kind.

This is a process of transformation from simple to the complex. The *einfache Formen* are the primary, most elemental manifestations of these fields of meaning; *kunst Formen*, artistic genres, are more complex and historically more recent representations of the same fields of meaning.

Jolles recognizes nine such semantic domains for the folklore forms. The holy is expressed in the legend; the family, in the *Sage*; the nature of the creation of the universe, in myth; the inquisitive spirit, in the riddle. Experience is represented in the proverb; morality, in the *Kasus*; factuality, in the *Memorabile*; naïve morality, in the *Märchen*; and the comic, in jokes.[47] He regards these genres as the finite elemental forms from which written literature has evolved. These are natural forms; they have the ability to multiply, mutate, and be transformed. The nine genres are the ultimate minimal and elemental forms that have generated all other kinds of literature. The primacy of the *einfache Formen* is cultural and historical. They appeared among the allegedly most primitive peoples and in ancient times. In the course of human progress and the advance of civilization they evolved into more complex forms, still maintaining the same field of meaning.

In most cases the criticism of Jolles has been trivial in its concern with the classification system or irrelevant in pondering the unverifiability of his metaphysical thesis.[48] Those who share Jolles's views on the evolution of narrative forms have often modified his theory to such an extent that the basic concept of genre has changed. For example, Jan de Vries adopts Jolles's notion of the transmutability of folklore forms in the context of changing historical circumstances but avoids the issue of origin and primacy of forms. In his view historical events, instead of fields of meanings, are at the core of any folk literary creation, within the confines of heroic legends, heroic poetry, myth, and *Märchen.*

According to de Vries, events that are inherently extraordinary are part of a heroic life, which "is a life *sui generis*" and does not belong to the narrative of history and cannot be lived by ordinary people. He suggests that heroic legends and heroic epics constitute the myths of society and culture and that they evolve in connection with the cult of the hero. However, as the distance between this initial situation and the present social condition grows, myth is transformed into a new genre, the *Märchen*; it loses its pathos and becomes a projection of wishful thinking rather than a sanctification of ritualistic acts, and the unrealistic optimism essential to this genre turns it into a trite and insipid narrative. In other words, de Vries suggests that the transformation of myths and heroic legends into *Märchen* is not a formal mutation of structure but a shift in social perspectives. This new vantage point eliminates the fundamental attitude towards myth, namely belief, and substitutes amusement. In the process, the recitation of songs moves from the royal court to the children's bedroom, and the narrators change from courtly bards to nursing maids and elderly women. The urbanization of society has historically whirled myths and heroic songs from the center to the periphery of culture. Thus, instead of evolution from primary to complex genres, de Vries postulates transformation of folklore genres, simple forms, into one another. But then, according to de Vries, myth, legend, song, and *Märchen* are no longer elemental; only the historic event retains a position of primacy. All four forms, however, are part of a sequence which is affected by social conditions and which centers around a single field of meaning, that of the heroic life.[49]

While de Vries conceived of Jolles's primary forms in historical terms, Kurt Ranke introduced to the theory of folklore genres a functional psychological dimension.[50] He regards the primary forms of folklore as expressions that have evolved in response to basic psychological human needs. Because these needs are fundamental to the individual and society, Ranke postulates that they have existed since the dawn of humanity and have continued into modern life. Consequently the folklore forms that evolved in response to these psychological conditions have not necessarily been transformed into a more complex form but have maintained their primary nature. Ranke assumes that genres—such as the tale, the legend, and the saga—all have "their own individual *enérgeia*, they transform [common motifs and narrative elements] into their respective particular expression and form." Thus, he is no longer concerned with the metamorphosis of genres themselves but with the transformation of themes and motifs as they adjust to the respective narrative frameworks of particular forms. Ranke's *einfache Form* is an "irreducible, genuine archetypal form, an integral whole in both content and structure."[51] Because these forms have a psychological rather than social or cultural basis, they are universal forms of human expression. Ranke thus maintains the primary nature of Jolles's *einfache Formen*, but discards their mutability into other complex forms. At the same time, though he substitutes the notion of a psychological function for a field of meaning, he conceives of the narrative-poetic effect of genres as if they are literary semantic fields. Any motifs, themes, or plots that drift into a particular genre transform to conform with the particular requirements and demands of the given kind of folklore. Thus, in developing Jolles's notion of *einfache Formen*, Ranke changes the concept of genre from an evolving to a permanent form and at the same time adopts some of the principles that underlie yet another notion of genre, that of genre as a form of discourse.

Genres as Forms of Discourse

Jolles's conception of forms in terms of fields of meanings generated a fourth concept of folklore genres, according to which they are distinct forms of discourse.[52] In this view each genre has its own rhetorical features, vocabulary, disposition toward reality, use of descriptive language, types of characters, and symbolic meanings—all of which mark it as a distinct form of discourse within oral tradition.

Such scholars as Max Lüthi and Lutz Röhrich have defined these forms of discourse by comparing them with each other so as to delineate mutually exclusive categories, for example the *Märchen* and the *Sage*.[53] Probably the first to approach and conceive of genre in this way were the Brothers Grimm, who observed that the *Märchen* is poetic, whereas the legend is historic.[54] They so designated these genres not only in terms of their respective contents but also in regard to an entire range of rhetorical characteristics, which they either mentioned or implied. The qualitative descriptions of the *Märchen* and the *Sage* —considered as forms of discourse—has multiplied and varied since then. They have served as a paradigm for many contrasting features: amusement and instruction, fantasy and reality, optimism and pessimism are but a few of the qualities of these respective forms. These attributes constitute a complete set of discourse features, symbols, subject matter, attitudes toward *Märchen* and *Sage*, and the conception of social and cultural and cosmic realities expressed in them. The *Märchen* plot takes place in an unspecified time and place, transcends natural laws, and is completely fictive; the legend is a discourse bound by empirical reality and the traditional concept of truth. As an expression of man, according to Lüthi, the *Märchen* embodies the relationship within the nuclear family, whereas the legend represents actions of man in society at large. As a form of discourse, any genre constitutes an ontological entity with a defined set of relations between language, symbols, and reality. Once a narrative motif or theme is incorporated into any such set, it is subject to the rules of discourse that prevail in the particular form. Thus genres are distinct entities, each dominated by unique qualities that transform all narrative features in accordance with its rules of discourse.

The Essays in This Symposium

Naturally, not all the participants in the symposium share the same concept of genre; they do, however, concur that the forms of oral tradition are not merely analytical constructs, classificatory categories for archives, file cabinets, and libraries, but that they are distinct modes of communication which exist in the lore of peoples. While sharing this same fundamental idea about folklore genres, the participants approach them from two different perspectives: literary-linguistic and ethnographic. These represent differences in emphases and scholarly traditions rather than theoretical conflicts.

Literary and Linguistic Analysis of Folklore Genres

Of the participants concerned with literary-linguistic analysis, Utley addresses himself to the question of tradition in literary forms. Although he aims at the pedagogical use of folklore in the teaching of literature, the implications of his essay reach beyond the confines of the classroom. His analysis implies that the tales, songs, and epics current in verbal circulation among completely or partially illiterate people have the same ability to aesthetically represent literary modes as written epic, prose, drama, and lyric. Hence, oral songs have critical aesthetic value not only to their indigenous audience in the community, but also to the readers of literature. Furthermore, Utley does not suggest that these "simpler forms" generate complex genres or serve as literary archetypes having the same modality; they simply coexist in the same language and geographical area, circulating on two distinct levels of society. Occasionally their paths converge to create crucial contact points between oral and the written traditions. Utley cites perhaps one of the most outstanding examples in the history of folklore of direct connections between oral tradition and written literature, that of Sir Walter Scott.

The deep devotion to the minstrelsy of the border that the middle-class lawyer and Scottish poet had was perhaps triggered but not caused by reading Percy's *Reliques of Ancient English Poetry*. Scott's childhood years on his grandfather's farm at Sandy-Knowe and the tales and songs he heard then, either from his grandparents, their servants, or other "rural folks," had a far greater impact upon his concern and love for tales and ballads than any literary influence.[55] Such direct contact seems to be at the core of much of the writer's later use of folktales, songs, and proverbs. Similarly Dostoevskij, whose attention to folklore is by no means a match for that of Scott, was able to reproduce popular songs, tales, and legends. His writings have many points of similarity with the spirit, ideas, and narrative structure of Russian folklore. At least partially, Dostoevskij is indebted for these similarities to social contacts he made with the "folk," to wetnurses who continued to visit his family and tell stories to the children and to storytellers he encountered in prisons.[56] In such cases the servant class constitutes a social bridge between oral and written genres. Maids and servants mediate between the traditions current in the nonliterate quarters of the city and those of the educated middle-class and so establish contact points between verbal and written literature. In other words, by extending Utley's thesis to the social domain it is possible to subject the relationship between folklore and literary genres not only to textual criticism but also to ethnographic research on the communicative channels in literate cultures. The oral and written forms have distinct social orbits, which criss-cross each other in a network of situations and contact points. If in the classroom oral genres are bridges to written literature, in the community they represent cultural connections between the two systems of communication and constitute, each in its own sphere, corresponding symbols.

In the essay "Aspects of the *Märchen* and the Legend," Max Lüthi addresses himself specifically to the question of the symbolic meaning of these two forms. While Utley demonstrates the relevance of folklore to literary criticism, Lüthi applies principles of literary criticism to folklore. Basing his generalizations upon numerous European texts, Lüthi conceives of these two forms as a pair of contrastive symbols: the *Märchen* embodies the world of the self, the individual, whereas the legend represents the harshness of the social and natural world external to self. Psychologically, the *Märchen* is a family narrative in dual terms: first, each of the actors in the story—the father, the mother, the helpers, and above all the hero himself—represents a Jungian archetype, and together they constitute personality; second, the tale is a projection of the maturation process of a child and his emergence as a social man, an equal member of the community and the family head. By following Lüthi's ideas, it is possible to regard the *Märchen* as not just "any development proceeding from villainy . . . or a lack . . . , through intermediary functions to marriage," as Propp states it,[57] but as a story of a child-hero that culminates with the phase in which the hero himself has children. Hence, the similarity in structural models of *Märchen* and myth, to which both Archer Taylor and Jan de Vries point,[58] is not accidental: both genres are concerned with and symbolize the growth of individual personality.

On the other hand, the legend is the story of the interaction of the self with the world outside the family circle. It is a reality full of obstacles, difficulties, and tribulations that have to be overcome; it is a world dominated by fears, anxieties, and suspicions, which it is possible to face only with the support of great religious faith. Consequently, the notion of belief is closely associated with this genre. These psychological, literary, and symbolic aspects of the *Märchen* and the legend which Lüthi discusses are applicable to the European narrative forms. Any extension of this interpretation to folklore genres of other languages and cultures would require further comparative analysis.

David Bynum's discussion, "The Generic Nature of Oral Epic Poetry," is comparative. He explores the possibilities of viewing the oral epic as a cross-cultural form that has similar properties of themes, composition, and performance everywhere. He is cautious in applying the term *epic* as Aristotle defined it to oral poetry in other languages, yet from his discussion it becomes clear that heroism as a theme, formula as a unit of composition, and musical accompaniment as a feature of performance are the earmarks of oral epic poetry. Bynum rightly concludes that basic cross-cultural research on this genre is still to be done. The year his essay originally appeared, Daniel Biebuyck and Kahombo C. Mateene published the text of an African oral epic, *The Mwindo Epic* (Berkeley and Los Angeles: University of California Press, 1969), in the original Nyanga and English translation, but further published texts are needed in order to establish whether the epic as an oral literary form is current among African peoples.[59] This is one genre in relation to which folklorists might have an actual sense of discovery. (Several years ago, for example, Arsenio E. Manuel found epic poetry in the hill lands of the Philippines;[60] texts from other countries undoubtedly will appear in print soon.)

Diffusion need not be considered the only factor that affected the distribution of this genre from a geographic center. Our awareness of the antiquity of the Greek epic and our veneration of it result from the historical development of Western civilization and could not serve, under any circumstances, as a proof for priority. The literary features of the epic depend on the musical mode of performance, the existence of historical-narrative traditions of combat, and the availability of social occasions for recitation.

Another musically based poetic genre is the blues, about which Harry Oster writes. Unlike the epic, it is a local Afro-American folk form of relatively recent growth. It emerged in the plantation fields and has flourished in cities and prisons. There are some further cultural and critical differences between the two genres. Whereas the epic adulates central cultural heroes and deities, the blues lament the tribulation of the marginal individual. Aesthetically the epic has been the subject of literary admiration and is considered a fundamental generic category; the poetic qualities of the blues have long been neglected. Oster's essay, "The Blues as a Genre," and his full-length study of this form, *Living Country Blues* (Detroit: Folklore Associates, 1969), are some of the first attempts to demonstrate the lyrical qualities, imagery, and irony of both classical and talking blues as they are sung in prisons and countryside. Since the blues is a poetic category of Black American culture, Oster's critical discussion actually amounts to a discovery of the literary features that the singers and the audience themselves aesthetically perceive in the songs; it is they who socially set the rhythmical confines of the genre and the range of applicable versification. His analysis of the form subsequently leads to discovery of the nonverbalized cultural aesthetics that generates such poetry.

In Oster's analysis of the blues, he deals with the text and texture, the surface features, of the form. Charles Scott's essay on the riddle focuses upon the deep structure of that genre. His is a polemic essay, arguing against the structural definition of the riddle that Robert Georges and Alan Dundes proposed several years ago.[61] He differs with them not only in the demarcation and proper identification of the structural unit of the riddle, but in the more fundamental conception of genre in general. Georges' and Dundes' starting point is the premise that generic forms have cross-cultural currency, but Scott assumes them to have validity only within the confines of particular languages. Riddles of separate cultures may differ not only thematically but also structurally. Moreover, since Georges and Dundes first formulated a structural definition of the riddle, further attempts in that direction have become entangled in a paradoxical situation.

While speakers of a language have little trouble intuitively distinguishing between riddles and proverbs,[62] students of folklore find it
increasingly difficult to account for this native distinction and often
conclude that "in form, riddles and proverbs come very close to each
other."[63] Quite possibly, by focusing on the deep structures of these
respective genres, it will be possible to find a solution to this dilemma.

The Ethnography of Folklore Genres

As pointed out earlier, literary and ethnographic methods in folklore
research complement each other. Yet the shift from the library to the
field not only adds new supplementary information but also changes
the perspectives of the text from linear narration to multidimensional
performance, from a tale to a telling. In this context folklore genres
are modes of verbal symbolic interaction, having rules and structures
which involve para-linguistic communicative components and established cultural attitudes. These are essential to the conception of genres, as much as themes and verbal structures are to literary-linguistic
analysis. As a result of the ethnographic study of folklore, basic concepts often must be changed. The article of Dégh and Vázsonyi,
"Legend and Belief," is a case in point. For years the notion of belief
has served as the basis for defining, explaining, and indexing the legend; it was the criterion *par excellence* of this genre. Yet, as Dégh's
field research reveals, ambiguities and even apparent contradictions
exist in the actual use of this concept by the people. It turns out that
the notion of belief has two, often incompatible meanings. On the
one hand, it connotes an attitude, a religious belief or faith; on the
other hand, it refers to beings or events which have their only reality
in the belief of the people. As Dégh and Vázsonyi demonstrate, the
attitude of belief is not the only way to relate to the *beings* which
exist in belief; people also parody them, joke about them, ridicule
them. Consequently, while all legends involve belief in both senses,
not all stories that are about beings that exist in belief are necessarily
legends. This clarification, which is based on ethnographic research,
has immediate application to ongoing projects of definition and classification of legends.

Similarly, Peter Seitel's approach to the proverb releases this genre
from the bonds of dictionaries and anthologies by which it has been

confined for years and permits examination of the proverb as an act of speaking. The notion of proverbs as metaphors is as old as Aristotelian rhetorics, which actually defines them as such: "Proverbs . . . are metaphors from species to species."[64] The sense of this expression is not altogether clear, but according to Bartlett J. Whiting "the meaning seems to be that the application of a proverb often depends upon a shift from the literal meaning of the incident or observation which was responsible for its origin."[65] Seitel accepts the Aristotelian conception of proverbs as given and, following theoretical and methodological developments in ethnoscientific and ethnolinguistic studies, he proposes to explore the use of proverb-metaphors in social interactions. The basic premise underlying such a research direction is that the use of proverb as metaphors for situations follows distinct discoverable cultural rules of communication. A clue to the viability of such an approach might well be taken from a traditional Fante saying: "there is no proverb without the situation."[66] Anthropologists, folklorists, and literary critics, such as George Herzog and C. G. Blooah, Raymond Firth, Ojo Arewa and Alan Dundes, Roger Abrahams, and Kenneth Burke,[67] have already followed this dictum. They have emphasized the relationship between spoken proverbs and social situations; Seitel proceeds to formulate a proposal for the discovery of the grammar of proverbs use.

The speaking of narrative genres requires the allotment of time and place, and it turns a telling into a total performance,[68] an artistic rather than merely informative act of communication. Yellowman, the Navaho storyteller who told Barre Toelken Coyote stories, encapsulates the transition from informing to performing.

I asked him [writes Toelken] how he would recognize the difference between a Coyote story and someone talking about Coyote if he were to hear only part of the total text; I asked whether it would be possible, by listening to a tape recording, to detect the difference between a Coyote story told within a myth, during a chant, or to someone's family. To the first question, he replied that conversations about Coyote would not use the "ancient" words one would associate with the tales; clearly then, subject matter is not the distinguishing factor. To the second, he replied that Coyote stories would be told about the same way under all circumstances, but that one might detect differing kinds of audience reaction.

In other words, distinct vocabulary and types of audience reactions are not just factors in converting conversation into performance, but within this type of communication they function also as generic markers of performances. Once students of folklore conceive of tales the way narrators and audience perceive them, as multidimensional communicative acts, they are likely to discover genre differentiation not only on a single level, such as text, but also in the performance, texture, and context.[69] V. Hrdličková demonstrates that such a research direction is possible, feasible, and it can, indeed, be fruitful and insightful. Her description of Japanese storytellers' performance clearly reveals that the notion of genre underlies acts of folklore communication. Genres are not merely kinds of narrative texts but types of performances, each of which has distinct and appropriate gestures, vocabulary, and formulas in addition to themes and plots. Moreover, in a complex society such as in Japanese urban centers, there is a high degree of performance specialization and each genre requires its own professional narrators. Both Toelken and Hrdličková explore storytelling events as dramatic mimetic communicative acts in which the narrative textual level constitutes one out of several symbolic systems which make up a performance.

The Classification of Folklore Genres

The focus upon the performing aspects of folklore naturally opens up new possibilities and presents new requirements for the classification of folklore genres. Roger Abrahams's essay, "The Complex Relations of Simple Forms," is a suggestive response to such a need. William H. Jansen was one of the earliest to consider the factor of performance as a classificatory criterion.[70] He drew a continuum between two polarities, performance and participation, which have an inverse relation to each other in every folklore genre. The forms with the lowest degree of performance factor are those which require the highest degree of participation, like collective group singing without an audience. Vice versa, genres having the highest degree of performance quality are those which have the lowest degree of participation.

The degree of specialization and skill in performance is greatest when the participation is least. Furthermore, the degree of performance quality in each case is effected by the requirements inherent in the form itself, by the function of the folkloric expression in the particular situation, and finally, by the social expectations of the speaker, assuming that people would like to live up to their role and image. Abrahams, on the other hand, regards performance as a constant factor in all genres; the variables are the extent and type of interaction between the speaker and the audience and the relationship between the performer and the folklore expression. These variables are scaled along a continuum from involvement to detachment, and from active participation to vicarious psychological identification.

My own essay shifts the focus from concern with analytical classification of folklore genres to the ethnic systematization of forms. Accordingly, genres are conceptual categories of communication not classification. They represent the principles of folkloric communication in a society. The discovery of these principles may confuse our archiving systems, but perhaps it will serve to improve our understanding of the process of folklore.

Conclusion

The essays assembled in this collection represent a new development in folklore-genre studies. The literary-oriented articles conceive of folklore forms not as the antecedents of literary genres but as richly symbolic expressions that are equally complex. They shun the anachronistic approach to folklore, still impeding many students of literature, which regards ballads, myths, and tales only as precursors of a Shakespeare, a Mann, or a Melville. The significance of oral epics, for example, is not in their being a literary model for the Miltons of world literature; they have intricate expressive complexities, the untangling of which can reveal the processes of creative composition, thematic transformation, and linguistic dexterity. An evaluative comparison of oral and written epics would do justice to neither. The evolutionary approach to folklore genres was inadvertently patronizing, for it assumed the latest to be the best. The search for legends, proverbs, or songs in the works of specific writers ultimately exhibits a primary concern with a literary work; the folklore genres are secondary. The present essays, it is hoped, will contribute to change this pattern.

The ethnographically oriented articles, as well as those dealing with classification problems, reveal dimensions of folklore often obscured from the student who is reading texts alone. For years we have known that the written page is but a pale reproduction of the spoken word, that a tale hardly reflects its telling; for years we have painfully realized that, no matter how carefully we record oral texts, much is left unprinted, even more is not understood. Certainly, the present essays neither intend nor pretend to present a systematic analysis of performance folklore in its cultural context; yet, we hope they do lead to an understanding of the forms of oral literature as multidimensional symbols of communication and to a conception of folklore genres as a set of systematically related conceptual categories in culture. Because genres constitute recognized modes of folklore, speaking their terminology and taxonomy can play a major role in such a study. What kinship terms are to social structure, genre terms are to folklore, both as communication and as scholarship. Their fluidity and multidimensionality undoubtedly make such an analysis rather complex; but then, we have not claimed that folklore genres are *einfache Formen*.

Notes

I am indebted to Charles Adams, Kenneth Ketner, and Barbara Kirshenblatt-Gimblett, who read parts of the Introduction. Their critical comments were extremely helpful.

1. Irvin Ehrenpreis, *The "Types Approach" to Literature* (New York: King's Crown Press, 1945), pp. 70–72, 80.

2. Richard M. Dorson, "The Growth of Folklore Courses," *Journal of American Folklore* 63 (1950) : 348.

3. Ibid., p. 354.

4. Ronald L. Bakér, "Folklore Courses and Programs in American Colleges and Universities," *Journal of American Folklore* 84 (1971) : 225.

5. Compare this list with Vladímir Propp, "Generic Structures in Russian Folklore," trans. Maria Zagorska Brooks, ed. Dan Ben-Amos and Philip Tilney, *Genre* 4 (1971) : 213–248.

6. Jerome R. Mintz, *Legends of the Hasidim: An Introduction to Hasidic Culture and Oral Tradition in the New World* (Chicago: University of Chicago Press, 1968).

7. *Deep Down in the Jungle: Negro Narrative Folklore from the Streets of Philadelphia* (Hatboro, Pa.: Folklore Associates, 1964), p. 16.

8. Alan Dundes, "Texture, Text, and Context," *Southern Folklore Quarterly* 28 (1964): 252.

9. Robert A. Georges, "The General Concept of Legend: Some Assumptions to be Reexamined and Reassessed," in *American Folk Legend: A Symposium*, ed. Wayland D. Hand, pp. 1–19.

10. Ibid., p. 19.

11. Alan Dundes, "Folk Ideas as Units of Worldview," *Journal of American Folklore* 84 (1971): 93–103. Reprinted in *Toward New Perspectives in Folklore*, ed. Américo Paredes and Richard Bauman, pp. 93–103.

12. Elias Schwartz, "The Problem of Literary Genres," *Criticism* 13 (1971): 113.

13. Claudio Guillén, "Poetics as System," *Comparative Literature* 22 (1970): 195.

14. Richard M. Dorson, "Current Folklore Theories," *Current Anthropology* 4 (1963): 93–112, and *Folklore and Folklife: An Introduction*, pp. 7–47.

15. See, for example, Stith Thompson, *Motif-Index of Folk-Literature*, 2d rev. ed. (Bloomington: Indiana University Press, 1955), I, 10; C. W. von Sydow, *Selected Papers on Folklore: Published on the Occasion of His 70th Birthday*, ed. Laurits Bødker, pp. 60–61, 127. It should be pointed out that during his travels Linnaeus himself recorded traditional materials and proposed systems of classification for them. See C. W. von Sydow, *Vara Folkminnen* (Lund: Domförlaget, 1919), p. 31.

16. Stith Thompson, *The Folktale*, pp. 413–427; Carl W. von Sydow, "Popular Prose Traditions and Their Classification," in *Selected Papers on Folklore*, pp. 127–145; V. Propp, *Morphology of the Folktale*, pp. 3–18.

17. For a discussion about Goethe's morphological ideas, literary genres in general, and their relationship to morphological and classificatory concepts in folklore, particularly those of Vladímir Propp, see Reinhard Breymayer, "Vladímir Jakovlevic Propp (1895–1970)—Leben, Wirken und Bedeutsamkeit," *Linguistica Biblica* 15/16 (1972): 59–66.

18. Archer Taylor, "The Classics of Folklore," *Arv* 20 (1964): 120–121. See also Thompson, *The Folktale*, p. 444.

19. Thompson, *The Folktale*, p. 22.

20. Kaarle Krohn, *Folklore Methodology: Formulated by Julius Krohn and Expanded by Nordic Researchers*, trans. Roger L. Welsch, American Folklore Society Bibliographical and Special Series, no. 21 (Austin: University of Texas Press, 1971), p. 158.

21. Lauri Honko, "Genre Analysis in Folkloristics and Comparative Religion," *Temenos* 3 (1968): 48–66.

22. Roger D. Abrahams, "The Complex Relations of Simple Forms," *Genre*

2 (1969): 104–128, and reprinted in this volume; Wolfgang Kosack, "Der Gattungsbegriff 'Volkserzählung,' " *Fabula* 12 (1971): 18–47.

23. See von Sydow, *Selected Papers on Folklore*, pp. 127–145.

24. Ibid., pp. 60–87.

25. Ibid., p. 243.

26. Ibid., pp. 50–51.

27. See ibid., "Kategorien der Prosa-Volksdichtung," pp. 60–85, and "Popular Dite Tradition: A Terminological Outline," pp. 106–127. Compare with Archer Taylor, "A Theory of Indo-European *Märchen*," *Journal of American Folklore* 44 (1931): 54–60, and the articles cited there.

28. Quoted in Stanley Edgar Hyman, *The Armed Vision: A Study in the Methods of Modern Literary Criticism* (1948; reprint ed., New York: Vintage Books, 1955), p. 247.

29. Edward B. Tylor, *The Origins of Culture* (1878; reprint ed., New York: Harper, 1958), pp. 89–90. Note that Tylor's concept of genres associated with religious beliefs and practices differs from what has been stated above. For example, he regards formal prayers as genres that evolved from charm-formulas. The contents of the two forms are similar, but their style and verbal renditions are different. See his *Religion in Primitive Culture* (1878; reprint ed., New York: Harper and Row, 1958), pp. 456–459. This position is consistent with his theory about the evolution of man's religions.

30. Alice Bertha Gomme, *The Traditional Games of England, Scotland, and Ireland* (London: David Nutt, 1894), I, 346–348.

31. See Thompson, *The Folktale*, p. 370.

32. Quoted in Murray B. Peppard, *Paths Through the Forest: A Biography of the Brothers Grimm* (New York: Holt, Rinehart and Winston, 1971), p. 50.

33. C. Scott Littleton, "A Two-Dimensional Scheme for the Classification of Narratives," *Journal of American Folklore* 78 (1965): 21–27.

34. See Bronislaw Malinowski, *A Scientific Theory of Culture and Other Essays* (1944; reprint ed., New York: Oxford University Press, 1960). For a recent discussion and assessment of Malinowski's contribution to theory in anthropology see Elvin Hatch, *Theories of Man and Culture* (New York: Columbia University Press, 1973), pp. 272–335.

35. Bronislaw Malinowski, *Magic, Science and Religion*, p. 101.

36. Edmund Leach, *Political Systems of Highland Burma: A Study of Kachin Social Structure* (1954; reprint ed., London: The London School of Economics and Political Sciences, 1964), pp. 264–278; Raymond Firth, "The Plasticity of Myth," *Ethnologica* n.s. 2 (1960): 181–188 (reprinted in *Tikopia Ritual and Belief* [Boston: Beacon Press, 1967], pp. 284–292); and Robert A. Georges, *Studies in Mythology* (Homewood, Ill.: Dorsey Press, 1968), pp. 168–198.

37. Thomas Rhys Williams, "The Form and Function of Tambunan Dusun Riddles," *Journal of American Folklore* 76 (1963): 95–110; quotations, pp. 106, 103.

38. Kenneth Burke, "Literature as Equipment for Living," in *The Philosophy of Literary Form* (1941; reprint ed., New York: Vintage, 1957), p. 253.

39. Roger D. Abrahams, "A Rhetoric of Everyday Life: Traditional Conversational Genres," *Southern Folklore Quarterly* 32 (1968): 44–59.

40. William R. Bascom, "The Forms of Folklore: Prose Narratives," *Journal of American Folklore* 78 (1965): 3–20.

41. Ibid., p. 5.

42. Alan Dundes, *The Morphology of North American Indian Folktales*, p. 112.

43. Robert A. Georges and Alan Dundes, "Toward a Structural Definition of the Riddle," *Journal of American Folklore* 76 (1963): 111.

44. For a discussion of structural analysis in folklore and the question of universals see Vilmos Voigt, "Some Problems of Narrative Structure Universals in Folklore," *Acta Ethnographica* 21 (1972): 57–72.

45. René Wellek, "The Concept of Evolution in Literary History," in *Concepts of Criticism*, by René Wellek, ed. Stephen G. Nichols, Jr. (New Haven: Yale University Press, 1963), p. 44.

46. For André Jolles's linguistic contribution to this concept see his essay "Antike Bedeutungsfelder," *Beiträge zur Geschichte der deutschen Sprach und Literatur* 48 (1934): 97–109.

47. André Jolles, *Einfache Formen: Legende, Sage, Mythe, Rätsel, Spruch, Kasus, Memorabile, Märchen, Witz*, Rhihe der Veröffentlichungen der Sächsischen Forschungsinstitut in Leipzig—Forschunginstitut für Neuere Philologie II (Halle: Niemeyer, 1930). For a biographical sketch and a brief evaluation of his work see Walter Thys, "André Jolles (1874–1946)," *Yearbook of Comparative and General Literature* 13 (1964): 41–48.

48. See for example von Sydow, *Selected Papers on Folklore*, pp. 60–64. For explicatory, mostly favorable discussions of Jolles's approach to the problem of folklore genres see Hermann Bausinger, *Formen der "Volkspoesie*," pp. 51–64; Walter A. Berendsohn, "Einfache Formen," in *Handwörterbuch des deutschen Märchen*, ed. Johannes Bolte and Lutz Mackensen, I, 484–498; Wolfgang Mohr, "Einfache Formen," in *Reallexikon der deutschen Literaturgeschichte*, ed. Werner Kohlschmidt and Wolfgang Mohr (Berlin: Walter de Gruyter, 1958), I, 321–328; Robert Petsch, "Die Lehre von den 'Einfache Formen,'" Deutsche Vierteljahrsschrift für Literaturwissenschaft und Geistesgeschichte 10 (1932): 335–369.

49. See Jan de Vries, *Heroic Song and Heroic Legend*, trans. B. J. Timmer; idem, *Betrachtungen zum Märchen besonders in seinem Verhältnis zu Heldensage und Mythos*.

50. Kurt Ranke, "Einfache Formen," in *Internationaler Kongress der Volkserzählungsforscher in Kiel und Kopenhagen 1959—Vorträge und Referate*, pp. 1–11; English translation by William Templer and Eberhard Alsen appeared in *Journal of the Folklore Institute* 4 (1967): 17–31.

51. Ranke, "Einfache Formen," *Journal of the Folklore Institute* 4 (1967): 27.

52. For a typology of discourse see Charles Morris, *Writings on the General Theory of Signs*, Approaches to Semiotics, no. 16 (The Hague: Mouton, 1971), pp. 203–232 (originally published in 1946). Morris does not refer to any folklore genre as a form of discourse, although he considers "mythical discourse" as a distinct type (pp. 213–214). The notion of "form of discourse" is used here more loosely than in the analytical system that Morris developed.

53. See Max Lüthi, *Das europäische Volksmärchen: Form und Wesen*; *Volksmärchen und Volkssage: Zwei Grundformen erzählender Dichtung* (Bern and Munich: Francke, 1961); *Once upon a Time: On the Nature of Fairy Tales*, trans. Lee Chadeayne and Paul Gottwald; "Aspects of the *Märchen* and the Legend," trans. Barbara Flynn, *Genre* 2 (1969): 162–178, and reprinted in this volume. Lutz Röhrich, *Märchen und Wirklichkeit: Eine volkskundliche Untersuchung*, and *Sage*. For an attempt to synthesize various approaches in the definition of the genre of the folktale see Marie-Louise Tenèze, "Du conte merveilleux comme genre," *Arts et Traditions Populaires* 18 (1970): 11–65.

54. See Jacob and Wilhelm Grimm, *Deutsche Sagen*, 3d ed. (Berlin, 1891), p. vii.

55. Charles G. Zug III, "The Last Minstrel: Folklore and the Poetry of Sir Walter Scott" (Ph.D. diss., University of Pennsylvania, 1968), pp. 1–45.

56. George Gibian, "Dostoevskij's Use of Russian Folklore," in *Slavic Folklore: A Symposium*, ed. Albert B. Lord, American Folklore Society Bibliographical and Special Series, no. 6 (Philadelphia: American Folklore Society, 1956), pp. 41–55.

57. Propp, *Morphology of the Folktale*, p. 92.

58. Archer Taylor, "The Biographical Pattern in Traditional Narrative," *Journal of the Folklore Institute* 1 (1964): 114–129, and see de Vries's works listed in the Selected Bibliography.

59. See Jan Knappert, "The Epic in Africa," *Journal of the Folklore Institute* 4 (1967): 171–190; Ruth Finnegan, *Oral Literature in Africa* (Oxford: Clarendon Press, 1970), pp. 108–110.

60. Arsenio E. Manuel, *The Maiden of the Buhong Sky: A Complete Song from the Bagobo Folk Epic Tuwaang*, rev. ed. (Quezon City: University of the Philippines Press, 1958).

61. Georges and Dundes, "Toward a Structural Definition," pp. 111–118.

62. Elli Köngäs Maranda, "The Logic of Riddles," in *Structural Analysis of Oral Tradition*, ed. Pierre and Elli Köngäs Maranda, p. 191.

63. Ibid., p. 223. See also Alan Dundes, "On the Structure of the Proverb," *Proverbium* 25 (1975): 965.

64. Quoted in B. J. Whiting, "The Nature of the Proverb," *Harvard Studies and Notes in Philology and Literature* 14 (1932): 277.

65. Ibid.

66. James Boyd Christensen, "The Role of Proverbs in Fante Culture," *Africa* 28 (1958): 232.

67. George C. Herzog and Charles G. Blooah, *Jabo Proverbs from Liberia*

(London: International African Institute, 1936); Raymond Firth, "Proverbs in Native Life, with Particular Reference to Those of the Maori," *Folk-Lore* 37 (1926): 135–153, 245–270; E. Ojo Arewa and Alan Dundes, "Proverbs and the Ethnography of Speaking Folklore," *American Anthropologist* 66, no. 6, pt. 2 (Special Publication, *The Ethnography of Communication*, ed. John Gumperz and Dell Hymes [1964]), pp. 70–85; Kenneth Burke, "Literature as Equipment for Living," in *The Philosophy of Literary Form: Studies in Symbolic Action*, pp. 253–262; Roger D. Abrahams, "A Rhetoric of Everyday Life," and "Introductory Remarks to a Rhetorical Theory of Folklore," *Journal of American Folklore* 81 (1968): 143–157.

68. For a systematic model of this transition, see Dell Hymes, "Breakthrough into Performance," in *The Communication of Folklore*, ed. Dan Ben-Amos and Kenneth S. Goldstein (The Hague: Mouton, 1975), pp. 11–74. See also Richard Bauman, "Verbal Art as Performance," *American Anthropologist* 77 (1975): 290–311.

69. See Dundes, "Texture, Text, and Context," pp. 251–265.

70. William H. Jansen, "Classifying Performance in the Study of Verbal Folklore," in *Studies in Folklore: In Honor of Distinguished Service Professor Stith Thompson*, ed. W. Edson Richmond, Indiana University Publications Folklore Series, no. 9 (Bloomington: Indiana University Press, 1957), pp. 110–118.

Part One

Literary and Linguistic Analysis of Folklore Genres

1. Oral Genres as a Bridge to Written Literature

FRANCIS LEE UTLEY

In most fields of learning, from biology to literature, the established contrast between the nineteenth and the twentieth century is that of origin and evolution versus structure and configuration. Brunetière, major nineteenth-century exponent of the theory of genres, began with a bow to the perfection of genres in the classical ages of Greece, France, and Rome, but he ended with full-fledged commitment to the evolution of genres. French tragedy, for instance, rose from Jodelle and Garnier to perfection in Corneille and Racine; after that we can trace only decline.[1] Today the major exponent of genre study is Northrop Frye, whose *Anatomy of Criticism* finds its climax in a formal and nonevaluative, a "structural" theory of genres.[2]

Similarly modern is the increased attention to genres in folk literature. It almost might be said that a preoccupation with formal classification is the indispensable badge of the professional folklorist today. Elsewhere I have suggested that the obvious way to avoid naïve judgments about the relationship of oral literature to the medieval Arthurian romance is to learn the difference between the *Sage* or local legend and the *Märchen*, both in their formal nature and in their methods of diffusion.[3] Literary students like Roger Loomis note that mountains and other natural objects named after Arthur or Gargantua appear after the romances rather than before and are hence derivative. This seems to imply, under the old unitary theory of *gesunkenes Kulturgut*, that all folk literature is derivative from aristocratic literature; the theory is unitary because it is only partly based on fact and because it involves a distortion of the evidence. No folklorist would for a moment deny that the ubiquitous but local *Sagen*, often mere fragments of onomastic fiction, show derivation from medieval literature. What he does insist on is that *Märchen* like the "Two

NOTE. Reprinted from *Genre* 2, no. 2 (June 1969): 91–103, by permission of the University of Illinois Press.

Brothers," "Cupid and Psyche," "The Dragon-Slayer," and "The Bird Lover" are older than the romances and contributory to their origins, form, style, and construction and that therefore these aspects of medieval literary history and criticism can be illuminated by study of the basic extant evidence, the modern oral representatives of medieval oral tales otherwise preserved only through their literary derivatives.

This, however, is only one application of oral-genre study to literature. The whole variety of oral structures can shed light on written structures. This variety is manifold: Aarne and Thompson's folktale types include a whole series of archetypal genres—the animal tale, the *Märchen*, the novella, the religious legend, the jest, and the cumulative tale. Almost any good book on folk literature, from Alexander Haggerty Krappe's eccentric but indispensable *The Science of Folklore*[4] through Jan Brunvand's modern and efficient *The Study of American Folklore*,[5] elucidates these and a great many more genres.

On the theoretical level there has been a significant controversy in German circles, which can be only briefly referred to here. Its modern phase begins in 1930 with André Jolles's concept of *einfache Formen*, which lie at the base of the more complex *Gattungen* of sophisticated literature,[6] where no genre classification can be fixed and inflexible. Jolles's forms are *Legende, Sage, Mythe, Rätsel, Spruch, Märchen, Witz*, or saints' legends, local legends, myths, riddles, proverbs or aphorisms, folktales, and jests. He adds two others, *Kasus* and *Memorabile*—essentially new concepts, which seem on the one hand to relate to exempla and the cases of moral casuistry (the German means merely "incident") and to report of fact (von Sydow's *Memorate?*) without any supernatural element on the other. The *Memorabile* is factual indeed, as opposed to *Sage, Legende*, and *Mythe*, but it must not be left out of the picture of folklore, since oral informants often are the best transmittors of historical truth, witness the recent interest in "oral history."[7] Beginning with Walter Berendsohn,[8] folklorists have protested that Jolles was bound in philological chains, that he paid too little heed to the oral literature, which in their minds unquestionably precedes written literature. Jolles had spoken of the creative factors both in terms of spirit and speech gesture. The saints' legend is the *imitatio* of the saint; the *Sage*, the family world of the Norse saga; the myth, the profound answer to questions about the essence of the universe; the riddle, a secret or problem to be solved as an initiation process; the folktale, the "suspension of an immoral reality"; and the joke "disengagement" and "the concomitant release of emotional tensions."[9] According to his critics Jolles slips into romantic views of language as a reified creative process, rather than as a reflex of life itself.

The best account of the controversy is that of Kurt Ranke, who made it a part of a brilliant inaugural address when he became president of the newly formed International Society for Folk-Narrative Research, which grew from the seeds planted at the Kiel and Copenhagen Congress in 1959.[10] Ranke, a peacemaker as well as a pacemaker, gives more credit to Jolles than some of his co-workers had; he objects to the overly-refined typologies of *einfache Formen* proposed by Berendsohn, Albert Wesselski, and Carl Wilhelm von Sydow. To Ranke, *einfache Form* means "an irreducible, genuine, archetypical form, an integral whole in both content and structure. . . . The folktale, the Sage, or the religious legend . . . can pick up the same motif, but by virtue of their own individual *enérgeia*, they transform this element into their respective particular expression and form." As a *Märchen*, "The Sleeping Beauty" has a happy ending; as saints' legend, "The Seven Sleepers" has a religious and didactic implication; as legends, the sleeping Rip Van Winkle and its German counterparts (Peter Klaus) stress the tragedy of transcience.[11] "As respective generic *topoi* we can point to the theme of the tragic dissolution of man into dust and ashes in the *Sage*, the concept of a blessed death in God in the religious legend, and the happy immutability of existence in the folktale."[12] Thus Ranke points to a broadening of the whole concept, beyond the simple barriers of written literature and beyond those of Indo-European–centered folklore.

The best recent contribution to the subject is Hermann Bausinger's *Forms of Folk-Poetry*.[13] It has appeared too recently to allow careful assessment here; I shall merely provide a table of contents. First it discusses *einfache Formen*, or the problem of folklore and literary origins, and then it divides the "forms" themselves into two major types, "Formel" and "Formen." Essentially this is a brave attempt to bring together the problems of oral formulae, ethnic formulae, metrics, and strict forms like the Wellerism with larger narrative, scenic, and musical forms—jest, *Märchen*, *Sage*, legend, example, anecdote, myth, song, and drama. As a handbook it would seem an excellent

European counterpart to Brunvand's *Study of American Folklore*, with special emphasis on the formidable theoretical background in Germany and on Jolles's seminal concept.

These are heady matters, of great concern to modern folklorists, whose need for both international stimulus and discussion, and international data as well, makes them perhaps the best transcenders of boundaries of all kinds and whose many recent positive discoveries in the realm of data and classification make them occasionally intolerant of theoretical coherence. In the rest of this essay I should like to work with one genre, the ballad, and its relationship to literature. My purpose is not theory but the humbler one of classroom relevance.

As we have seen, the debate has centered on the relationship between folklore and literature. This debate, like too many of those surrounding these two interdependent disciplines, is often circumscribed by the "trained incapacity" of the participants—by the folklorist's dislike of theory and his lack of interest, not perhaps in literary masterpieces themselves, the *Iliad* or the *Miller's Tale* or *Finnegans Wake*, but rather in the subtleties of contemporary literary history and criticism. The student of literature, in turn, is repelled by type and motif numbers, the predominance of German monographs on the folktale, and the basically scientific and statistical aims of some kinds of folklore study. As a folklorist I am biased, and I would argue that, since the folklorist is more frequently forced by bread-and-butter considerations to join literary departments than the literary student is forced to make the simple intellectual leap to the sister discipline, the greater incapacity shows up among the littérateurs. Nowadays the folklorist, angry at his treatment by literature and anthropology departments, tries to create his own institutes (Pennsylvania, Indiana, UCLA, and Texas) and to declare his independence of the Modern Language Association and the American Anthropological Association by holding his own separate but equal American Folklore Society meetings. On the whole this is a healthy development, but it could further impede exchange between scholars who need to talk to one another. As a medievalist aware of the difficulty I have in getting my students to learn Latin and Old French, *or* folklore, I greatly fear the results of further departmental barriers.

Hence it is timely to suggest a few simple ways in which folk genres can be used to aid in the teaching of literary genres.

We have long known that some of the great ballads are worthy of the name tragedy, and no English curriculum can survive without a few ballads on its reading list: "The Wife of Usher's Well," "The Cherry Tree Carol," "Sir Patrick Spens." One shudders sometimes to think of the peculiar notions of the ballad which may be taught by the teacher of the survey course who knows nothing of folklore. Yet perhaps he knows more than we think; the modern folksong movements, with which a young instructor can scarcely escape some contact, cannot always teach untruth.

In any event, it would be hard to miss some of the valuable lessons one can learn from "The Wife of Usher's Well," to take but one example. Most anthologies contain Child A,[14] the version recorded by Sir Walter Scott, with its master touches of allusion and subtle suggestion:

> "The cock doth craw, the day doth daw,
>> The channerin worm doth chide;
> Gin we be mist out o our place,
>> A sair pain we maun bide.
> Fare ye weel, my mother dear!
>> Fareweel to barn and byre!
> And fare ye weel, the bonny lass
>> That kindles my mother's fire!"

Doubtless Scott added his own handiwork to this poem. The "channerin worm" is a linguistic rarity which goes direct to the point and hints at a host of horrors: chewing, chattering, and channeling.[15] It is expert diction. The bonny lass appears nowhere else in the ballad or in its variants; she suggests a whole second tragic subplot of lost love on the part of the youngest revenant. Thus the author of *Waverley* hovers over the poem he reports from "an old woman residing near Kirkhill, in West Lothian." We can never be sure where the old woman left off and Scott began. So much for folksong "authenticity," which deserves this word, but not a dirty word, since no folklorist would deny that a master collector like Scott can improve folk art a bit.

The element of tragedy remains. Here is a woman, a wealthy carline wife, a peasant with the financial strength of a bourgeois. She is not one of the heroes of high place whom Aristotle found in Sophocles, yet she has a character which in personal vigor is worthy of tragic stature. So much for our first point. As a second one we observe that her sons are worthy of their mother. They are "three stout and stalwart sons," sailors we presume, since they are sent "oer the sea" for no specified reason, and we may select the most obvious of the implications. By the simplest kind of incremental repetition the growth of a mother's fears about their death is revealed:

> They hadna been a week from her,
>   A week but barely ane,
> Whan word came to the carline wife
>   That her three sons were gane.

> They hadna been a week from her,
>   A week but barely three,
> Whan word came to the carline wife
>   That her sons she'd never see.

By one week they are "gane," by three she'll "never see" them again. The audience, reasonably pessimistic, knows that "gane" can mean "dead"; yet a mother's hopes war with her fears, and "gane" to her in one mood means only what we know when we heard that they had gone o'er the sea. To us "never see" is final, and to her it is as good as final, for even if they were alive and in prison they are as if dead to her. One can compare this progression with the growing apprehensions of Oedipus as truths begin to come to him, or those of Lear as he discovers the malevolence of Goneril and Regan, or the false evidence submitted to Othello by Iago. Even more dramatically we can recall the importance of having Hamlet's interview with Ophelia precede that with Gertrude. Here the language is simple; in those tragedies it is complex. Yet all five examples reveal the human condition.

Now we come to a third point: the mother's hubris, her defiance of the gods, of the elemental powers:

> "I wish the wind may never cease,
>   Nor fashes in the flood,
> Till my three sons come hame to me,
>   In earthly flesh and blood."

It is part of her strength that she can so blaspheme; it is part also of her *mana* or spirit power that her words have real effect, for the sons do come back. But the verbal invocation is, as usually in folklore and always in tragedy, equivocal. The sons come home indeed, but the Wife forgot to ask that they should come home to stay. This they do not; they are mere revenants. Of the "earthly flesh and blood" we are not told for certain. Since the sons have been at the gates of Paradise and as a result wear birchen hats, they are otherworldly and may be mere shadows of the strengthless dead. Yet they feast, they sleep in bed, and the worm threatens to eat them.

By a masterpiece of understatement we encounter the over-protective mother, who by her blaspheming grief has already damned herself and perhaps her sons as well:

> And she has made to them a bed,
> She's made it large and wide,
> And she's taen her mantle her about,
> Sat down at the bed side.

As for the bonny lass or the maidens who blow the fire, they have no chance at all in this maternal empire. Thereupon we find that, whatever their nature, the sons are doomed to return to the otherworld. They are subject to the dawn and its crowing cock. The otherworld is no longer Paradise; that they have lost by their mother's actions. Now it is the cold grave itself, the burial mound of pagan belief, where "the channerin worm doth chide." Perhaps they did come in earthly flesh and blood. Perhaps that is all they ever will have: an earthly corpse to be eaten by Gifer the worm. With tragic irony the Wife has in her impetuous motherhood triumphed for a moment over the heavens, only to lose all for both herself and her sons in the end.

To this little masterpiece we may in our pedantic way compare the great tragedies and their own ironies: the supersubtle and scholarly Hamlet, enemy of pagan vengeance, forced to a mountain of carnage; Macbeth, the poet whose dreams, inspired by witches, outdistance his needs and who by pushing destiny brings unwanted destiny upon himself; Othello, brave and prudent general whose mind is clean of doubt, led into a bedchamber pettiness of suspicion and climax of murder; Oedipus, martyr to his people, who is so incredulous of prophecy that he weaves about him his own web of destruction. Against all these we may set our Wife, no minor rival of theirs but a woman who packs in herself all the verities of maternal strength and weakness. In the sudden shift from bedroom to grave, rest from pain to painful resting, lies peripeteia; in the horrid revelation of the two speaking sons, anagnorisis; in the leaping and lingering drama, the three acts of beginning, middle, and end; and, in the crucial episode, one night of action, are unities of place and action. The great simplicities which are so hard to control in the sprawling drama are easily retained in the folk ballad. One need not belabor the point: any classroom where ballad is juxtaposed to tragedy will find the simple form a highly efficient prelude and paradigm for the form of greater complexity.

But there is yet more to learn from folklore and from this ballad in particular. Both ballads and literary works have variants: *Hamlet* and *Ur-Hamlet*, ballads Child ABC and D and often many more.[16] "The Wife of Usher's Well" has its counterpart in D, "communicated, 1896, by Miss Emma M. Backus, of North Carolina, who notes that it has long been sung by the 'poor whites' in the mountains of Polk County in that State."[17] This time the American Child was good to us; usually he had no American variants, and their discovery in mass was the later triumph of a host of collectors from Cecil Sharp to Edward Ives, Vance Randolph, and Bertrand Bronson today. But now Child gives us enough for a meaningful comparison, capable of defining the difference between irony and sentimentality, tragedy and melodrama.

Our Scottish Wife is strong and carline, her sons strong and stalwart, her attitude to the heavens one of defiance. What of the heroine of Child D?

> There was a lady fair and gay,
>   And children she had three:
> She sent them away to some northern land,
>   For to learn their grammeree.

Falling to the language of genesis, we may speak here of a downward evolution, a mighty loss between Child A and D. Genesis of course is not our problem, for ballads may go down, as this one does, or up, as does "The Foggy Foggy Dew." The real thing is the tone, which says something very plain to the literary student. We have moved from a vigorous peasant woman to a stereotyped "lady fair and gay," whose breeding does not guarantee strength of character and suggests something rather effete and delicate. That is our first point again. The second concerns the sons, who have become "three little lonely babes," learning their grammar in school. Sickness takes them, rather than the virile perils of the sailor on the sea. The death is plainly labeled, with no maternal nuances. The tragic spirit admires the matured human being who owes something to the world because the world has given him life, the man who is capable of decision, even though, being human, he may abuse it. *Posse non peccare*, to use Augustine's words. In turn the sentimental spirit loves to weep over the babe, the powerless infant—pure emotion uncontaminated with reason. But emotion, called on so often, becomes stereotyped, and these babes are the creatures of stereotype, pathetic creatures rather than men of potency who could be a tragic loss to the world that bred them, as well as to the grieving mother.

Nor is our gentle Lady Gay capable of the Wife's defiant blasphemy; her appeal is to the conventional medieval and Christian heaven:

> There is a king in the heavens above
>> That wears a golden crown;
> She prayed that he would send her babes home
>> To-night or in the morning soon.

Martinmas, a colorful day with deep pagan overtones recalling animal ritual sacrifice and a vigorous saint, patron of tavern keepers, beggars, vine growers, and reformed and unreformed drunkards,[18] is in Child A the day of the boys' return. In the American version the shift from Martinmas to Christmas reflects Protestant culture, but the new festival, with no discredit to that happy season, not yet commercialized in the Piedmont, increases the poem's blandness. When the college student Hickman killed "Little Marion Parker" (a ballad of the 1920's in America) he did it on Christmas Day, and that was the worst of all. Or are we to make something of the Infancy and the returning babes? Possibly, but the inference seems not only bold but meaningless. What is gained except emasculation, already present in the babes themselves, who will not—like the other Babe—grow to drive the moneychangers out of the temple? That Babe triumphed over death; these do not. Always remembering that we are speaking to students, we might say something here about the difficulties of Christian tragedy. Christianity has but one tragedy, and that leads to the Divine Comedy.

The Lady Gay does not see the babes even in inferable earthly flesh and blood; she only dreams of them. They do not feast as the Wife's sons had done; they are under tabu against eating earthly food. All they can think of is "our Saviour," a worthy object of reverence, of course, but not a common allusion in tragedy. She does dream that she makes them sleep; a nuisance this double dream-state. Then the eldest wakes them all; the symbolic cocks are not there to do it. Absent is the "channerin worm," since the babes seem to have a secure enough place in heaven if they do not eat. Absent too is the bonny lass and the maidens; they have no place in this kindergarten, *pace* Sigmund Freud. The moral is wholly Christian:

> "Green grass grows at our head, dear mother,
>   Green moss grows at our feet;
> The tears that you shed for us three babes
>   Won't wet our winding sheet."

This last line seems a little fudged. The truth is that the Lady's weeping really does pain the babes; it does wet the winding sheet,[19] as in "The Unquiet Grave" (Child, No. 78):

> " 'Tis I, my love, sits on your grave,
>   And I will not let you sleep;
> For I crave one kiss of your clay-cold lips,
>   And that is all I seek."

> "You crave one kiss of my clay-cold lips;
>   But my breath smells earthly strong;
> If you have one kiss of my clay-cold lips,
>   Your time will not be long."

The *mana* of tears preserves relics of pagan belief, but the moral is Christian.

In the history of genres nothing is more striking than the way in which Christianity took the motive out of the ancient elegy for the dead. Immortality makes elegy redundant and superfluous, since the better life is infinitely to be preferred to this one, the human condition. Our babes are not yet in heaven, and the tears pain them in their green graves. The greenness itself is significant. It may be a sign of fertility and resurrection, a happy sign that immortal life is to come; it may also be a mere natural result of the weeping. In any event we have a Christian poem in Child D, acceptable to all good people, meaningful in the light of the conventional, but sentimental, nontragic, and almost banal to the discriminating reader. Its lovely tune, as sung by Andrew Rowan Summers and John Jacob Niles, in part excuses the bathos. To the student who has come close to the tragedy of "The Wife of Usher's Well" in Child A, there has been an unconscionable falling off.

Thus, by comparing a simple form in its variants with a complex Elizabethan tragic form, we may highlight irony and tragedy as opposed to the blander tone of a less heroic age. One could make many more such demonstrations: how, for instance, the Grimm version of "The Fisherman and His Wife" reveals the technique of tragic inevitability. A tormented sea and sky, the forces of nature, reinforce the mood as does the storm in *Lear*; the increment of such forces, rising in intensity, prophesies the final defeat of the wife who through her husband asks the Fish for hut, castle, kingdom, empire, papacy, and finally equation with God. Yet all along we know that something will explode in the end, and we sit on our seats waiting to see what limits there are to this woman's greed and to heaven's tolerance. Both folktale and ballad are useful to the critical forum and to the classroom.

We are often asked why new modes of artistic apprehension come more quickly with the plastic arts than they do with the literary, why the Fauves caught on more speedily than did Joyce or Eliot or even the literary Dadaists like Tristan Tzara. Why does Pollock make millions while the Little Magazines have to be subsidized? The answer is easy: one comprehends the structure of a work of art on sight—more easily of course if one is a connoisseur, but easily enough unless one closes one's mind (as too many do) to the impression there to take for a song. By contrast the work of literature, the long poem or novel, must be sat with for hours, and only the connoisseur comes close to anything like an appropriate sense of its structure, because only he can put in the hours with efficacy. Our hedonistic students today are vastly more visual than they are verbal; the Fine Arts course gets across much more swiftly than the Survey of Literature. We need, therefore, the simple forms of folk art as a prelude and touchstone for the literary master work. Once one has the strategy and the terms, the grooving emotion and excitement, one can proceed by graded effort to the ultimate initiation, the ultimate catharsis. With the ballad and the folktale so ready to hand, why not use them?

Notes

1. René Wellek, *A History of Modern Criticism: 1750–1950* (New Haven: Yale University Press, 1965), IV, 65–68. For a brilliant attack on evolutionary theories as applied to the drama see O. B. Hardison, Jr., *Christian Rite and Christian Drama in the Middle Ages* (Baltimore: Johns Hopkins Press, 1965).

2. Northrop Frye, *Anatomy of Criticism: Four Essays*. See also the article "Genres" and articles on the specific genres in Alexander Preminger et al., eds., *Encyclopedia of Poetry and Poetics* (Princeton: Princeton University Press, 1965), pp. 307–309.

3. Francis Lee Utley, "Arthurian Romance and International Folktale Method," *Romance Philology* 17 (1964): 596–607.

4. Alexander Haggerty Krappe, *The Science of Folklore*.

5. Jan Harold Brunvand, *The Study of American Folklore*.

6. André Jolles, *Einfache Formen*, 3d ed. (Tübingen, 1965).

7. Jan Vansina, *Oral Tradition: A Study in Historical Methodology*, trans. H. M. Wright (Chicago: Aldine, 1961).

8. Walter A. Berendsohn, "Einfache Formen," in *Handwörterbuch des deutschen Märchen*, ed. Johannes Bolte and Lutz Mackensen, I, 484–498.

9. Kurt Ranke, "Einfache Formen," in *Internationaler Kongress der Volkserzählungsforscher in Kiel und Kopenhagen 1959—Vorträge und Referate*, pp. 1–11. Translated by William Templer and Eberhard Alsen in *Journal of the Folklore Institute* 4 (1967): 17–31. For the treatment of the genres in particular see *JFI*, p. 20. The other articles in this issue of *JFI* treat related matters: Max Lüthi, "Parallel Themes in Folk Literature and Art Literature," pp. 3–16; Isidor Levin, "Vladímir Propp: An Evaluation on His Seventieth Birthday," pp. 32–49.

10. See note 9.

11. The examples, with an American increment, are taken from Max Lüthi's *Es war einmal: Vom Wesen des Volksmärchens*, 3d ed. (Gottingen: Vandenhoeck & Ruprecht, 1968). A translation by Lee Chadeayne and Paul Gottwald,

with an introduction by Francis Lee Utley, has appeared with the title *Once upon a Time: On the Nature of Fairy Tales.*

12. Ranke, "Einfache Formen," *JFI* 4 (1967): 28.

13. Hermann Bausinger, *Formen der "Volkspoesie."*

14. Francis James Child, ed., *English and Scottish Popular Ballads*, reprint 5 vols. in 3 (New York: Pageant Books, 1956), I, 238–239 (no. 79).

15. See *OED* under "channer"; Sir W. A. Craigie, *A Dictionary of the Older Scottish Tongue*, under the same. Not in Kurath and Kuhn's *Middle English Dictionary.*

16. For American versions, see Tristram P. Coffin, *The British Traditional Ballad in North America*, rev. ed., American Folklore Society Bibliographical and Special Series, no. 2 (Philadelphia: American Folklore Society, 1963), no. 79.

17. Child, *English and Scottish Popular Ballads*, V, 294. The D version was added in the notes by George Lyman Kittredge. It is not clear whether it was originally in Child's notes and not used or was newly collected by someone known to Kittredge.

18. See "Martinmas" in Maria Leach, ed., *Funk & Wagnalls Standard Dictionary of Folklore, Mythology and Legend*, 2 vols. (New York: Funk & Wagnalls, 1950), II, 682.

19. Child D is eccentric, and Kittredge suggests emendation. The usual American variants, usually of the same sentimental cast, agree in making the tears wet the shroud. See, for instance, Arthur Kyle Davis, *Traditional Ballads of Virginia* (Cambridge, Mass.: Harvard University Press, 1929), pp. 279–287 (variants A, E, F, I—though G on p. 285 makes the babe consider the tears as "dear," another apparent reversal of the superstition); Alton G. Morris, *Folksongs of Florida* (Gainesville: University of Florida Press, 1950), pp. 281–282 (A and B); Vance Randolph, *Ozark Folksongs* (Columbia: State Historical Society of Missouri, 1946), I, 123–124 (A and B). For the agony of excessive grief for the living as suffered by the dead see Child, *English and Scottish Popular Ballads*, I, 234–236, and Lowry C. Wimberly, *Folklore in the English and Scottish Popular Ballads* (Chicago: University of Chicago Press, 1928), pp. 103–110, 230–233.

2. Aspects of the *Märchen* and the Legend

MAX LÜTHI

In the introduction to a recently published collection of Breton folk-tales the editor, Geneviève Massignon, noted the remark of one of her informants that these *Märchen* were so old that one couldn't know if they ever were invented by anyone: "contes si vieux que l'on ne sait pas si personne les a jamais inventés."[1] The remark of this woman of Lower Brittany, in particular the choice of the word *inventé*, shows exactly the feelings of countless hearers and narrators of folk tales and also those of many scholars: these stories could not have been invented; they must somehow have created themselves. "Composition" (*Zubereitung*) in literature and "spontaneous creation" (*Sichvonselbstmachen*) in folk literature are the formulations Jacob Grimm used to express this.[2]

Under the influence of the theory of *gesunkenes Kulturgut* such views later fell into disfavor. We have not become weary of repeating that it is not any mystical folk mind which creates poetry, but that in every single case it is a certain individual. When in his large-scale and careful investigation of the tale of the Animal Bridegroom, which appeared nearly fifteen years ago, Jan-Öjvind Swahn arrived at the assumption of some kind of collective origin for this tale type, of which "Amor and Psyche" is the best-known representative, critics immediately objected that his arguments were taken from the "moth chest of Romanticism."[3] Now the Breton storyteller whose avowal we cited at the beginning of this article has certainly not come in contact with that notorious chest at any time. Yet even modern research has again approached the position of Jacob Grimm in a sense, proceeding from a completely different hypothesis. Advocates of the so-called

NOTE. Reprinted from *Genre* 2, no. 2 (June 1969): 162–178, by permission of the University of Illinois Press; translated by Barbara Flynn. Originally published in *Germanisch-Romanische Monatsschrift*, N. F. 16, no. 4 (1966): 337–350.

Märchen biology, which investigates the life of the tale, that is, the function and role of the tale and of its narrator in the community, say that not only the narrator but also the audience participate in the construction and wording of the tales. The narrators pay attention to the needs and desires and also to the immediate mood of the listeners. Creative personalities wanting to innovate are restrained by their generally more conservative public. Less skillful narrators are corrected and encouraged to improve the story. The Hungarian scholar Gyula Ortutay said flatly, "The audience takes part in the creation of variants."

In this way modern *Märchen* biology comes to conclusions similar to those of modern folksong research. This stresses that one might go so far as to designate folksongs as collective creations, since only those songs could become folksongs which from the outset are planned according to a current idea and which are created according to a current form or which can adapt themselves to this form in the course of transmission. The effect of repeated singing may either be destructive (*Zersingen*) or corrective (*Zurechtsingen*). The *Märchen* biologists observe a corrective way to tell a tale (*Zurechterzählen*), as well as an incorrect and destructive way (*Zerzählen*). Once again I will quote Ortutay: "We have . . . learned that a ballad or a tale begins to degenerate, to become bad, when the audience is no longer present, when the item is preserved only by the individual memory, which becomes more and more unsure." The audience spurs the narrator on to a better, finer performance and spurs his rivals to emulate him.[4]

Beside the folkloristically and sociologically focused *Märchen* biology stands *Märchen* psychology. Today this is supported above all by developmental psychologists and by the members of the Jungian school. In another way and in another sense than *Märchen* biology, psychologists too shore up the theory of the collective origin of folktales and with it the old theory of polygenesis, which is admitted for simple tales, but which has been given up almost as universally for more complicated creations. Psychologists detect in *Märchen* symbols of emotional events that in essence are common to all men, even if they are also differentiated according to the individual, race, and stage of culture. Because even complex psychic events, above all the maturation processes, take place in a similar way everywhere and at all times, relatively complex stories, which mirror these events, could have originated independently from one another everywhere and at all times.[5]

The continuing argument over the question of how far tales and legends are of collective and how far of individual origin shows that the impression that *Märchen* and legends have not been arbitrarily created, not *inventé*, but somehow arose and grew by themselves, an impression occurring again and again among simple peoples just as among scholars, really contributes to the fascination of this creation.

In the present essay, which by no means attempts to discuss the problem in a fundamental manner, the apparent or real spontaneous creation of objects in folktales can serve as a point of departure. Even now it has become clear that the most varied sciences are interested in the *Märchen*. The literary scholar attempts to investigate the history, that is the origin, development, spread, and changes of the tales, but he also asks about their structure and style and about the view of man and the world contained in them. The folklorist seeks not only traces of old customs and rites in the *Märchen* and legend, but as a biologist he investigates their place in the life of the community; he is interested in the tales and in the relation of the tales to their environment. The sociologist also promotes *Märchen* and legend biology, and beyond that he sees in legends and tales reflections of the disputes of the different social groups. Historians of religion and mythologists take tales and legends as evidence of the relation of men to the supernatural, and psychologists, educators, and psychiatrists try to understand them as the expression of emotional development and complexities and to investigate their effect and influence on healthy people and on patients, on children and on adults. Thus tales and legends are a field of activity (at times one might say a playground) for many sciences.

Since in *Märchen*, and especially in legends, standards are also set and ethical demands advanced, one could think that even philosophy would allow herself to be tempted out of her ivory tower. So far this has not happened. Instead, folkloristics is concerned with this side of the legend, with the moralizing and ethical standards in the legend. The folklorist is the most comprehensive caretaker of tales and legends. He is not only their investigator but at the same time their collector and usually also their editor. Each science investigates the folktale from a different standpoint; each makes other aspects visible. We have already touched on a few of these, and we will touch on a few others, but essentially we are limiting ourselves to the literary method of observation. This also has more than one side and has the advantage of a certain objectivity. *Märchen* psychology easily leads to speculation. Whether the various figures of the tales represent various parts of the personality is a matter for discussion.

Since each action of a man is also an argument of this man with himself, it seems to me that one cannot deny the supposition that the family in the folktale is a symbolic representation of the total personality—"Each person is a little society"—a supposition that is at least relatively justified. But it still remains a supposition, whereas the descriptive statement that the family as an organizing principle plays a greater role in the *Märchen* than in the legend is in the realm of the observable. That it is the nuclear family which forms the folktale (nephews, cousins, or aunts scarcely ever appear) contributes to the strictness of the narrative form. At the same time, something of its world view manifests itself in the way the *Märchen* presents the family. The family in the *Märchen* is full of tensions, full of inner conflicts. The hero and heroine are better sheltered in universal nature than they are in family. Animals and stars are usually more trustworthy and helpful partners than brothers and sisters, sons and parents; to scarcely any of the usual helper figures does the hero of the *Märchen* have a closer relation than to the helpful animals. These are sober statements. But whether a helpful fox symbolizes a specific side of the unconscious allows for a difference of opinion. Because psychologists lean toward bold theories, they have so far encountered from folklorists and literary scholars almost as strong a rejection as that encountered by the Nature Mythologists of the last century. However, their contribution to the knowledge of the folktale should not be underestimated. If in this literary essay little is said of them, this should not be taken as a value judgment.

To the question of what is spontaneously created in the *Märchen*—we will speak of it next—one might answer: the manner of narration, the style. Whoever acknowledges that the characteristic mark of a work of art is the harmony of all its elements in a unified style[6] will state, perhaps with a certain bewilderment, that in the European folktale, which in the form finally transmitted to us is certainly not the work of a single person, such a harmony of stylistic elements establishes itself as though spontaneously. The folktale likes everything to be sharply defined, of specified form. It likes to speak of staffs, swords, guns, feathers, and animal hairs—all things whose form approaches the linear. It often mentions little boxes, nuts, eggs; not only costly clothes or spinning wheels, but whole castles are enclosed in a nut or an egg and therewith are confined in a circle with a clear outline. One of the best-known folktale motifs is that of the life in the egg; the innermost life of the giant or a cannibal is not in his body but somewhere far away in a well-hidden and well-protected egg. Only the one who breaks or crushes this egg can kill the giant. In our context one recognizes at once that the egg occurs here not only because it is an ancient symbol of life, but also because as a stylistic element it is well suited to the total style of the folktale. The folktale also likes to speak of rooms, houses, and castles, all things with sharp borders and horizontal and vertical interior lines. The castle, a mentally projected geometric conception, is a sort of emblem for the folktale, just as the cave with its uncertain form lost in the darkness of the earth is an emblem for the legend. Correspondingly, in the *Märchen* clothing plays a greater role than the body—whose presence we often feel very clearly in the legend.

To the partiality for sharply outlined, clearly formed things is added the *Märchen*'s general preference for hard and clear-colored metals such as gold, silver, copper, and iron; for minerals—stone and glass; and for bold colors, especially red, white, and black, above all, and the metallic colors. Mixed colors and shades are almost completely lacking. In addition to this come the formulaic numbers (3, 7, 12, 100), formulaic openings and conclusions, transition sentences, charms and magic verse, the habit of formulaic repetition, multiplication, contrast, and the tendency to push everything to its farthest extreme—the punishments as well as the rewards, the social types (the hero is either prince or swineherd) as well as character types (the hero and heroine are good, their opponents evil). The hero and heroine stand not only at the extreme ends of the social order but also at the extreme edge of the family. They are the youngest and apparently the weakest and most unpromising.

The same sharp formation, precision, clarity, and stability reign in the design of the action. Things such as the forest or the city into which the hero enters are only named, not described. The figures are isolated; they set out into the world alone; the action is developed in far-reaching lines, whereas by preference the events of the legend occur within one place. The folktale action has marked junctions, tasks, commands, prohibitions, and restrictions; the hero is guided by advice, gifts, and assistance, not by emotional impulse or the decisions of his conscience. The terse conclusion is in accordance with the clarity marking the narrow line of action. The sudden transformation, as well as any sort of miraculous happening, also fits into the total style. It is a style of precision and clarity. The episodes rank themselves together, not haphazardly, and not in unspecified numbers, as happens so often in the sweeping oriental tales, but usually in three divisions, with the stress on the last. As a whole the folktale is frequently in two parts. The order of episodes is in accord syntactically with the parataxis of the sentences. But many other tales also tend toward a clear diagram, which makes everything visible, makes everything proceed smoothly, and translates qualities into deeds, relationships into gifts. Neither the inner life nor the social life of the characters, neither their surroundings, origin, or posterity are presented. The characters of the *Märchen* are cut out of the context of their existence; they have no real surroundings, no real inner world, no posterity, no ancestors. And the isolation of the characters accords with the isolation of the episodes, which are sealed off in themselves, often so much so that reference or allusion to earlier events is avoided and instead these events are told again in the same or slightly different words. Certainly this is one of the means of prolonging the tales without having to lose oneself in descriptions. But it is at the same time suited to the whole style of the folktale. Indeed stylistic pressure is rather stronger than the need to expand the tales.

When one considers that all this happened again and again in oral tales, among more and more different narrators, and among the most varied peoples, then one will involuntarily say that the tale has obviously risen spontaneously. That is, it arises not only or even predominantly from the necessities of oral transmission and the primitiveness of the narrator. Folksong and legend have different styles than the *Märchen*. In folksong the colors of living nature, green and brown, occur frequently; in the *Märchen* mention is made of neither the green of the deciduous forest or the pine forest nor the brown of tree trunks, fields, or hair, but rather they speak of golden hair and coppery-colored forests. This is not because these are easier to tell of or more convenient to transmit but because they belong to the style of this class of tale.

Thereto it happens that a picture of man automatically results from this style of the European folktale, which I have tried to sketch comprehensively or at least to indicate.[7] At the center of the *Märchen* stands the hero or heroine. All other characters, no matter how sharply drawn, are only opponents, helpers, or motivators of him, or they contrast to him. Now the central character, the hero, appears, in accord with the total style of the folktale, as one isolated. He is the outermost, most dispensable member of the social order as well as of the family. Within the family he bears the stigma of stupidity or laziness; not infrequently he is the only child, born to parents who have been childless for a long period; he is a stepchild or a Tom Thumb; magical conception may mark him and single him out—he appears as the offspring of an animal or even as half-man. He leaves his parents and by no means always returns to his father's house, as Hansel and Gretel do. Hansel and Gretel are abandoned; others leave voluntarily, travel under completely different pretexts out into the unknown world and encounter adventures alone. But precisely because they are nowhere firmly rooted, they are free to accept each new relationship, free to enter into and dissolve every tie; they receive gifts and help from otherworldly characters easily and surely.

In its heroes and heroines the *Märchen* delineates man as isolated and, because of this, capable of universal relationships. The hero of the *Märchen* is isolated but not at the mercy of the world; instead he is simply the gifted one, who receives gifts and aid at every step and is able to accept them, in contrast to his unendowed older brothers and sisters. He is isolated but not lonely, because he doesn't feel himself to be alone; all important contacts are made without difficulty. Because this representation of man results from the whole style of the *Märchen*, it recurs in each tale. Psychologists, who try to interpret the *Märchen* symbolically, refer to particular statements of different tales, to maturation and growth processes, to struggles with bonds to mother or father, to the search for the core of the true personality, to the devotion to unconscious spheres and neglected possibilities, to conflicts within the unconscious. We completely believe that such things are reflected in the *Märchen*. It is indisputable that the *Märchen* plainly invites symbolic interpretation. Everyone sees that the beautiful princess symbolizes a high value and that dragons, witches, and ogres symbolize evil powers. But in the interpretation of special traits opinions can differ, and arbitrary judgment easily slips in. However the general picture of man, which is peculiar to this genre can be immediately gathered from the tales.

The legend also gives a description of man. It is different from that of the *Märchen* because the viewpoint of the legend is different. The *Märchen* considers man; the legend considers what happens to man. The *Märchen* outlines the narrow road of the hero walking through the world and does not dwell on the figures meeting him. But the legend looks fixedly at the inexplicable which confronts man. And because it is monstrous—war, pestilence, or landslide, and especially often a numinous power, be it nature, demons, or spirits of the dead —man becomes small and unsure before it. The legend sketches suffering man, stricken and perplexed, questioning, brooding, explaining, but also struggling with a difficult decision, losing himself in wantonness or rising to a sacrificial act. More than once it has been shown that the historical legend in particular sketches man as someone enduring fate rather than shaping or mastering it.[8] But the man of the legend is not more passive than he of the *Märchen* in every respect. In thinking and interpreting, in the spiritual conflict with the powers meeting him, he is far more self-reliant and active than the hero of the *Märchen*, who accepts almost everything as self-evident. Not only his thoughts, misgivings, and fears arise out of his own soul, but also his decisions and deeds, whereas the hero of the *Märchen* is guided and moved through gifts, instructions, obstacles, and aids. In the distant view of the *Märchen*, men, animals, and otherworldly beings change into mere shapes. The legend, however, is close to man, animal, and spirit. It has another viewing distance and another line of sight. In its center stands not man as such, but his difficult-to-comprehend partner.

Both the slight distance and the attention to the supernatural partner automatically produce another description of man. It also produces another manner of narration. In this way, as the man of the legend is a groper, a questioner, a small thing surrendered to the grip of monstrous powers, so also is the manner of narration groping and fragmentary. It is debatable whether one could speak of a special legend style. "When dealing with the legend, there is . . . no point in asking after the form of the tale and after its generic style," declares Leopold Schmidt. "There is no such thing; in the legend, everything is content."[9] Such an attitude apparently does not differentiate at all, or not enough, between folk belief and legend. In folk belief everything is content, but the folk legend is a narrative form and as such has its style. In another place I have tried to describe this style more precisely as a mixture of elements of certainty and uncertainty, a mixture which the divided, uncertain attitude of the man of the legend matches.[10]

As narrative the *Märchen* is richer than the legend. As simple as it seems, it is differentiated in its way. It is aware of the contrast between being and appearing; especially is it aware of the two-facedness of a thing. The forest, the castle, and the forbidden room are at the same time places of danger and of important adventure, the wild animal can change to a grateful helper or to a radiant bridegroom, death can bring release or transformation to man. A more central bearer of the theme of appearance and reality is the hero of the *Märchen*, who appears to be stupid, lazy, dirty, awkward, ugly, and abnormal but then proves himself to be one who outshines all the others.

Other important themes also appear in the *Märchen*, such as the meeting with oneself. We have already encountered the motif of the hidden life; the tales in which it is contained are known under a variety of names, such as The Giant without a Heart (and are Number 302 in the Aarne-Thompson Type Index).[11] The giant, ogre, or cannibal has hidden his life somewhere outside his body, usually far away in a berry, a bee, a bird, or a fish, in a sword, or especially in an egg. He who gets it in his power has power over the life of the giant. The secret of where the life is placed being conveyed to the hero through the maiden stolen by the giant, he finds the egg and crushes it so that the giant must die. In many variants it is the case that the death of the giant ensues only when one hurls the egg against the giant's own forehead. The giant dies by his own hand, as it were. It is noteworthy that the most different types of folk narrative, not only the *Märchen*, tend toward such a fateful self-encounter. As in "Hansel and Gretel" the witch must burn in her own oven, in this manner other monsters also perish through their own evil methods; in the *Märchen* of the Romanic countries, for example, Bluebeard and the evil mother-in-law of Dornröschen perish in this manner.

Especially impressive is a legend of a nightmare, recorded in many

Swedish variants. A farmer or squire finds his horse—sometimes it is designated as his favorite horse—sweat-covered every morning and standing shivering in its stall. He suspects the horse is being ridden by a nightmare and uses a device appearing in many such legends to ward off the nightmare. He ties a scythe, with its cutting edge up, upon the back of the horse. In the morning the farmer is found dead in the stall. Night after night, without knowing it, he has gone to oppress his horse himself, and he has now been slain by his own weapon. There are many legends about nightmares with the motif of a knife or scythe with its edge turned upward. Then on the next morning one finds a member of the household or village, either male or female, who was wounded during the night and because of this is now unmasked as one who "goes riding" at night.

In the Swedish group,[12] where not a man but a horse is ridden, the possibility is open for the owner himself to injure his horse and by this to inflict harm on himself as well. The highest and most decisive form of this possibility is the death of the man through his own preventive measures. This goal is not reached in all narratives. There are versions in which a servant ties the scythe to the horse and in the morning finds his master dead or only wounded in the stall and others in which the farmer binds the scythe and then encounters the servant dead or injured. In this manner the variants oscillate around a goal which many of them reach, while others don't completely achieve it. But it is obvious that striving toward this goal is inherent in the legend group and that it aims there as the highest development of the conception of a tale held by the group. We encounter here a special form of the corrective way to tell a tale.

There are not only original forms (archetypes) from which the variants were derived; there are also end forms (*Zielformen*) to which they strive. For many decades it has been the chief work of the so-called Finnish school to ascertain the original form of a tale type through a comparison of all its known variants. Scarcely anyone has concerned himself with what one could call an end form. In our example, when certain versions stress that it is not just any horse which causes the squire's death, but his favorite, it means an accentuation of reference to himself. Similarly in the cycle of tales about Oleg or Orvar Odd, which also proceed toward the destruction of the hero through his own doing, there are climax forms in which the vehicle of doom is not just any one of his horses or perhaps only a predatory animal, but his favorite horse, whom he loves and who has previously saved his life.[13]

From Jeremias Gotthelf's "Schwarze Spinne" we know about the plugging up of demons of contagion. As a spider or smoke, the demon is shut in a crack, a knothole, or a dowel hole of a wooden house. Years later someone pulls out the plug, and then the disease breaks out anew.[14] Here also variants tell how the actors destroy themselves. Thus in a version from Uri recorded by Josef Müller:

> As the Black Death reigned in the land, they built at Spiringen a house in Sticki or in Butzli. During the construction a worker was stricken by the disease. His thumb was already black. Deciding quickly, he cut it off and placed it in a dowel hole which he closed securely. Soon afterwards he went abroad. Ten years later he returned home. As he came to the Sticki-house he wondered about his thumb. He opened the dowel-hole and the finger leaped at his forehead. Then he was stricken by the pestilence and died in a few hours.[15]

Here there are no ogres; only the theme of insolence and hubris, which often occurs in the legend, is a slight reminder of them. But the picture of the unfortunate man's own thumb leaping at his forehead is the legend's analogue to the *Märchen's* picture of the life in the egg which is hurled against the forehead of the giant and which brings death to him. Both are pictures of self-destruction.

Also in the plague legend many variants reach the ideal form only approximately. "As the Black Death overran the Jen Valley," so it is reported, "a woodsman in the forest was stricken by it. He saw the black swellings, removed them with an ax, bored a hole in a fir tree and shut them inside. A year later he was laughing about them again and said he wanted to see what they were doing. He opened the hole; then a blue smoke came out and then he was finished."[16] Thus the shape of a certain theme, here that of ruinous self-encounter, works itself in many legend types into the body of variants within a certain place, and, as if by chance, one version comes closer to and others farther from the goal contained by entelechy within the motif constellation. Let us understand "goal" as a thematic concept, not as a quality of form.[17]

Among treasure legends is a group in which the spirit guarding the treasure must be forced to release itself. Every time the ghost commands the daring treasure hunter to do something, he must induce the spirit to be released to do it himself: "Lead the way yourself!" "Untie yourself!" "Chop it yourself!" Johann Wilhelm Wolff, who in 1853 published such a legend recorded in Hessen, notes, "The spirit leading the way is in such cases the main point, since otherwise the spirit would probably leap on the neck of the one he accompanies or inflict evil in another way."[18] This realistic explanation is certainly completely plausible. But, against the background of all the other tales that are aware of the theme of self-encounter, the motif at once acquires a fuller meaning.

A sort of evolution of material toward a goal inherent in it also appears in the legend which during the nineteenth century in northern Germany attached itself to the murder of an unpopular landowner.[19] In many variants the event words for itself an impressive final picture: the lord must dance himself to death on the sherds of his own wine bottles. In one case the real point of departure is that the man has been tortured to death with scissors, glass fragments, and rods; in one other, that the sticks with which he had previously thrashed people are used on his body and beaten to shreds. In this way what so often occurs in tales has here happened in reality—the hard-hearted man perishes through his own instruments of torture. The narrative fantasy, however, even in this case tends toward the optically significant and symbolic final picture—the dance of death of the lord on the fragments of his own wine bottles. In another case a variant combines both: "Si hebben de Wienfläschen intwei smäten, un he hat so lang up de Schörwen danzen müsst, bet he doot wäst is. Mit de Pietsch hebben se em dräben." The tyrant is not murdered, he must dance himself to death, and his own whip drives him to it.

Another kind of self-evolution of material we meet in the wide circle of variants on the death of Great Pan.[20] In the writings of Plutarch about the fall of the oracle we read how the helmsman of a Greek ship is called to from an island, "When you come to Palodos, announce that Great Pan is dead." As the helmsman then does this, "one hears a great lament, not from one, but from many voices." Modern legend collections have recorded numerous similar tales. Austrian legends tell how a *Fänggin*, a young forest-woman, serves as maid to a farmer. A man going through the mountain forest suddenly hears a hoarse voice call to him, "Tell the Stutzfärche, the Rohrinde is fallen and dead." In the house of the farmer the wanderer tells of his unusual experience; and then the maid rises, begins to howl and lament, runs swiftly to the mountain forest, and is seen no more. The names change in other versions of the tale and in different traditions, but they usually have reference to trees; vegetation spirits have been inferred—in reflections on Pan as well—and the mourning of the death of Nature spirits in autumn has been thought of. But in northern Germany the same story is told about kobolds, and in England and Ireland it is even told about cats. Mutual relationships are not clarified; the northern form can just as well be the original as the southern.

As early as 1922, the American scholar Archer Taylor advocated the opinion that the bearers of the action are less important than the story itself. In each landscape the legendary beings entrusted to it are simply inserted as figures. What interests us in our connection is the circumstance that the change of the figures automatically changes the story. The forest beings of the south usually begin to mourn with the reception of the tidings of death; the cat of the north, however, rejoices over the news of the death of the King of the Cats because now it will become the king's successor. Or it leaps at the throat of the lord, who along the way has killed a wild cat, and chokes him. In the *Märchen* one can exchange figures almost arbitrarily; it has no influence on the course of the action whether a minister or a coachman plays the usurper and claims to have killed the dragon. The less easily flowing legend, however, feels the force of the changing characters and adapts itself to their individuality. The nature beings of the Alps are sensitive. But cats are considered witches' animals and have a bad reputation, especially in Celtic regions. Thus under their influence the tale takes another direction, as by itself it approaches dark tragedy, whereas in the Alpine legends the prosperity that the *Fänggin* has brought to the farm continues after her departure. In the English version, the earliest-known variant of which arises in the middle of the sixteenth century, when the man who along the way has killed the unknown cat tells his deed at home himself and through it proceeds to his own destruction, a theme well known to us again appears.

We have called our essay "Aspects of the *Märchen* and the Legend." From the point of departure of spontaneous creation a number of different aspects have come into view; others have remained unmentioned. We now refer back to one of the tales previously mentioned and consider in particular a few more points. The legend group last discussed, that of the death of Great Pan, above all shows much of the individuality of the legend: projection of a mysterious and completely different world into the profane world of everyday, the uncanny actions, the astonishment of the perplexed, the incomprehensibility of the unknown world. This unknown world, however, manifests itself in a very precise sentence, cited exactly from the most ancient to the most recent records. All this is evidence for that mixture of definite and indefinite elements of which we have already spoken.[21]

"D'Jochrumpla söl hêmkô, der Muggastutz sei tôd." "Kilian ist tot!" "Balthasar est mort!" or "Burlotte est morte." "Commend me unto Titton Tatton and to Pus thy Catton and tell her that Grimalkin is dead." Ὁπόταν γένη κατὰ τὸ Παλῶδες, ἀπάγγελον‘ὅτι Πὰν ὁ μέγας τέθνηκε. There follows a very definite reaction, whose meaning, however, remains doubtful—here again is the characteristic entwining of defined and vague. This tale type is fully explainable neither as the expression of a vegetation cult (Wilhelm Mannhardt)[22] nor as a mere consequence of auditory illusion (Taylor), but only as the expression of that common experience of a hard-to-explain but strongly felt and unfamiliar world breaking open the borders of our profane existence. But from this completely different world emanate normative effects. In the legend group that tells of the death of an otherworldly being this is expressed only by way of suggestion; it is expressed more clearly in the plague legend, which punishes the curiosity of the hero. A warning against presumption and hubris is a component of many legends. Moralizing takes from the supernatural legend as well as the historical legend a part of their terror, because through moralizing the events acquire a tangible sense.

But also in moralizing, the comment of a particular social group makes itself noticeable. If in the Mecklenburg legend of the tyrant's dance on the wine bottle sherds as well as in many legends of tyrants and castles in Switzerland there is a social protest from the lower class, there is in the Alpine legend in which cowherds criminally waste milk, butter, and cheese an important warning from the upper class—the owners of the mountain pasture wish to frighten their cowherds away from carelessly or wastefully handling the goods entrusted to them. He who carelessly or perhaps maliciously allows a cow to fall into a chasm must go around after his death and Sisyphus-like draw the fallen animal out of the chasm again and again. Removers of boundary stones must wander—here the community expresses itself in criticism. Whoever enlarges his farm goods at the cost of the *Allmend*, the communal property, is stigmatized particularly sharply (much in contrast to today, where one is accustomed to cover tax evaders with the mantle of understanding).

If social criticism can emanate from different classes and groups in this manner, so too different epochs naturally make themselves noticeable in the legend and the *Märchen*. Where in antiquity the death of Great Pan is spoken of, Christian thought can later make its way. While cutting wood, servants hear a bird sing, "Stutzi Mutzi! Tomorrow we must go to church, the chief is dead!" Thus in the legend the otherworldly realm is not only moralized but also Christianized. Historical changes can also be identified in the *Märchen*, though mere shifting of elements, such as the substitution of swords with guns, of the inn with the hotel, affect only the surface area of the *Märchen*. But it is believed as well that one can find traces of historical developments in its structure. In the tale of The Giant without a Heart, frequently alluded to here, the hero receives from the animal helpers the ability to take on their shape. It is thought that this shifting of shape is older than the magical summoning of animals usual in other tales. In the contact with the beasts of prey one suspects an older level than in contact with domestic animals.[23] But descriptive research may say that younger and older layers unite in the *Märchen*; each element is woven into the whole.

The historian, as well as the psychologist, moves in the realm of conjecture and, like him, is exposed to severe disappointments. Thus one ventured to conclude from the old-Germanic–sounding rhythm of the verse "Rapunzel, Rapunzel, lass dein Haar herunter" that the Rapunzel tale extended back into a relatively early time—if not into the Germanic, then somewhere into the tenth, eleventh, or twelfth century. And then it turned out that that coining of the verse originated with Jacob Grimm and that in the source (the model text of which moreover is not a German but a French *Märchen*) there is no verse at all but a clumsy and completely unmagical prose: "Rapunzel, lass deine Haare runter, dass ich rauf kann"—the awkward translation of the French "Persinette, descendez vos cheveux que je monte." Other scholars assume a relationship between the tower of the Rapunzel *Märchen* and the puberty house of many primitive peoples and believe it is possible to ascertain the age of the tale in this way.[24]

In my exposition I have refrained from such daring hypotheses and have tried only to show what lies open today, what yields itself, as it were. In what appears obvious are many problems and many aspects. To consider a few of them, if only in a quick survey and without systematizing them in any way, was the intention of this essay.

Notes

1. Geneviève Massignon, *Contes traditionnels des tailleurs de lin du Trégor* (Paris: Editions A. et J. Picard, 1965), p. 12.

2. Cf. André Jolles, *Einfache Formen*, ed. A. Schossig, pp. 183 ff.

3. Jan-Öjvind Swahn, *The Tale of Cupid and Psyche* (Lund: Gleerup, 1955). See also the reviews of this book by Walter Anderson in *Hessische Blätter für Volkskunde* 46 (1955): 118–130, and by Kurt Ranke in *Arv* 12 (1956): 158–167.

4. Gyula Ortutay, *Ungarische Volksmärchen* (Berlin: Rütten & Loening, 1957), pp. 51, 54. For *Märchen* biology, see Linda Dégh, *Folktales and Society: Story-Telling in a Hungarian Peasant Community*, trans. Emily M. Schossberger (Bloomington: Indiana University Press, 1969). For folksong scholarship, see Erich Seemann, "Volkslied," in *Deutsche Philologie im Aufriss*, ed. Wolfgang Stammler, 2d ed. (Berlin: Rütter & Loening, 1960), II, 350–373.

5. Cf. Hedwig von Beit, *Symbolik des Märchens*, 3d ed., 3 vols. (Bern and Munich: Francke, 1967).

6. Cf. Emil Staiger, *Grundbegriffe der Poetik*, 7th ed. (Zürich: Atlantis, 1966), pp. 255–256, and "Versuch über den Begriff des Schönen," *Trivium* 3 (1945): 192–193.

7. Max Lüthi, *Das europäische Volksmärchen*, 3d ed. (Bern, 1968), and *Volksmärchen und Volkssage: Zwei Grundformen volstümlicher Erzählung*, 3d ed. (Bern and Munich: Francke, 1975).

8. Cf. Hermann Bausinger, "Volkssage und Geschichte," *Württembergisch Franken* 41 (1957): 1–24 (see especially pp. 20, 22).

9. Leopold Schmidt, *Die Volkserzählung: Märchen, Sage, Legende, Schwank*, p. 108.

10. Cf. Max Lüthi, "Gehalt und Erzählweise der Volkssage," in Lüthi, *Volksliteratur und Hochliteratur: Menschenbild Thematik Formstreben* (Bern and Munich: Francke, 1970), pp. 26–37.

11. See Antti Aarne and Stith Thompson, *The Types of the Folktale*, 2d ed., rev. (Helsinki: Suomalainen Tiedeakatemia, 1961), pp. 93–94.

12. See Carl-Herman Tillhagen, "The Conception of the Nightmare in Sweden," *Humaniora: Essays in Literature, Folklore and Bibliography Honoring Archer Taylor on His Seventieth Birthday*, ed. Wayland D. Hand and Gustave O. Arlt (Locust Valley, N.Y.: J. J. Augustin, 1960), pp. 323–325. For further reports I wish to express my thanks to Dr. Bengt of Klintberg, Stockholm.

13. Cf. Max Lüthi, "Parallele Themen in der Volkserzählung und in der Hochliteratur," in Lüthi, *Volksliteratur und Hochliteratur*, pp. 90–99 (in translation "Parallel Themes in Folk Narrative and in Art Literature," *Journal of the Folklore Institute* 4 [1967]: 3–16). See also Lüthi, "Zum Thema der Selbstbegegnung des Menschen," ibid., pp. 100–113.

14. Jeremias Gotthelf, "Die Schwarze Spinne," in Gotthelf, *Bilder und Sagen aus der Schweiz* (Solothurn: Jent & Gossman, 1842), pp. 11–12.

15. Josef Müller, *Sagen aus Uri*, ed. Hanns Bächtold-Staübli (Basel: Schweizenische gesellschaft für volkskunde, 1926), I, 56.

16. Ibid.

17. For entelechy in another sense see Hugo Kuhn, "Gattungsprobleme der mittelhochdeutschen Literatur," in *Dichtung und Welt im Mittelalter* (Stuttgart: J. B. Metzler, 1959), pp. 56–61.

18. Johann Wilhelm Wolff, *Hessische Sagen* (Göttingen: Fr. Chr. Wilhelm Vogel, 1853), pp. 200–201.

19. See Gisela Burde-Schneidewind, "Der Sagenkreis um den mecklenburgischen Gutsherrn Georg Haberland," *Deutsches Jahrbuch für Volkskunde* 5 (1959): 8–23. See also Burde-Schneidewind, *Herr und Knecht, Antifeudale Sagen aus Mecklenburg* (Berlin: Akademie-Verlag, 1960), pp. 97–110.

20. See Archer Taylor, "Northern Parallels to the Death of Pan," in *Washington University Studies*, Humanistic Series, 10 (1922): 3–102, and Inger M. Boberg, *Sagnet om den store Pans dod* (Copenhagen: Levin & Munksgaard, 1934).

21. Lüthi, "Gehalt und Erzählweise der Volkssage."

22. Wilhelm Mannhardt, *Wald- und Feldkulte*, 2 vols. (Berlin, 1875–1877).

23. Cf. Lutz Röhrich, *Märchen und Wirklichkeit: Eine volkskundliche Untersuchung*, 2d ed. (Wiesbaden: Franz Steiner, 1964), pp. 81–102.

24. Will-Erich Peuckert, *Deutsches Volkstum in Märchen und Sage, Schwank und Rätsel*, pp. 19–20. Cf. Lüthi, *Volksmärchen und Volkssage*, pp. 62–96.

3. The Generic Nature of Oral Epic Poetry

DAVID E. BYNUM

In 1875 the Ottoman Empire was still an unfamiliar and forbidding realm to Europeans, and its possessions in the Balkans were still, as they had always been, a disturbing intrusion in Christian Europe. No matter what their nationality, Europeans seldom had any desire or reason to travel in the Balkan provinces of Turkey, and few ever did. But in the summer of that year, two adventurous young Englishmen made a journey into the northernmost parts of Turkey-in-Europe, going more than two hundred miles across the *vilayet* of Bosnia and Hercegovina southward from the Austrian frontier in Croatia to the southern Dalmatian coast of the Adriatic. Armed with a letter of permission from the Turkish governor, **Derviş Paşa**, the two insisted upon traveling the whole distance on foot, thinking they would learn more of the country by walking through it than they could by using any vehicle. Their eccentric eagerness to walk when they might have ridden alarmed the local authorities along their route and occasionally exposed the two men to personal danger because of political unrest in the *vilayet*, but it also did bring them within reach of some unique features of Bosnian culture which they could not otherwise have seen. Not least among these was a modern custom of singing epic poetry.

The two travelers that summer of 1875 were brothers, Arthur and Lewis Evans, and they were very young. Arthur, the elder brother, was only twenty-four. Still it was not their first visit to Turkish Bosnia, for they and an older friend had spent a day together in the Turkish border town of Kostajnica during a tour of Austria four years earlier, in 1871. Destiny held great things in store for Arthur Evans, who later in his life founded Minoan archaeology by excavating the ruins of a certain very old palace at Knossos in Crete.[1] But, although he had still not even come of age in 1871 and did not begin his work at

NOTE. Reprinted from *Genre* 2, no. 3 (September 1969): 236–258, by permission of the University of Illinois Press.

Knossos until 1900,[2] Arthur's destiny had already snared him in her web that day in Kostajnica. Between the summers of 1871 and 1875, he had seen much of Europe: France, Venetia, Germany, Hungary, Roumania, Bulgaria, Serbia, and even Sweden, where he crossed into the Arctic Circle to visit Lapland. But of all the places he had seen, Kostajnica meant most to him. As his biographer Joan Evans later explained it:

> The romance of the distant and the unfamiliar had always a peculiar charm for Arthur Evans; and in the curiously primitive town of Costainiča he for the first time encountered the enchanting contrast and blend of east and west, Turkey and Europe: an enchantment that was to hold him for the rest of his life. He bought a complete Turkish outfit and donned it in triumph, and spent all his remaining money in a bazaar where the shops held hardly anything he had ever seen before. It was a visit of a single day, and a case of love at first sight. Thereafter Arthur Evans set the Balkans before any country in the world.[3]

So Arthur and his brother came to Bosnia again in 1875 for a deeper excursion into those colorful, mountainous, and culturally unexplored districts of the Ottoman realm. Striding southward from the Sava River toward Travnik and Sarajevo, Arthur in a larger sense was taking the first steps along a way that would lead him on to his work in Crete nearly a quarter-century later.

Arthur was a first child in a prosperous family that had ridden the tide of nineteenth-century British industrialization to a position of comfort, security, and fine personal accomplishments by the time of his birth in 1851. His mother had died when he was a small boy, and from his earliest childhood his mind had been shaped to the mold of serious antiquarian, historical, and political interests, first by the companionship and constant example of an expert and resourceful father, and later by Harrow and Oxford. He had grown up tuned to react in a lively and sober way to excitements of the kind his journey through Bosnia would give him.

Although such walking trips as his enjoyed a certain Victorian, not to say Byronic, vogue, Arthur Evans's walk through Bosnia to the sea was an uncommon experience even for a man of his character. Few westerners and fewer natives ever chose the northern Balkans as the scene for this Romantic sport, for while it was sometimes a warmly hospitable land, it was also a land mined with fierce xenophobic suspicions that demanded more endurance of the mind as well as of the legs than most men would steel themselves to.[4] Thus the brothers Evans were generally mistaken for spies and provocateurs by Christians and Moslems alike everywhere they went in Bosnia, a country divided against itself in its religions as well as its political hopes. More than once in the few weeks they traveled there the Evans brothers were physically threatened by hostile Moslems and were glad they had firearms to defend themselves. It was an exceptional journey not only because Arthur Evans made it, but because it happened at all.

Eighteen seventy-five was almost the last moment to see the *vilayet* of Bosnia while it was still Turkish, as it had been for four hundred years. Under the Treaty of Berlin, Austria occupied the province in 1878 and introduced far-reaching changes in it. But when Evans was there, it still had the reputation of being the most stubbornly conservative and traditionalist corner of the Turkish Empire.

Arthur Evans kept a journal of his adventures with his brother in Bosnia, and, after some rewriting of it, he published it in 1876.[5] The historical moment when it was written is enough by itself to make the journal an entertaining and useful document; but Evans was no ordinary nineteenth-century journalist, and he wrote of things other men would not have noticed. A substantial part of his journal is a kind of ethnography, often startlingly accurate and detailed even by modern standards. If no native Bosnian or Turk living in Bosnia could credit Evans's political detachment or understand rightly why he was in their country, nevertheless his purposes really were disinterestedly intellectual, even scholarly. He was a keen and thoughtful observer despite his youth. With the sharp eye of a classicist searching out ancient reliques and monuments, Evans recognized many cultural remnants of Roman Illyria in both material objects and in the customs of Bosnia, and he even noticed some of the archaic features of Bosnian life which link it to the culture of mainland Greece and the Peloponnesos reaching back in time well into the pre-Christian era.

Evans had been walking in the country hardly a week when he accidentally discovered a curious rural festival celebration taking place on an uninhabited mountaintop near Komušina in the northern Bosnian uplands. It was the Fifteenth of August, Assumption Eve, and a festival of the local helot-like Christian population, or *raya*. Evans recognized the Christian occasion of the festival, but he had never seen anything like the form it took. He described it thus in his journal:

> Beyond here we forded the Ussora, and now began to fall in with long trains of Bosnian rayahs, a troop of small Bosnian horses laden with bales and human beings, all streaming in the same direction as ourselves. It was evening when we began to ascend a small wooded mountain, escorted by this motley troop; the women and children mostly on foot, the men usually on horseback, and with their bright red turbans—worn about here by even the poorest classes—forming a brilliant foreground to the surrounding foliage. We followed the current, and an hour's winding ascent brought us to the summit of a mountain, normally lonely and devoid of habitation, but now thronged to overflowing by a gorgeous array of peasants from the uttermost recesses of Christian Bosnia, and some even from beyond the Serbian frontier. The summit of the mountain formed a long flat neck capacious enough to accommodate many thousands, and rising to its highest point towards its north-western extremity. As each detachment of peasants arrived they tethered their horses, and made straight to the summit of the ridge, which was surrounded by a rude shrine. This was the central point of the vast assemblage, and the reason of this great Christian gathering. . . .

> As the night drew on the whole neck of the mountain was lit up by cheery bonfires, round which the peasants clustered in social circles. Our Zaptieh provided us with blazing logs for ourselves, over which we performed our own culinary operations, supplemented by a generous haunch from a sheep, roasted in the usual Bosnian fashion. . . . A goodly portion of the assemblage seemed determined to make a night of it, and what with carousing, dancing, singing and playing, I will not deny that they succeeded.

> The first dance I saw was of a comic kind, performed by two men, and there were so many varying figures that one fancied they must improvise them as they went on. The accompaniment on a ghuzla, the one-stringed lute of the Serbs, was of the dole-

fullest. . . . The Kolo, however, or round dance of the Sclaves, was more elegant, and chiefly danced by the girls, who formed themselves in a ring and danced round and round, sometimes in a very spirited manner.

. . . .

We heard much playing of ghuzlas and double pipes and flutes, and much vocal accompaniment with lyric songs and long epic ballads. . . . One of the many minstrels was enchanting an audience of Bosniac maidens with a lyric, whose measure, unless my ears deceived me, was identical with that of Anacreon's song. . . . the long expenditure of breath renders a pause a physical necessity for the recovery of wind at the end of every two lines, so that the lays were generally divided into couplets. Much that looks Procrustean, and many apparently capricious full stops in classic metres, might, one would think, be referred to similar causes. Nearly a minute would sometimes elapse after one couplet before the singer had recovered breath to continue.

But what carried one back into epic days at once was a larger gathering, forming a spacious ring lit up by a blazing fire, in the middle of which a Bosniac bard took his seat on a rough log, and tuning his ghuzla began to pour forth one of the grand sagas of his race. Could it have been an unpremeditated lay? Without a book or any aid to memory he rolled out the ballad for hour after hour, and when I turned to rest, not long before sunrise, he was still rhapsodizing. I do not pretend to know what was the burthen of the ballad. . . . The hearers of the bard to whom I was listening seemed never to grow weary. Every now and then an ecstatic thrill would run through the whole circle, and find utterance in inarticulate murmurs of delight.[6]

Arthur Evans's lucky encounter with Bosnian festival poetry is a typical example of the European discovery of oral poetry in the nineteenth century. There were not many affluent, intellectual Europeans like Evans who went to the distant places such as the Balkans, central Asia, Sumatra, or the extreme north of Russia where long narrative oral poetry could be found. Nor were the difficulties of travel and the political hazards of those places always so easy to overcome as they were for the Evans brothers in Bosnia. Moreover, men who made such journeys did so for any other reason than to observe or record oral poetry; and if they did meet with it in the course of other business, the meeting usually surprised them no less than it did Arthur Evans.

Arthur's self-imposed mission in Bosnia was to collect sealstones. His comments on them are among the longest and most knowledgeable in his journal. By contrast, his description of the festival poetry on Assumption Eve is an exercise in innocent imposture; in this too he was typical of his era. The festival was a high point in his journey —one senses that plainly in reading his travelogue—yet he found it hard to say exactly why it so impressed him. This educated young Englishman's mind was an almost perfect marriage of alert curiosity and unlimited confidence in his own understanding.[7] It was a rare moment when the two qualities were at odds, as they were on this occasion. While he never for a moment faltered in reliance on his English literary upbringing to provide a sufficient explanation for what he had seen, still there was something vaguely wonderful and baffling in the Bosnian poetry ("Could it have been an unpremeditated lay?") which he would not simply dismiss as a pointless anomaly. Instead, the strangeness of it moved him to write as circumstantial an account as he could of an actual performance of oral epic poetry. It may seem a niggardly and faltering account by twentieth-century standards, but in 1876 it was unusual for its fullness of detail.

By Evans's time, the existence of oral poetry in the Balkans and elsewhere in the East had been known in western Europe for decades. There were even translations into English from the Serbo-Croatian tradition that Evans witnessed for a moment in Bosnia.[8] But while bits and samples of that poetry circulated abroad like pinned and lifeless specimens of some exotic fauna, the manner of its performance (and hence its real nature) remained an unbreached mystery outside the remote regions where it was sung. Natives invariably knew the institution of epic singing in their own countries and could with some embarrassment describe the rudiments of it to interested Europeans, but they generally considered it a homely and unnoteworthy fact of their culture; and since, as one can see in Evans's own account, epic singing was an intimate social custom and not a public spectacle staged for strangers, the rare foreigner who came to these lands had little chance to observe it, even if he wanted to.

Evans's description of oral poetry in the Bosnian hinterland a century ago has been amply confirmed by the work of collectors who have recorded texts and other ethnographic information in those regions since his visit. Their confirmation of the facts he reported gives assurance that the detailed studies of Balkan oral epic singing in recent decades do indeed faithfully portray a traditional form of art, and not an innovation or a late, epigonic deformation of some older form.

During the past century and a half, others like Arthur Evans have found other oral traditions of long narrative poetry many places in eastern Europe, Asia, and even in Africa. Like Evans, they too have usually been followed by still others who have confirmed their observations and written down further examples of the poetic traditions concerned. Thus a considerable number of oral metrical narrative traditions have been collected in modern times during two or more successive generations. Partial inventories of these modern oral traditions are easily accessible in the comparativist writings of Cecil Bowra and Albert Lord.[9] But no full catalog of them has ever been compiled, and there are at least three good reasons why that has not yet been undertaken.

As might be expected, the amount and the character of the oral narrative poetry that has been accumulated by different hands at different times and from widely separated modern traditions are highly various from one part of the old world to another. Even superficial comparison reveals such a diversity among the modern oral poetries conventionally called "epic" that the name no longer clearly means any one thing, if it ever did. In what sense, for example, is this modern Balochi poem of twenty-one verses "epic," as its editor calls it, and is it indeed comparable to the Moslem epics in Uzbek or Serbo-Croatian[10] that run to several thousands of verses?

> O khumēth nosh khan thīraghē dānā
> Bāz khanē phīlī gardan o rānā
> Tikkaen wāgān dē kumundēnā
> Whashīyā azh Sēviyā mawā gardān.
> Shakhalo sarphurān sohāgīyān

Pha murādē ma dēravā dā<u>th</u>āṅ
Bosht maṅ shazhmēhā harēvīyā
War gadēmā maṅ hā<u>dh</u>irē jam <u>kh</u>āṅ
Azh ba<u>dh</u>āṅ khoheṅ thīwarē sham <u>kh</u>ān.
Hakk o nāhakkā pha<u>dh</u>a gardāṅ
Jagh nāwhasheṅ ki basthagheṅ bandāṅ
Ma hawāṅ dēhā ke alē gindān.
Kaul-eṅ go haisī chotavo phāghāṅ
Yabarē bushkāṅ maṅ bāzeṅ shēfāṅ
Jānī azh bal nēzaghāṅ gark bī.
Biyāith hawāṅ nar ki wā<u>dh</u>āē ā<u>kh</u>taī
Kadahē phur bī<u>th</u>aī hasēvānī
Man dī azh Shāheṅ Qādirē lotāṅ
Sobh pha Sēvī phutureṅ Rindāṅ
Gēshtar azh hir'-phā<u>dh</u> thanakh-rīshāṅ
Azh-pha<u>dh</u>ā chukh jano Mughal ro<u>kh</u> bī.[11]

Mir Chakur, son of Shaihak, sings: the King of the mighty Rinds sings: in reply to Gwaharam he sings.[12]

O my bay! eat your grain from your nosebag; make your neck and legs as stout as those of an elephant; swiftly, giving you the reins to mount the cliffs, I will return from Sibi. For you I have stored in my tents the sweet camels' milk. Stand in your stall with six pegs, eat of the wheat and satisfy your heart. Strengthen yourself for the enemies' mountains, for right or wrong I will come back again. The folk are displeased that you should be tied up in that land where I see the brave.

I swear on my head and hair and turban, once I get free I will lay many low; lives will be overwhelmed among the spears and lances. Let the man come on, whose hour is come, the cup of whose reckonings is full! I too ask from my King and Creator victory for the true Rinds at Sevi, rather than for the slender-footed thin-beards. Hereafter the Mughal youths and maidens will receive enlightenment!

Mr. Dames, who knew a good deal about the oral poetry of the Balochi, placed the short poem just quoted among the "heroic or epic ballads" of this Iranian-speaking people in central Asia. Yet whatever local validity his judgment may have had, the poem is surely not a narrative, but rather more akin to the so-called praise poetry of Bantu Africa, which also has sometimes been called epic.[13]

Thus what is called epic poetry in the oral tradition of one region is not necessarily commensurate with other poetry scholars call epic elsewhere. The specialists working with each modern tradition have devised their own procedures independently of each other and decided for themselves what their generic nomenclature would be. No one man or group has been arbiter among us in these matters because no one has been so well acquainted with enough of the many modern traditions to speak persuasively enough about their universal likenesses. There has been no conscious community of oral epic scholars comparable to the diffusionist school of folktale scholarship.

Although the differences of form and substance among well-recorded modern oral poetries make it difficult to give them names with common, universal meanings, that difficulty by itself is not too great to overcome. But it is compounded by others. Some modern oral traditions of so-called epic poetry are so remote from the knowledge even of specialists that no one presently could render a satisfactory description of them in their own terms, much less classify them comparatively with oral poetry in other parts of the world. In some cases this difficulty is one of inadequate collection; in other cases it is merely neglect. Finally, a third and even greater obstacle everywhere hinders progress in comparative studies of oral epic poetry. This is the barrier of languages, which sets stricter limits on the ambition of a comparative epicist than it does on practically any other branch of folklore scholarship. More than any other genre of folklore, modern oral epic poetry is typically so massive and so elaborate a form both thematically and in the techniques of its composition that translations and synopses in learned languages can rarely be extensive or detailed enough to support sound judgment about traditions in languages one does not himself know. So every scholar who would range beyond more than a very few modern narrative traditions must to some extent share Arthur Evans's imposture in writing about an oral poetry whose language he could not understand. Cecil Bowra admitted the same fault in his comparison of oral poetic traditions in his book *Heroic Poetry*:

> In some cases, where no texts have been available, I have used information about them from books of learning, though I have not often done this, and then only when I have had full confidence in the trustworthiness of the author. I fully realize that this is by no means a perfect method. It would certainly have been better to work only with original texts in every case and not use translations at all. But a work of this kind would require a knowledge of nearly thirty languages, and not only am I myself unlikely ever to acquire such a knowledge, but I do not know of anyone interested in the subject who has it. So I must ask indulgence for a defect which seems to be inevitable if such a work is to be attempted at all.[14]

Sir Cecil's caveat notwithstanding, his own book makes plain how hazardous the method may be. But we must all at least confess the same limitation, with only the further extenuation that today, without cutting ourselves off from a sizeable part of our subject as Bowra did in limiting his interest to heroic poetry (supposedly a subcategory of epic), the number of germane languages one may be ignorant of should be numbered nearer fifty than thirty.

To some extent, then, every comparative epicist may sometimes have to proceed as Arthur Evans did on his mountaintop above Komušina. Guided only by the ideas of poetry he had gotten in study of the Classics, he listened and watched closely and could confidently propose some distinctions of genre in Bosnian oral poetry solely from the dissimilarities in its performance. And once he had recognized a narrative in the long, concentrated singing of a "Bosnian gleeman," he called it epic (what else could be so long?).[15] Admittedly, he also called it saga, ballad, and heroic lay, mixing nomenclature in a chaotic manner that shows as much uncertainty of exactly what the names mean as of the precise nature of the poetry he heard. But his first impulse and his later uncertainty both were perfectly contemporary. When he noticed differences of kind in Bosnian poetry, which he did not understand, he did not hesitate to classify the kinds by reference to the genres of a literature he did know, ancient Greek. So too modern collectors generally have appropriated the words *heroic* and *epic* from ancient

Hellenic learned tradition to designate long narrative in verse wherever it has been discovered in Eurasia in modern times and regardless of the peculiar features of particular modern traditions.

So the name "epic" is only a more or less metaphorical expression as applied to oral poetry in many parts of the modern world. Under these circumstances, it would not be helpful to attempt yet another imperfectly informed synthetic description of epic as a universal class of modern oral poetry, and I shall not. Indeed, the best hope of progress in that grand task seems to be rather in reaching a more exact understanding of individual modern traditions than has been attained in most cases. As the great age of collecting draws toward its inevitable end, the paramount need is to determine the processes of each tradition itself, the dynamics of its thematics and composition. The older critical preoccupation with historical, social, and psychological implications of oral traditions have been productive and deserve every encouragement. But the hope of comparative studies rests in a better science of oral poetics, the analysis of oral poetry from an internal point of view rather than in relation to various other learned disciplines.

Amid the wide array of modern oral poetries, where does one begin? Any reasonably well-recorded tradition will serve, but so-called epic oral poetry has been collected most fully in modern times from three regions of the Old World: northern Russia, central Asia, and the Balkan Peninsula.

In the case of northern Russia and central Asia, most of the collections are from districts that now fall within the Soviet Union, and they consist mostly of texts in Russian, Turkic, and Mongolian languages. A large portion of the Russian collections have been published, but many of the Turkic, Mongolian, and other Siberian traditions have been published only in small specimens. There are nevertheless very extensive resources in unpublished manuscripts and sound-recordings in the Soviet Union, particularly of non-European traditions, which may be of the greatest value to comparative studies of oral epic poetry. Profitable collecting is still possible and is still going on many places in the Soviet Union, chiefly in its Asiatic regions. These resources deserve much more attention in the West than they have been given, despite the burden of learning little-known and remote languages which their use imposes on western scholars.[16]

The third great district of epic collection in the Old World is the one Arthur Evans visited in 1875. From the Turkish Conquest until the nineteenth century, the Balkans remained as shut off and as little known to Europeans as other eastern lands thousands of miles farther from Europe. But for all its isolation, Turkey-in-Europe was not enormously distant from the literary centers of the west. Of all the Orient, it remained among the geographically most accessible places that were attractive to Romantic tastes for rare things like oral poetry. As the alien presence of Turkish power gradually retired from Europe in the nineteenth century, western Europe's best information about flourishing oral poetry came from the Greek and Slavic peoples of the Balkans, and the interest that information stimulated in western literary circles gave incentive to the new emulative intelligentsia of the post-Ottoman Balkans to value and collect the folklore of their own peoples.[17]

There was never a large, organized effort to collect folklore in the Balkans, but many individuals of diverse backgrounds have worked separately at different times during the last two hundred years to gather whatever each could discover and thought good. Many of the separate collections have in time found their way into larger archives, and today the material that has thus accumulated in South Slavic, Roumanian, Modern Greek, and Albanian recordings and manuscripts constitutes the fullest documentation of traditional oral literature from any one region in the world. In this body of material, oral epic poetry is the most prominent genre both in amount and by virtue of the technical excellence of the many singers represented in it. The study of oral epic tradition in this region presents some of the same problems as the traditions of Asia (unpublished collections in remote languages), but it rewards its students with an unexcelled geographic density and historical range of recorded data. For these reasons, Balkan epic tradition is presently a court of review for hard issues in oral epic studies, because it is the court where the fullest brief can be compiled for most arguments.

With regard to the question of what oral epic poetry essentially is, whether in a local or comparative sense, the study of Balkan tradition offers yet another estimable advantage. This is the only region where the name "epic" is not merely metaphorical or a simile, because in the first instance epic poetry means the poetry of Homer in archaic

Greek. If epic poetry is any one thing, it is a genre of Balkan folk-lore, being indigenous in the Balkans from before the age of litera-ture.

Without understanding the Slavic poetry he heard on the crest of a mountain in northern Bosnia, Arthur Evans could not rightly make any more exact comparison between it and Homer's *Iliad* or *Odyssey* than he did implicitly in calling it epic. But today, there is no longer reason to doubt that the performance he saw was a fair analogue of the poetic performances that once produced sung ver-sions of the Homeric epics in Greece, less than six hundred miles southeast of Bosnia and probably about twenty-seven centuries ago. After Milman Parry, Albert Lord, and their Oral Theory, poetry made in this manner[18] is called Oral Traditional Epic Poetry, and it is a recognized genre of folklore. The name of the genre distinguishes it from all of written literature on the one hand, and from all other kinds of oral composition on the other hand. Moreover, it makes those distinctions not once but twice over, because the name Oral Traditional Epic Poetry is a tautology made necessary in modern times by the peculiar history and doubtful authority of the older, simpler name, Epic Poetry.

The word *epic* is the eldest component in the present-day name of the genre, and it is derived from Greek ἐπικός, "that pertains to (F)ἔπος: an utterance, something said." The word therefore origi-nally meant neither more nor less than "oral," except that ἔπος was Homer's name for spoken words and "oral" is our later expression.

In Homer's time and earlier, when his tradition of poetry was formed, any utterance was unmistakably oral and writing had no part in its creation because writing was not used for that purpose. When writing was used in Homer's age, it was to keep records, not to com-pose any kind of speech, narrative or otherwise. So Homer himself had no occasion to differentiate between speaking and telling a story. For him, each was an inseparable aspect of the other, and ἔπος meant just spoken words in general.

Thus the word ἔπος is found first in the poetry of the earliest and best among the many recorded oral poets of the Balkans. But, where-as Homer used the word rather frequently, he never used it to mean a specific kind of poetry or genre of literature, and he never used the adjective ἐπικός at all. Nor is there any other evidence that *epic* ever meant a form of poetry in ancient Greek oral tradition. Indeed, there are practically no words to designate poetic genres in all that survives of the Homeric lexical stock: not in the *Iliad*, nor in the *Odyssey*, nor in the several small poems and fragments that are commonly attributed to Homer as the eponym of ancient Greek oral tradition. But the reason for the lack of such words is not far to seek.

Just as writing was not used to make poetry in archaic Greece, neither was there any writing of literary criticism when Homer dictated the *Iliad* and *Odyssey* to someone who used his writing skill to make a record of Homer's poetry. In Homer's time there was hardly anything even analogous to criticism that was not a part of ἀοιδή, Homer's and his fellow singers' own art of minstrelsy. But the ancient Greek minstrel's criticism of his own art was confined within close bounds. Homer was interested in the problem of choosing stories that people liked and in telling them well. Like any good singer, he also commented in his songs on the sense of things in them, as in Penelope's speech to Medon in the *Odyssey* (4. 686–693):[19]

> You, who keep gathering here, and consuming away much livelihood,
> the property of wise Telemachos, nor have you listened
> to what you heard from your fathers before you, when you were children,
> what kind of man Odysseus was among your own parents,
> how he did no act and spoke no word in his own country
> that was unfair; and that is a way divine kings have, one
> will be hateful to a certain man, and favor another,
> but Odysseus was never outrageous at all to any man.

Here Penelope's remarks on the nature of kingship represent a class of obiter dicta in Homeric poetry that is Homer's own comment on the meaning of details in his tradition. But these were the limits of criticism in Homer's day. For the ἀοιδόι there simply was no branch of criticism like our modern interest in genre classification. Men who make poetry in an oral tradition are not concerned with choosing one poetic form or another in which to compose, nor are they bothered by generic distinctions between their own poetry and anyone else's. The generic categories of their poetry are determined for them by the pre-existing forms of tradition when they learn it, and any changes in the tradition which they may make while they practice it are accomplished solely through their own traditional manipulation of traditional forms and ideas. When there is no writing, those who are poets make poetry as tradition dictates and those who are not poets are not concerned with poetics.

Arthur Evans's "many minstrels" at a Bosnian festival in 1875 are a case in point. Their selections of meter, music, and things to sing about were not matters of their own choosing. The minstrel who "was enchanting an audience of Bosniac maidens with a lyric" used a lyric measure because he was singing to women. That circumstance or context of his performance validated the meter, tune, and subject of his song and invalidated any others not customary in that context. As an oral traditional poet, he could not have chosen to do otherwise, and his audience of Bosniac maidens otherwise could not have been "enchanted." Similarly, Evans's singer of long narrative used the bowed *gusle* and sang a long song in decasyllabic meter with a rapid recitative delivery because singing to a peer group of adult men could be done only that way. So there was no more problem of genre for Evans's Bosnians than there was for Homer. For them, the selection of one poetic form or another was perfectly governed, like everything else in their traditional life, by contexts of propriety. Only the outlandish stranger seated among them, only Arthur Evans, had any reason to think of genres, because he could not compose such poetry himself, nor could he understand the contextual propriety that invisibly governed each performance he heard. We should not look to oral tradition of any age for words to name its genres, because the literary idea of genre has no true counterpart in oral tradition.

So to Homer *epos* meant "oral utterance," or "simply speaking," and was not a word to designate genre in the earliest recorded Balkan oral tradition. But once Homer's poems had been written down, they took on an entirely new character—they became literature, and as literature they long outlived remembrance of their author's age, even in ancient Greece. In the heyday of classical Greece, the orality of Homer's poetry was first ignored and then forgotten. Thus by the time of Aristotle, four centuries after Homer, the Homeric poems had assumed a very different function in Greek culture than they had when Homer sang them. By that time writing had replaced ἀοιδή as the usual means of poetic composition, and the *Iliad* and *Odyssey*

together with other oral poems in written form had become corner-
stones of civic education and literary tradition. For the sake of helping
the young and their tutors to understand and emulate certain putative
qualities of Homeric poetry, it became important to characterize and
classify its genre with respect to the other kinds of poetry at large in
the Greek polity. In fourth-century Greece, it was the content of the
Homeric poems in writing that was important and memorable, not the
oral poetic tradition that had originally produced them. So Aristotle
gave them a name, ἐποποιίαι (epic poems), and then examined their
fixed texts to determine what he meant by "epic" and how it was different from other kinds of literature. Criticism in the sense we know
it had begun.

Aristotle set forth in the book *Poetics* what he thought distinctive of
Homer's poetry. His well-known and problematical theory of imitation need not detain us long. In regard to Homer, it was a typical post-
Platonic attempt to understand things of pre-Platonic origins and not
a perfectly consistent attempt either. His comments on epic show Aristotle uneasy in discussing it, not sure of its exact nature nor of his own
analysis of it. Four centuries had been a long time, and he plainly knew
nothing firsthand about Greek oral epic tradition.

In the *Poetics*, Aristotle wrote that people commonly called any
hexametric poem epic (*Poetics* 1. 8–11). He rejected that careless, vul-
gar usage as inaccurate and said that meter alone is not enough to denote poetry. Aristotle revealed that he did not know the oral origin of
Homeric poetry when he included it among the arts that imitate only
in words, or meter (*Poetics* 1. 7). That is indeed true if epic exists, as
it did for Aristotle, only in fixed form. But had he like Arthur Evans
ever heard an oral epic performance, he would surely have placed it
too among the arts that imitate by rhythm and perhaps also harmony
(*Poetics* 1. 13–14). For Aristotle, epic, together with the genre of
tragedy, was "a metrical representation of heroic action," but he
thought it different from tragedy in being unlimited in the duration of
the action imitated in it and, more importantly, in using narrative,
which he thought foreign to tragedy (*Poetics* 5. 7–11).

Philosophers were not better critics of literature in ancient Greece
than in modern times. Aristotle wrote that "narrative imitation excels
all others"[20] but later asserted the superiority of tragedy over epic as a
form of literature (*Poetics* 26. 9–15), despite its lack of narrative

(*Poetics* 6. 2). And if that were not inconsistency enough, he also said that the elements of epic are all found in tragedy, but not all the elements of tragedy are in epic (*Poetics* 26. 9, and 5. 10–11); in this instance he seems to have been thinking of tragedy's many varieties of rhythm and its tunes or song (*Poetics* 1. 13), which he did not know as rightful parts of oral epic tradition.

Although it is mainly unrewarding to a modern folklorist to follow Aristotle's reflections on epic poetry, nonetheless two items of information in his *Poetics* deserve attention. The first is the popular usage which Aristotle reports from his era, whereby *epic* meant simply poetry in epic meter, Homer's hexameters. The second bit of information is in his intriguing reference to some epic poems as pathetic. He cited the *Iliad* as an example of such epics, whose plots center on grief-provoking disaster (*Poetics* 24. 1–3). The same idea attaches to some modern Balkan oral epic tales, whose singers designate certain of their best songs *žalosne* in a comparable sense. This notion may in fact be one of the few real glimpses of ideas from oral tradition concerning genre in all of Aristotle's treatise on poetry. It is, at any rate, an idea about varieties of story that is found in the minds of many persons actually in modern oral storytelling traditions, even as far from the Balkans as North America. Morris Opler quoted a Jicarilla Apache informant on this subject in the preface to his excellent collection *Myths and Tales of the Jicarilla Apache Indians*:

> The winter was the time when stories were told most, for then the nights were long and the people got tired of lying around. The story of the emergence can be told any time, day or night, and during any season, but it was most often told during the long winter nights. It is not dangerous to tell it at any other time, however. The story of the killing of the monsters by Killer-of-Enemies or stories about the bear, snake, any monster, or any of the evil ones can be told during the winter only, for then those dangerous ones go high in the mountains and are not where the people live. And those stories are always told at night.
>
> The stories are of different kinds. Some make you happy, some make you sad; some frighten you. They have a little feast when stories are being told . . .[21]

Thus Jicarilla Apache storytelling was governed by certain seasonal and temporal contexts of propriety relating to the local economy and the Jicarilla system of beliefs. But within those contextual determinants was a peculiar scheme of genres based not on the poetic form nor on the social function of stories, but rather on the attitudes their performance traditionally evoked. In this connection one remembers again Evans's enchanted "Bosniac maidens" and the ecstatic thrill that ran through the whole circle of the "Bosnian gleeman's" listeners, and their "inarticulate murmurs of delight." One remembers too the famous scene of Odysseus weeping at the Phaiakian court:

> These things the famous singer sang for them, but Odysseus,
> taking in his ponderous hands the great mantle dyed in
> sea-purple, drew it over his head and veiled his fine features,
> shamed for tears running down his face before the Phaiakians;
> and every time the divine singer would pause in his singing,
> he would take the mantle away from his head, and wipe the
>   tears off,
> and taking up a two-handled goblet would pour a libation
> to the gods, but every time he began again, and the greatest
> of the Phaiakians would urge him to sing, since they joyed in his
>   stories,
> Odysseus would cover his head again, and make lamentation.
> There, shedding tears, he went unnoticed by all the others,
> but Alkinoös alone understood what he did and noticed,
> since he was sitting next him and heard him groaning heavily.
> At once he spoke aloud to the oar-loving Phaiakians:
> "Hear me, you leaders of the Phaiakians and men of counsel.
> By this time we have filled our desire for the equal feasting
> and for the lyre, which is the companion to the generous
> feast."   *Odyssey* 9. 83–100

The epic singer whose tale causes Odysseus to weep is Demodokos, who sings a narrative Aristotle would have called "pathetic." Odysseus weeps not only because the narrative tells of his own deeds at Troy, but because it is a tale that should sadden its hearer, whoever he is.

The idea of "a story that should sadden its hearer" is essentially a category of criticism, even though it may happen to have no special terminology to express it in an oral traditional culture and may appear to be no more than an emotional or (even worse) a merely sentimental reaction to poetry. But it should not be forgotten that even sentiment and the emotions are subject to the law of contextual propriety when custom demands them. Oral traditional storytelling is nothing if not a custom, and, like our own solemnity in church or at a flagraising, reactions of pity or delight may be no more than proper in the context of hearing one traditional tale or another. Any folklorist who has tried to collect oral traditional narratives and failed to react to them in a proper mode of appreciation knows the consequences, no matter how generous an allowance for his outlandishness his informant may be willing to grant him. And in a deeper sense too, without emotional reactions dictated by custom, even literature as we know it would be only the empty folly Tolstoy said it is in the essay "What Is Art?" Tolstoy's argument for an ethnically religious dimension in literature would be a self-evident proposition in oral-traditional cultures, and the contextually conditioned, customary emotions that go hand-in-hand with that religious dimension of oral tradition may be far more exact and far more universally applicable as criteria of genre than they appear to be to us in our modern secular tradition of literary criticism that began with Aristotle.

The notion of pathos as a generic distinction within epic poetry is so briefly stated in Arisotle's *Poetics* that it is really only a suggestion. In fact, the idea had not come to him in connection with epic at all, but rather it was something he borrowed from his earlier, much fuller analysis of the genre of tragedy (*Poetics* 10 and 11). In doing this, Aristotle was at least true to himself, for his whole discussion of epic poetry is only a species of appendix to his remarks on drama. Aristotle's evident uncertainty in writing about the generic nature of epic and his marked preference for tragedy may be the reasons why his treatment of epic is so brief. It occupies only a few lines in the shortest treatise of all he wrote that have survived, although some parts have been lost from the book during its long history. But whatever the reasons for it may be, the Aristotle we know is actually a rather slight critic of ancient Greek epic poetry for all the weight his opinions have subsequently come to bear.

Homer had made no distinction between the art of epic singing and the songs themselves. His word ἀοιδή meant both. In an oral tradition there is no difference between them. To Homer ἔπος was even less definite; it meant words in general. Probably partly out of respect for great Homer, Greeks after him called any hexametric poetry epic. But whatever else ἔπος and ἐπικός may have meant to Greeks in the four centuries between Homer and Aristotle, after Aristotle the words were permanently charged with two more-or-less exact meanings: epic poetry had simple (i.e., single) meter and consisted of long (i.e., unlimited) narration.

Aristotle's literary confinement of the meaning of the words *epic* and *epos* brought about their metamorphosis into genre designations and launched them on a long career of literary and philosophical reinterpretation that has not yet ended and that probably will not end as long as we have literature. But through the whole long history of the words' peregrinations since Aristotle, his legacy has remained in the central sense: long verse narrative sharing qualities of the *Iliad* and *Odyssey*.

With this meaning, the genre-designation "epic" (and its congeners in other languages) was ready-to-hand when modern collecting began in living oral traditions. Yet the name came so loaded with the burden of long literary reinterpretation that it could not be used to designate any folk tradition of long verse narrative outside of literature without summoning to mind myriad irrelevant and misleading literary associations. This was unobjectionable so long as the Romantic idea of folklore as *gesunkenes Kulturgut* prevailed. But as the collections of oral tradition piled up through the nineteenth and twentieth centuries, it became necessary to distinguish between literary epic and the accumulating evidence of something like it yet different, the folk genre of epic that Arthur Evans found in a northern Bosnian manifestation. To make this distinction, the word *oral* was prefixed to *epic* as a delimiting term. Originally, it did not name the genre of folk epic more precisely than the word *epic* alone. Its value was only to strip away from *epic* the heavy encrustation of literary implications that had gathered around it and to denote a nonliterary kind of epic whose real nature was in fact unknown. In this century, Milman Parry and Albert Lord have made two important steps forward from that position. They dispelled the mystery of how oral epic could be maintained in tradition over long periods of time without any use of writing and defined it accordingly as verse narrative of unlimited length, (re)composed at each telling, and having certain characteristic structures of words and ideas (called formulas and themes) in its composition that betray the processes of traditional poetics. To indicate the difference between oral transmission of poetry that has been made in writing, with its telltale lapses from traditional poetics, and poetry recomposed at every performance from traditional formulas and themes, Parry first and Lord after him added the further delimiting word *traditional* to the name "oral epic," and so the modern designation of this genre of folklore came into being: Oral Traditional Epic Poetry.

The revolution in criticism wrought by the Oral Theory has irreversibly made the study of oral epic poetry a study of entire epic traditions, in which individual texts derive their importance chiefly from their service as testimony about the processes and meanings of a whole tradition of metrical storytelling. No matter how grand it may be in itself, no separate text, not even a text so magnificent as the *Iliad* or *Odyssey*, is thought to carry more than a fraction of the significances in the tradition that formed it. Literary tradition consists more in its masterpieces, which shape its changing character from age to age. But the masterpieces of an oral tradition vanish no sooner than they are made, and the tradition changes less because it consists more in poetry than is usual. That understanding has been hard for literary people to reconcile with conventional habits of literary thinking, whose mighty authority yields slowly to such changes. Thus it happens that the massive modern collection of oral traditions has been in progress and spreading around the world for a century and a half, whereas the Oral Theory is scarcely a generation old and is still confined to the demonstration of a few bare principles in European oral epic traditions. We have only begun to understand the whole wonderful panoply of oral poetics. We have come a long way since Aristotle and Arthur Evans, but there is yet much to be done.

Notes

1. Sir Arthur Evans, *The Palace of Minos: A Comparative Account of the Successive Stages of the Early Cretan Civilization as Illustrated by the Discoveries at Knossos*, 4 vols. and index (London: Macmillan & Co., 1922–1936).

2. Arthur Evans first visited Crete in 1893 on the same business that was most rewarding to him in Bosnia and Hercegovina in 1875—collecting seal-

stones. He might never have gone to Crete had the Austrian authorities in Dalmatia not reacted as they did to certain political indiscretions of his youth and banished him from Ragusa in 1882, thereby effectively ending his intended career as journalist, activist, and general connoisseur of Yugoslav lands and peoples. Between 1893 and 1900 he was on Crete several times but did not begin to excavate until 1900, "when local political conditions made it possible"; see J[ohn] D[evitt] S[tringfellow] Pendlebury, *The Archeology of Crete* (London: Methuen, 1939), p. 18, and chapter 14, "Paradise Lost," in the biography of Arthur Evans by his half-sister, Joan Evans, *Time and Chance: The Story of Arthur Evans and His Forebears* (London: Longmans, Green & Co., 1943), pp. 239–258.

3. Evans, *Time and Chance*, p. 166.

4. Arthur Evans himself knew about the trying moments of a journey in 1634 by another Englishman, Sir Henry Blunt (Blount), who had "stayed a day or two in 'Saraih,' the metropolis of the kingdome of Bosnah": Sir Henry Blount, *A Voyage into the Levant: A Briefe Relation of a Iourney lately performed by Master Henry Blunt, Gentleman, from England by way of Venice into Dalmatia, Sclavonia, Bosnah, Hungary, Macedonia, Thessaly, Thrace, Rhodes and Egypt, unto Gran Cairo*, 3d ed. (London, 1638). The desire to visit these places had been nurtured in the Evans family for generations; Joan Evans tells of the legacy to young Arthur from his grandfather (*Time and Chance*, p. 165): "One of Arthur Benoni Evans' favorite books of travel had been Walsh's *Overland Tour from Constantinople to Vienna*, which he had bought in 1835. This had survived to inspire his grandson as a boy with an interest in Turkey in Europe." The book was by Robert Walsh (1772–1852), published at London, 1828 (3d ed., 1829, and again in 1831). For an account of a native's journey on foot in Bosnia written by himself, see Matija Mažuranić, *Pogled u Bosnu ili kratak put u onu krajinu učinjen 1839–40 po Jednom Domorodcu* (Zagreb, 1842; 2d ed., Zagreb, 1938). The motives of this journey, too, were Romantic and in many ways like Evans's; but unlike Evans's, Mažuranić's travelogue became a literary monument.

5. Arthur J[ohn] Evans, *Through Bosnia and the Hercegovina on Foot During the Insurrection, August and September, 1875*, . . . (London, 1876). It contains a number of valuable drawings by the author.

6. Evans, *Through Bosnia*, pp. 130–139.

7. Joan Evans had much more material at hand by which to judge the young Arthur than the journal of his first trip into Bosnia. Although she was a lady of level judgment as well as a most sympathetic biographer, she wrote of his conceit even more strongly than I have: "Arthur Evans at twenty-four was a fantastically conceited young man who knew better than anyone how great were his especial gifts; and he had to set about using them, and making the world value them, as best he could" (*Time and Chance*, p. 163).

8. Arthur derived his opinions about the substance of Bosnian oral poetry from the translations of John Bowring, which he cited: *Narodne srpske pjes-*

me: Servian Popular Poetry (London, 1827). Bowring was somewhat an impostor. He tried to give the impression that he had translated from Slavic, when in reality he had only translated from other translations in German, whose authors he cites but does not credit in his Introduction. In their nearly total ignorance of Slavic, Bowring and Evans were birds of a feather; but Bowring, the less candid of the two, gulled Evans no less than he did many another Englishman in the nineteenth century, imposing on them a view of Balkan oral poetry colored almost beyond recognition by the dense filter of German Romanticism. Evans faithfully reflected that Romantic view in his journal when he ventured beyond the evidence of his own senses into thoughts about the putative content of Bosnian oral poetry. No doubt the most disastrous single mistake men have repeated throughout the annals of oral epic scholarship is just such reliance as Evans's upon the distorted view of a previous commentator with doubtful credentials, which in turn is derivative in a succession of misconceptions going back into the very abyss of confusion. The root of the fault is, of course, in the hardship for men of letters of learning the exotic and, except for studies in oral poetry, the rather useless dialects that are indispensable to sound judgment in this branch of learning.

9. Cecil M. Bowra, *Heroic Poetry* (London: Macmillan & Co., 1952). A[lbert] B[ates] Lord, "Homer and Other Epic Poetry," in *A Companion to Homer*, ed. Alan J. B. Wace and Frank H. Stubbings (London and New York: Macmillan, 1962), pp. 179–214. Albert B. Lord, "Epic Poetry," in *Collier's Encyclopaedia*.

10. Concerning the length of composition in these traditions, see V. M. Žirmunskij and X. T. Zarifov, *Uzbekskij narodnyj geroičeskij èpos* (Moscow: Ogiz, 1947), p. 24 and passim; and David E. Bynum, "Themes of the Young Hero in Serbocroatian Oral Epic Tradition," *PMLA* 83 (October 1968): 1296–1303.

11. The Balochi text and English translation of this piece are from M. Longworth Dames, *Popular Poetry of the Baloches*, 2 vols. (London, 1907), I, 24–25; II, 29–30.

12. This is a prologue in mixed meter, which Mr. Dames printed as though it were prose. The first two lines are formulaic, but short:

> Mir Chakur Shaihak gushi:
> sari Rind Badshah gushi:
> Gwaharamar phasave dath gushi.

13. H. F. Morris, *The Heroic Recitations of the Bahima of Ankole* (Oxford: Clarendon Press, 1964), and Trevor Cope, James Stuart, and Daniel Malcolm, *Izibongo: Zulu Praise-Poems* (Oxford: Clarendon Press, 1968).

14. Bowra, *Heroic Poetry*, p. vi.

15. Evans, *Through Bosnia*, pp. 139 and 141.

16. Concerning the Russian tradition, see V[ladímir] Ja[kovlevič] Propp, *Russkij geroičeskij èpos* (Leningrad: Leningrad University Press, 1955). See

the essays on Asiatic and Caucasian traditions in I. S. Braginskij, A. A. Petrosjan, and V. I. Čičerov, eds., *Voprosy izučenija éposa narodov SSSR* (Moscow, 1958).

17. See the splendid account of these facts in Miodrag Ibrovac, *Claude Fauriel et la fortune européenne des poésies populaires grecque et serbe* (Paris: Didier, 1966).

18. The description is in Albert Bates Lord, *The Singer of Tales* (Cambridge, Mass.: Harvard University Press, 1960, and later editions).

19. Quotations from the *Odyssey* here and throughout are from the new translation by Richard Lattimore, *The Odyssey of Homer* (New York: Harper & Row, 1967).

20. The Greek is a clause of consequence, meaning that "narrative is best of all imitation" in regard to those particular features of it enumerated in the preceding sentences: "περιπὴ γὰρ καὶ ἡ διηγηματικὴ μίμησις τῶν ἄλλων." This is a good example of the difficulty of interpreting the *Poetics*.

21. Morris Opler, *Myths and Tales of the Jicarilla Apache Indians*, American Folklore Society Memoir Series, no. 31 (New York: American Folklore Society, 1938), pp. viii–ix.

4. The Blues as a Genre

HARRY OSTER

If in defining "blues" with texts we include all the forms and types of songs folk performers call by that name, the result is much broader than the conventional definitions. The form may be any one of the following.

1. Talking Blues.

A semi-rhythmic speaking or a mixture of speaking and singing is accompanied by rhythmic guitar playing. The speech has a fluid conversational flow, though it is more rhythmic than ordinary conversation. At the same time it is less rhythmic than an Afro-American folk sermon or than the talking blues of white performers in the Southern Appalachians, which usually have the poetic stresses coinciding exactly with the accented beats of the accompaniment. In black talking blues the lines are of approximately equal duration in time but may vary considerably in the number of words. When the talking blues include singing, the performer slips from speech to song and back so naturally that the shift is scarcely perceptible. The genesis of the form lies in the tendency in a nonliterate society to make less separation between speaking and singing than is typical in literate cultures.

Sung:
Well, my mules is gaited down,
Boy, I walk the field all day long,
Lord, I'm gonna plow this team, baby, Lord, an' I ain't gonna
plow no mo'.

NOTE. Reprinted from *Genre* 2, no. 3 (September 1969): 259–274, by permission of the University of Illinois Press.

Spoken:

Lookă hēre, yŏu knōw oňe thing, Ĭ sēarched thĭs whōle rĭvĕr
   bŏttŏm ōvĕr,
Aň' Ĭ aĭn't fŏund ănŏthĕr mūle nō whēre, măn, plōw lĭke thēse
   mūle plōw.
I'm gŏnnă hāng ŭp my̆ lĭne, I'm gŏnnă tālk tŏ 'ĕm frŏm hēre ŏn oŭt.
"Yŏu bĕttĕr gēt ōvĕr ă lĭttlĕ bĭt, haŭgh."
Thăt's gŏin' tŏ yŏur lĕft, yŏu knŏw whăt I'm tālkiň' ăbŏut,
   Yŏu's ă plōwhănd. . .

Sung:

Wĕll, I'm gŏnnă plōw ŏn băby̆, wŏh, I'm gŏnnă m̆ake thĭs dăy,
Yŏu knŏw thĕ sūn ĭs sīnkiň' lŏw, măn, ăn' my̆ tēam ĭs dŏne gŏt slŏw.

Spoken:

Bŏy, thĕy wālk lĭke thĭs ăll dăy, Ĭ gŏt ĭt măde, aĭn't Ĭ? . . . [1]

2. Classic Blues.

The melody consists of twelve bars, usually in 4/4 time, broken
up into three units of four bars each. The first phrase is built on
the tonic chord, the second on the subdominant, the third on the
dominant seventh. To go with each musical phrase is a line of text.
The second verbal line repeats the first, sometimes identically, sometimes with a slight variation for rhetorical emphasis. The third
line, which rhymes with the first and second, resolves the thoughts
expressed in them—if they express grief, it gives a reason for it, or it
concludes the verse in startling or epigrammatic fashion. The verbal
phrases take up less than four bars each, leaving a break in which the
instrument answers the voice or embellishes the melody. The singer
"worries" the third and often the seventh and/or the fifth of the
scale, wavering between flat and natural. The same effect is heard in

the accompaniment, readily accomplished on a guitar by pushing the strings sideways and distorting the pitch or by sliding a hard object along the strings so that pitches not in the European scale are sounded and notes are "bent." The effect is approximated on the piano by rapid alternation between major and minor intervals and by superimposing a minor third over a major chord while remaining in a major key. Although ideally the blues is an improvised form, frequently the singers perform a song essentially as they have before, or as they have heard it on a record. Further, it is important to note, the emotion expressed may be sad, happy, or a combination of both.

Ĭ sáy thĕ blūes lĕft Texăs, lópin' líke ă mūle, *(guitar response)*
Ĭ sáy thĕ blūes lĕft Texăs, lópin' líke ă mūle, *(guitar response)*
Tákes ă high brówn wómăn, Ĭ swéar she's hárd tŏ fóol.
   (guitar response)

Yŏu căn fáll frŏm thĕ móuntain, dówn ĭn thĕ déep blŭe séa,
   (guitar response)
Yŏu căn fáll frŏm thĕ móuntain, mámă, dówn ĭn thĕ déep blŭe séa,
   (guitar response)
Yóu ain't dóne nŏ fállin', bábў, till yŏu fáll ĭn lóve with mé.
   (guitar response)[2]

3. Free-Form Three-Unit Blues.

These songs are a rough fluid approximation of the classic form but with variations from verse to verse in the number of bars, the length of verbal phrases, and the instrumental breaks between lines, within a verse, and between verses. The chords may differ from those in European harmony, or the order of chord resolutions may be essentially the same as in the classic blues but with the proportions varied to suit the whims of the singer.

You know it was a dark cloud risin', baby, risin' in the west,
You know it was a dark cloud risin', baby, rose up in the west,
You know the storm rose up from the Gulf, baby, Lord it rolled
   out 'cross the world.

I was standin' in my cell, the ole cell begin to roll an' rock,
The wind was howlin' for miles aroun',
Lord, I wonder why do that storm rise this away.

You know it fell over Cameron, washed that poor town away,
You know it was mothers, sons, and daughters, Lord, didn't have
no place to stay,
You know that mothers, sons, and daughters, fathers, all outside.

Woh, the wind was howlin', man, yes, the lightnin' begin to
flash,
Lord, the wind was howlin', yes, the lightnin' begin to flash,
Well, I fell down on my knees, I cried, "God, help poor me."[3]

4. Blues of Two Lines, Four Lines, and Variable Numbers of Lines.

Some songs are not in a three-unit form but are similar to more standard blues in the sentiments they express, their language and verbal
conventions, and the instrumental style of the accompaniments. In
this category the most common forms are two line, often with a chorus, and four line. The former approximates an eight-bar construction
when there is no chorus, and the two lines rhyme. The latter is usually around sixteen bars, with the opening verbal line sung three times
and a rhyming concluding line, a favorite form in revival spirituals.
The third group intermixes stanzas of different lengths at the expressive whim of the performer.

Two line with chorus:

Yonder comes a man with a great big knife,
Somebody been messin' with his wife.
Chorus: Now you can't get drunk no mo',
You may try, you can't buy,
You can't get drunk no mo'.[4]

Four line:

Well, dig my grave with a silver spade,
Well, dig my grave with a silver spade,

Well, dig my grave with a silver spade,
You may let me down with a golden chain.[5]

Stanzas with variable numbers of lines:

Lord, looka here, baby, oh darlin', what do you want pore Bob
  to do?
Oh baby, what you want pore Bob to do?
You must want me, baby, Lord, for to lay down an' die for [you].

If you ever been down, baby, you know just how this pore [boy
  feels],
If you ever been down, woman, you know how it is.

Wonder why, woman, you wanna treat me this way,
Oh, I wonder why, baby, you wanna treat me this way.

I'm worried, woman, I ain't got no place to go,
Let's go out an' have some fun, baby, we gonna ball all night
  long,
Let's go out and have some fun, darlin', we gonna ball to the
  break of day.
If the river was wine, me an' my baby be drunk all the time.[6]

Structure, Imagery, and Wit. In both talking blues and blues more
rigid in structure, most lines are made up of two sections of approximately equal duration with a caesura more or less in the middle.
Often there is a striking contrast between the first and second halves
of a line or between the opening line of a verse and the last line.
Sometimes balanced contrast reaches the extreme of appearing both
within single lines and between separate lines. The result of these elements in combination is a quotable verse, complete in itself; it is often
aphoristic, rhythmically appealing as the words trip easily off the
tongue, and readily remembered—roughly analogous to the heroic
couplet of the eighteenth century, if we disregard the repetition of a
line in the blues. Note, for example Alexander Pope's statement in
"An Essay on Criticism":

True wit is Nature | | to advantage dress'd,
What oft was thought, | | but ne'er so well express'd.

As in the heroic couplet, in blues the final line completes the thought
initiated by the first, in a way which is witty, dramatic, or evocative.

Since such a verse or line is a satisfying unit in itself, a singer who is making up a song as he goes along by free association can fit into the mood of what he is saying a stock aphoristic or witty verse that deals with the situation on his mind, lines like:

> When you see me comin', baby, raise yo' window high, . . .
> When you see me leavin', hang yo' head an' cry.[7]

Comin' contrasts with *leavin'*, and *raise yo' window high* has meanings on several different levels. Because the man enters through the window he is a secret lover, and raising the window is an active image for welcome, though ironically different from flinging a door open in welcome. Finally the phrase has sexual overtones: the window through which the male enters is a vagina symbol. All the connotations attached to *raise yo' window high* are contrasted with *hang yo' head an' cry*.

> Hey, when you see my comin', put yo' black dress on, . . .
> I swear the graveyard gonna be yo' restin' place an' hell gonna be
>   yo' home.[8]

Here the arrival of the lover is ironically different from that in the previous example. This time the woman has been unfaithful to him, rather than, as in the preceding case, unfaithful to her regular lover. The only contrast is an implied contrast between dread, fear, and gloom at the approach of the lover and the joy a woman should feel at his arrival. Fundamentally the verse is composed in terms of balance. The idea in the first line—get dressed for mourning and death —parallels the ideas in the final line; *graveyard* is balanced by *restin' place*, *hell* by *home*. Rhetorically, the effect is movement toward a climax, a progression in importance from adopting a garb suitable for death, through resting in the graveyard, to suffering for all eternity.

A more dire evocation of death occurs in:

> Tombstone landin', baby, an' ole dry bone, . . .
> They are before me, when I am dead an' gone.[9]

The graveyard is presented in highly specific and forbidding terms: *tombstone landin'* and *ole dry bone*, which are the objective correlative of the abstract *dead an' gone*. In this instance, the usual order of an abstract statement followed by a concrete image is reversed. The effect is somewhat less exciting.

In another blues concerned with death the singer (speaking to his woman, who is dying of TB) presents an equally horrifying scene:

Graveyard ain't nothin', Lord, but great lonesome place, . . .
You can lay flat on your back, little woman, and let the sun shine
    in your face.[10]

Nothin' is balanced by *great lonesome place*; the first line, which is relatively abstract, is balanced by a concrete picture in the second; and the second line is balanced within itself. The last line begins with a phrase which has pleasurable connotations—*lay flat on your back* suggests either rest or love-making—but the end of the line twists the meaning ironically toward a dreary, painful isolation in which her only companion is the South's broiling hot sun.

Another singer, a prisoner, faces the fear of extinction in these lines:

Yes, I'm goin' down slow, somethin' wrong with me,
I've got to make a change while that I'm young,
If I don't I won't never get old.[11]

The vagueness of the first line is appropriate because the ailment is not any particular physical disease but the psychological and emotional effect of hopelessness and despair in prison. Making a change and being young are contrasted with not doing so and not growing old. The effect is aphoristic and witty.

A deftly structured verse dealing with love for another man's wife runs:

Lord, I love you, baby, but I'm scared to call your name,
Lord, you're a married woman, I love you just the same.[12]

The first half of each line contrasts with the second half. In the order of proper climax, the strongest idea comes at the end. Equally pointed and tightly constructed is another verse dealing with infidelity:

Woman rocks the cradle, I declare she rules the home, . . .
But a man rockin' other men's babies, an' the fool think he
    rockin' his own.[13]

Woman's position is presented in the first line, man's contrasting one in the second. She is strong and sinful, he is weak and gullible. The final statement, *the fool think he rockin' his own*, is rhetorically powerful.

Because the proper order of climax is movement upward in the scale of importance or dramatic impact, the following achieves a comic effect through the use of anticlimax:

> Now I have pawned my shoe, I even down an' pawned the suit
> off my back,
> I woulda pawn my sock', but they got holes in 'em.[14]

In poetic terms the lines are stronger, more stirring to the imagination, because they occur in a context in which the humor is tinged with sadness; the fact that the singer is a compulsive gambler gives the lines ironic overtones.

An example of wit is:

> I ain't gonna tell you what the Dago tol' the Jew, . . .
> Don't like me, baby, be sure don't like you.[15]

The impact stems largely from the clever construction of the stanza.

A lover speaks of the coldness of his woman in a homely but memorable image drawn from farming:

> But there is no mo' potatoes, you see the frost have killed the
> vine,
> An' the blues ain't nothin' but a good gal on your min'.[16]

Among the poor, potatoes are one of the foods which are the staff of life. The two portions of the first line balance well, and the metaphor appropriately and poetically suggests that her coldness has killed what he needs for sustenance. In epigrammatic fashion the final line sums up his situation and amplifies the meaning of the first line.

A drunken woman is described in these arresting lines:

> Heyah, heyah comes that woman, oh Lord, she's so bad drunk
> again,
> Lord, her pocket full o' money, an' her belly full o' gin.[17]

The second line strikingly expands and makes specific the implications of the first. The combination of both a full pocket and a full belly raises the nasty suspicion of prostitution, a thought subtly suggested rather than crudely stated.

Wanderlust finds eloquent expression in:

> One day I was walkin' out on the career,
> Lookin' at the birds, how they was treadin' the mighty air,
> I looked at automobile', how they was runnin' the track,
> It looked sweet to me, decide I better run the highway.[18]

Coming from a talking blues, these lines are more conversational in their flow than most verses in blues of more classical structure, but there are caesuras in three of the lines; *how they was treadin' the mighty air* and *how they was runnin' the track* are completely parallel, but at the same time there is contrast between the sky and the earth. *Treadin'* is used in a metaphorically fresh way, suggesting a solid, purposeful movement in contrast to the soaring and swooping usually associated with birds on the wing.

An equally memorable statement of the urge to hit the road is:

> When the moon jumps on the mountain, Lord, I'm gonna be on
> my way,
> I'm gonna be on this ole highway until ole dollar a day.[19]

Although both lines are complex sentences (that is, have an independent and a dependent clause), the order is reversed in the final line, contrary to the impulse toward parallelism, but whoever coined the verse in this form had a keen instinct for poetic effect. (It is possible that the form resulted from a desire to find a rhyme for *way*, but the lines are so well constructed that I doubt this was the reason.) *When the moon jumps on the mountain*, like *birds treadin' the mighty air* in the previous example, uses a verb startlingly in contrast to those generally associated with the moon. The moon would more typically *come*, *glide*, or *rise*, all smooth and unstartling movements; *jump* fits the mood of the singer, his yearning for quick motion, for getting rolling right away. *I'm gonna be on my way* and *I'm gonna be on this ole highway* deal with movement, though not notably, and, then, in contrast to the three previous clauses comes *until ole dollar a day*, an elliptical, compressed, and colorful way of suggesting that sooner or later the wanderer is going to have to stop somewhere and plod through a dull job.

Rhyme and Versification. As regards another basic structural element of poetry, in most blues it is customary though not invariable for the opening lines of a stanza to rhyme with the final line. The tendency in Afro-American folk speech to make the vowels come close to each other in sound and the practice of dropping consonants not only at the ends of words but often also in the middle of them make it easy for a singer to create rhymes even in the course of original improvisation. Sometimes too there is rhyme by assonance, that is, the singer uses near rhymes, for example, time / min(d), joint / pint, say / here (heyah), gol(d) / boa(r)d, tone / gone, bone / gone, sign / town, frien(d) / man, train / name, gone / town, and min(d) / cryin(g).

Improvisation, Personal and Social Context, the Logic of Association. Because the basic elements of most blues, verses like those discussed earlier, are standardized bricks which can be used to construct a wide variety of buildings, it is revealing to discuss the creative process at work, to describe the circumstances in which songs were improvised, and to examine how individual performers of varying creative abilities handle their raw materials. Note, for example, "Brownskin Woman," improvised by Willie B. Thomas during a jam session which I taped.

1. Got a mind to ramble, got a mind to settle down, (2)
   Gonna leave this town, I'm gonna be Alabama boun'.

2. My mama told me, papa told me too,
   Brownskin woman gonna be the death of you.

3. I can't count the time I stole away and cry,
   My baby she don't love me, and I can't see why.

4. She's long and tall, she's six feet from the groun',
   Oh baby, she's long and tall, she's six feet from the groun',
   She's strictly tailor-made, and she ain't no hand me down.

5. She got eyes like diamonds, teeth shine just the same,
   She got sweet ruby lips, she got hair like a horse's mane.

6. I asked the ticket agent how long the train had gone,
   Well, I asked the ticket agent how long the train had gone,
   Well, the same old train, my baby left me alone.

7. I didn't have no money, I walked back through the do',
   Say my baby is gone, she won't come home [no mo'].

8. If I had wings like a jaybird in the air,
   I would find my woman if she's in this world somewhere.[20]

In terms of the social context of the performance, the musicians were affirming their identity with the group, enjoying the interaction between themselves and their friends, who laughed, shouted encouragement, clapped their hands, or sometimes danced. The music primarily expressed a feeling that they were glad to be alive. In this song Willie B. Thomas is essentially a synthesizer, although in his speech he shows impressive fluency and color. With the single exception of the last part of the opening line, which in the context would typically be "got a mind not to settle down," all the stanzas are standard in Afro-American tradition; the particular combination, however, is Willie's, for it took shape spontaneously as he was singing. Later, although he was aware that he had produced an excellent song, he could not repeat it but had to listen to the tape recording to find out what he had sung. Frequently I have found that blues singers have only a rough idea of what they have just performed, and, when I ask them what they would like to call the song, they wrinkle their brows in perplexity and on occasion give any name that happens to occur to them.

Being improvised of standard components, the text is not a directly personal statement, but it is nevertheless autobiographical in its psychological associations. Having a family of seven young children, three by his current marriage and four by his wife Martha's earlier marriage, all of whom he finds it difficult to support, he fantasies at times on the theme of being a free wanderer from town to town, but at the same time he feels drawn to his settled state. The marriage, however, is a troubled one, and Willie, as suggested by this blues, would like to believe that his lighter-skinned wife is the cause of the difficulties. (She insists that on weekends when he gets drunk he often tries to kill her.) The fourth stanza probably rose to his tongue because he is only 4′ 10″ tall, and as a result of a childhood accident he is slightly hunchbacked. To a man who is both plain and undersized, an attractive tall woman like Martha is apt to seem particularly desirable. Possessing her is a source of special pride to Willie, and probably this fact explains why this verse crops up in many of the improvised blues he sings. The last three stanzas suggest his fear that his wife will leave him.

A similar principle of organization, though accompanied by more creativity, is apparent in the "Bulldog Blues" of Robert Pete Williams.

1. You know I'm gonna buy me a bull dog, I want to watch you whiles I'm gone.
   I'm gonna buy me a bulldog, darlin', I want to watch you whiles I'm gone,
   I'm gonna tie him in my front yard so he won't let nobody in.

2. Well, I want you to tell me, baby, is you got in your mind to treat me right?
   I want you to tell me, darlin', is you got in your mind to treat me right?
   Well, (if) you ain't, baby, we just want to part right now.

3. If I could holler just like a mountain jack,
   I'd get up on the mountain, God knows I'd call my baby [back].

4. I go up on the mountain so high, I seen grass growin' on a dollar bill,
   I been on the mountain so high, I seen grass growin' on a dollar bill,
   I wanta tell you, woman, you know I was dead on your trail.[21]

In "Bulldog Blues" the singer's first thought is to try to keep his woman faithful by stationing a bulldog in the yard to frighten lovers away—a standard blues image. Then he threatens to leave her if she won't be true, but, with a twist of thought characteristic of the blues, he wants her back again. The image he uses is powerful though conventional: if he had the wild scream of a mountain jackass to express his anguish, he would climb high above the world and summon her. The reference to a mountain leads to another image which includes a mountain, this time embodying a shift from abject despair to vindictive pursuit. Instead of being a mournful wailing animal, he is a beast of prey with fantastic keenness of vision. Thus he has cleverly extended his metaphor. The rhetorical exaggeration of "on the mountain so high, I seen grass growin' on a dollar bill" is freshly imaginative and powerful. This fanciful image may well be an inspired reworking of the relatively commonplace lines in one of Leroy Carr's later versions of "How Long, How Long" (Vocalion, c. 1934):

> I can look and see the green grass growin' up on the hill,
> But I haven't seen the green back of a dollar bill,
> For so long, so long, baby, so long.

Sustained Irony. Although most blues follow a logic of emotional association, sometimes singers spin out a blues that follows a more tangible central thread. In Otis Webster's "I Know How to Do Time" the unifying theme is an extended ironic interplay between two frames of reference—one of a childlike old-fashioned plantation Uncle Tom who has faith in the paternalistic benevolence of his boss, the other of a worker who thinks for himself, whose fault is that "he just don't know how to do time," that is, he won't put up with a way of life which is like being in prison.

Spoken:

Yes, you know, boy, I'm a raggety,
I ain't never had no good clothes,
The man I used to work for, you know,
He used to give me my room an' board,
You know I thought that was a good man to work for me,
He asked [me] to go out, find another boy like me.
I went out, talk to that ole boy about tryin' to come out, find him
    a job,
The first thing he holler, "What that man pay?"
"Oh partner, don't worry 'bout the pay,
I guarantee you be satisfied."
"I don't know whether I be satisfied or not,
'Lessn' I know what I'm gettin'."
"Oh, you silly, son, you don't know like I do.
I didn't know what I was gonna get either
Till I went there. I tell you,
Give him a day an' a half, two days,
See how you like it."
"Well, I believe I'll go down there an' try him one time."

Sung:

My mule won't pull my plow, oh Lord, he's reined up too tight,
Say, my mule won't pull my plow, oh, the captain say he reined
   too tight,
Lord, I begin to look at my next partner over there, he seem
   to be doin' all right.

Spoken:

You know last night me an' that new boy went out to have some
   honeymoon,
He didn't know what drinkin' was.
I says, "Son, now get yourself a half pint o' wine now."
"They don't sell no half pints o' wine."
"Oh, you don't know what you talkin' about, you green!"
"Yeah, that's all right, don't worry about my time, do yours."
"That's a fine way to be!"

Our boss told him, "Gonna give you about two and a half a day,
You reckon you worth that an' board?"
"I don't know about that board proposition. What you got to
   eat?"
"Oh, we have a few rice, beans, 'taters, cucumbers, onions—"
"What you mean name all that kind o' stuff?
Tell me what you got to eat."
"If you don't want that, you know what you can do."

Sung:

Oh, Bossman, I believe I got you another man again,
Oh, Bossman, I believe I got you another man again,
Ain't but one thing I found wrong with him, he just don't
   know how to do time.

Spoken:

Yes, I went to my bossman, just for a pair o' blue jean',
He looked at me, says, "Son, what do you do with all your
   money?"
I say, "Boss, I blow that stuff in."
"Why don't you do like that boy over there?

He got good clothes."
"Ain't been on long, long as I is."
"Yeah, but you better count that money,
Gonna be in debt, can't get out."
"Well, if I can't get out I'll always have a good job,
'Cause you won't run me off, I know."

Sung:

Sometimes I wakes up in the mornin', baby, I just can't eat for
    cryin',
Well, I wakes up so early in the mornin', baby, little woman,
    I just can't eat for cryin'.
Well, you talk about a wise man know, I declare I know how to
    do time.[22]

Satisfied with his cooperative, naïve, overworked, underpaid, and ragged field hand, who assumes he has a good job, the boss sends him out to find another worker just like himself. The potential new worker wants to know specifically what he is going to get paid. Unlike the narrator, whose "mule is reined too tight," who is too confined by a repressive system, the modern black moves freely. When the two go out to drink together for the first time, the new man finds it hard to believe that wine is sold in such penny-pinching quantities as half-a-pint. Also the latter wants to know what his board will consist of, and he is openly scornful of fare which consists of only cheap vegetables.

The traditional scene in which the penniless sharecropper goes to the boss to beg for an advance presents several ironies. The boss chides him for spending money which in actuality he never had and rebukes him for dressing so badly, whereas the new man is dressed decently because he has just started the job. The farm hand ironically finds solace in the thought that if he gets into debt he can always depend on the boss for a good job.

The song ends in a burst of anguish as the singer faces the full bitterness of his servitude—a life which is like serving time in prison.

Blues as Catharsis. Finally, it is important to note that the surface of blues is deceptive. The texts emphasize such disturbances as frustration, anger, aggressiveness, sadness, oppression, hunger, sickness, the pangs of the cuckold, and the restlessness of the wanderer, but the form takes on a different significance when it is considered in relation to the social context within which the music is performed. Meaning and function emerge more clearly in the light of these additional quotations from the remarks of country blacks I have recorded. Georgianna Colmer said, "I'd sing them old moans until I got happy"; Hogman Maxey, "When you sing the blues jus' right, why you feel like a million when you may not have a dime"; Robert Pete Williams, "I want you to be happy and take the blues like me." Thus a major function of the blues is akin to Aristotle's view of tragedy. If one can convert sadness into a blues, the effect is a catharsis of troubled emotions.

Blues as a Means of Gaining a Sense of Belonging. Although part of the time the blues singer performs for his own ears, frequently he sings and plays for a crowd of listeners and dancers. In such a situation, in a jam session at a little country shack, Roy Jenkins stated, "The blues ain't blue; it's keepin' it all to yourself. Now tell 'em, guitar, 'cause they might not understand me. Maybe if you was to come out, tell 'em what you mean, they might get it." This quotation suggests another important function of the blues: communication of feeling in order to gain a sense of being part of a cohesive group, a vital value also when a preacher shouts his sermon with the encouragement of his congregation, who punctuate each line with exuberant cries of "Preach on, Rev," "Hallelujah," "My Lord," or when the leader of a work gang in prison chants ironically and is answered rhythmically by the chorus of his mates. In all these instances the performer finds his burden easier to bear as a result of musical communion with a group; he is no longer alone.

Although some blues express unrelieved sadness, the overall mood of most of them is an affirmation through sensuality of life, love, and hope.

Notes

1. Roosevelt Charles, "Mule Blues," Louisiana State Penitentiary (hereafter referred to as Angola), November 19, 1960. I recorded all the blues referred

to in the notes. The full texts are available in *Living Country Blues* (Detroit: Folklore Associates, 1969).

2. Robert (Guitar) Welch, "Out in West Texas," Angola, March 27, 1959.

3. Roosevelt Charles, "Hurricane Audrey Blues," Angola, November 19, 1960.

4. James (Butch) Cage and Willie B. Thomas, "You Can't Get Drunk No Mo'," Zachary, Louisiana, October 10, 1960.

5. Tom Dutson, "Dig My Grave with a Silver Spade," Angola, June 5, 1959.

6. Robert Pete Williams, "I'm Lonesome Blues," Angola, February 22, 1959.

7. Charles Henderson, "She Was a Woman Didn't Mean No One Man No Good," Zachary, Louisiana, February 16, 1960.

8. Charles Henderson, "61 Highway," Zachary, Louisiana, March 15, 1961.

9. Smoky Babe and Sally Dotson, "Dell on the Mountain," Scotlandville, Louisiana, February 25, 1960.

10. Robert (Guitar) Welch, "TB Blues," Angola, February 27, 1959.

11. Robert Pete Williams, "Prisoner's Talking Blues," Angola, March 21, 1959.

12. Matthew (Hogman) Maxey, "Fiddle Blues," Angola, April 14, 1959.

13. Herman E. Johnson, "Crawlin' Baby Blues," Baton Rouge, Louisiana, November 3, 1960.

14. Roosevelt Charles, "Georgia Skin," Angola, November 19, 1960.

15. Charles Henderson, "Rock Island Blues," Zachary, Louisiana, February 5, 1961.

16. Herman E. Johnson, "C. C. Rider," Baton Rouge, Louisiana, May 12, 1961.

17. Leon Strickland, "How Long Blues," Killona, Louisiana, November 27, 1959.

18. Roosevelt Charles, "Trouble Followin' Me," Angola, November 19, 1960.

19. Leon Strickland, "Key to the Highway," Killona, Louisiana, November 27, 1961.

20. Scotlandville, Louisiana, October 5, 1960.

21. Angola, February 10, 1959.

22. Otis Webster, "I Know How to Do Time," Angola, November 26, 1960.

5. On Defining the Riddle:
The Problem of a Structural Unit

CHARLES T. SCOTT

That an adequate definition of the riddle as a folkloristic (literary) genre has never been well formulated should not surprise those who view a theory of genres as a legitimate concern of a broader theory of literature. On the other hand, it may indeed be something of a surprise that a genre as minor as that of the riddle should command serious scholarly attention with respect to questions of definition.

The search for a satisfactory definition of the riddle is, of course, simply one instance of the larger, continuing problem of defining the genres of folklore and literature—a problem which appears to have a limitless capacity for aligning those with a "taxonomic itch" against those who consider labeling of any sort to be a perverse undermining of creativity in art.[1] It is not difficult to understand, however, why the riddle should be a likely candidate for examination in attempts to develop general methodological principles for genre definition. First of all, the texts of riddles are characteristically short enough to investigate with a certain degree of ease and efficiency. Because they are short, they can also be examined in relatively large numbers, thereby providing samples that could be statistically significant if one chose to approach the study of them from that point of view. Secondly, riddles are often sufficiently stylized to exhibit a variety of recurrent formal characteristics, which suggest therefore that general formulaic patterns can be extrapolated from the texts. Finally, even within the relative stability of the form, there is enough flexibility to challenge the ingenuity of the analyst and to attract his interest.

The status of the riddle as a minor genre of folklore can probably be attributed to several rather widely held conclusions about riddles in general. One is that their primary function is mere entertainment or amusement. A second is that they are most often associated with

NOTE. Reprinted from *Genre* 2, no. 2 (June 1969): 129–142, by permission of the University of Illinois Press.

the games of children rather than with the presumably more serious preoccupations of adults. A third conclusion is that their content and language tend to focus predominantly on concrete, homespun details rather than on the more abstract features of human relations and behavior which one expects, for instance, in proverbs and aphorisms. Doubtless, there is considerable accuracy in these conclusions, but there is also no doubt that each of these conclusions can be challenged as valid generalizations. For example, the concept of amusement (play) as function is open to more serious connotations than the layman is normally willing to grant,[2] and consequently the amusement function of riddles is not necessarily as trivial as some would choose to believe. Additionally, it has been well demonstrated that, for some societies, riddles have a social and didactic value that clearly transcends the entertainment or amusement function.[3] There are clear cases also where riddles are regarded far more seriously than as simple child's play, as evidenced, for instance, in the Old English riddles of the *Exeter Book* or in numerous Persian and Arabic riddles which carefully conform to the stylistic requirements of the *c̆ar bayti* tradition of much Islamic lyric poetry.[4] The third opinion, that riddles focus unduly on concrete details rather than on abstract features, is, of course, no argument to disprove the possible sophistication of riddles as an art form. On the contrary, in numerous instances a case could well be made in favor of their sophistication in terms of compactness of imagery, appropriateness of analogies, and so on. It does not seem too fanciful a notion to suggest that certain qualities of imagery that we might associate with good examples of Japanese *haiku* are shared by the following Persian riddles: "A lion's thumb, a gazelle's jump, an ass's cry. —Frog" or "A blue napkin full of pears. —Sky." In short, while we may continue, for whatever reasons, to regard riddles as a minor genre of folklore, we need not interpret *minor* to mean "trivial," nor do we need to underestimate the actual and potential sophistication of the genre.

A central problem in the theory of genres concerns the extent to which definitions proposed for specific genres are valid. In particular, the claim is occasionally made, or more frequently implied, that suggested definitions of genres are universally valid. Alternatively, but less commonly, some researchers prefer to limit their proposed definitions to a specific sociolinguistic context. The latter approach is characteristic of researchers trained in the empiricist tradition of the social sciences—a tradition which has been attacked in recent years, at least in its applications to psychology and to linguistics, for lacking sufficient explanatory power in its formulations.[5] Nevertheless, the empiricist approach[6] is essentially a reaction against genre definitions which purport to isolate classes of literary or folkloristic discourses solely on the basis of their social function or on the basis of culturally biased aesthetic values or perhaps simply on the basis of the semantic content of the discourses. For the empiricist, the alternative point of view is to claim that intuitively perceived distinctions in classes of literary or folkloristic discourses (as in all other discourses) should be subject to verification through correlated formal distinctions in the overt manifestations of these discourse classes. Thus, the problem of genre definition can be expressed as follows: what (overt, formal) characteristic or set of characteristics will unambiguously differentiate this class of discourses from some other?

Once an empirically based and inductively derived definition has been proposed, the empiricist must wrestle with the question of the extent of validity of his definition. Given his normally inductive approach to sociocultural problems, including those of language and literature, the empiricist would probably posit as an initial hypothesis that genre definitions are valid only for specific linguistic communities. In a recent issue of *Genre* Professor Eliseo Vivas states the hypothesis quite unequivocally: "a genre, since it is derived inductively, is valid only for the members of the class from which it was obtained and cannot be extrapolated beyond them."[7] In *Persian and Arabic Riddles*, I clearly demonstrated that, within the requirements for well-defined terms in tagmemic theory, it was impossible to claim universal validity for the definition of any genre.[8] Still, these conclusions are no more than reiterations of a plausible hypothesis that remains open to empirical investigation.

But, if the empiricists have not been notably successful in establishing their claim, neither have those who would at least imply universal validity for genre definitions. Archibald Hill has remarked on the absurd extremism of Arnold's totally subjective and culturally biased definition of literature itself.[9] Subjectivism, imprecision, and conflicting criteria are no less clear in traditional attempts to define the riddle. Thus, Archer Taylor's statement that "a true riddle consists of two descriptions of an object, one figurative and one literal, and confuses the hearer who endeavors to identify an object described in conflicting ways"[10] is an intuitively correct characterization of the nature and function of riddles as a type of discourse, but it provides no formal criteria for isolating the riddle as a distinct genre of folklore. Similarly, the classic definition given by Gaston Paris is even less acceptable: "L'énigme est une métaphore ou un groupe de métaphores dont l'emploi n'a point passé dans l'usage commun et dont l'explication n'est pas évidente."[11]

Within the tradition of those who would claim universal validity for genre definitions, Robert A. Georges and Alan Dundes have made the most serious effort of all to state a formally unambiguous definition for the riddle. They conclude that "a folk riddle is a traditional verbal expression which contains one or more descriptive elements, a pair of which may be in opposition: the referent of the elements is to be guessed."[12] Although I have given elsewhere a fairly detailed criticism of this definition,[13] the burden of the essay here will be a further elaboration on that criticism, not for the purpose of restating old arguments, but for the purpose of examining, from quite a different point of view, a crucial issue raised in the Georges-Dundes study. This issue concerns the nature of the "structural unit" which must be posited if structural analysis is to be applied successfully to problems of genre definition. Although it is probably superfluous to say so, the remarks that follow are not intended to place the Georges-Dundes study in a bad light. Rather, they are meant to point up a number of problems in their formulation which have serious consequences, not only for the adequacy of the particular definition proposed, but also for the general methodological principles to be developed for genre definition.

Before proceeding further, however, a few preliminary comments are in order:

1. It is apparent that the success of the definition proposed by Georges and Dundes rests squarely on the adequacy of the term *descriptive element*, since this is posited as the basic "structural unit" of discourses such as riddles and proverbs (and possibly many other types of discourses as well). The question, in other words, is whether the unit "descriptive element" is itself a well-defined term.

2. Both the number and status of the descriptive elements are mat-

ters of concern. In short, is obligatory or optional status to be assigned to these descriptive elements and what is the minimum number of such elements required for the riddle qua genre?

3. The last clause of the Georges-Dundes definition, "the referent of the elements is to be guessed," would appear to invalidate their claim that "the best way to arrive at a definition of the riddle is through structural analysis, since definitions based on content and style have proved to be inadequate."[14]

The problem in (1) is especially crucial, since the definition has no value unless the unit "descriptive element" can be isolated and quantized. This involves analytic procedures of segmentation, grouping, and distribution, which Georges and Dundes do not provide—at least not in any explicit way. Their suggestion that the unit "descriptive element" consists of a "topic" and a "comment" ("The *topic* is the apparent referent. . . . The *comment* is an assertion about the topic, usually concerning the form, function, or action of the topic")[15] merits consideration, however, since it potentially points the way to a methodological procedure for isolating descriptive elements. Still, no strong claim can as yet be made for its utility.

In (2) the problem is more immediate. Even if we grant the viability of the unit "descriptive element," it is still clear that the Georges-Dundes definition, as it stands, does not differentiate riddles from proverbs in any "structural" sense. The clue to this difficulty is to be found in an earlier article by Dundes, where he states that "proverbs are traditional expressions in which there is a *topic* and a *comment*. The simplest form of the proverb would thus be 'Money talks'."[16] Since a descriptive element consists of a topic and a comment (cf. above), we can infer that the minimal unit of proverbs is also the descriptive element.[17] Furthermore, since the simplest form of proverb is "Money talks," then we must conclude that the structure of proverbs is such that they consist of at least *one* descriptive element. That is, one descriptive element (DE) is obligatory; presumably, and optionally, there may be others. We can express this conclusion formally with the rule:

$$\text{Proverb} \longrightarrow \text{DE}_1 \, (\text{DE}_2 \ldots \text{DE}_n)$$

where parentheses are a notational convention indicating the optional status of "$\text{DE}_2 \ldots \text{DE}_n$." The Georges-Dundes definition of the riddle, though, states that the riddle contains one or more descriptive elements; that is, at least *one* DE is obligatory. Thus:

$$\text{Riddle} \longrightarrow \quad DE_1 \, (DE_2 \ldots DE_n)$$

When we assign optional and obligatory status to the descriptive elements, therefore, we see that there is in fact *no structural difference* between proverbs and riddles. As the Georges-Dundes definition is presently stated, it fails to distinguish between the two genres.

Notice that the further remark in the Georges-Dundes definition, "a pair of which may be in opposition," has no bearing on this conclusion because this is merely an *optional* condition imposed on the descriptive elements, applicable only in case there are at least *two* descriptive elements. But the number of descriptive elements is itself optional, as we have seen.

This leads to the problem in (3), which concerns the last clause of the definition: "the referent of the elements is to be guessed."[18] Given the identity of the rules expressed above for the structure of the proverb and riddle, we would have to conclude that this last clause is the only characteristic of the definition which serves to distinguish riddles from proverbs. But, since this clause is clearly a statement of *function* rather than of structure (that is, the function of the discourse in terms of speaker-hearer roles), it seems inescapable that Georges and Dundes have, after all, relied on functional analysis for their definition, rather than on structural analysis, contrary to their claim and original intention.

A structural approach to the analysis of discourses (no matter what the content nature of the discourse) assumes the identification of discrete units, which, as Dundes has correctly noted, must be "standards of one kind of quantity."[19] Not only is this intuitively appealing, but it is also mandatory, for structural analysis presupposes a treatment of raw data from the point of view of a quantum mechanics.[20] The identification of such units, however, requires explicit procedures for segmenting and grouping the data. Once the units have been properly isolated, a structural analysis would then proceed to state the distribution of the relevant units, either by expressing the permitted combinatorial possibilities of the units relative to each other and to the discourse as a whole or by expressing constraints on the combinatorial possibilities.

The descriptive element proposed by Georges and Dundes might well be a useful and relevant unit of discourses. (Surely *descriptive elements* itself is an arbitrary term, but this is of no great importance.) Let us suppose, for present purposes, that the descriptive element is the basic unit of discourses. How is it to be isolated? Georges and Dundes suggest that the topic-comment criterion may be applied to this question. Thus, the proverb "Money talks" consists of one descriptive element because it has the constituent structure shown in figure 1.

Fig. 1. Constituent structure of the proverb "Money talks"

In this case, the notion "descriptive element" is identical to the grammatical notion "sentence," as expressed in figure 2.

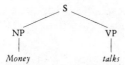

Fig. 2. Constituent structure of the sentence "Money talks"

Now consider the application of this criterion to texts of riddles, for example, "A blue napkin full of pears. —Sky." In "A blue napkin full of pears," how many descriptive elements are to be identified? If one applies the topic-comment criterion to this text, where is the topic-comment cut to be made? Traditional immediate constituent (IC) analysis would no doubt suggest the division shown in figure 3.

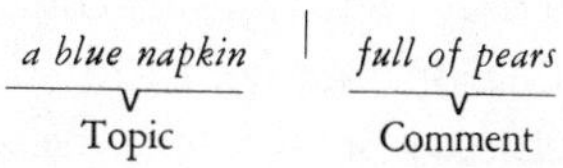

a blue napkin | full of pears

Topic   Comment

Fig. 3. IC analysis of the phrase " a blue napkin full of pears"

Notice two facts here: (1) the analysis meets the functional conditions for topic-comment suggested by Georges and Dundes, and (2)

the analysis accords with traditional IC analysis in that, in constructions like the above, post-nominal phrasal modifiers are normally cut
first. Thus, once again, the discourse unit "descriptive element" is
identical to a grammatical construction—in this case, a nominal.

But suppose we choose to analyze the nominal construction as deriving from the (abbreviated) deep structure of figure 4.[21]

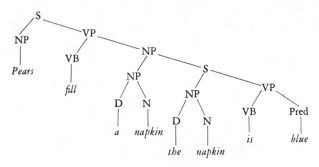

Fig. 4. Deep structure representation of the phrase " a blue napkin full
of pears"

This would yield a deep structure representation for the text, which
might be spelled out as "Pears fill a napkin (the napkin is blue)." In
the derivation of the surface structure of the construction, we would
then assume application of a series of transformational rules, which
would produce the following intermediate structures:

a. *Pears fill a napkin (the napkin is blue)* [deep structure]
b. *Pears fill a napkin (which is blue)* [relative clause T-rule]
c. *Pears fill a napkin (blue)* [relative pronoun and copula deletion T-rule]
d. *Pears fill a blue napkin* [adjective inversion T-rule]
e. *A blue napkin full of pears* [nominalization T-rule]

The point of all this is that we can now say that (1) the topic-
comment structure is formally equivalent to any concatenation of
NP and VP immediately dominated by a node S, (2) since topic and
comment are the required constituents of a descriptive element, the
descriptive element itself is formally equivalent to any S-dominated
structure, including an embedded S, and (3) there are as many descriptive elements in a discourse as there are S nodes in the deep struc-

ture of the discourse. In the example above, therefore, there are *two* descriptive elements (represented in *a* by the two underlying simple sentences, one of which is embedded in an NP constituent of the matrix sentence), not *one* descriptive element as might have been supposed originally if topic-comment analysis had been treated as equivalent to first-cut IC analysis.

Consider now a second example, cited at the beginning of this essay: "A lion's thumb, a gazelle's jump, an ass's cry. —Frog." From any point of view, there would appear to be no difficulty in claiming *three* descriptive elements in the text of this riddle, since the structure of the text is clearly one of conjoined nominals with optional deletion of the conjunction *and*, as illustrated in figure 5.

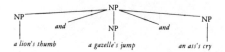

Fig. 5. Deep structure representation of the conjoined nominals "a lion's thumb, a gazelle's jump, an ass's cry"

In each of the descriptive elements, however, what is the topic and what is the comment? Traditional IC analysis has always had difficulty in handling genitive constructions like the above; that is, in "a lion's thumb" should the ICs be isolated as *a lion's | thumb* or *a lion | 's thumb*? A way out of this dilemma is to suggest cuts based on the equivalent constructions listed in figure 6.

		Topic		Comment
a lion's thumb	⟶	the thumb	|	of a lion
a gazelle's jump	⟶	the jump	|	of a gazelle
an ass's cry	⟶	the cry	|	of an ass

Fig. 6. Transformally related surface structures of the nominals "a lion's thumb, a gazelle's jump, an ass's cry"

This procedure suggests that the correct IC analysis for the original genitive constructions is: *a lion's | thumb, a gazelle's | jump*, and *an ass's | cry*. Either way, the topic-comment relation is described as formally equivalent to the (grammatical) head-modifier relation, so that the topics of the three constructions are *thumb, jump*, and *cry*, and the comments are *a lion's | of a lion, a gazelle's | of a gazelle*, and *an ass's | of an ass*. We could ask at this point whether such a conclusion accords with the Georges-Dundes semantic criteria: "The *topic* is the apparent referent. . . . The *comment* is an assertion about the topic, usually concerning the form, function, or action of the topic."

Notice further that the above constructions have been treated in terms of their alternative surface structures, that is, as nominals. But the alternative nominal constructions can be viewed as transformationally derived from underlying simple sentences (see figure 7).

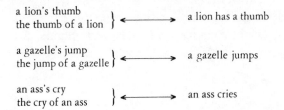

Fig. 7. Transformational relationships between nominals and sentences

In this view, the resultant deep structure of the riddle text is that of a discourse consisting of conjoined sentences (see figure 8).

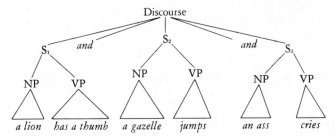

Fig. 8. Deep structure representation of the discourse "A lion's thumb, a gazelle's jump, an ass's cry"

Clearly, what happens now is that nominalization transformations are applied to S_1, S_2, and S_3 to convert these deep-structure sentences to their equivalent surface-structure nominals.

This analysis, however, suggests several conclusions: (1) DE_1, DE_2, and DE_3 are formally equivalent to S_1, S_2, and S_3. This reinforces the conclusion reached earlier that the descriptive element is formally equivalent to any S-dominated structure; (2) the topic-comment structure is formally equivalent to any concatenation of NP and VP immediately dominated by an S-node (a conclusion also reached earlier); and (3) the topics, therefore, for the three descriptive elements in this riddle text are *a lion, a gazelle,* and *an ass.* The comments for the three descriptive elements are *has a thumb, jumps,* and *cries.*

Conclusion 3, of course, is just the reverse of what was stated previously in the analysis based on surface-structure ICs. This reversal of conclusions is not a trivial matter by any means, since once again we could ask whether the conclusion just reached accords with the Georges-Dundes semantic criteria for identifying the topic and the comment. The two approaches to analysis yield the following sets of data:

Analysis A [based on surface-structure ICs]
    Topic Set A: thumb, jump, cry
    Comment Set A: a lion's / of a lion, a gazelle's / of a gazelle, an ass's / of an ass
Analysis B [based on deep-structure S's and T-rules]
    Topic Set B: a lion, a gazelle, an ass
    Comment Set B: has a thumb, jumps, cries

For the three descriptive elements of the riddle text, which of the analyses yields topics that could be said to be apparent referents and comments that could be said to be assertions about the topics? The conclusions of Analysis A would appear to contradict the semantic criteria of Georges and Dundes, since, in the given context of the riddle, terms like *thumb, jump,* and *cry,* rather than being referents themselves, seem to be better interpreted as assertions "concerning . . . form, function, or action. . . ." The conclusions of Analysis B seem to correspond more closely than those of Analysis A to the semantic criteria established by Georges and Dundes.

But, if Analysis B is selected, then the previously stated theoretical conclusions associated with this analysis should also be recognized. These can be restated as follows:

(1) *Descriptive element* is a totally ad hoc label for a unit of discourse whose basic structure is that of an underlying simple sentence in the deep-structure representation of the text.

(2) The term *unit* is justified here, since the structure under consideration meets the requirements of "standards of one kind of quantity"; all such units are at least characterized by the deep constituent structure of figure 9.

Fig. 9. Minimal deep structure of any sentence

(3) The topic-comment criterion as a methodological principle for unit ("descriptive element") identification is open to varying interpretations and is, therefore, useless for such a purpose. Clearly, however, the topic-comment relation is identical to the deep-structure subject-predicate relation. Because this latter relation can be determined unambiguously, it must replace the topic-comment criterion.

Two corollaries to these conclusions, both of which are relevant to the question of defining the riddle, are the following: (1) it is possible to replace vague and imprecise semantic criteria, of the sort that Georges and Dundes have proposed, with specific formal correlates, and (2) the "descriptive element" proposed by Georges and Dundes for the definition of the riddle is clearly *not* uniquely characteristic of either riddles or proverbs or both; it *may*, however, in its reinterpretation as given here, be a viable unit for discourse analysis in general.

Quite obviously, no attempt has been made here to reformulate a definition of the riddle. It seems quite clear that no form of functional analysis can really account for an intuitive ability to discriminate successfully between riddles, proverbs, and other folkloristic or literary genres. The challenge of accounting for this intuitive ability, therefore, would appear to depend upon the success of structural analysis—the characterization of the structure of discourses in terms of their identificational and contrastive features. Structural analysis, however, presupposes the availability of structural units which can be isolated in accordance with explicit criteria for their identification. This essay has done just that for one such unit. The actual role of this unit in the task of defining the riddle, as well as other discourses, must still, of course, be determined, and its utility must be tested.[22]

Notes

1. In this essay I deliberately avoid discussion of the motivation for a theory of genres, and consequently for the definition of genres, because this could not be done without resort to a lengthy excursus. Moreover, the very nature of this symposium would seem to make such an excursus unnecessary.

2. See, for example, Johan Huizinga, *Homo Ludens: A Study of the Play-Element in Culture*, trans. R. F. C. Hull (Boston: Beacon Press, 1955).

3. See, for example, John Blackling, "The Social Value of Venda Riddles," *African Studies* 20 (1961): 1–32.

4. Charles T. Scott, *Persian and Arabic Riddles: A Language-Centered Approach to Genre Definition* (Part 2 of the *International Journal of American Linguistics*, October 1965).

5. Noam Chomsky, Review of *Verbal Behavior* by B. F. Skinner, *Language* 35 (1959): 26–58, and *Aspects of the Theory of Syntax* (Cambridge, Mass.: M.I.T. Press, 1965).

6. For example, Scott, *Persian and Arabic Riddles*.

7. Eliseo Vivas, "Literary Classes: Some Problems," *Genre* 1 (1968): 103.

8. Notice, however, that this conclusion was a natural consequence of descriptive method within the conventions of tagmemic theory, not one which could be said to be empirically motivated on independent grounds.

9. Archibald A. Hill, "A Program for the Definition of Literature," *University of Texas Studies in English* 37 (1958): 46–52.

10. Archer Taylor, "The Riddle," *California Folklore Quarterly* 2 (1943): 130.

11. Gaston Paris, Preface to *Devinettes, ou énigmes populaires de la France*, by Eugène Rolland (Paris, 1877), p. viii.

12. Robert A. Georges and Alan Dundes, "Toward a Structural Definition of the Riddle," *Journal of American Folklore* 76 (1963): 113.

13. Scott, *Persian and Arabic Riddles*, pp. 16–21.

14. Georges and Dundes, "Toward a Structural Definition," p. 113.

15. Ibid.

16. Alan Dundes, "Trends in Content Analysis: A Review Article," *Midwest Folklore* 12 (1962): 37.

17. Indeed, Dundes has specifically claimed this in a personal communication: "[The descriptive element] is also an EMIC unit of proverbs . . ."

18. Strictly speaking, as a consequence of the preceding discussion, the last clause should read: "the referent of the element(s) is to be guessed."

19. Alan Dundes, "From Etic to Emic Units in the Structural Study of Folktales," *Journal of American Folklore* 75 (1962): 96.

20. Martin Joos, "Description of Language Design," *Journal of the Acoustical Society of America* 22 (1950): 701–708.

21. The grammatical notions of *deep structure* and *surface structure*, referred to throughout the remainder of this paper, are used in the sense in

which they have been developed by Chomsky in *Aspects of the Theory of Syntax* (Cambridge, Mass.: M.I.T. Press, 1964).

22. I would continue to maintain that the tentative definition of the riddle I proposed in *Persian and Arabic Riddles* is superior to the Georges-Dundes proposal in at least one important respect: it differentiates riddles from proverbs, which theirs does not, by using the obligatory binary structure of the riddle as a differentiating characteristic. In the notation used in this essay, this can be expressed as follows:

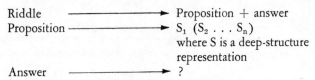

Riddle $\longrightarrow$ Proposition + answer
Proposition $\longrightarrow$ S_1 $(S_2 \ldots S_n)$
where S is a deep-structure
representation
Answer $\longrightarrow$?

Thus, the appropriate rewrite for the final rule must still be determined. Additionally, the characteristic of "partially obscured semantic fit" between the Proposition and the Answer constituents must still be formalized. It now seems possible that this could be done by means of semantic feature analysis, in which case the problem would be not unlike the formalization problems involved in stating grammatical rules such as those concerning co-occurrence restrictions, agreement, government, and so on.

Part Two

The Ethnography of Folklore Genres

6. Legend and Belief

LINDA DÉGH & ANDREW VÁZSONYI

In the course of the last decade, folk-narrative scholars who had been interested primarily in the *Märchen* switched their attention to scrutiny of the folk legend. Leopold Schmidt hailed this new epoch of legend research[1] and emphasized the need for a more up-to-date method of approach. This genre is so immense, said Schmidt, that it touches upon the whole spectrum of folk culture. Whether settlement or house, whether proverbs or manners of speech, there is no part of folklife that does not relate in one way or another to legend. Also, important neighboring fields such as cultural history, art history, and literature are saturated with the aura of folk legendry.[2] Folklorists have been long aware of the difficulty in describing the legend and in delimiting this capricious genre from other forms of folk prose. Those who experimented with a variety of methods in the effort to pin down the extent of the legend form had to realize that it floats uncontrollably and might materialize within any kind of human communication, not allowing itself to be fixed formally.[3]

Those who have amassed variants of the same legend have found that identical contents might be expressed by a wide range of texts, from informal everyday talk through well-organized and structured *Märchen*-like compositions. Formal divergencies depend in most cases on the skills of the occasional narrator and on the concern of his audience. Attacking pedantic form-analysts, Schmidt declared with disappointing sobriety that legend is all content and has no fixable form at all.[4] At the same time, a number of specialists, guided by the classical statement of Jacob Grimm,[5] tried to discern the style of legend by contrasting it with *Märchen*.[6] Interest in the form and the

NOTE. Reprinted from *Genre* 4, no. 3 (September 1971): 281–304, by permission of the Faculty-Student Association of the State College of Arts and Sciences, Plattsburgh, New York.

style of legend called also for the establishment of some kind of a system for ordering the available texts preserved in archives and printed in collections. Based on the Aarne and Thompson principles of classification, motif and type lists were prepared quite early by isolating minimum (motif) and maximum (type) story-units within limited regions of distribution. Because these indexes lacked a common principle and goal, they had little practical use. More recently, an international cooperative worked out a tentative topical list of legend categories that became the foundation for a few experimental index-proposals,[7] this without the participants ever having agreed on what kinds of legends would fit into this kind of classification.[8]

Beside these concerns and some others, the belief factor became one of the principal issues. Legend scholars have considered belief an indispensable ingredient of legend narration. The multifarious aspects of belief in a real or a fancied fact as expressed by the legend, the legend transmitter, and the supporting society was and still is viewed as one of the keys to the scholarly comprehension of the genre.[9]

In the numerous definitions of the folk legend, contacts with reality and attitudes toward it are pointed out as essential criteria. Friedrich Ranke, the first legend theorist who urged fieldworkers to observe the legend in its natural environment, wrote: "The folk legend is a popular narrative with an *objectively untrue* imaginary content. It is presented in the form of a simple account as if it would have really happened."[10] "The legend, by its nature, claims *to be given credit on the part of the teller as well as the listener*; it will communicate truth, things that really have happened."[11] Another influential theorist, C. W. von Sydow, asserts that legends, "in the form they have taken, . . . *cannot have happened*, rather they have been formed by the fabulating gift of the people."[12] Several folklorists have agreed with Ranke and von Sydow that the story of the legend does not contain objective truth[13] and that, nevertheless, the narrator and his audience believe it to be true.[14]

Even at a glance, however, it is difficult to accept these two features as essential to the genre in question. The truth of the legend and the belief of its bearers are by no means of equal value in all kinds of folk legends, and their usefulness in the definition needs some reconsideration.

The *objective truth* of a belief and of the story based on this belief cannot be effective enough to justify its inclusion in the definition of legend. The teller does not, and in most cases cannot, know about the veracity of the legend. Neither can nor would his listeners do research to find out about the factual truth. The widely popular stories about unidentified flying objects, for example, that tell about the visit of benevolent Martians or about the wonder weapons of Planet Men undoubtedly belong in the realm of legend. At the same time, the board of experts engaged in the investigation of UFO sightings have not as yet come to a unanimous resolution as to the origin and the nature of these phenomena. It might well be that future research will prove or disprove beyond doubt the truth of the floating legendlike stories. Would the genre of UFO stories change *subsequently* if it turns out that at the time of their spread they happened to coincide with the objective truth?

Here is another example. Three distinct legends are known about Petőfi, the great Hungarian poet and national hero who perished at the age of twenty-six fighting in the 1848–1849 War of Independence. One of the legends tells that he was killed on the battlefield and is buried in an unidentified mass grave nearby. Mortally wounded, Petőfi gathered strength and wrote with his heart's blood the word *Hazám* (My Country) in the dirt before he collapsed. (This scene was immortalized by a painting which helped keep the legend alive, for oleograph copies of the painting were popular for a century, finding their way to farm houses all over Hungary.) Another legend tells us that Petőfi was not killed in action. He was captured by the Russians and lives on in Siberia. A third legend also claims that the hero did not die, that he is still around in a hideout and appears occasionally disguised as a wanderer. Quite obviously the second and third Petőfi legends are untrue in all their details. However, the first might in its essential part be true. Recently a team of scholars began a search for documents that could solve the mystery of the poet's death. Archives were consulted for leads, and mass graves close to the battlefield were opened. In the event that the bones of Petőfi cannot be found, can we say that the story is a legend? And if his remains can be identified, can we say that the legend of 120 years ceased to be a legend, retroactively?

Nevertheless, other examples seem to confirm the correctness of the definition. If a story had been spread around in the fifties about people who visited the moon and later returned, it would have been accepted as untrue; that is, it would be a legend by definition. Today, however, when people have visited the moon, the legend is now the story we have heard from quite a few people, namely, that the astronauts never reached the moon, that the pictures are fakes, and that the whole lunar expedition was nothing more than political propaganda. Is it possible, then, that the mere presence or absence of the objective truth determines whether a story is a legend? Such a mechanical distinction seems unlikely. There must be another decisive factor to be considered. The information—"People were on the moon"—had been officially communicated in print and by radio and television. The legend informants of the fifties, on the other hand, could have received their false information only through mouth-to-mouth gossip, as would be true of someone who today credits the whispered rumor that no such thing happened, despite all the accounts of the mass media.

For purposes of legend definition, the fact that recipients acquire their information (which is a potential legend-core) through specific communicative channels is much more significant than the question of objective truth. The way in which the intricate process of legend transmission typical of the genre is conducted might be termed the *legend conduit*. (We use the term *conduit* rather than *channel* to avoid confusion with *channel* as used in several other disciplines.)

By *legend conduit* we understand the sequence of individuals who qualify as legend receivers and transmitters. If the legend goes off its track and ends up on another conduit, its fate might be multifarious. The legend might, for example, be developed into another genre; it might be shaped into a *Märchen* or a joke; it might be reduced to a rumor. Wandering from conduit to conduit, eventually the legend may retrieve its lost track as likely as it might become mutilated and distorted or wither away into nothingness. The procedure by which legends are being generated, formulated, transmuted, and crystallized by means of communication through the legend conduit might be called the *legend process*. The legend carriers—believers or nonbelievers—usually accept, pass on, and are fed back the verbal communication they themselves have launched. Thus, sometimes it might be the echo of their own statement that acts as substantial proof for the legend, rather than the real facts. If this reasoning is acceptable, then theoretically we must accept that a truthful story, passed through the *legend process* and handed down through the *legend conduit*, can become a legend. We believe that the specific mechanism of legend transmission is a *sine qua non* within the *climate*[15] in which legends occur.

In the outskirts of Bodrogkeresztúr, a small town in Hungary, near the railway station there is a hill with a memorial column at the top. This column, as can be read on the inscription, commemorates a victorious battle. For some reason, local people think, and tell the legend, known to every child in the region, that the column marks the scene of a lost battle and that the hill was raised above the bodies of the slain soldiers. That the story is contrary to the facts written on the memorial is *proof* that here we have a legend. There are similar stories with erroneously conceived facts as their core. Bedford, Indiana, high-school boys tell of a woman buried under a haunted tombstone they occasionally visit, although the inscription indicates that a man is buried in the grave.[16] Terre Haute, Indiana, college students spin stories about a face imprinted in a wall they frequently pass, although no face is there at all.[17] But we still could not say that an *erroneous* belief makes the story a legend. Even if by accident the story did agree with the data of the column (the tombstone, the wall) and was spread through the means of the legend conduit, even if it did not look for, but intentionally avoided, the objective data, the legend would not lose its legend quality. The decision that this is or is not a legend cannot depend on whether its first proponent has read the inscription correctly or incorrectly.

In general, educated people—including folklorists—know whether the subject matter of a legend is true or false. One can even say that they are those who might know for sure, not the bearers of the legend. Of course, educated people might also be wrong. However, it would be unwise to reformulate the definition to read: "The subject of the legend is a statement which the legend specialist and other educated people know is untrue, providing their information is correct." It would be more sensible to drop the requirement of objective truth from the definition of the folk legend. Similarly, the requirement that both narrator and his audience have to *believe* in the truth of the legend ought to be dropped.

Let us first talk about the narrator. How can we find out whether he really believes in the truth of the story he tells? The most logical answer would probably be: from the text of the legend. But does the text convince us that the teller believes the story? Because the story is told as a declaration, as an explanation, put in the past tense and made formally to seem true? These stylistic devices of narration might be applicable to most prose genres and would be rather unremarkable in any of them, not affecting their fictional status. Or would the conviction of the teller be shown by his statement concerning the place, the date, and the witnesses of his story? Not all legend tellers use such details in their narratives, but, where one does, the only conjecture we can make is that the teller is trying to convince his audience and to make his listeners believe what he is telling. It does not mean that he himself is convinced of its truth. The teller might lie, he might make fun of the believers, he might pretend in order to attract public interest or to gain popularity, or he might simply be following tradition by making use of the available formulae common to oral genres of narration. The text alone cannot tell us whether the raconteur believes his story.

There seems to be no way other than to contact the teller of the legend and to find out from him whether he believes his own statements. Lutz Röhrich states that the legend is called "facts" or "old facts" by the folk.[18] Indeed, we also found legend referred to as "fact." But, because Röhrich bases his observation on a single experience and our sampling is likewise limited, we would hesitate to agree with him that the term is used "by the folk." We suppose that the reference to legend as "fact" is not generally known. It is used in contradistinction to the *Märchen*, which, on the other hand, is referred to in many areas as a "lie."[19] Are these two names to be taken literally? It would seem unlikely. Everybody knows that a *Märchen* is not "true" in the general sense of this word and that the narrator does not want to make it appear true. The traditional and indispensable introductory formulae are especially destined to call the attention to this fact, to create the particular *indexical context* (*Zeigfeld*)[20] of the *Märchen*. The formulae for the legend implying "fact" or "old fact" are also elements in the traditional paraphernalia of the genre and are bound to create the specific *Zeigfeld* of the legend. The legends are as little "true" as the *Märchens* are "lies."

An informal, relaxed interview situation should be established, not always an easy task but, theoretically, not impossible. If the teller of the legend is cooperative and willing to answer questions, we have to make sure of his sincerity. It is questionable how sincere the informant can be, to what extent he is capable of a profound, almost psycho-analytical insight that overcomes inhibitions, ambivalent feelings, overcompensation, or other disturbing psychological phenomena. Intensive questioning of the narrator would be time-consuming, and the result would hardly clarify our problem.

Unconditional belief, coherent in its content and permanent in its intensity, is a category of religion. Wherever the power of a dogma does not reinforce a convention, as in the vague and vast realm of folk religion, the quality and quantity of belief is mutable and very much dependent on social and personal contingency. As we shall see in greater detail later, some people believe in one story, others believe in another; someone might take one portion of a legend for granted but reject the rest. It is possible both to believe unconditionally and to believe with some second thoughts, with a trace of doubt or with mixed feelings. This fluctuation in the attitudes toward belief cannot be discerned from the text of the legend alone. Nor can it be traced with certainty by means of statements solicited from the legend informant.

The belief of the legend carrier cannot be related directly to the dissemination of the legend. Even the nonbeliever can stimulate legend dispersion (see the figure on page 118). A story was going around among our Lake County informants in 1964–1965 about a miracle that occurred in one of the big cities.[21] It said that Jesus Christ descended in the middle of the main square, where all the worshipers gathered for the sight and for the expression of their devotion. As the miracle caused a traffic jam, a policeman appeared and wanted to arrest Jesus, who, instead of following the cop to the police station, chose to ascend to Heaven. Informants stated that they had read this in the newspaper and that it really did happen. After some searching we traced the newspaper story. It was a humorous sketch concerning the gullibility of people: "They would give credit to all kinds of nonsense, such as, let us say Christ would descend in the middle of the main square. . . ." No matter how incredulous the dispenser of a legend is, no matter how much he emphasizes that his story is untrue, the receivers might accept it as truth. A further convincing example of this point is that of the atheist museums that had been set up in some old churches in Soviet Russia for the enlightenment of the religious masses. According to reports, visitors nevertheless knelt down and worshiped in front of showcases that they assumed contained relics of their beloved saints, whose legends they cherished. The suggestion offered unintentionally by the nonbeliever is similar to infection of others by a germ carrier who is himself not afflicted with the disease.

Available legend collections remain silent about the belief of the audience, whose participation in the performance is largely ignored. It might well be that the legends were addressed to believers who expected to gain confirmation in their belief. Conversely, legends might have been addressed to nonbelievers, whom the teller tried, with or without success, to convince of the justification of his belief. To accept that the audience has to acknowledge the legend as truth would mean that the inevitable qualms expressed by some persons would divest the narrative of its legend character and place it into another genre category.

That part of the legend definition dealing with belief, therefore, could not contain more than this: "The legend is a story which, according to many folklorists, is believed to be true both by the teller and the audience." This, however, does not sound very convincing. It seems, also, that the problem of believing needs to be elaborated on the sociocultural level, that is, to be pursued beyond the actual belief attitudes of individual legend carriers.

Curiously, legend definitions and descriptions focusing on the element of belief hardly ever consider those whom the legend concerns— the teller and his audience—to say nothing of their cultural environment. Nothing but the text was consulted by folklorists who dissected and analyzed its content and made assumptions about the belief from items preserved in print. The folklorist never knew who the teller was, or when, where, and why the story was told, who was present, and what kind of feelings were roused by the legend-telling situation. Texts for scholarly study were selected from collections of different nature and quality. The only thing that mattered was whether they comprised the text the scholar needed for his specific interest.

Most of the available collections reflect the idea of their editors about what a legend is. It is no wonder that these anthologies support preconceived theories. However, legend collections are unfit for scientific study not only because of the arbitrariness of selection principles, but also because the published texts are incomplete, mutilated by the collectors, who concentrated exclusively on the plot of the story. Even the verbal part of the complex performance of the legend was hardly ever recorded. That is to say, the lack of adequately recorded legends has caused false impressions about the extent of this genre and yielded erroneous speculations. In most cases, the description of the complex performance of the legend has been unavailable for the legend analyst.

Legends are seldom limited to the mere relation of the plot. In most cases the narrative itself cannot be separated from the circumstances of telling, the introductory remarks of the teller, interjected comments, and reflections of both teller and participants that parallel the performance to the end. Furthermore, the closing remarks, explanatory, supplementary or contrasting stories, analogous cases, and modifications or straight refutation of the story in question are also inseparable parts of the legend. In regard to the legend context, the network of minor motifs carries no less weight than the epic itself. As we would like to show in the following discussion, these motifs often modify and sometimes even change radically the aspect of the legend. If inadequately recorded texts have allowed the conclusions discussed in the foregoing paragraphs, complex recordings will show an entirely different picture. They will demonstrate that legend carriers do not always believe their story beyond dispute and that the question of objective truth is not an ingredient of the genre definition.

The folklorist who records and observes legend telling as a complex event[22] will have to realize, above all, that in the act of legend creation cooperation between the speaker and his audience is much closer than in the composition of any other prose-narrative genre. One might say that the intimate participation and involvement of the listeners is one of the inherent features of the legend. The teller is not a self-conscious artist who is recognized and admired for his creative fantasy, like the storyteller.[23] He is just one of the group, whose other members share the same knowledge and act as audience or often as associate contributors to his story. At best the teller might differ from the others in one particular area of knowledge in which he possesses extra information and expertise the others do not have, so that he is considered more competent.

Except for some uncommon individuals,[24] the legend teller has a rather limited repertoire. The average community raconteur knows ten to fifteen legends, but many repeat only one. The teller of only one story can be as popular as anyone else; he is welcome to speak up at the usual community get-togethers. The participants take turns and stay in the spotlight as long as their piece lasts, then they resume their place among the audience. Obviously, the legend teller does not claim authorship for his story, like the tale raconteur, but refers to others from whom he received his information. He usually assures his audience that this information is accurate and that nothing was changed of what was passed on to him. He cites eyewitnesses and comments on the statements of others. He might express his opposition or his uncertainty or he might simply repeat with the dispassionate neutrality of a chronicler what others were telling. Max Lüthi is correct in his statement that the legend raconteur is a researcher who offers enlightenment and explanation by his story elaboration,[25] rather than an inspired inventor. In his effort to round off the narrative, to convince the sceptics or to disavow the believers, the narrator needs the data contribution and support of all who are present.

Folklorists who observe legend-telling sessions will realize the difficulty in determining what is and what is not believed by the participants. It is also hard to tell whether their belief has, or does not have, an objective foundation. In view of the roles played in the act of legend performance and the ad hoc interpersonal relationship manifest during the tenure of the event, even the following questions will have to be raised: Who is the narrator and who belongs to the audience? Is there an audience at all? Or is the legend a genre that has to be performed collectively, with the contribution of different individuals?[26] Later we will try to answer these questions.

Albert Wesselski has already pointed out the necessity of common awareness[27] as a prerequisite for legend formation. Leopold Schmidt recently emphasized that well-established familiarity with the legend topics is as important as the act of telling.[28] This means that the community would not produce legends without possession of a common ground that supports them. The interaction of the participants brings the legends to life, and the nature of each telling-event acts upon the actual quality of belief. The actual belief manifest at the time of the telling is always the result of the dichotomous relationship between the communal belief system, inherited in tradition and sanctioned by enculturation, and the personal belief of the individual performers. The shared knowledge of the network of belief makes its presence felt in an overt or covert form in all phases of legend communication. The attitudes of the participants might express agreement or disagreement through open statement but more often by implication only. In a natural context, this common frame of reference[29] absolves the speakers of the need to include minor details of their story or to explain things commonly known within the group. This accounts also for the brevity and the fragmented style of the legend.[30]

Modern collectors favor the use of intensive questioning. But this method would not work in the survey of natural-context narration because a face-to-face conversation with the collector would force the informant to change his story: he would feel that he has to add enlightening remarks to help the outsider to better understanding. The questions interjected by the interviewer to satisfy his scholarly interest would do no good either; questions would confuse the teller and interrupt the natural flow of his story. If *Märchen* tellers are hard to divert from the well-trodden track of their repertoire pieces, legend bearers are sensitive to the smallest eventualities. The collector should not manipulate the situation; he should not obstruct the natural context.

The text below does not involve the collector.[31] She did not participate in the general talks on that winter evening, December 30, 1962, when she recorded the continuous conversation between people who were swapping legends. It went on without interruption from eight o'clock until a little before midnight. Eight adult women, four elderly, and two young men were present in the living room of the small peasant cottage. The women were spinning hemp; the men sat smoking around the table, sipping wine. The tape recorder was outside of the room, and the microphone was camouflaged with a shawl; only the hostess knew of its presence. The following example was a part of the session and was told in the second hour of the recording.

For an adequate analysis of the legend-telling event one would obviously need much more information than we are able to offer now. Information concerning the socioeconomic background of the community, the personality of the participants, their social status, their roles in the given situation, and their reasons for joining in are all pertinent to the understanding of the legend and its function. However, as we want only to give an example of the collective formulation of the verbal part of the legend and the individual attitudes expressed in this act, we will limit ourselves to the tape-recorded conversation. Besides Mr. K, the twenty-two–year–old male proponent of the main legend, there were two principal contributors: Mr. A, a thirty-year-old man, and Mrs. Sz, a fifty-eight–year–old woman. The other contributors were Mr. E, the host; Mrs. E, the hostess; Mrs. F, R, and S, three elderly women; and Mr. T, an old man. Also present were two men and three women who did not take part in the conversation.

Mr. K.	Now listen to this, folks. In M. there is a woman. She is hundred and four years old. An old woman of hundred and four years. If anyone would shake hands with her would get three thousand forints.
Mr. E.	I have heard four thousand.
Mr. T.	What? Four thousand? You don't say!
Mr. K.	Sure. Whoever would shake hands with her. I mean, take her hand.
Mr. T.	What the hell! Why not? For four thousand?
Mr. K.	She cannot die until someone shakes hands with her.
Mr. T.	This is a joke.
Mr. E.	She is a witch.
Mrs. S.	Oh no . . .
Mrs. F.	This is the truth. Everybody knows about it.
Mr. T.	Why shake hands with her? What for?
Mr. A.	She cannot get rid of her power. She cannot die until someone takes over, do you understand, uncle? But no one wants it.
Mr. T.	Her power?
Mrs. E.	And her sins. She is a sinner.
Mr. K.	My father tells me that he would be willing to take her hand and squeeze it. But it had to be only the two of them. No one else can be present. Only the one who will do the handshaking and the old woman. And the fence around her orchard is something peculiar. No one on this earth has seen anything like this . . .

Mrs. S.   Oh come on . . . what can be so peculiar?

Mr. K.   Just listen to this: that orchard is full of apples and if one would reach out for one, I mean someone would pick up an apple from under the tree, his hand would shrink. One could not pick up the apple with one's hand. No one ever guards that orchard. No one takes care of their horse. They turn it loose, nothing on earth . . . I was . . .

Mr. F.   God protect us!

Mrs. R.   I have heard it too, but I am not sure about it.

Mrs. E.   God would not let this happen. I wonder . . .

Mrs. S.   Who is it?

Mr. K.   (*to Mr. A*) You know them, why don't you speak up?

Mr. A.   Of course. She lives close by the Catholic Church.

Mr. E.   On the corner, next to the cemetery?

Mr. K.   That's right. And you know about her son? She has a son, a handsome young man.

Mr. A.   He doesn't get a wife, no matter how handsome he is.

Mr. K.   He cannot marry, neither can her daughter. No one wants her daughter.

Mrs. F.   No, because of her mother. The witch.

Mrs. S.   I don't believe this.

Mr. T.   I do, I do . . . This is a good excuse for the boys. Is it not more sensible to stay a bachelor? (*He laughs.*) Smart fellow, didn't let himself to get pushed around.

Mrs. Sz.   Don't talk rot, old man. There were others like this. There was a man. But he is dead now. He lived somewhere close to these people. They say he was on his deathbed for very long, maybe for two weeks . . .

Mrs. E.   (*whispers*) He was tortured by the devil . . .

Mr. T.   O.K., haven't you ever heard about people who were dying away slowly? The teacher's mother had cancer . . .

Mrs. Sz.   . . . but he was tortured so much that the down comforter flew up from his body into the air, in the house, then, high up into the attic and again down. As if it would have been smashed into the middle of the room, onto the floor. Of course, they did not know what it was

	about. The one was there, who went to see the sick, grabbed it and put it on the bed. As soon as it was on it, the puff jumped away again.
Mrs. F.	He got it I am sure, his sin or what, his power was taken over by the one who picked up the puff and put it on his bed.
Mrs. Sz.	The man could not die before that.
Mr. T.	All right, all right. You were saying they got to shake hands. How does the puff know that? This is all a big—big stuff of nonsense.
Mr. K.	Of course they have to touch hands until they get even with him.
Mrs. Sz.	Yes, yes, but nobody wanted his hand, no one went near to him. This is why the puff flew down the floor. As it was there, they had to put it back on its place. There was no other way.
Mrs. S.	How in God's name can a puff fly up to the attic?
Mr. T.	They were dreaming.
Mr. A.	But who would shake hands with a woman like this? Anyone would be scared.
Mr. E.	I wouldn't dare.
Mr. A.	She looks awful. She is only skin and bones. Only her big eyes. Her hand like a skeleton, only the skin keeps her together not to fall apart. She can't take a step all day, at night she still is not in her bed.
Mr. T.	Where is she?
Mr. A.	Who knows? They carry her all around.
Mrs. S.	People talk so much of these things, one is confused what to believe of it.
Mr. T.	Talk, talk, too much waste of time. I have never seen anything, you can take my word on that.
Mrs. E.	Who carried her around?
Mr. E.	The devil, the evil one. Her partner.
Mr. K.	That's why she can't die and rest in peace.
Mrs. Sz.	They carry her all over. Those are dragged to the middle of the Tisza [river], into the willows, the thickets, on the top of the houses, over hills and valleys, ditches and bushes, they drag those everywhere.

Mr. K.	Well, of course, these have to go, to settle with the devils. This is real truth, Aunt Emmy.
Mr. T.	How you can lie!
Mrs. R.	Maybe those things happened to our ancestors. Not today. Wasn't that one of your father's stories?
Mr. K.	You can visit and see for yourself. I am not making this up.
Mr. A.	Now listen to this. Do you know who was the one who told this to me? The man who built the house of the B's, over in E. I don't know whether you know the man. The name is M. Do you know the M. boys?
Mr. E.	Why, sure.
Mrs. E.	Aren't we related? We baptized one of the boys.
Mr. A.	Well, they've called them to finish up the house, the house of the old woman. They offered some eight thousand forints for the finishing and the painting of the house from the inside and the outside. And they didn't dare do it. Such an easy job for so much.
Mr. T.	What a dope.
Mr. A.	If you don't believe, why the hell don't you do the job? For that money?
Mr. T.	I have no time for fooling around.

This brief episode of a legend-telling session demonstrates some important characteristics of legend composition and the variable attitudes expressed parallel to the process. The form seems to be unstable and subject to the actual feelings and the interaction of the people who happened to be present. This is to say that the personality composition of the group was responsible for this particular event. Each legend-producing session has to be viewed as unique. In our case, the informal talk crystallized in three different, though related, stories, two of which complement each other, whereas the third corroborates both. The three tellers—the proponent and the coperformers—as well as all the other speakers contributed to the legend as they expressed their feelings evoked in the different stages of the telling. None of the three legends comprised in the complex telling-situation reached such formal perfection as is the case with most of the texts in printed collections. We usually find unbroken individual stories in those collections, not spasmodic, amorphous formulations jointly shaped like those of the members of this group. Nevertheless, our example is typical, for the legend appears often in this kind of intricate, so to say polyphonic, form. It would be hard to disentangle the counterpoint parts of the choir in this performance. An arbitrary dissection, the elimination of the "superfluous" voices, would be as difficult as it would be senseless to reduce the whole complex into single, homogeneous, conventional, and unified stories.

Our example shows that it would be even harder to characterize the attitudes expressed by the members of the group during the telling. The differences are rather indistinct—and this is the answer to our question raised earlier: who assumes the role of the narrator and who accepts the role of the listener? These two roles alternate, and there are many degrees of participation between the principal speaker and the silent listener, whose nonverbal reactions we had to exclude from our present considerations. The speaker is influenced, stimulated, assisted, and encouraged or, conversely, discouraged, intimidated, challenged, and forced into argumentation by the comments of the listeners. Sometimes a member of the audience can make the speaker interrupt the narrative in progress and hand it over to someone else. In this case the speaker continues his participation in the further formulation of the legend as one of the audience. As was pointed out earlier, and as we have hoped to demonstrate by our example, the relationship between the tale teller and his audience differs from that between the legend teller and his audience. In the first we have the relationship between the entertainer and the entertained where the reflections of the audience are rather that of the excited admiration, enchantment, criticism, and so on, stimulated by the story and the manner of its telling.[32] On the other hand, the legend mostly occurs in conversation,[33] with audience participation in the formulation. In a legend-telling situation, the various types of participants—the proponent, the contributor, the expander, the stimulator, the critic, the challenger, and so forth—play equally important roles, and often switch them.

Would it even be possible to find out what was the true belief of the participants in this legend-telling event? In our case, besides the principal speakers, Mr. E, Mrs. E, and Mrs. F expressed unconditional belief. Among them, Mrs. F was motivated by her profound religious

conviction. It is interesting to note, on the other hand, that Mrs. S'
hesitancy to accept the existence of witches came also from her religious devotion, for the Church was strongly against such superstition.
Mrs. R was undecided, and Mr. T tried to ridicule the whole idea. He
dismissed the truthfulness of the incident and tried to make it look
funny and to find a rational explanation. However, his readiness to
shake hands with the witch for four thousand forints at the beginning
of the talk loses its impetus at the end, when he refuses to do the
painting job at the witch's house for eight thousand because he has
"no time for fooling around."

At any rate, the attitudes toward belief displayed on this particular
occasion can be considered as valid only for this case. The respondents
would have reacted differently on other occasions and would have reacted differently to other legends. The question, whether the proponent and the respondents do or do not believe in the legend, would
seem to be overly simplified for those who have observed similar legend-telling occasions.

Between the two extremes of unconditional belief and absolute denial a wide variety of accidental personal opinions might well prevail.
It often happens that the teller and his audience will open or close
the telling of a legend with an inconclusive discussion of its truth.
One might say the question of belief-nonbelief is an active problem
in any community where legends are told.

Because legends are deeply rooted in social reality, their appreciation is not only territorially limited but also influenced by age, sex,
religion, occupational groups, and the like. Conflicts between these
groups possessing different sets of legendry might erupt and be expressed through the different attitudes toward their respective legends. The generation gap makes itself felt when young people make
fun of the backwardness of their elders. While we recorded the witch
legends of an old woman in Crown Point, her daughter, who sat with
us, was ready with improvised counter stories immediately after each
piece, to discredit her mother's stories. Iván Balassa gives account of a
case where young people scared an old man out of his wits. The man
used to tell about a revenant, and, when he left his audience one night
and walked home, he met a boy posing as the spook.[34] In peasant
communities under the impact of industrialization, men, who are

more exposed to modernization than the women, discredit the legend. The more sedentary women, who are tied up with household chores, adhere to the old. As Károly Gaál puts it, it would have been a shame for a man to tell a legend without including disparaging remarks, as it does not become a man to prove himself a coward.[35] In urban communities young people display a variety of attitudes toward their legends, and partial belief is often concealed by humorous release of tension built up by the telling of horror legends.[36]

As a point of departure, for an assessment of the unsolicited statements uttered before, during, or after the story concerning its truth for the teller, we will quote a few of the most common types. One proclaims with a solemn pledge that "This happened to me, it is true as the Gospel."[37] Unwavering belief is also expressed by the teller who substitutes for the Bible a creditable witness: "My father saw this and he never told a lie." Another wants to impress by distinguishing between credible and noncredible things: "I do not believe in witches, but this really happened to my brother, who was a God-fearing man, may he rest in peace." There is no trace of doubt in the following statement either, although there is no reference to a known person: "It happened here in our place to someone." Another teller moves the legend event to somewhere else, or far away in the past: "Not here, to be sure, this occurred in another town, not ours"; "In olden times these things used to happen." In a number of statements witnesses are mentioned in general terms, without naming individuals: "Old people always used to talk about it," or "I heard that this is true from people older than we are," or "So many people believe in that, it must be true." The one who put it this way, "G. N. who is supposed to have been possessed of the Devil," yields some doubt, as does this introductory remark to a story: "I am not sure whether it was true or not, I have heard it from others." A lady, in a letter relating the story of the woman on the railroad track looking for her head, expressed herself this way: "I have never heard this, until my teenage daughter came home and told me, so it is *probably* only a tale."[38] Conversely, this contention reveals a trace of belief within the doubt: "Well, I don't know as there's anything to that, but there's somethings that works kind of funny." Some tellers become convinced of the truth of the story by the power of evidence, or at least do not dare to deny its probability: "From the stories I've heard, and from looking on the Bridge, that kinda makes you wonder if it is really haunted." A similar confession of belief is split into two parts, beginning with this: "People in our place tell . . . I did not want to believe it. . . ." The end of the statement follows after the story: "Since that time I believe in the Wild Hunt." Those who accept only a part of a story and reject the rest say, "There is something to it but only a part of it might have been true," or, "There are no haunted houses. This is foolish to believe . . . but there were witches in our village."[39] An interesting type is represented by "I do not believe in such silly superstition. Anybody can tell you that mermaids could not survive under the ice of Lake Michigan in winter. . . . Mermaids live in hot waters, somewhere around Florida."[40] Some would go along with the plot of the legend but would not accept the fantastic explanation because of their rational way of thinking: "It is not true that the Flying Saucers come from Mars. They are nothing but spy ships, and spies ride on them and make snapshots of our military bases," as one of our Gary informants put it. From the simple uncertainty of "I doubt it," "I really don't think," "Superstitious people took this for granted," the absolute denial does not lie far away. Such responses as the following exemplify the attitude of the nonbeliever: "They are just a bunch of stories that a bunch of guys made up to have some fun"; "I don't really believe that stuff, but it is pretty neat to tell all your friends"; "If that isn't the biggest lie you've ever heard in your life, I don't know what is"; "How could anyone believe this? It is only a tale."

The foregoing statements made by legend narrators concerning their belief did not affect essentially the plot of the stories they were telling. Nevertheless, the attitude of the individual narrator might account for decisive changes in the story that has been passed on to him. If legend collectors had cared to record the variants of the same legend instead of contenting themselves with a single version, if they had not picked the text they considered the most "complete" and discarded the others as "corrupt," we would have more data for the study of the processes of legend formation. We cite two examples that give an idea of how the personal opinion of the teller might affect legend variation:

a. There is a legend about a rich man who kept his dead wife in a glass casket surrounded by blue lights and displayed it on his porch for years.[41] This is one of the numerous variants known to us. Another among the variants says also that many courageous people visited the premises at night and found no casket on the porch: the owner of the house had installed a greenhouse on the porch, where he used sun lamps to grow his exotic plants. A third version also disproves the idea of the dead wife and adds that the old man was a miser and a hoarder who used sharp blue lights to keep people away from his property. The irrational as well as the rational versions of the legend underwent the legend process, and no doubt all three are genuine legends, stemming from the same root, however distinct from each other. They must be considered as different stories and not the complement of each other.

b. The two outstanding *Märchen* tellers of Kakasd, who were not too good at legend telling, shared parallel versions of one common story about a nightmarish experience.[42] In Mrs. Palkó's version, she claimed an apparition haunted her father, whereas that of her nephew stated it was he who was plagued. While the old woman's story, told in third person, was meant to relate an experience she believed to be true, her nephew's personal story aimed at the refutation of the supernatural encounter. He emphasized that it was the only time he was scared, because he saw a fiery frog of which his grandmother (not he) said that it was an evil spirit. He added a second episode to his story to reaffirm his scepticism. It was about another nocturnal fishing adventure: this time he was scared by his little dog that hid in the sleeve of his fur coat.

In addition both to the statements surrounding the legend plot and to the individual variation of stories that reflect personal attitudes (which may influence the composition of independent legends), we consider now the problem of belief and nonbelief as expressed by the narrative *content* itself. This concerns a whole group of well-established legends that are built up against communally known and confirmed belief concepts with the intent to discredit them. Explicitly or implicitly, each of these legends includes another legend, or rather two (or more) amalgamated legends form another. The difference in reality values is, properly speaking, the subject matter of the legends in this group.

The folklorist has been acquainted with negative legends; he has not paid much attention to them. They have been considered as "anti-legends,"[43] pseudo–belief-legends, transition forms, mixed forms, corruptions, travesties, and the contrast pairs of positive narratives that came to life as symptoms of the dissolution of folk society and the crumbling of its old values. The idea that prior to modern industrialization values expressed through folklore were unanimously accepted by individual members of the society would support the contention that legends must be believed. Contrary to this, folklorists now know for sure that there are and always were individuals of "rational mind" opposed to the belief in supernatural or uncommon events. Even the most backward society has its unbelievers; born sceptics, searchers for truth, and knowledgeables are recognized folk characters. The topic of the legend is raised as an unuttered question that is being discussed at the legend-telling session by supporters and nonsupporters. As we have previously stated, positive attitudes do not cause a story to become a legend, nor do negative attitudes destroy the same legend. Tellers might indicate feelings different from those expressed in the pieces of their repertoire, for they do not tell only the legends they believe to be true.

The simplest kinds of negative legends usually tell of a horrible experience that implies a supernatural encounter but release tension by finding sober explanation of the adventure. Most such legends tend to generalize. If they show evidence that in particular cases supernatural phenomena did not occur, the conclusions of the legends may suggest that "Supernatural phenomena do not exist." (The conclusion is similarly erroneous in many positive legends: "It is believed, consequently true.") Such legends are very common and might relate to all walks of life. Many revenant sightings end up with the realization that the pursuing evil spirit in the form of a cow, a cat, a dog, or other domestic animal was nothing but a stray; the heavy footsteps of the invisible evil was the rhythmic echo of the man's own footsteps, strengthened by the rustle of his raincoat; the dead coming out of his grave at midnight turns out to be a rabbit nesting in his hole; Jack-o-lantern is nothing but the lamp of a wagon invisible because of the fog; the fisherman who cannot pull out his net realizes it is the other fisherman's net entangled with his, rather than the devil caught in the haul; and the woman scared by a witch-cat that jumped in through the chimney realizes that it was her own black cat. Similar stories are told by the wiseacre who always finds some pseudo-scientific explanation for the unexplainable, such as the one who at the wake interprets the sound from the dead as air leaving the collapsing organism. In another story the remarkable mystery of the umbrella lost at the shores of a tarn and retrieved at the seaside is explained by the underground communication between the two. Also the mysterious chain on the tombstone is explained by an informant by the possibility that the raw, uncut stone had the print of a chain pressed into it at the quarry.

Among the more elaborate negative legends, many are extremely popular in both rural and urban communities because of their applicability to important social functions. They might be used for educational, ritual, and fear-stimulating purposes, to name just a few. It should be determined how these legends relate to true belief and how social functions reinforce them.

Stories that frighten credulous people, especially stories about sham ghost encounters, are internationally known. Besides the ones already cited, there are several dramatized ghost stories. The "ghost" wrapped in white sheets and carrying an illuminated pumpkin is the hero of variable stories. One tells how the "ghost" was killed by believers trying to harm the real revenant; another "ghost" who tried to frighten his rival away from his girlfriend likewise met a sad end. The pseudo-ghost might also be successful in teaching a lesson, as exemplified by the old woman who, in another story, kept trespassers away from her yard by masquerading as a ghost. In yet another story, it is not the living dead who urges his brother from under the window to fulfill his last wish but a friend who assumes the role of the deceased.

Legends might serve as simple enjoyment of the chill of fear.[44] An Austrian informant tells how scary stories were passed around in the mill at night when men were waiting for the flour to be ground. Those who were visibly frightened were scoffed at. People still laugh when remembering that some fifty or sixty years ago a soldier was scared to death by a spook. The story is still used as a teaser: "Soldiers are cowards." To be scared and still be a man is the idea of the utilization of this set of negative legends.[45] The tests-of-courage stories about haunts follow a definite pattern both in rural and urban cultures and are currently extremely popular.[46] The quality of belief is variable also in this group. The extent of diversity might be noted by reference to two well-known legends. One of them is the story of the girl who proves her courage by visiting the cemetery at midnight and dies of shock when her apron is caught on a stone because she thinks it is the hand of the dead.[47] The other narrative is a parallel opposite to the Fatal Initiation legend. It accumulates all the possible horrors of a haunted house, to make the frustration of the man pursued by the floating *coffin* palpable, only to surprise the audience with an abrupt end in laughter: The *coughin'* was stopped by cough pills.[48]

This latter legend might be viewed as a pun as well, although it has several divergent versions, many of them with a tragic ending. But even if we consider it as a joke, the narrative contains almost all attributes that qualify for a legend, including that it does take a stand on the question of belief and truth the same way as legends do. What it communicates in the language of the legend is that the floating coffin is not real but just the product of a play of words or that it is real but became eliminated by a pun, or, if you like, word magic. In the course of the past few years folklorists have attempted to relate legends to age groups and have found a number of stories generally popular among Indiana schoolchildren between six and ten. In one of these a ghost or monster scatters people by repeating the words, "One black eye!" until a tough child rebuts it by saying, "Shut up, or you're going to have two black eyes!" In other stories the ghost cries, "Bloody fingers!" until he is silenced with the words, "Cool, man, cool, go get a Bandaid!"[49]

There is a legend dressed up as a joke. It is about a girl who at about midnight must pass by a cemetery on her way home and is badly frightened. She is relieved when she beholds an elderly lady walking ahead of her. "May I join you?" asks the girl. "I am ashamed for being such a coward, but I am afraid to pass here by myself." "Don't be ashamed, dear," answers the lady, "I used also to be superstitious when I was alive." Were this story put in the past tense, it would also formally qualify as a legend. But even in this form, what the joke really spells out, in legend terms, is this: there are ghosts, and whoever thinks that the belief in them is superstition is wrong.

The little we know about negative legends allows us to believe that they are not "corruptions" of "real" legends but rather belong in one important group of the genre.[50]

Finally, we would like to summarize the main inferences we have made so far from the available materials before us: contrary to the generally acknowledged rule, the bearers of legend tradition do not always believe in the truth of their story; the attitudes toward belief range from absolute acceptance through many intermediary stages to absolute rejection; nevertheless, the attitudes are not merely *affirmative* or *negative* (which, from a subjective standpoint corresponds to belief and nonbelief, including intermediary stages) but can be also *universal* or *particular*, *hypothetical* or *categorical* in all stages and according to all combinations of these qualities and quantities.

That legends are not always believed has been stated before now. That they might reflect different degrees of belief also is not new, for it was first suggested by von Sydow. However, von Sydow's ideas were mostly utilized in the attempt to determine and isolate subcategories within the genre, ranging from the simple relation of a remarkable experience through the well-organized, relatively stable narrative. According to this construction, absolute belief decreases gradually through the process of genre development.[51] When Max Lüthi, on the other hand, stressed that the loss of belief does not transform the legend into a tale, he also pointed out that the style of the legend is affected by the presence or the absence of the belief of its carriers.[52]

It would not be possible to depict the relationship of the legend and its bearers on a thermometerlike vertical line placed between the freezing point of total negation and the boiling point of total belief. Nor would it be possible to put this relationship into a horizontal plane. One must utilize a three-dimensional space. Points in the inside of a coordinate shaped as a geometrical solid would represent the position of the legend bearers. This point does not stand motionless during the act of telling; it changes its situation in space as the legend bearers relate differently to the diverse parts of the legend.

Some terms used here suggest the vocabulary of the classical-scholastic syllogistics. It might well be that our reference to this method of formal logistics is not unjustified. As a matter of fact, the legend always *states* something and often *attests* its statements. In some cases, it formally relates statement and attestation in the manner of deductive reasoning. Most legends might be reduced to an inference that strives to reach *conclusions* from *premises*.

The premises, of course, are often erroneous or, like the enthymeme, incomplete, and the conclusions are, as already mentioned, often faulty. This, however, does not disturb the actors of the legend performance. If one of the premises is incorrect or missing, the common reference takes care of its correction and completion. Common knowledge may be represented as sounding like the fixed pedal point with the moving voices of the legend, earlier characterized as polyphonic. At any rate, the conclusion is usually preconceived, and the argument making it feasible serves only as the ostensible verification of what had been anticipated. Consequently, the implications inherent in the legend are mostly, if not always, erroneous. Nevertheless, they accomplish and furnish the necessary proof of the legend within its actual indexical context.

Theoretically speaking, as many kinds of attitudes toward the legend can be presumed as points can be placed in the inside of the geometrical solid; that is to say, the variables are unlimited. In other words, this means that, even without consideration of this perpetual change, the relationships of the legend bearers and the legend can be so manifold that they practically cannot be assessed.

To simplify the matter, let us suppose that we can place any of the participants in the legend process—that is, the propopent of the legend, the receiver, and the transmitter—into any of essentially five categories: (1) believers, (2) indifferents, (3) sceptics, (4) nonbelievers, and (5) opponents. In accordance with our considerations, we have reached the conclusion that any member of these categories might participate in the process of legend formation and in the legend transmission. As was also made clear, the belief of the narrator (and the quality and quantity of his belief) is not the condition or the prerequisite of the legend. Accordingly, doubt, unbelief, or direct opposition does not prevent the legend from coming into existence by the legend process and from being passed through the legend conduit.

This conduit, demonstrated by the accompanying figure, is an intricate labyrinthlike formation. We think that the first stage of legend formation is when the *event* falls into the frame of reference of an appropriate person. This person is the *proponent*, who has the ability to create the legend, however imperfect its form, from the combination of the *event* and his earlier familiarity with related questions of belief. It is usually not one but several proponents who learn about

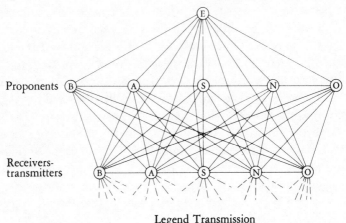

Legend Transmission

E = Event   A = Ambivalent   N = Nonbeliever
B = Believer   S = Skeptic   O = Opponent

the event in question practically at the same time and start the chain, possibly in interaction with each other.

The proponent obviously does not need to believe his story. He can add his doubts, his disbelief; he can tell it with a negative sign. The germ wrapped in the shell of incredulity might fall into fertile soil. It might happen that the incredulous proponent passes the rudimentary beginnings of a legend to a firm believer. If the story coincides with the common frame of reference of the man who has the believer's disposition, he will transmit his version with the addition of a positive sign. However firm his belief, it is uncertain at this point what the response of the next receiver will be to what was passed to him— scepticism, ambivalence, or whatever. And so the legend passes through the legend conduit: the continuation is endless as more and more people of diverse personality take part and shape the legend into untraceable variations.

We have stated that the subjective belief of the legend carriers is not a necessary ingredient of the legend and that, moreover, it is unessential in the process of creation and transmission. Does this not contradict the recognition that the legend always states (or denies) something, that it thus expresses the intent of persuasion if not the conviction of belief? We do not think so.

What does the legend want to make us believe? Statements that can be positive, negative, or hesitant. It wants to convince its adherents, for example, that there *are* ghosts (the narrator has seen one or heard about one from others), that there *are no* ghosts (the apparition turned out to be a natural phenomenon, or a trick), that *supposedly there are* ghosts ("I don't believe in them, but I don't know what to believe of a case that really has happened"), that there are no such things now but there *used to be*, or they happen *somewhere else*, and so on. Several legends not only discredit the truth of their plots but also emphasize their absurdity.

Every legend states something. The statement, as we recognized, might contain a second thought, it might display strong doubt, but it nevertheless remains a *statement*, whether negative or positive. This is distinctive in comparison with tale categories. Although objective truth and the presence, quality, and quantity of subjective belief are irrelevant, it is all the more relevant that any legend, no matter how fragmentary or corrupt, makes its case. It takes a stand and calls for the expression of opinion on the question of truth and belief.

We emphasize again: it is not necessarily the belief of the narrator or the belief of the receiver-transmitter that we have to consider; rather we must consider, abstractly, so to speak, the *belief itself* that makes its presence felt in any kind of legend. The legend tells explicitly or implicitly almost without exception that its message is or was believed *sometime*, by *someone*, *somewhere*: "by the neighbor," "by an old woman," "by grandfather," "by somebody," "by people somewhere else," "long time ago." As much as it seems proven that the personal belief of the participants in the legend process is irrelevant, it also seems to be a rule that general reference to belief is an inherent and the most outstanding feature of the folk legend. The questions of the origin and of individual and sociopsychological meanings of this phenomenon will have to be raised some other time.[53]

Notes

1. Leopold Schmidt, "Vor einer neuen Ära der Sagenforschung," *Österreichische Zeitschrift für Volkskunde* 19 (1965): 53–74.

2. Leopold Schmidt, *Die Volkserzählung: Märchen, Sage, Legende, Schwank*, p. 107.

3. C. W. von Sydow's categorizing of legends from *Memorate* through *Fabulate* was reinterpreted and further elaborated by a group of Scandinavian scholars who have tried to isolate further subgenres. See Lauri Honko, *Geisterglaube in Ingermanland*, Folklore Fellows Communications, no. 185 (Helsinki: Suomalainen Tiedeakatemia, 1962); Brynjulf Alver, "Category and Function," *Fabula* 9 (1967): 62–69; Otto Blehr, "The Analysis of Folk Belief Stories and Its Implications for Research on Folk Belief and Folk Prose," *Fabula* 9 (1967): 259–263; Juha Pentikäinen, "Grenzprobleme zwischen Memorat und Sage," *Temenos* 3 (1968): 136–167.

4. Schmidt, *Die Volkserzählung*, p. 108.

5. In the Introduction to his *Deutsche Sagen* (1816), Grimm claimed that the difference between *Sage* and *Märchen* is that the *Märchen* is more poetical, whereas the *Sage* is more historical.

6. The determination of the distinctive form and style of the tale and the legend as formulated by their diverse artistic aims had been offered in the works of Max Lüthi, *Volksmärchen und Volkssage: Zwei Grundformen erzählender Dichtung*, and "Aspects of the *Märchen* and the Legend," trans. Barbara Flynn, *Genre* 2 (1969): 162–178 (reprinted in this volume).

7. Following the decision reached at the Budapest session of the International Society of Folk Narrative Research in 1963, classification proposals were prepared in several countries. To mention just a few: Gisela Burde-Schneidewind, Ina-Maria Greverus, Ingeborg Müller, and Lutz Röhrich, "Deutscher Sagenkatalog. X. Der Tod und die Toten," *Deutsches Jahrbuch für Volkskunde* 13 (1967): 339–397; Alan Bruford, "Scottish Gaelic Witch Stories: A Provisional Type-List," *Scottish Studies* 11 (1967): 13–47; Tamás Körner, "Mutavány a készülö magyar hiedelemmonda-katalógusból" [A chapter from the Hungarian folk-belief legend catalog in preparation], *Ethnographia* 81 (1970): 55–87; Ilona Dobos, "A történeti mondák rendszerezéséröl" [On the classification of historical legends], *Ethnographia* 81 (1970): 97–111.

8. Critical remarks and general evaluations were made by Maja Bošković-Stulli, "Beitrag zur Diskussion über die Katalogisierung der Volkssagen," *Fabula* 8 (1966): 192–207; Fritz Harkort, "Volkserzählungstypen und Motive und Vorstellungsberichte," *Fabula* 8 (1966): 208–223; Vilmos Voigt, "A mondák müfaji osztályozásának kérdéséhez" [Some questions of cataloging folk legends], *Ethnographia* 78 (1965): 200–220.

9. See Lutz Röhrich, *Märchen und Wirklichkeit*, 2d ed. (Wiesbaden: Franz Steiner Verlag, 1964). Concerning the reality factor of the folk legend, it should be noted here that the typical division of legends into minor or major subgroups as suggested by many authors ("Sage" in *Folk Literature* [*Germanic*], ed. Laurits Bødker, pp. 255–258) might have its practical use but would not be applicable in our theoretical survey of the genre. The generally known main categories—mythological (or belief), historical, and etiological

legends—are entities depending on whether the factual core of the story is a subjective belief, a visual object, or a historical fact. In reality all three are of equal quality as legend cores. Moreover, they are inseparable and might occur jointly in the legends.

10. Friedrich Ranke, "Grundfragen der Volkssagenforschung," *Niederdeutsche Zeitschrift für Volkskunde* 3 (1925): 14. Italics ours.

11. Ibid., p. 13. Italics ours.

12. Carl Wilhelm von Sydow, "Kategorien der Prosa-Volksdichtung," in *Volkskundliche Gaben John Meier zum sibzigsten Geburstage dargebracht*, ed. Erich Seemann and Harry Schewe, p. 74. Italics ours.

13. Explicitly stated in Will-Erich Peuckert, *Sagen: Geburt und Antwort der mythischen Welt*, pp. 21–36; Lutz Röhrich, "Die deutsche Volkssage: Ein methodischer Arbiss," *Studium Generale* 11 (1958): 664–665; Carl-Herman Tillhagen, "Was ist eine Sage?" *Acta Ethnographica* 13 (1964): 10; and implied in the definitions in Maria Leach, ed., *Funk & Wagnalls Standard Dictionary of Folklore, Mythology and Legend* (New York: Funk & Wagnalls, 1950), II, 612; Wayland D. Hand, "Status of European and American Legend Study," *Current Anthropology* 6 (1965): 441; and Jan Harold Brunvand, *The Study of American Folklore*, p. 87.

14. Several authors further elaborate Ranke's definition, such as Schmidt, *Die Volkserzählung*, p. 108; Will-Erich Peuckert, "Die Welt der Sage," in *Vergleichende Sagenforschung*, ed. Leander Petzoldt, p. 173; Julius Schwietering, "Volksmärchen und Volksglaube," *Dichtung und Volkstum* 36 (1935): 68–70; Röhrich, "Die deutsche Volkssage," p. 664; Gottfried Heilfurth, *Bergbau und Bergmann in der deutschsprachingen Sagenüberlieferung Mitteleuropas* (Marburg: Elwert Verlag, 1967), II, 36; Hand, "Status of Legend Study," p. 441; Tillhagen, "Was ist eine Sage?" p. 441; Brunvand, *Study of American Folklore*, p. 87.

15. The description of the atmosphere, the "Klimata . . . in denen Sagen gedeihen," is well elaborated by Peuckert, *Sagen*, pp. 37–45.

16. William M. Clements, "The Chain," *Indiana Folklore* 2, no. 1 (1969): 90–96.

17. Ronald L. Baker, "The Face on the Wall," *Indiana Folklore* 2, no. 2 (1969): 29–46.

18. Röhrich, *Märchen und Wirklichkeit*, p. 9.

19. Linda Dégh, *Folktales and Society*, trans. Emily M. Schossberger, pp. 86–87.

20. The term was borrowed from the psycholinguistic study of Karl Bühler, *Sprachtheorie: Die Darstellungsfunktion der Sprache* (Jena: G. Fischer, 1937), pp. 79–82.

21. This and following examples from the Gary–East Chicago area are from the collections of Linda Dégh and Andrew Vázsonyi in 1964–1968.

22. The first attempt to record the cycles of legend telling in their entirety was made in shorthand notation by Otto Brinkmann, *Das Erzählen in einer Dorfgemeinschaft* (Aschendorff: Münster, I. W., 1933).

23. The personality of the legend teller has not been studied as thoroughly as that of the storyteller. Among the very few works worth mention are Leza Uffer, *Rätoromanische Märchen und ihre Erzähler* (Basel: Schweizerische Gesellschaft für Volkskunde, 1945), pp. 80–87; Matthias Zender, "Quellen und Träger der deutschen Volkserzählung," in *Vergleichende Sagenforschung*, ed. Leander Petzoldt, pp. 119–123; and Honko, *Geisterglaube*, pp. 123–125.

24. One notable legend teller recognized in his community is László Lénárt. His 120 texts were collected and published by Iván Balassa, *Karcsai mondák* [Legends of Karcsa] (Budapest: Akadémiai Kiadó, 1963). A few of Lénárt's legends are included in Linda Dégh, *Folktales of Hungary* (Chicago: University of Chicago Press, 1965), nos. 33, 35, 47, 48, 49, 51, 60, and 69.

25. Lüthi, *Volksmärchen*, p. 15.

26. Pentikäinen, "Grenzprobleme," p. 155, emphasizes that the intensive analysis of individual bearers of legend tradition and their audiences is an important future task. Only a frequency analysis, aiming at understanding of the roles of the diverse types of tellers, can cast light on the genre itself.

27. Albert Wesselski, "Die Formen des volkstümlichen Erzählguts," in *Die deutsche Volkskunde*, ed. Adolf Spamer, I, 219–220.

28. Schmidt, *Die Volkserzählung*, p. 108.

29. The term of Th. M. Newcomb is used to indicate the ground "which actually influences the way in which perception is structured" (*Social Psychology* [London: Tavistock, 1952], p. 94) and is utilized in the study of folk belief by Honko, *Geisterglaube*, pp. 94–99.

30. According to Zender, "Quellen und Träger," p. 129.

31. From field-work materials tape-recorded in northeast Hungary by Linda Dégh.

32. Dégh, *Folktales and Society*, pp. 112–119.

33. Linda Dégh, "Processes of Legend Formation," *Laographia* 22 (1965): 85–86.

34. Balassa, *Karcsai mondák*, p. 38.

35. Károly Gaál, *Angaben zu den Aberglaubischen Erzählungen aus dem südlichen Burgenland* (Eisenstadt: Burgenländisches Landesmuseum, 1965), p. 23.

36. Linda Dégh, "The Haunted Bridges Near Avon and Danville and Their Role in Legend Formation," *Indiana Folklore* 2, no. 1 (1969): 54–89.

37. If not otherwise stated the quotations were taken from the following collections: Balassa, *Karcsai mondák*; Richard M. Dorson, *Buying the Wind* (Chicago: University of Chicago Press, 1965); Karl Haiding, *Österreichs Sagenschatz* (Vienna: Molden Verlag, 1965); Gottfried Henssen, *Sagen, Märchen und Schwänke des jülichen Landes* (Bonn: Rohrscheid Verlag, 1955); and Roger E. Mitchell, "George Knox from Man to Legend," *Northeast Folklore* 11 (1969), and *Indiana Folklore* 1 and 2 (1969).

38. The legend reported is from Frankfort, Indiana, in 1970.

39. From a Gary informant of Hungarian background.

40. Linda Dégh, "Approaches to Folklore Research among Immigrant Groups," *Journal of American Folklore* 74 (1966): 555. A similar statement, concerning mermaids in Lake Balaton, was made by an informant in Hungary.

41. Linda Dégh, "The House of Blue Lights Revisited," *Indiana Folklore* 2, no. 2 (1969): 11–28.

42. The texts were published in Linda Dégh, *Kakasdi népmesék* [Folktales of Kakasd], 2 vols. (Budapest: Akadémiai Kiadó, 1955, 1960), I, 106–108, and II, 218–219. Comments: Dégh, *Folktales and Society*, pp. 135–138.

43. Kurt Ranke, "Schwänke und Witz als Schwundstufe," in *Festschrift für Will-Erich Peuckert* (Berlin: Erich Schmidt Verlag, 1955), pp. 41–59; Röhrich, *Märchen und Wirklichkeit*, pp. 47–62.

44. The enjoyment of fear by legend telling is discussed by Heilfurth, *Bergbau und Bergmann*, p. 42. In more detail, see Linda Dégh, "Neue Sagenerscheinungen in der industriellen Umwelt der USA," in *Probleme der Sagenforschung*, ed. Lutz Röhrich, pp. 43–48.

45. Gaál, *Angaben . . .*, p. 24.

46. Dégh, "The Haunted Bridges," pp. 77–81; Carol A. Mitchell, "The White House," *Indiana Folklore* 2, no. 2 (1969): 97–109; and Linda Dégh, "The 'Belief Legend' in Modern Society: Form, Function and Relationship to Other Genres," in *American Folk Legend: A Symposium*, ed. Wayland D. Hand, pp. 63–66.

47. AT Type 1676 B, "Clothing Caught in Graveyard."

48. William M. Clements, "The Walking Coffin," *Indiana Folklore* 2, no. 2 (1969): 3–10.

49. John Vlach, "One Black Eye and Other Horrors: A Case for the Humorous Anti-Legend," *Indiana Folklore* 4 (1971): 97–102. Numerous additional variants were selected by Sylvia Grider and Linda Dégh in 1974.

50. The problem of negative legends is discussed in more detail in Linda Dégh and Andrew Vázsonyi, "The Dialectics of the Legend," *Folklore Preprint Series* 1, no. 6 (December 1973): 12–14.

51. See note 3 in the main. Others, like Zender ("Quellen und Träger," pp. 119–120) and Röhrich ("Die deutsche Volkssage," p. 664), distinguish between individual attitudes of the legend teller and those of the audience.

52. Lüthi, *Volksmärchen*, pp. 24–25.

53. Since the completion of this essay we have discussed other aspects of legend in "The Dialectics of the Legend" and in "The Memorate and the Proto-Memorate," *Journal of American Folklore* 87 (1974): 225–239.

7. Proverbs: A Social Use of Metaphor

PETER SEITEL

This essay will present a system for viewing proverbs as the strategic social use of metaphor, that is, as the manifestation in traditional, artistic, and relatively short form of metaphorical reasoning, used in an interactional context to serve certain purposes. It will be the task here to show why it is reasonable and interesting to view proverbs in this way, to suggest areas of investigation which present themselves in this light, and to offer some preliminary conclusions drawn from my own researches. The proposed method is a development from the ethnographic approach used by other investigators, who have taken as their goal the explication of meaning in proverbs through a description of the cultural context in which they appear. George Herzog and C. G. Blooah, in *Jabo Proverbs from Liberia* (London, 1936), give ethnographic details concerning the content of most proverbs presented and often the social situations to which they may be applied. In an article on Maori proverbs, Raymond Firth has stated the general principles of this type of approach.

> The essential thing about a proverb is its meaning—and by this is to be understood not merely a bald and literal translation into the accustomed tongue, nor even a free version of what the words are intended to convey. The meaning of a proverb is made clear only when side by side with the translation is given a full account of the accompanying social situation—the reason for its use, its effect, and its significance in speech.[1]

In an article entitled "Proverbs and the Ethnography of Speaking Folklore,"[2] E. Ojo Arewa and Alan Dundes expand on this basic idea. They not only delineate the various aspects of the "social situation" of proverb use but also see proverbs as part of the total communica-

NOTE. Reprinted from *Genre* 2, no. 2 (June 1969): 143–161, by permission of the University of Illinois Press.

tion system operative in a given society. As a mode of social communication, proverbs may then be handled within the framework outlined by Dell Hymes in an article entitled, "The Ethnography of Speaking."[3] When applied to proverbs, this general method for describing the cultural patterns of language use yields the following questions:

> One needs to ask not only for proverbs and what counts as a proverb, but also for information as to the other components of the situations in which proverbs are used. What are the rules governing who can use proverbs, or particular proverbs, and to whom? upon what occasions? in what places? with what other person present or absent? using what channels (e.g. speech, drumming, etc.)? Do restrictions or prescriptions as to the use of proverbs or a proverb have to do with particular topics? with the specific relationship between speaker and addressee? What exactly are the contributing contextual factors which make the use of proverbs or a particular proverb, possible or not possible, appropriate or inappropriate?[4]

The core of interest in the Arewa and Dundes article is essentially the same as that of the earlier work by Firth; that is, to reach an understanding of proverbs by thoroughly describing the ethnographic context, Arewa and Dundes have extended and delineated more precisely the questions to be asked concerning the relevant aspects of social context.

The system for studying proverbs presented here owes much to Hymes's "ethnography of speaking" approach. Rather than viewing proverbs as an instance of patterned speech to be fit into a system designed to handle a much broader range of data, however, I shall take an alternate approach by setting a goal of proverb study and then adducing whatever methods seem appropriate to the attainment of this goal. This does not in any way question the validity of the "ethnography of speaking" method; the system presented here merely takes as its first step the consideration of proverb usage itself, to determine whether certain problems arise that are characteristic of it alone or whether in proverb usage certain general problems are most readily accessible to investigation.

This essay takes as its central question: Given that a person has memorized a certain number of proverb texts, by application of what set of rules does he speak them in a culturally appropriate manner and by what criteria does he judge the correctness of another's usage? Alternately stated, the goal of the method presented is to delineate the culturally shared system which enables a person to use proverbs in a socially acceptable manner.

With this central concern, a certain line of investigation may be followed. First, what is a proverb? That is, how does one recognize that which he is going to study? Second, what is the data available for the study? Third, what are the tools available for the analysis of the data? Fourth, what conclusions may be drawn on the basis of the data?

It will become evident that the first two questions in practice cannot be separated. Definition of a phenomenon for study depends, of course, on the type of data available. An investigator who observes proverb usage in a natural conversational setting and in his own language will define *proverb* differently from an investigator whose data are collections of texts. Proverbs in English may be provisionally defined as short, traditional, "out-of-context" statements used to further some social end. That proverbs are short and traditional is a generally accepted feature of definition. That they are used for a social end or a "strategy" has been noted by Kenneth Burke.[5] What is meant by "out-of-context" is simply that a proverb in some way violates the "usual" rules of conversation; a proverb may be acceptable at a given time within the order of a conversation, but the proverb's syntax, subject matter, or other features violate in some (acceptable) way the "usual" context. "A stitch in time saves nine" applied to the need for minor automobile repairs before a long trip introduces the subject of sewing into a context where it appears to have no place. "Seeing is believing" in judgment of a purported statement of fact stands out from the normal conversational flow because of its unusual syntax. "Business is business," applied to the morality of New York Chemical Bank's role in the economy of South Africa, violates usual English rules which specify the permissible combination of words. Leaving the definition at present to the criteria mentioned above, let us consider how the data available for the study limited the application of this definition.

Proverb use among the Ibo people of Eastern Nigeria was studied through library materials. Three types of data were used: ethnographic, textual, and literary. The ethnographic materials were the monographs of Victor Ch. Uchendu[6] and G. T. Basden,[7] as well as other books and articles on Ibo society. Also employed was a collection of 1022 proverb texts made by Northcote Thomas as part of his report on the Ibo-speaking peoples of Nigeria.[8] Three novels of Chinua Achebe[9] provided examples of proverb uses in traditional contexts. While the ethnographic and textual works are generally accepted as "hard" scientific data, an explanation must be given of how and why one may use novels as repositories of factual information.

The rationale that allowed the use of novels as sources for the realistic portrayal of proverb use was essentially this: if it could be shown that the novelistic depictions of cultural features (exclusive of proverb use) were substantially accurate, then it would not be unreasonable to assume that accounts of proverb usages were similarly true to life. To this end, novelistic description of such things as social organization, residence rules, burial customs, cosmology, and performances of items of verbal art other than proverbs were compared with accounts from the ethnographic sources on the same cultural features. The novels were shown to be accurate in every instance, with allowance for the fact that variations exist within what was then Ibo territory.

Using novels as ethnographic data on proverb use has certain inherent limitations. Aside from the fact that the rational foundation rests on the inductive leap outlined above, only certain proverbs and aspects of proverb use are available for study. If, for example, there are Ibo proverbs set off from usual context by unusual syntax or violation of permissible combinations of words, one could not detect this because all the proverbs appear in English translation. One manner of departing from the normal context, however, does remain recognizable even in translation—the abrupt shift in subject matter when a proverb such as "a stitch in time . . ." is used. This kind of "out-of-contextness" is recognizable in a novelistic setting because the contexts in which proverbs appear are described. Many proverbs deal with animals, but few if any of the novelistic contexts of proverb use have animals in them. With respect to the definition first proposed, then, the proverbs will be limited to those set off by subject matter. This type of proverb has been termed the *metaphorical proverb* because the relationship between it and the situation to which it is applied may be termed metaphorical.[10] The novels yielded 150 instances of proverb use in social contexts (uses of proverbs in the authorial voice for descriptive purposes were eliminated).

The features of the context of proverb use were then recorded, with the selecting out of as many social features mentioned by Arewa and Dundes as the smallness of the sample allowed. For example, the relative age of the speaker and intended hearer and their relative social status and sex could be employed because of the few discriminations needed on each dimension. But a category such as kin relationship could not yield significant results because of the relatively large number of possibilities in relation to the small size of the sample. Also recorded was the intention of the speaker in using the proverb— knowable in most cases because it is the craft of the novelist to make internal motivations evident. The type of occasion was noted—ceremonial, formal reception of a visitor, village meeting, informal discussion, and so on—as was the presence or absence of introductory phrases such as "the elders have a saying that . . ."

It should be noted that all of these categories refer to the situation in which a proverb is spoken, henceforth called the *interaction situation*. An equally important aspect of proverb use to be described is the metaphorical relationship between the situation presented literally in the *proverb* and the *context situation* to which the proverb refers. To understand proverb use one must understand the mechanism of this metaphor and how it is manipulated to serve social ends. As an aid to developing a conceptual terminology with which to analyze this relationship, consider the heuristic model shown in the accom-

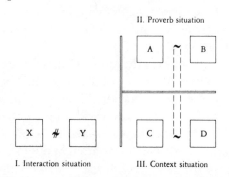

Social and Metaphoric Relationships in Proverb Use. Two of the three domains were labeled differently in this essay as it appeared in *Genre*. The names there and their equivalents here are as follows: social context = interaction situation, and social context = context situation.

panying figure. X and Y are, respectively, the speaker and the intended hearer of a proverb, and ⤴ represents the relationship which obtains between them—features of which are age, sex, status, and the like. Part I of the diagram thus represents the interaction situation of proverb use. Parts II and III represent, respectively, the proverb situation and the context situation to which the proverb is applied.

The symbol ∿ refers to a relationship which is seen by the speaker as obtaining both between the objects (or people) in the social world (C and D) and between the concepts in the imaginary proverb situation (A and B). Because the diagram represents a *logical* structure, the symbol ∿ represents a relationship of a logical nature which obtains between the substantive terms of the proverb situation (A ∿ B) and also between the substantive terms of the context situation (C ∿ D). This relationship may therefore be named by relational words such as *implies*—to characterize the relationship between the substantive terms *smoke* and *fire* in a usage of "where there's smoke there's fire." Another example is the relational word *equals*—to relate substantive terms in "a penny saved is a penny earned." The relational word may also name an action which is occurring or has occurred between the substantive terms, as does the word *recognition* in a usage of "it is a wise parent who knows his own child." The symbol ∿ can never stand for a substantive term.

The parallel dotted lines drawn between the relationship symbols (∿) in II and III represent the drawing of an analogy between the two relationships. Thus, we may visualize that X says to Y that A is to B as C is to D (or A : B :: C : D).

To give an example of how the model represents the areas of investigation of proverb use: A father is discussing with his adolescent son the advisability of the son's associating himself with a certain group of boys, one of whom has earned a very bad reputation. To his son's argument that all of the rest of the members are reputable individuals, the father may answer, "If one finger brought oil it soiled the others." Here X and Y are the father and his son. The relationship between them (⤴) has dimensions of age, status, kin relationship. The interaction situation (I) may or may not be relevant—formal teaching session, informal discussion over a meal, or whatever. The proverb situation (II) is made up of the term "finger which brought oil" (A) and the term "other fingers" (B). The relationship between them (⌢) is "soiling." The context situation described (III) is a boy of bad reputation (term C) bringing disrepute (the relationship ⌢) to the other members of his group (term D). The fact that the relationship in the context situation is seen by the father as somehow the "same" (that is, "soiling" in both cases) is shown by the parallel dotted lines.

If the son objects by saying that this doesn't apply to him personally, the father might say, "If you lie with the puppy you'll get fleas." In this example, the interaction situation (I), remains the same as in the first case, but here the proverb situation is made up of the term "you, lying with the puppy" (A) and the term "fleas" (B), the relationship (⌢) being "getting." The context situation (III) here consists of the son's associating with the aforementioned group (term C) and a bad reputation (term D), the relationship (⌢) here also one of "getting." The parallel dotted lines represent the drawing of the analogy: "you, lying with the puppy" is to "fleas" as "you, associating with that group" is to "a bad reputation." This example may be seen as being of the same rational structure as the first, but with one significant difference. In the second instance the son appears in two places —as the hearer (X) and as a subject in the context situation (C).[11] The dual role of the son in this instance points up another aspect of proverb use—one which I have termed *correlation*.

By correlation I mean the manner in which the speaker "matches up" the terms in the proverb with the people in the context situation and possibly in the interaction situation. This may be described with a set of terms borrowed from language grammars: first, second, and third persons, singular and plural. To see how these apply to proverb use, it is easiest to give examples of a single proverb used in several of the six types of possible correlation. If I journey to a friend's house on an urgent matter, during the course of preliminary exchanges of courtesy (as an Ibo) I might say, "A toad does not run in the daytime unless something is after its life." The meaning would be clear—I have come because I have a matter to discuss ("the toad running in the daytime" is to "something which is after its life" as "I, visiting," is to "matter to be discussed"). The correlation would here be first person singular because the person to whom the "toad" refers is "I."

However, if you come to see me, and I say this proverb to you, the correlation is second-person singular, because the person to whom the "toad" refers is then the person to whom the proverb is spoken (you). Further, if I speak to you about the frequent visits a third person makes to a certain house, alluding to the fact that I feel suspicious activities are going on, I may use the same proverb. Here the correlation is third-person singular, because the person referred to is neither the speaker nor the person to whom the proverb is addressed. I leave it to the reader's imagination to construct hypothetical situations for using this proverb in the plural correlations of first, second, and third person; that is, the "toad" as we, you (pl.), and they.

Although the above six types of correlations were most often found in Achebe's novels, other types, made up of a combination of the six, are also possible. If there are two terms within a proverb which one wants to correlate with two people in a certain social situation, this usage is possible and may be handled within the correlation scheme. Consider, for example, a situation in which a man of high status visits a man of lower status, and the latter treats the former with generous hospitality. When the man of high status expresses his gratitude, the man of lower status may reply with modesty, "[don't thank me because] a woman can place only so much of her leg over her husband." That is, beings of lower status can do only so much—very modest indeed. The correlation here is both first- and second-person singular, for terms referring to both the speaker and hearer are present in the proverb usage. The importance of correlation to understanding proverb usage may be noted by imagining a reversal in the correlation of the above proverb.[12] Suppose, in reference to the same situation, that the man of high status speaks the proverb to the man of lower status. The usage would then be, rather than a modest statement, a blatant insult. Note that in a first- and second-person correlation, the social context is the same as the social situation. It appears that proverb use of this kind is one of great delicacy.

Another concept important to the description of proverb use is "strategy." By strategy I mean essentially what Kenneth Burke proposed the term to mean—a plan for dealing with the situation which the proverb names. As an answer to an implied (or perhaps stated) question, "what to do?" the proverb is an attempt to resolve the personally felt conflicts which arise from perceived contradictions in a social situation. That is, a conversational proverb use is an attempt to solve a situational problem the speaker perceives in a manner which the speaker believes is most suitable. This is most evident in proverb usages where advice is being given: "look before you leap" is usually used as an attempt to resolve the perceived contradiction between quick decisive action and thorough weighing of alternatives; "he who hesitates is lost" (although perhaps not used metaphorically in all cases) is often an attempt to resolve the same contradiction. Proverb usages such as the one described above for "if one finger brought oil it soiled the others" give advice regarding the proper choice of alternatives—here an admonition to break off what is perceived to be a damaging relationship. Proverbs may also be used to resolve the contradictions between what a person feels an interaction situation should be and what he perceives it to be at present. The usual use of "the toad does not run in the daytime unless something is after its life" is an attempt to bridge the gap or to mediate between a simple social visit and a situation in which an important matter may be discussed. The speaker perceives the initial situation as mere greeting behavior; he has a desire for a different kind of situation. The proverb is spoken to resolve this felt conflict—in favor of the speaker's desire. Proverb usages in which the context situation described is the same as the interaction situation of use are manifestations of this kind of conflict resolution.

For Ibo proverb usages, and perhaps for proverb usages in general, a speaker may attempt the resolution in what may be seen as two mutually exclusive ways. First, he may propose to defeat one side of the contradiction, giving victory to the other; this is the intent for the usages described in the preceding paragraph. Second, he may propose that the contradiction which he perceives in a situation and which the intended hearer also perceives is in fact the natural state of the world and must be endured. This type of strategy, which might be called "restraint" or "consolation," is evident in the instance of one elder seeking to comfort another, described by Achebe in *Arrow of God* (p. 213). When the speaker hears of the disappointment his friend has experienced because of an abnormal domestic relationship between his daughter and son-in-law, he consoles him by saying, "[don't let this bother you because] there are more ways than one of killing a dog." That is, there are more ways than one of ordering a domestic relationship. This proverb usage also indicates the difficulty one would have in ascribing strategies to proverbs on the evidence of the text alone.

The major areas of the proposed method for studying proverb usage are the interaction situation, the proverb situation, the context situation, and the concepts of correlation and strategy. These will be used in the next section, first in a brief report of the library research on the Ibo materials and then in a discussion of ways of implementing the approach in a field research context.

It must be repeated that the results of the library research rest on the inductive leap discussed before, and hence must be taken as provisional; however, several interesting patterns do emerge from the materials. As one might suspect from the examples given above for the case of double correlation, there is a significant connection between the speaker's intent and the type of correlation employed. For example, for proverb usages in which animals are correlated with people, the rule appears to operate that for first person correlation the intent is a justification of one's own actions or position on a given social issue. The proverb quoted above, "the toad does not run in the daytime unless something is after his life," is usually used in first-person correlation to state one's intention of and justification for bringing up a matter for discussion.[13] "The lizard that jumped from the high *iroko* tree to the ground said he would praise himself if no one else would" is spoken by a man who has come to request the sponsorship of an elder in beginning his yam garden. With this proverb usage he states that he must mention his own personal attributes and feels justified in doing so.[14]

A second-person correlation for proverb usages in which animals occur may be found only a few times in Achebe's novels. In each case, however, the proverb is used in a negative appraisal of the intended hearer's actions and with intent which may be characterized as insult. One of these instances is especially interesting because the proverb cited here for a second person occurs in other usages in a first-person correlation. "A toad does not run in the daytime unless something is after its life" is spoken by an elder who has received a visit from a younger relative of his.[15] The elder is quite displeased with the youth's discourteous manner, which violates not only norms for respectful treatment of elders but also the cordial relationship which is supposed to obtain between people who stand to one another as kin of the mother's-brother / sister's-son type. To add to the elder's expression of displeasure he introduces the proverb with "we have a saying that . . . ," implying that either the youth does not know the proverb—the most frequently used one in the novels—or that the elder is paying ironic over-courtesy.[16]

Third-person correlations for animal subjects, as one might expect, are used in the novels for negative judgments. "Unless the wind blows we do not see the fowl's rump" is used of friends who desert when adversity arises.[17] "Did you expect the leopard sired to be different from the leopard?" remarks negatively on the resemblance between father and daughter.[18] "When the mother-cow is chewing grass its young ones watch its mouth" remarks upon bad habits passed from parent to child.[19]

These examples should not be construed as evidence for a general rule that proverbs are used in support of oneself and against others. These examples are drawn only from those proverb usages that include animal subjects—30 out of 150.[20] The results are given here merely to suggest the aspects of proverb use which are part of the proposed method of investigation. Among the remaining 120 are usages which support the actions and opinions of others and some which are self-deprecatory for the purposes of courtesy and humor.

A somewhat similar pattern emerges for those proverbs in which a word such as *child* or *boy* occurs. First-person correlation of *child* is common and has no negative connotations.[21] Second- and third-person correlations are deprecatory[22] with one basic exception—when the proverb is addressed to a child. In such a usage, the elder may be reprimanding the child, but in no sense may his remarks be taken as insult. "A boy who tries to wrestle with his father gets blinded by the old man's loin cloth" is spoken to a son to warn against disobeying his father.[23] Were this said by one grown man to another, it would clearly be aggressive and derisive in tone. Unfortunately, no such pairs of interaction situations and context situations exist in the novels for the same proverb. But an indication of the shift in the speaker's intention and in the application of the metaphor may be found in two instances of the same proverb—one in the Northcote Thomas collection and one in *Things Fall Apart*. "A baby on its mother's back does not know the way is long" is said by a priestess to a young child whom she wishes to comfort just before she will carry the young girl the long distance to an oracle cave.[24] This proverb also occurs in the Thomas collection in the section "Wealth and Poverty," where it is translated as "the child which is carried on the back does not know that travelling is a labor."[25] The proverb is to be applied "to a spend-thrift son" or, it would appear, to any person who lives on the wealth of his parents rather than by his own labor. This is another clear instance of a change in application signaling a change in the speaker's intent and in the very meaning of the metaphor. The more specific problem of proverb use to children will be taken up below.

The extension of this type of study to field research requires that the lines of investigation suggested in the heuristic model of proverb use be followed in two ways. First, in interviews with proverb speakers, hypothetical uses should be constructed for a single proverb. Each situation should differ from another by a single value on one of the dimensions cited—type of correlation, socially defined characteristics of the person to whom the proverb applies (age, sex, social standing, etc.), aspects of the interaction situations in which the proverb is spoken, and so on. The informant should be asked whether the proverb may be used in this way; if it can, he should give an exegetical statement (if possible) which approximates the meaning of the usage. Questions should be asked, such as, if the usual use of the proverb is a first-person correlation, is it possible to use it in a second-person correlation, and what does it mean so used? If a proverb is usually used by one senior in age to a junior, can it be used in any other way? Does a proverb have the same meaning whether applied to a man or a woman? Can this proverb be spoken if people who stand in certain kin relationships to the speaker are present? For any single proverb, the distinctions to be made for proper use, and the consequent questions to be asked, are great in number. The aim is to construct usages of the same proverb in which a minimal difference in application signals a difference in meaning. When this information is available for a representative number of proverbs, patterns of use will emerge as they have to a limited extent for the Ibo materials.

The second way of applying the proposed method to field studies is to record instances of proverb use in their natural social contexts. The participants might be questioned at a later time as to the relevant factors that caused the choice of one proverb as opposed to another.

This would provide the frame for questions regarding the interchangeability of proverbs under certain circumstances. In both types of study, the aim should be to isolate the minimal differences in the features of interaction situation and context situation which signal a change in proverb meaning and proverb selection.

Recalling the short discussion of the proverb "a child on its mother's back does not know the way is long," we may ask whether the proposed method can offer a framework for dealing with special use of proverbs to children. That children occupy a special status in a system of proverb usage is suggested by a few reports on African societies. Otto Raum states that proverbs are not to be used at all to children below a certain age among the Chaga; stories are thought to be the proper mode of moral instruction.[26] From a personal account I have the fact that among certain Swahili-speaking cultures on the coast of Tanzania a proverb use to a child is usually accompanied by a story said to "explain" the meaning of the application of the proverb. What these examples seem to suggest is that the metaphorical reasoning employed to understand proverbs is thought to be acquired by a process of developmental learning and, also, that cultural concepts in the system of metaphorical proverb use (the proverb terms) must be invested in the child's mind with proper cultural meanings.

The process of metaphorical reasoning has been discussed as the application of an imaginary (proverb) situation to a real (context) situation through a process of correlation. If one wanted to simplify this process so that it could be learned by a child, he would try to make the desired correlation as unambiguous as possible. One of the ways to do this is to "literalize" one of the proverb terms; that is, to make part of the proverb nonmetaphorical. This is what is evident in the usage of the proverb "a child on its mother's back does not know the way is long" directly to a child. In the Arewa and Dundes article, twelve proverbs are given which are said to relate to child rearing. Although no definite indication is given as to which proverbs are regularly addressed to children, it is interesting to note that ten of the twelve have the words for *child* or *mother* in them. The problem of a "literal" correlation in usage to children may offer evidence on indigenous ideas of developmental growth of reasoning capacity.

To discuss the educational process of investing proverb terms with proper cultural meanings, it is necessary to refer again to the heuris-

tic model of proverb usage. It will be recalled that the process of metaphorical reasoning requires drawing a parallel or an analogy between the relationships that obtain between A and B and between C
and D. But how are these relationships known? Of what are they
made? And how does one communicate this to a child?

I believe that the direction in which these answers may be sought is
indicated by drawing an analogy. It will be recalled that in the interaction situation (sector I of the diagram) the symbol $\twoheadrightarrow$ represents the relationship between the speaker and the hearer (X and Y
respectively). It is, as we have seen, a shorthand representation for
the sum of the culturally defined features of the relationship which
obtains between them. That is, for example, if both are male, features of the relationship are: relative sex of speaker and hearer—
same; sex of speaker (or hearer)—male. Their relative and/or absolute ages also comprise features of the relationship, as do the political, ritual, and social statuses of the participants. It is to be emphasized, first, that these features are culturally defined and, second, that
the sum of these features comprises the relationship between speaker
and hearer. The composition and definition of the relationship
($\sim$) which obtains between the proverb terms, A and B (sector
II), may be understood in an analogous way.

A proverb term, for example "child," is characterized by a number
of cultural features which together comprise the metaphorical concept "child"—dependence, innocence, irresponsibility, ignorance, and
so on. These are ascribed differentially from society to society; children in one society may be thought to be completely irresponsible,
whereas they may not be thought so in another. Terms are invested
with culturally defined features by virtue of appearing or of having
once appeared in a certain culturally recognized environment. For
"child," the feature of dependence may come as a result of the environments connected with suckling and later feeding by the mother.
Irresponsibility as a feature may result from cultural practices and beliefs regarding the entrusting of certain tasks to children. In a similar manner other features come to define the metaphorical concept
"child." But cultural environments are not exclusively social or natural settings. We have, for example, the expression "the child who
cried 'wolf,'" a possible feature of the concept "child" which comes
not from any social environment but from a story told to warn chil-

dren. That the tortoise is slow but steady is a feature of our concept of "tortoise," which also derives from a story. The environments that invest proverb terms with features (alternately stated, symbols with associations or "valences") may be social, imaginary, or naturalistic. Thus, we may state that terms in a proverb, just like the participants in a proverb-speaking interaction situation, are invested with culturally defined features which are relevant for proverb usage.

When two terms appear in juxtaposition within the proverb situation, the sets of features characteristic of each combine so that features which correspond between the terms make up the relationship ($\sim$), whereas others, for which there is no correspondence between the terms, drop out. That is, each term may have a very large number of features associated with it, but when both are part of the same stated situation only certain of the features apply. To follow the example of "child": if one says of an incompetent employee, "you shouldn't send a child to do a man's work," certain features of "child" are implied because of the juxtaposition with "man,"[27] that is, indecision, incompetence, and the like. In the previously discussed proverb "a child on its mother's back does not know the way is long," however, "child" is invested with slightly different features by virtue of juxtaposition with "mother" (or "mother's back"): ignorance of the ways of the world in comparison with an adult and dependence on an adult. A proverb such as "a child cannot pay for its mother's milk" sets up a relationship between child and mother (mother's milk) which has the features of exclusivity, nurturance, inappropriateness of certain social forms that imply distance between individuals (paying), and the relationship among certain groups of kin in Ibo usage.[28] These examples are adduced to suggest that the relationship between proverb terms consists, then, of the sum of the logical correspondences in the culturally defined features characteristic of the terms, just as the relationship between the participants in the interaction situation of proverb use consists of the sum of the culturally defined features characteristic of the participants.

This provides a hypothesis to explain the problem of proverb usage to children. Because it is necessary for the hearer of a proverb to know the features of the terms (so that he can understand the relationship and, hence, the metaphor), a child is told stories either along with proverbs or instead of them so that he can see the terms, later to be used in proverbs alone, in the environments which define their features. Alternately, proverb use is general or the use of particular proverbs is delayed until a child is thought to have had sufficient social experience, to have observed the social environments which invest proverbs with their proper features.

In this short essay I have attempted to present a method for dealing with the phenomenon of proverb use. It has been my purpose to extend proverb study beyond the perusal of texts, and beyond a check list of questions to be answered, to the construction of a heuristic model of proverb use, with focus on the central problem of the social application of metaphor. The aim of the system is understanding, here taken to mean the ability to produce and to interpret proverb usages in culturally acceptable ways. The purpose of presenting this method is to show the boundaries of the area for investigation and to suggest a few of the problems therein.

As a necessary by-product of the presentation, a vocabulary for talking about proverb usages was developed. I have tried to make it as simple as possible, introducing only the widely used concepts of person and number from an "outside" discipline. The other words used—*situation, relationship, feature, term, correlation*, and *strategy* —have been given their usual meanings or a restricted part of their usual meanings. The discussion of the use of literature for ethnography, the short examples of results from a study of Achebe's novels, and the concept of the nature of metaphor (as part of the discussion on child proverb usage), may be taken as useful spin-off or as Shandyesque digressions.

And yet it appears that the most important question that might be raised about proverbs has been neither asked or answered: why study them at all? Again let me answer with an analogy: as white rats are to experimental psychologists and as kinship terms are to cultural anthropologists, proverbs can be to folklorists. By pushing around these small and apparently simply constructed items, one can discover principles which give order to a wider range of phenomena. Proverbs are the simplest of the metaphorical genres of folklore—song, folktale, myth, folk play, and so forth—and the genre which clearly and directly is used to serve a social purpose. By investigating the relatively simple use of metaphorical reasoning for social ends in proverbs, one can gain insight into the social uses of other, more complex metaphorical genres.

Although relatively simple in their application of metaphor, proverbs are one of the most complex genres in that they are most sensitive to social context. That is to say, the social rules one must master in order to use and interpret proverbs correctly are probably the most numerous and complex of those for any genre. Given a logical and workable method, they can be ascertained, and if this is possible for the most complex genre—proverbs—it will also be possible to write rules for the use and interpretation of less context-sensitive genres.

The simple, yet subtle and complex, nature of proverb use makes its study an important step in understanding the general problem of the social uses of metaphor. To a person interested in the social purposes that literature of all kinds may serve, the investigation of proverbs can offer significant insight.

Notes

I would like to thank David Sapir for his comments and helpful suggestions.

1. Raymond Firth, "Proverbs in Native Life, with Particular Reference to Those of the Maori," *Folk-Lore* 37 (1926): 134.

2. E. Ojo Arewa and Alan Dundes, "Proverbs and the Ethnography of Speaking Folklore," *American Anthropologist* 66, no. 6, pt. 2 (1964): 70–85.

3. Dell Hymes, "The Ethnography of Speaking," in *Anthropology and Human Behavior*, ed. Thomas Gladwin and William C. Sturtevant (Washington, D.C.: Anthropological Society of Washington, 1962), pp. 15–53.

4. Arewa and Dundes, "Proverbs and Ethnography," p. 71.

5. Kenneth Burke, *The Philosophy of Literary Form*, pp. 3–4.

6. Victor Ch. Uchendu, *The Igbo of Southeast Nigeria* (New York: Holt, Reinhart and Winston, 1965).

7. G. T. Basden, *Among the Ibos of Southern Nigeria* (London: Seeley Service, 1921) and *Niger Ibos* (London: Seeley Service, 1938).

8. Northcote Thomas, *Anthropological Report on the Ibo-Speaking Peoples of Nigeria*, 6 vols. (London: Harrison and Sons, 1914).

9. Chinua Achebe, *Things Fall Apart* (London: Heinemann, 1958), *No Longer at Ease* (London: Heinemann, 1960), and *Arrow of God* (London: Heinemann, 1964).

10. W. R. Bascom, "Stylistic Features of Proverbs: A Comment," *Journal of American Folklore* 78 (1965): 69.

11. Although the proverb has the syntactic form "If you lie with the puppy . . ." it should not be thought that the son in the usage described appears in three places: as hearer (X), as a term in the social situation (C), and also as the term *you* in the proverb situation. To the contrary, the *you* of the proverb term (A), "you, lying with the puppy," is the X *you* of impersonal statement, not the *you* of second-person address. The proverb usage would have exactly the same logical structure were the proverb to read "lying with the puppy brings fleas."
Two points must be emphasized. First, the model proposed does not describe or explain syntactic or surface structure; it is designed to investigate the logical structure and the rational process that underlies proverb use. Second, a term in the social situation (C or D) can never also be a term in the proverb situation. The proverb derives its essence, and the metaphor its meaning, from the fact that the terms A and B are related to each other in one system (imaginary), and this very relationship is said to characterize the relationship between two terms, C and D, in another separate system (social).

12. In the first usage the metaphorical analogy is man : wife :: man of high status : man of low status; the speaker is the man of low status, and thus the correlation is second person–first person. In the reversed usage, the analogy remains the same, but the speaker is the man of high status, and thus the correlation is first person–second person.

13. Achebe, *Things Fall Apart*, pp. 19, 282, and *Arrow of God*, pp. 171, 254.

14. Achebe, *Things Fall Apart*, p. 20.

15. Achebe, *Arrow of God*, p. 25.

16. This pattern is also reported by Arewa and Dundes for Yoruba proverb usage ("Proverbs and Ethnography," p. 79).

17. Achebe, *Arrow of God*, p. 72.

18. Ibid., p. 91.

19. Achebe, *Things Fall Apart*, p. 65, and *Arrow of God*, p. 213.

20. It should be noted that the results given here are for single-type correlations. A double correlation for animal subjects, "A fowl does not eat into the belly of a goat" (Achebe, *Arrow of God*, p. 93), does not follow the rule for single correlations of animal subjects. It resembles the example of double correlation given above in the text in that social context equals social situation and the metaphorical analogy refers to the differential statuses of the speaker and hearer.

21. See, for example, Achebe, *Things Fall Apart*, pp. 61, 151.

22. See, for example, Achebe, *No Longer at Ease*, p. 75.

23. Achebe, *Things Fall Apart*, p. 123.

24. Ibid., p. 92.

25. Thomas, *Anthropological Report*, proverb no. 28.

26. Otto Raum, *Chagga Childhood* (London, 1940).

27. Similarly for the term "man," which not only has associations of competence when juxtaposed with "child" but is also used in a juxtaposition like "are you a man or a mouse?"

28. Achebe, *Things Fall Apart*, p. 151.

8. The "Pretty Languages" of Yellowman: Genre, Mode, and Texture in Navaho Coyote Narratives

BARRE TOELKEN

Probably no other character is encountered throughout such a broad range of Navaho legend, chant, and folktale as Ma'i (Coyote).[1] Yet, even though he has been the subject of scholarly comment in nearly every serious ethnographic investigation of Navaho culture and literature, a close critical analysis of Ma'i in Navaho lore, based on good data, has yet to appear. The scope of such a study is of course far beyond the capabilities of a single essay, or probably of a single writer. Some literary observations on the narratives, however, are possible to make at this time: their appearance in such a wide spectrum of Navaho tradition makes it obvious even to someone of my limited acquaintance with them that their stylistic attributes reach far beyond the so-called Coyote Tale and into the whole concept of Navaho literary expression.

For purposes of focus here I will illustrate my remarks primarily by reference to tales told by one Navaho raconteur. In spite of the severe limitations we must place on generalizing from the data provided by one informant, I would rather work from material I have collected myself (for reasons which will become more apparent below) and from comments made to me by a single good informant than to cope badly with the uncountable critical problems which arise in the use of transcribed texts, no matter how serious or how august their collector may have been. The Navaho propensity toward playing subtle tricks on outsiders on the one hand, or the occasional school-sponsored attempt, on the other, to apologize rhetorically for one's own very knowledge of the tales (for example, overuse of the term *zhini*, "they say"[2]), when added to the already dizzying profusion of transcription techniques, makes the close literary use of published texts critically hazardous for anything beyond synopses.

NOTE. Reprinted from *Genre* 2, no. 3 (September 1969): 211–235, by permission of the University of Illinois Press.

For another kind of focus, directly related to the fact that this is an essay, not an anthology of Navaho tales, I will use one particular tale as exemplar of the literary conditions I plan to discuss. The reader will have to accept my choice of this tale as, first, typical of the Coyote stories and, second, as broadly representative of the stylistic and structural matters which are not always present in every tale but which become familiar to one who has heard many of the tales over a period of time. Admittedly, even such brief remarks as I can make here will be a considerable load for such small evidence; the aim of this piece, then, is to be provocative, not definitive. Even so, the observations I make here, as far as I can check them through other data available to me, are not exceptional in nature to those which could be made were I to offer twenty or fifty such tales as textual evidence.

First, a word about the narrator and my acquaintance with him, since these matters have an important bearing on the reliability of the data and on my position as collector and evaluator of them. It has been my distinct good fortune to have lived among the Navaho on the Northern Reservation (chiefly in southern Utah) off and on for thirteen years, for three of these years under the most intimate conditions and for nearly all of one of these years (1955–1956) as an adopted member of a family who lived far from roads (in the then-remote Aneth district, in Montezuma Canyon) and who spoke no English. This was the family of Tsinaabạạs Yazhi (Little Wagon), which consisted of the old man and his wife, their daughter (then about 25 years old), her husband, Yellowman (then about 40), and several of their small children. My adoption by the old man put me in the position of participating fully in the entire activities of the family, including arising before sun-up to perform dawn chants and pollen throwing.[3]

During a rather severe winter we spent most evenings sitting around the fire in Little Wagon's large *hogaan* listening to the old man tell tales, legends, and miscellaneous yarns. It was under these circumstances that I first observed, albeit unwittingly, something of key importance about Navaho mythic narrative. A small family passing by on horseback had stopped for the night, according to the usual custom. Outside it had begun to snow lightly, and one of the travelers' children asked where snow came from. Little Wagon, in answer, began a long and involved story about an ancestor who had found a piece of beautiful burning material, had guarded it carefully for several months until some spirits (*ye'i*) came to claim it, and had asked then that the spirits allow him to retain a piece of it. This they would not allow, but they would see what they could do for him. In the meantime he was to perform a number of complicated and dedicated tasks to test his endurance. Finally, the spirits told him that in token of his fine behavior they would throw all the ashes from their own fireplace into Montezuma Canyon each year when they cleaned house. Sometimes they fail to keep their word, and sometimes they throw down too much; but in all, they turn their attention toward us regularly, here in Montezuma Canyon. When this long story had been completed there was a respectful silence for a moment, and then the young questioner put in: "It snows at Blanding, too. Why is that?" "I don't know," the old man replied immediately, "You'll have to make up your own story for that." I of course assumed that the whole story had been made up for the occasion, and so it seemed, but I have encountered other students of the Navaho since then who have been subjected to the same or a similar story. The literary point came to me later, as Little Wagon commented after the travelers' departure that it was too bad the boy did not understand stories. I found by questioning him that he did not in fact consider it an etiological story and did not in any way believe that that was the way snow originated; rather, if the story was "about" anything, it was about moral values, about the deportment of a young protagonist whose actions showed a properly reciprocal relationship between himself and nature. In short, by seeing the story in terms of any categories I had been taught to recognize, I had missed the point, and so had our young visitor, a fact which Little Wagon at once attributed to the deadly influences of white schooling.

In these nightly sessions Little Wagon usually held the floor, with his son-in-law, Yellowman, telling only a few tales now and then. It was not until recently, when Yellowman had moved his family to Blanding, Utah (after two desperate years of near-starvation on the reservation), that I visited him during the winter, when the tales can be told, and found him an apparently inexhaustible source of tales, legends, astronomy, and string figures, narrating almost nightly to his family with a finesse I have not encountered in any other informant. Yellowman has now had thirteen children, and all of those old enough have gone to school. Yet English is not spoken by the children at home, and although Yellowman lives in a frame house on the edge of town, has made moccasins at the Utah State Fair, works for the Forest Service during the summers, and has numerous contacts with whites, he still does not speak English—probably out of cultural aloofness. He still brings up his children in the Navaho way, still dances in the *Ye'i bichei* ceremony each year, carries his babies in a cradle-board, and acts the part of cultural advisor to many nearby Navaho. His wife still grinds corn and berries on a flat stone, dresses and weaves in traditional fashion, cooks and serves the usual Navaho fare: coffee, mutton, *naneeskaadi* (a tortilla-like dry bread). Because of these and many other elements of cultural conservatism, as well as for his striking talents at storytelling, I consider Yellowman an outstanding and, for our purposes, culturally reliable informant. In addition, he has shown a very cheerful willingness to respond to questions about Navaho stories and storytelling; thus I have been able to check on a number of matters which otherwise would have remained quite indistinct in my mind.[4]

I have mentioned these details at length because they have much to do with the kind of evidence I mean to bring forth in this article. Most anthropological data on the Navaho I have read to date are plagued, as suggested partially above, by two great areas of distortion. The first is the well-known tendency of our culture to see things chiefly in terms of its own existing categories, and thus to classify data in its own terms. This leaning may have as much to do with normal thought processes as it does with cultural myopia, and we may never be able to cure it, but we should be aware of its effects on what we suppose to be our objectivity.[5] The second possibility for distortion lies in the Navaho view of information and how it may be transmitted. Sometimes an attitude may be communicated in a statement which is technically false but which uses humor as a vehicle (such as when an elderly Navaho began to refer to me as his great-grandfather because of my beard); sometimes aloofness or an unwillingness to be impressed is communicated by statements designed to make the listener appear stupid or to imply he has missed the point of one's remark (such as when a man heard me say I was from the East—literally, from near where the sun comes up—and commented, as if to someone else, "It must be pretty hot there"); still other information which may fall into a rather large ritual category must be specifically requested four times (the Navaho "special" number) or it will not be given. Professor David Aberle found, for example, that some of his information relating to peyotism was affected by his initial un- awareness that some potential informants assumed his single question indicated that he did not really want an answer. Very likely he as- sumed they were reluctant to answer and like a gentleman changed the subject.[6] I cannot safely say that my own work is immune to such problems, or to still others I have not myself isolated or yet recog- nized, but my first-hand experience with Navaho humor, my presence (and occasional participation) at a good number of Navaho cere- monials, and my continued and ready access to my adoptive family have made me sensitive to such areas when it has come to making generalizations about the data.

With these preliminary remarks, then, let me present a typical "Coyote tale" for consideration here. The story is one I identify de- scriptively by characters and plot direction, for to my knowledge it has no formal title: Coyote, with the aid of Skunk, plays dead in order to kill and eat some prairie dogs.[7] This particular text was recorded at Blanding, Utah, on the evening of December 19, 1966, as Yellow- man told the tale to several of his children; the translation which appears here was made with the valuable help of Annie Yellowman during the summer of 1968, for use in this article.

In the tale presentation the narrator's actions, styles, and devices will appear in parentheses, the audience's reactions in brackets. These references make it necessary to place other information—linguistic, for example—in notes; since this is at best a burden on the reader, I will provide notes only for those points which bear on the story or on the subsequent discussion of it.

(Slow, as with factual conversational prose; regular intonation and pronunciation; long pauses between sentences, as if tired) Ma'i was walking along once[8] in a once-forested area named after a stick float- ing on the water. He began walking in the desert in this area, where there were many prairie dogs, and as he passed by them they called him mean names, but he ignored them. He was angry, even so, and it was noon by then, so he made a wish:

(Slower, all vowels more nasalized) "I wish some clouds would

form." He was thinking about killing these prairie dogs, so he wished for clouds, and there were clouds. [*smiles and silent laughter*]

Then he said: "I wish I could have some rain."[9] He said: "I wish the ground to be damp enough to cool off my hot feet." So the rain came as he wished and cooled off his feet.[10]

"Now I want a little more, so the water will come up between my toes." [*quiet amusement, exchange of glances*] Every time Ma'i wishes something it comes about.

(Pause, four seconds)

"Now I want the water to come up to my knees." When it reached his knees, he wanted it to be even deeper so that only a small part of his back would show. Then he said: "I wish the water would rise some more so that only the tips of my ears will show." [*amusement, heavy breathing to avoid open laughter*] Now he began to float. Then he said: "I wish I could float until I come to a stop along with some flood debris near the middle of the prairie dogs' area." [*quiet laughter*] So that happened.

The pile of debris was made up of sticks, pine cones, and other fragments of vegetation, and mud. When he came floating to that place it had stopped raining. Ma'i lay there for a long while, pretending he was dead.

Skunk[11] was on his way by that place to get some water. [*silent laughter, knowing looks*] Ma'i was pretending he was drowned [*quiet amusement*] and Skunk didn't know he was there. [*open laughter; two girls now giggling almost constantly throughout the rest of this scene*] Skunk had a dipper, and put it into the water.

"Shiłna'ash"[12] *(speaking very nasally, through side of mouth, lips unmoving and eyes closed, in imitation of Ma'i).* [*open laughter, lasting three or four seconds*]

Skunk turned around in fright, but he didn't see anyone. So he put his dipper in the water again, and Ma'i said:

"Shiłna'ash" *(nasal, eyes closed, mouth unmoving, as before).* [*quiet laughter*] He said it four times,[13] and on the fourth time Skunk came to that place where Ma'i was lying *(normal intonation).*

(Still nasal, lips unmoving, eyes closed, for Ma'i's speech) "Go back to the village and tell the prairie dogs that you were on your way to get water and you came across the body of a dead coyote that

got drowned, Shiłna'ash. Tell them, 'It looks to me like he's been there for some time because it looks rotten and wormy.' Before you go there, get some *t'loh ts'osi*[14] and stick some under my arms, in my nose, in the corners of my mouth [*mild amusement*], in my ears [*quiet laughter*], in the joints of my legs; tell them how rotten I look. Tell them, 'He must have come down the wash and got drowned.' [*quiet laughter*] And one last thing before you go there: go make some clubs, four of them, and put them under me. Tell them, 'Since the coyote is dead, why don't we go over there where he is and celebrate?'[15] When they get here, have them dance around in a circle. Keep one of the clubs, and, when the prairie dogs beat me with their clubs, you do it, too. When they start dancing and beating, don't forget to tell them to take it easy on me; beat me slowly and not too hard," he said. [*laughter*]

(*Normal tone*) So Skunk went back to the prairie dogs' village and told the whole story as he was directed by Ma'i. He said: "I was just now on my way to get water, and I came across the body of a dead coyote that got drowned. It looks to me like he's been there a long time because it looks rotten and full of worms. He must have come down the wash and got drowned. Why don't we go over there and have a ceremonial to celebrate his death?"

(*Normal conversational tone, perhaps a bit more slowly pronounced than usual*) At the village there were also jackrabbits, cottontails, ground squirrels, and other small animals that Ma'i usually likes to eat. They couldn't believe it. They said (*nasal, high pitch*), "Is it really true?" "Is it true?" "Is it true?" "I don't know; why doesn't someone besides Skunk go over there and see?"[16] (*back to regular discourse, somewhat nasalized*). So the jackrabbit went over to where Ma'i was and came back and told them it was all true. Then the cottontail went over there and came back and said it was all true. Then one of the prairie dogs went over there and came back and said, "It's true." On the fourth time they all went over there and gathered around Ma'i to celebrate. They began to dance around him; we don't know exactly what they were singing, but the noise sounded like they were all saying, "Ma'i is dead," as they danced around and beat him slowly and gently. As they danced, more of them came along, and Skunk began to get ready to say what Ma'i had told him to say when he had said, "Don't forget to do all these things at this time, Shiłna'-ash."

(*Nasal whine*) Skunk said then, "Look! Way, way up there is a *t'ajilgai*[17] far above us." He said it four times, so the prairie dogs all looked up, and Skunk let out his scent[18] into the air, and it came down right into their eyes. [*laughter*] So the prairie dogs were fooled and they were busy rubbing their eyes.

Then Ma'i jumped up and said, "How dare you say I'm dead?" [*laughter*][19] He grabbed the clubs under him and began to club the prairie dogs. [*laughter and giggling*] He clubbed all the prairie dogs to death. [*extended laughter, including Yellowman for the first time*]

(*Pause, after laughter, about four seconds*)

"Let's start roasting the prairie dogs, Shiłna'ash. You dig out a place in the sand."[20] So Skunk began to dig a place and build a fire, and he put the prairie dogs in to cook.

"Let's have a race, Shiłna'ash. Whoever gets back first can have all the fat prairie dogs." [*laughter*]

(*Nasal whine*) "No, I don't want to. My legs aren't long enough."

But Ma'i insisted. Skunk complained that he couldn't run as fast as Ma'i, so Ma'i gave him a head start. So Skunk ran off. Skunk ran beyond a hill and hid under a rock.[21] Soon after that, Ma'i passed by, running as fast as he could. He had tied a burning stick to his tail so as to make lots of smoke.[22] [*laughter, including Yellowman*]

Skunk watched until Ma'i had gone completely out of sight and then went back to where the prairie dogs were buried. (*From this point on until midway in the next scene, the narration gets faster, with pacing related entirely to audience reaction, much in the manner of a stand-up comedian in a night club.*) He dug up all but the four skinniest prairie dogs and took them up onto a nearby ledge. [*laughter*] And while he was eating he watched for Ma'i, who soon came running as fast as he could. [*laughter, including Yellowman*] He wanted to make a good finish to show how fast he was, so he came running very rapidly and jumped right over the fire. [*laughter, including Yellowman*]

"Whew!!" he said. [*peak laughter, much extended, including Yellowman*] "Shiłna'ash, the poor old man with the stinking urine is still coming along." [*extended laughter*] Even though he was anxious to begin eating he didn't want to look greedy, so he paced back and forth in the shade making lots of footprints which would show he had waited for a long time. [*laughter, including Yellowman*]

Then Ma'i went to the fire and began digging with a stick to find the prairie dogs. He found a tail from one of the small prairie dogs and pulled on it. "Oh oh, the tail must have come loose from being overdone." [*laughter*] He took out the skinny carcass and threw it over his shoulder toward the east, and said, "There will be fatter ones than this."[23] [*laughter*]

Now, digging around with the stick,[24] he came onto the second skinny prairie dog and threw it toward the south, and said, "There will be fatter ones here."

(*Far more slowly, almost drowsily*) He came to the third one and threw it toward the west, and the fourth one he threw toward the north. Then he dug around and around with the stick and couldn't find anything. He walked around and around and finally decided to go find those skinny ones he threw away. So he ate them after all. [*quiet laughter*]

Then he started looking for footprints.[25] [*quiet laughter*] After a long time he found some tracks leading away from the roasting area to the rock ledge. He walked back and forth along this line several times without seeing Skunk, until Skunk dropped a small bone down from the ledge. [*quiet laughter*]

Ma'i looked up. (*nasal whine*) "Shiłna'ash, could I have some of that meat given back to me?" [*quiet laughter*] He was begging, with his eyes looking upward. [*laughter, including Yellowman*]

(*Pause, seven seconds*)

(*Admonishing tone, very slowly delivered*) "Certainly not,"[26] said Skunk to the begging coyote. He finally dropped some bones down and Ma'i gnawed on them. [*moderate laughter*]

(*Pause, about five seconds*)

That's what they say.[27]

Lawrence Hennigh has demonstrated recently the decisive importance of informant commentary in our critical approaches to the understanding of folktales which might seem at first easily classifiable in our terms; his study shows vividly that any consideration of folktale meaning made without reference to the informant's own critical

and cultural observations is not only weak, but actually invites error.[28]
Even though oral informants often disagree on the nature of the same
materials, and even though it is probably impossible for a literate,
scholarly audience ever to approach an oral tale from an oral culture
with anything like a traditional mental "set," no matter how much
informant material is available, we still may say that the informant's
conception of his own art can open possibilities to us which we might
otherwise never suspect and can save us from the blunder of inserting our own culture's aesthetic prejudices where his belong. With
these possibilities and limitations in mind, it is instructive to look into
some areas of literary discussion which have come up in my conversations with Yellowman.

For one thing, I had noticed that a good many words and phrases
used in the Ma'i stories were not familiar to me from regular conversational Navaho. I had found when I played tapes of these stories to
Father H. B. Liebler, a man with some twenty years' fluency in Navaho, that he too missed a good part of the meaning.[29] I asked Yellowman, therefore, if he used a special vocabulary when he told the
tales. His answer, not surprisingly, was yes; his explanation was essentially that these were "older" words and phrases and that he used
them because they were the vocabulary he had always heard used in
the tales.[30] But then he added with a smile a comment which I have
taken to mean "They are beautifully old-fashioned." Certainly the
Navaho reverence for beauty and for ancient things is well known,
but a slightly new dimension emerged when I talked with Yellowman's children about this matter. They reported that the vocabulary
was so familiar to them that they understood it readily (they had
heard it so often), that it did seem to add the valued sense of antiquity to the stories, but that in addition it lent to the narratives a kind
of pleasant humor, a comfortable quaintness that seemed to provide
(this is my interpretation of their remarks) a ready context for the
humorous scenes within the story. The element of humor will come
into deeper consideration below.

When I asked whether he told the tale exactly the same way each
time, he at first answered, "yes," but when evidence from compared
tapes was brought into the discussion it became clear that he had
understood me to be asking him whether he changed the nature of the
prototype tale of his own volition; the wording was different each

time because he recomposes with each performance, simply working from his knowledge of what ought to happen in the story and from his facility with traditional words and phrases connected, in his view, with the business of narrating Ma'i stories. He did not mention it, but it is quite obvious from tapes made of his stories when no children were present that the audience plays a central role in the narrative style. Without an audience, his tales are almost entirely lacking in the special intonations, changes in speed, pacing, and dramatic pauses which are so prominent in the specimen text given above. Speaking in solitude to a tape recorder, Yellowman gives only a rather full synopsis of characters and incidents; the narrative drama, far from being memorized, emerges in response to the bona fide storytelling context.

Does Yellowman consider these to be chiefly children's stories? Not at all, although he spends more time telling them to his own children than to anyone else. Adults in the audience do not remove themselves; they are as emotionally involved as the children. And, as Yellowman points out, stories of Coyote and his role in the Creation, the Emergence, the placement of stars and in the continuing fortunes of men and animals are told during the most serious of adult circumstances (that is, in ceremonies, myth recitations, chant explanations, and so on), because he is an extremely important personage in the Navaho belief system.

Why, then, if Coyote is such an important mythic character (whose name must not even be mentioned in the summer months), does Yellowman tell such funny stories about him? Yellowman's answer: "They are not funny stories." Why does everyone laugh, then? "They are laughing at the way Ma'i does things, and at the way the story is told. Many things about the story are funny, but the story is not funny." Why tell the stories? "If my children hear the stories, they will grow up to be good people; if they don't hear them, they will turn out to be bad." Why tell them to adults? "Through the stories everything is made possible."[31]

Why does Coyote do all those things, foolish on one occasion, good on another, terrible on another? "If he did not do all those things, then those things would not be possible in the world." Yellowman thus sees Coyote less as a trickster per se and more as an enabler whose actions, good or bad, bring certain ideas and actions into the field of possibility, a model who symbolizes abstractions in terms of real entities. Moreover, Freud notwithstanding, the narrator is in large part conscious of this function.[32] When in one story Coyote loses his eyes in a gambling match or gets them caught on a tree branch during a game, he replaces them with amber pitch-balls, and the story ends by explaining, "That's how Ma'i got his yellow eyes." But I exasperated Yellowman on one occasion by pursuing the question of how coyotes could actually see if their eyes were made of amber balls. It turned out just as it had with Little Wagon's snow story: the essence of the tale was not on the surface at all. Yellowman explained patiently that the tale allows us to envision the possibility of such things as eye disease, injury, or blindness; it has nothing to do with coyotes in general; and Ma'i himself may or may not have amber eyes, but since he can do anything he wants to, the question is irrelevant—he has eyes and he sees, period. I have found since that time that most Navaho of my acquaintance know the story, with minor variations, and none of them takes it to be etiological.

On the basis of such comments as these (and there are many more like them in my notes), I can suggest several important points: that Coyote tales are not simply entertainment; that they are phrased consciously in such a way as to construct an interesting surface plot which can act as entryway to a more subtle and far more important area of consideration; that the telling of, and listening to, Coyote stories is a serious business with serious consequences, no matter how much the humor might lead an outsider to feel otherwise; that, in short, the structures and styles we find meaningful in lettered literature are likely to be misleading, or at least irrelevant. I am suggesting that the significant part of the Coyote stories resides in their texture, not their structure, and that excessive attention to structure and stated content may actually stand in the way of our seeing those subtle moral implications and conceptual patterns which seem to be the Navaho's main reasons for telling the story. For one thing, such approaches in the past have led even a strong scholar like Clyde Kluckhohn to say of Navaho narratives: "Folk tales are secular in that, although things happen in them which could never occur in ordinary life and are hence part of the supernatural order of events, they are told primarily for amusement and entertainment. . . . Folk tales have none of the high seriousness of the myths. . . ."[33] Or the statement by W. W.

Hill: "Navaho folklore can be divided into two principal parts: accounts which deal with religious subjects, and stories with morals but which are told primarily for amusement."[34] If both of these do not misunderstand what the Navaho consider a religious subject, they at least fail to detect those textural elements which might have connected amusement with religion.

Alan Dundes has suggested that texture in a traditional text is the language employed: the particular phonemes, morphemes, rhymes, stresses, tones, pitches, and so on.[35] I would expand this somewhat and describe texture as *any* coloration given a traditional item or statement as it is being made. In narrative it would certainly include linguistic features, as well as any verbal manipulations which evoke, suggest, and describe or those which in any way qualify, modify, expand, or focus the rational structure by reference to or suggestion of emotions, mores, traditional customs and associations, aesthetic sensitivities and preferences, and so on.[36]

Dundes is correct in pointing out that "the more important the textural features are in a given genre of folklore, the more difficult it is to translate an example of that genre into another language,"[37] and, I would add, the more difficult it is for an outsider even to understand what, in fact, the given item or text means in its own language and the more difficult it is to delineate genre (since genre, in our culture at least, is usually distinguished on the basis of structure). Admittedly, the concept of genre in our own culture has been cloudy. When we have been able to see clear differences in the way things look on paper (even or uneven right-hand margin) or in fields of focus (novel versus short story), we have been able to make some clear distinctions. But there remains a considerable gulf between those who, like René Wellek and Austin Warren,[38] classify on the basis of form and structure, and those like Northrop Frye who prefer "the radical of presentation."[39] This has complicated our approach to the oral literatures of people for whom the material is not limited to particular forms (especially visible ones) and for whom the radical of presentation is always oral.

I found in questioning Yellowman that his own concept of the Coyote materials was based almost exclusively on style, rather than on content or structure. Among other questions, I asked him how he would recognize the difference between a Coyote story and someone talking about Coyote if he were to hear only part of the total text; I asked whether it would be possible, by listening to a tape recording, to detect the difference between a Coyote story told within a myth, during a chant, or to someone's family. To the first question, he replied that conversations about Coyote would not use the "ancient" words one would associate with the tales; clearly then subject matter is not the distinguishing factor. To the second, he replied that Coyote stories would be told about the same way under all circumstances, but that one might detect differing kinds of audience reaction. On these and other topics it became increasingly clear to me that Yellowman sees the Coyote stories not as narratives (in our sense of the term) but as dramatic presentations performed within certain cultural contexts for moral and philosophical reasons.[40] He thus does not place the materials in a separate category excepting only with respect to the way they are performed; that is, his central consideration is not one of structure/genre but of texture/mode, not because he is unaware of genre (for he distinguishes clearly among song, ceremonial chant, story, and oratory), but because in the case of the Coyote materials generic distinctions are far less relevant than are those textural keys which allow the listeners to gain access to the important levels of meaning.

Following Yellowman's lead here, let us take a closer look at some of the more easily discernible textural elements in the tale presented above. Probably most noticeable are the various recitational devices suggested by my descriptive comments in parentheses. These include a dramatic intonation assumed by the narrator as he takes the parts of central characters; a kind of special nasalized delivery of all vowel sounds throughout the story (this may be a part of the "archaism" effect); a variation in phrasing, in which the opening and closing of the story are delivered quite slowly, while the climax is in a passage of rapid delivery; the use of appropriate gestures, facial expressions, and body positions in taking the parts of various central characters; and, very importantly, a kind of contractual interaction developed by the narrator with his audience which tends to direct these other aspects of recitation and which seems based in their mutual recognition of the story type, its central characters and their importance in the Navaho world view, and their expectation that this particular performance will cause important ideas to come alive in exciting ways.

Another aspect of texture is, of course, language, and, in this department, without recourse to the special print necessary to make clear the fine shades of oral Navaho, we are limited to a few broad comments. Of basic importance to our understanding of the effect of the Coyote materials on a native audience is the observation that Navaho has no indirect discourse, and it has nothing quite like our infinitive. Thus, one does not say, "He said that he would come"; rather, one says, " 'I will come,' he said." Similarly, if one is asking another whether he needs help, one does not say, "Do you want me to help you?" Instead, one says, " 'Help me,' is that what you mean to say?" In other words, one must think of how the other person would phrase it, then say it that way and add *ninizinya?*—which is often translated "you want it?" but really means something more like "Is that what you have in mind?" This is a linguistic feature, not an artistic device. Nonetheless, in dialogue where there are questions being asked, or where information is imparted, especially in scenes where Coyote is trying to trick or take advantage of someone else, this formation, in company with the audience's appreciation and perception of the dramatic context, produces humorous irony.

I have already mentioned the intentional use of language patterns for their pleasantly archaic effects on the story, and they need not be treated again here. There is, between these two areas, another interesting facet of artistic manipulation of a native linguistic feature: in the text above, in three scenes there is an unusual overabundance of the nasal *ąą* in the words chosen by the narrator.[41] This is a sound which occurs naturally in a number of Navaho words, and one which I have heard used widely in informal conversation by itself as an equivalent to the word for "yes": *Aoo'*. Often it is used, in my experience, while someone else is talking, by way of assent, or in order to show that one is listening and following—much as one uses *mhm* in informal English. Its implication, when used alone, is "That's correct," or "I agree," or "Yes, I understand." In the Coyote tales of Yellowman, there is a heavy use of words containing this sound in passages where Coyote is illustrating (by observance or nonobservance) some Navaho tabu, in passages where truth is being discussed, and in passages which seem to contain some key action in the development of the story line. There may be other appearances of this device, but I have not been able to catalog them clearly, mainly because the sound itself is fairly well distributed throughout all texts I have collected; yet suddenly one hears perhaps a whole sentence, or as many as three or four sentences, which feature this vowel sound almost to the total exclusion of others. In the tale above, the first such scene is the one in which the small animals are trying to determine the truth of Skunk's report of Ma'i's death; the second instance is the scene in which Skunk hides under a rock, and we know he will be the first to claim the roasted prairie dogs (this would be the climax of the surface story and will be discussed below); the third use of nasal *ąą* comes in strongly as Ma'i begins to exhume the skinny prairie dogs and moves into position for his "come-uppance." The impact of such passages is at least threefold: first, on the story (structural) level we have a morpheme used as part of a word which communicates a particular meaning, with its normal range of denotation and connotation; secondly, we have on the "moral" (textural) level a morpheme used to suggest certainty, reliability, "truth" within the local context; thirdly, we have a complicated set of reactions based on the combination of the other two levels, for while we get a subliminal chant that implies "Yes, there it is, now we know, this is what they say," we are perceiving simultaneously the irony of the situation— which in nearly every case is based on our recognition that things are not as the story characters see them: Coyote is not dead, a race is not really in progress (and betrayal is at hand), and the gluttonous Coyote gets finally four skinny and sandy prairie dogs. There is, in short, a simultaneous assignment of two different phonemes by use of the same morpheme; because it is done consciously and in particular story contexts, because it is done with the same intent each time (insofar as one can determine such things), and because the effects are quite appropriate to the dramatic context, it is difficult to believe that it happens by accident. The morpheme, nasal *ąą*, would seem to constitute a usable, understandable textural formula which establishes a bridge between story and meaning by helping to create irony.

Another great body of textural reference lies in the area of traditional and cultural association, that is, in those words, colors, sequences, and actions which inevitably bring about reactions based on cultural values, mores, custom, and so on. The sequence of fours, as noted above, is—for a Navaho audience—loaded with traditional associations. Not only does a Navaho audience see in the sequence an automatic progression ending on something important at the fourth step, but the ritualism of four-ness in so many other areas of Navaho life now carries over to suggest an almost ceremonial significance for the actions of the characters in the tales. More subtle, for the outsider at any rate, is the high incidence of broken customs, or traditions ignored and transgressed. Admission of hunger or tiredness is considered an extreme weakness and is subject to laughter;[42] begging help from someone of lesser talents (as Coyote does in the above tale) is idiotic and is subject to ridicule; begging for food is contemptible and brings laughter; any kind of extreme, overinquisitiveness, obtrusiveness, intrusiveness, gluttony, and the like, is considered the sort of weakness which must be cured by ceremony and is often in the meantime subject to laughter, especially when it has been carried out by someone who should know better; betrayal is wrong, and anyone who practices it is asking for betrayal in return, which, if portrayed as a come-uppance in kind, is considered funny; in addition, any trick is thought to be funny in itself, no matter by whom or on whom it is played.

If we consider even these few textural possibilities and their presumable impacts on a traditional Navaho audience, and if we play them off against what we see happening on the structural (plot) level, we will find that the structure has acted simply as the vehicle. The structural climax, that point at which we can see the outcome of the story line—that is, when Skunk hides and then doubles back to get the prairie dogs—brings an appreciative look to the faces of the audience, but their heavy laughter begins when Ma'i goes racing by with his self-confident torch blazing. And the heaviest laughter of all comes when Ma'i throws himself down, exhausted, and reveals his weariness by saying, "Whew!!" It is not enough to point out that because the audience has heard the story so many times before they already know the outcome; after all, the "Whew!!" has been heard many times before as well. The audience's attention throughout has been on Ma'i, his actions, and his reasons for those actions, that is to say, on culturally moral subjects which have little to do with "how the story comes out." To put it another way, the attention is chiefly on texture, and the textural climax comes when Ma'i, in a strong symbolic tableau of all weaknesses and excesses brought out in the narrative, provides a "releaser" for all the laughter that has been built up through the story. What might seem to us a frivolous action not directly related to plot development turns out to be, for the native audience, symbolic of the central concern of the story.

What remains, then, is to posit some relationship between humor, as we have seen it operate above, and "meaning" in the Coyote materials. W. W. Hill suggested that Navaho humor was used in religious contexts in a secondary way, to prevent a "lag in interest," but that in "lay stories" humor was centrally present for the sake of amusement. Thus, for Hill, humor in Navaho ceremony was a digression, even though he did note that humorous episodes are often integral parts of ritual acts and in spite of the fact that one informant pointed out to him that "It was not done just because of the fun; it was a part of the ceremony."[43] Hill did, however, recognize something of extreme importance in the social function of Navaho humor: "The difference between ourselves and the Navaho is that in their society institutionalized humor is not a vestigial survival but a functioning organ. Among them humor forms a recognized important adjunct of most formalized social exchange and religious performance."[44] It is unfortunate, it seems to me, that Hill did not follow the ramifications of this idea further, for, if humor can be so much a part of religious exercises, it does seem hasty to class all things centrally humorous as "lay" or "secular." It would be illogical to assume that all humor among the Navaho is religious, of course, but we do need to be ready for classifications other than our own.

In the tale above, and in all other Coyote tales I have heard, one is struck by the presence both of humor and of those cultural references against which the morality of Coyote's actions may be judged. We may certainly agree with Hill that the humor does prevent a lag in interest, but far beyond that it functions as a way of directing the responses of the audience vis à vis significant moral factors. Causing children to laugh at an action because it is thought to be weak, stupid, or excessive is to order their moral assessment of it without recourse to open explanation or didacticism. What Hennigh says about moral reactions to Eskimo incest tales is exactly applicable here: to enjoy moral defections in a tale, "a listener must be given the opportunity to tell himself, 'I wouldn't do a thing like that.' Thus assured, he can enjoy both the vicarious pleasure of witnessing a tabu being broken and the direct pleasure of moral superiority."[45] Why, though, would one want to feel superior to one of his own deities? What is there about Coyote in particular that he can be both the powerful force he is and the butt of humor in these tales?

First of all, the Navaho did not invent Coyote, as we all know; he is a common character in the tales of many American Indian tribes. Also, as Paul Radin and others have shown, there is something psychologically compelling about trickster figures that seems to work beyond the local plot structure of any particular trickster story. These matters have been dealt with amply by others, and I do not propose to open up these topics again here. The real question is that of how the Coyote stories function within the Navaho view of things in addition to, or in spite of, the universal traits treated by comparatists.

It is important to know that the central Navaho religious ideas are concerned with health and order; very likely, to the Navaho mind, these two concepts are in fact inseparable. Moreover, the kind of order conceived of is one primarily of ritual order, that is, order imposed by human religious action, and, for the Navaho, this is largely a matter of creating and maintaining health. Health, on its part, is seen as stretching far beyond the individual: it concerns his whole people as well as himself, and it is based in large part on a reciprocal relationship with the world of nature, mediated through ritual.[46] The world is seen as an essentially disordered place, which may bring to man at any time bad dreams, encounters with unhealthy animals and situations (lightning, ants), and all sorts of unnamed hazards. Man himself may run afoul of nature by not being under control; that is, his own natural desires, if allowed full rein, can cause disease (the best example, of course, is excess of any sort). In fact, one common way of envisioning evil among the Navaho is to describe it as the absence of order, or as something which is ritually not under control.[47] Man, in other words, uses his rituals to establish an island (the Navaho might call it a "world") of stability and health in what is essentially—to his view—an unpredictable universe. Man's ability to survive culturally is related directly to his ability to impose the resources of his mind, ritually directed, on an otherwise chaotic scene. Nature, of course, is distracting, and in its way fights against regularization. In the myths and stories one finds continual evidence that the concepts of order are continually being challenged (and thereby authenticated in importance) by exponents of that Nature which exists outside man. Hill, for example, quoting Matthews's earlier account, discusses the clown's antics during the Night Chant: "Thus with acts of buffoonery does he endeavor to relieve the tedium of the monotonous performance of the night. . . . His exits and entrances are often erratic."[48] What he does not mention (and appears not to have known) is that the Night Chant uses what we might call monotony to establish order, and full attention to the entire proceedings is of considerable importance; as with the other rituals, the efficacy of the ceremony is seen as lying in direct proportion to the attention of the participants (which include even the onlookers). Missing a part brings about weakness in the whole. As Reichard points out of the Night Chant, even within the myth itself inattention to ritual details is dramatically denounced.[49] The clown, then, as far as the serious participant is concerned, does not play the part of a comic reliever but acts as a test, a challenge to order.

I think the position of Coyote in the tales I have been discussing here is roughly analogous to this kind of challenge. If Coyote really were, as Reichard suggests, the exponent of irresponsibility, lust, and lack of control, his continued central role in moral stories would be puzzling, except, as noted above, for purposes of establishing a sense of moral superiority. But certainly one could feel even more easily superior to a nondeity if that were all there is to the matter. And why would a deity be, as Reichard describes him, "sneaking, skulking, shrewd, tricky, mischievous, provoking, exasperating, contrary, undependable, amusing, cowardly, obstinate, disloyal, dishonest, lascivious, sacrilegious," to quote a few of the traits attributed to him?[50] Indeed, Coyote seems almost the demonic opposite of a white Boy Scout (or of a white God, for that matter).

For whatever it is worth, Yellowman sees Coyote as an important entity in his religious views precisely because he is not ordered. He, unlike all others, experiences everything; he is, in brief, the exponent of all possibilities. Putting this together with Yellowman's comments, mentioned above, that Coyote makes it possible for things to happen (or for man to envision the possibility of certain things occurring), it seems to me that Coyote functions in the oral literature as a symbol of that chaotic Everything within which man's rituals have created an order for survival. Man limits (sometimes severely) his own participation in everything but remains responsive to the exercise of moral judgment on all things. Man, in ordering his life, thus uses certain devices to help conceive of order—in this case stories which dramatize the absence of it. The Coyote materials, then, may be seen as ways of conceptualizing, of forming models of those abstracts which are at the heart of Navaho religion.

It is not off the subject, I hope, to mention that when I lived with Yellowman's family in Montezuma Canyon, I once came down with what appears to have been pneumonia and was diagnosed by a Navaho practitioner as one in need of the Red Ant ceremony. A medicine man (in Navaho, literally, a "singer") was sent for who knew the ceremony, and I was later advised I was being treated for red ants in my system, which I had no doubt picked up by urinating on an ant hill. Some time after the ritual, which was quite successful I must point out, I had occasion to discuss the treatment with the singer: had I really had ants in my system did he think? His answer was a hesitant, "no, not ants, but Ants" (my capitalization, to indicate the gist of his remark). Finally, he said, "We have to have a way of thinking strongly about disease." I now take this to be a ritual counterpart of the functions I have described above in the Coyote materials. As ways of thinking and ordering they seem consciously symbolic (but not the less "real" to the users) and much more akin to what I would call artistic modes of thought than they are to anything we can classify by our normal concepts of genre. At least they are not the simple tales of amusement that so many have taken them for in the past. It would seem difficult indeed to remove them from the total context of Navaho religious thought.

Notes

This essay incorporates parts of a paper presented at the 1967 annual meeting of the American Folklore Society at Toronto. Travel grants to support recording and further study have been generously provided by the Department of English and by the Office of Scientific and Scholarly Research of the University of Oregon. For supplying first aid to the author's failing Navaho language and for providing excellent comments on the nature of this investigation, a recognition of indebtedness is due Annie Yellowman and Helen Yellowman Yazzie, daughters of the informant, and the Reverend H. Baxter Liebler, long-time Episcopal missionary to the Navaho.

1. By way of only a few examples, see Gladys A. Reichard, *Navaho Religion* (New York: Pantheon, 1950), Concordance A; Leland C. Wyman, ed., *Beautyway: A Navaho Ceremonial* (New York: Pantheon, 1957), p. 131, and *The Red Antway of the Navaho*, Navaho Religion Series, no. 5 (Santa Fe: Museum of Navaho Ceremonial Art, 1965); David P. McAllester, ed., *The Myth and the Prayers of the Great Star Chant, and the Myth of the Coyote Chant*, Navaho Religion Series, no. 4 (Santa Fe: Museum of Navaho Ceremonial Art, 1956), pp. 91–105; Father Berard Haile, O.F.M., and Mary C. Wheelwright, eds., *Emergence Myth*, Navaho Religion Series, no. 3 (Santa Fe: Museum of Navajo Ceremonial Art, 1959), p. 130.

2. See note 7, below, concerning Sapir's text of the tale used in this study.

3. Perhaps it is well to explain that this adoption featured none of the Hollywood elements which might be imagined by the reader unfamiliar with the Navaho. Tsinaabąąs Yazhi simply announced at an evening meal that he was going to be my father and that henceforth I was to be known to others as Tsinaabąąs Yazhi Biye' (Little Wagon's Son). After that point my address to him was *shizhe'e* ("my father") instead of the joking *chichei* ("my grandfather"); my form of address to his daughter, therefore, became *shaadi* ("my older sister") and to her husband, Yellowman, *shiɫna'ash* [the ɫ here is pronounced like the Welsh *ll*; that is, a voiceless lateral fricative] ("my kinsman," "my cousin").

4. His comments have been augmented by those of his daughters, one of whom supplied me the title of this paper during a session in which Yellowman attempted to explain his choice of vocabulary in the Coyote tales. I was having difficulty with a certain phrase, when Helen Yellowman interjected in English, "He just means he uses those pretty languages."

5. Melville Jacobs made this observation in his extremely valuable study *The Content and Style of an Oral Literature: Clackamas Chinook Myths and Tales* (New York: Wenner-Gren Foundation for Anthropological Research, 1959), p. 128; but even Jacobs's title betrays the fact that our culture makes a distinction between sacred and secular which is not so clearly marked in most Indian tribes (and particularly the Navaho).

6. David F. Aberle, *The Peyote Religion among the Navaho* (Chicago: Aldine, 1966), p. 103 n. Aberle notes that some people did respond to only one question, which may mean the custom is breaking down. It is difficult to determine, however, how even the occasional recourse to this custom may affect data drawn from questionnaires as they are subjected to statistical analysis.

7. Elsie Clews Parsons presented a text of this story with the title "Coyote Plays Dead," in "Navaho Folk Tales," *Journal of American Folklore* 36 (1923): 371–372, and related it to a Pueblo tale of suspected Spanish origin which appeared in her earlier article, "Pueblo-Indian Folk-Tales, Probably of Spanish Provenience," *Journal of American Folklore* 31 (1918): 229–230. A

very awkward native text is given in Edward Sapir and Harry Hoijer, eds., *Navaho Texts* (Iowa City: University of Iowa, 1942), pp. 20–25; entitled "Coyote Makes Rain," it employs the self-conscious *zhini* ("they say") thirty-nine times in what appears to me a much collapsed form of the story.

8. The Navaho wording here is complex and refers to this story as one of a series of repeated actions. The closest English equivalent I can think of would be "in one of the episodes," but I have avoided that translation because it implies something more objectively literary than does the original. The point, however, is more than linguistic: Yellowman here limits himself to one incident in Coyote's career but opens the narration in such a way as to remind his listeners of the whole fabric of Coyote legend. Compare the presumable effect of this on native listeners with that of Sapir's text, mentioned above (note 7), where the narrator is telling a tale to an outsider in which the first phrase translates, "Long ago Coyote was trotting along, they say."

9. *Yellowman*: Ma'i does not want to alert the prairie dogs, but in order to get the desired results he must speak these wishes aloud. Therefore he phrases them as if he were seeking only personal respite from the heat.

10. The word *Yellowman* uses here would normally be translated "palms"; it is one of several indications throughout the Coyote canon (and supported by Yellowman in conversation) that Coyote is not always envisioned as a coyote.

11. *Golizhi*, lit., "one whose urine stinks."

12. I retain this term for lack of a proper English equivalent and because it is distinctive to the speech of Coyote. Meaning literally "My maternal male cousin on uncle's side," it is used familiarly among male friends in the figurative sense of "cousin," or even something like the English "old buddy." Essentially it is a term of trust as well as of friendship or relation. Coyote uses the term constantly, especially when he is trying to put something over on someone else; thus its appearance usually creates a sense of irony, and its retention here may help signal its literary function for the English reader. As noted above (note 3), the ł is pronounced as a voiceless lateral fricative.

13. Four is the number in Navaho narrative, custom, and ritual that corresponds to three in European-American folklore. Usually the fourth position "carries the weight," and normally the narrator works up to the fourth, utilizing (as we do in "Cinderella" or "The Three Pigs") the audience's recognition of the sequence to build tension. Here, however, Yellowman condenses the sequence with this descriptive comment. It seems to me that a possible aesthetic explanation for it might be that the humor (as the laughter suggests) has been chiefly connected to the first position; the rest, being important but anticlimactic, is wisely telescoped. I neglected to consult Yellowman on the matter, however.

14. Literally, "slender grass," a certain variety of desert grass, the heads of which look like small, twisted green worms. I have not been able to find a botanical name for it.

15. The phrase uses *hatał* (voiceless lateral fricative ł), "sing"—which

usually implies a ceremony connected with healing or purifying.

16. In this discussion of "what is true" there is a predominance of the vowel sound *ąą*, with and without nasalization. The textural ramifications of this feature will be discussed below. See also notes 21 and 23 for similar passages.

17. *Annie Yellowman*: "It's a special kind of bird."

18. Literally, "urine."

19. *Annie Yellowman*: Now he can have revenge because their previous insults have been made even more serious by this false claim that he is dead.

20. As usual, Ma'i cons someone else into doing the work.

21. Heavy use of *ąą* throughout the description of Skunk hiding and Ma'i running past; see also notes 16 and 23.

22. *Yellowman*: He ties the burning stick to his tail in order to show off how fast he can run. (Readers familiar with Navaho lore will recognize in this scene an important motif in the story of Coyote's theft of fire.)

23. There is heavy use of *ąą* in the exhumation scene; see notes 16 and 21.

24. Probably to avoid being burned; Ma'i avoids discomfort.

25. This is humorous in part because he has already covered the ground with his own footprints, the mark of a poor hunter, and thus subject to ridicule.

26. Emphatic: *dóóda héé!*

27. This is Yellowman's favorite ending-formula. In my references to the narrator's change of tones and styles I have included only those variations of importance to the present study. The reader will note that most of the highly nasalized passages occur in the speech of characters; it can be assumed here that passages which are not marked were delivered in a regular narrative tone, which for Yellowman's rendition of the Coyote stories is slightly more nasalized than normal conversation and somewhat more slowly delivered.

28. This is not a new idea, of course. Hennigh puts it in a succinct cross-cultural context which nicely demonstrates the central point. See Lawrence Hennigh, "Control of Incest in Eskimo Folktales," *Journal of American Folklore* 74, no. 312 (1966): 356–369.

29. Father Liebler, called "priest with long hair" by the Navaho, is founder, builder, and former vicar of St. Christopher's Mission to the Navaho at Bluff, Utah. Now in "retirement," he and a small group of faithful retainers built the Hat Rock Valley Retreat Center, near Oljeto. His familiarity with Navaho language and culture is long-standing; see his "Christian Concepts and Navaho Words," *Utah Humanities Review* 13 (Winter 1959): 169–175, and "The Social and Cultural Patterns of the Navaho Indians," *Utah Historical Quarterly* 30 (Fall 1962): 299–325.

30. Reichard (*Navaho Religion*, p. 267) points out that such language may not actually be archaic; its special usage sets it apart, and its users might attribute its effects to archaism, but it is still in wide use and is understood by all native speakers, including children.

31. This is a literal translation of the idiom; it may also mean "They make things simple, or easy to understand."

32. Reichard (*Navaho Religion*, pp. 147 ff.) has a good discussion of Navaho symbolism. My own acquaintance with the symbols themselves, especially in relation to particular rituals, is spotty enough to prevent a full evaluation of Reichard's comments, but I can say that her willingness to allow for conscious art seems quite sensible; see especially her discussion of the Navaho awareness of word as symbol (p. 267).

33. Clyde Kluckhohn and Dorothea Leighton, *The Navaho*, rev. ed. (Cambridge, Mass.: Harvard University Press, 1962), p. 194.

34. W. W. Hill, *Navaho Humor*, General Series in Anthropology, no. 9 (Menasha, Wis.: Banta, 1943), p. 19.

35. Alan Dundes, "Texture, Text, and Context," *Southern Folklore Quarterly* 28, no. 4 (December 1964): 251–265.

36. By structure I mean the formal framework, the lineal or organized form of a traditional text. In narrative, it is that particular sequence of events that makes up the story line and plot; structure, then, is the rational design of the story. Although in actual artistic practice texture and structure are tightly interrelated, one can separate for purposes of discussion what is being said from how it is being said. It is usually on the basis of structure that definitions of genre are founded in literature.

37. Dundes, "Texture, Text, and Context," p. 254.

38. René Wellek and Austin Warren, *Theory of Literature*, pp. 235, 241, for example.

39. Northrop Frye, *Anatomy of Criticism: Four Essays*, pp. 246–248.

40. Jacobs has suggested (*The Content and Style*, pp. 211 ff.) that our conceptions of drama much more closely match the characteristics of folk "stories," for in most cases (at least in most Indian materials) a tale is not told in its entirety; rather, certain key features and actions are described in such a way as to cause the audience to envision a drama in progress. The audience creates a mental stage upon which characters manipulated by the narrator play their scenes. I suspect that this may be true of all oral "narrative," including such things as the ballads and tales of our own culture, and that our penchant for applying generic terms based on visible form to oral materials has led us constantly away from the essence we seek.

41. See notes 16, 21, and 23, above.

42. See Reichard, *Navaho Religion*, p. 90.

43. Hill, *Navaho Humor*, p. 23.

44. Ibid., p. 21.

45. Hennigh, "Control of Incest," p. 368.

46. On order and Navaho ritual, see Reichard, *Navaho Religion*, pp. 183, 80–81. In the remainder of this discussion it is important to keep in mind that culturally the Navaho consider themselves nomadic, that their whole view of

life seems based on a sense of where they stand in relation to a changing land-scape. As Hoijer has pointed out, this characteristic is reflected deeply by the Navaho language, which defines position by withdrawal of motion and which often uses substantives that are actually descriptions of movements: *hanibąąz*, lit., "a hooplike object has rolled out," means "full moon." See Harry Hoijer, "Cultural Implications of Some Navaho Linguistic Categories," in *Language in Culture and Society*, ed. Dell Hymes (New York: Harper and Row, 1964), pp. 142–148.

47. Reichard, *Navaho Religion*, p. 5.
48. Hill, *Navaho Humor*, p. 23.
49. Reichard, *Navaho Religion*, p. 119.
50. Ibid., pp. 422–426.

9. Japanese Professional Storytellers

V. HRDLIČKOVÁ

The complex investigation of oral literature should consider, in addition to the verbal components, also oral realization, that is, the recitation milieu and the audience reactions. Only in such a way is it possible to comprehend the real aesthetic value of this art. This approach is particularly valid in connection with an attempt to characterize various storytelling genres and to grasp the storytellers' own notions of their artistic problems. On the basis of experience gained in a study of professional storytelling in China and Japan, I have reached the conclusion that the idea of a story in isolation from its actual narration has been, for too long, a conception of scholars, one not shared by the storytellers themselves. For them it is often more important *how* a story is told than *what* the story relates. Chinese storytellers have always stressed that a good storyteller can turn a bad story into a great one and that, on the contrary, an inexperienced artist can "kill a good story."[1]

In Tokyo I showed the storyteller Yanagiya Sansuke the printed edition of a collection of humorous tales still told on the stage. He said at once that the book was not intended for the storyteller but mainly for the reader, because storytellers learn a narrative not by reading but by listening as their masters relate it to them orally.

Another storyteller, Hayashiya Shozo, was clearly surprised when I asked him whether an apprentice could learn a story from a written text. He replied simply, but pointedly, "A book—that's only words! A storyteller must know how to tell the story, when he is to make a certain gesture, in which direction he is to turn his head, how to hold the fan. And that is what is most important in the storytelling!"

Chinese and Japanese materials are especially instructive for the understanding of certain aspects of oral literature, for here it is a

NOTE. Reprinted from *Genre* 2, no. 3 (September 1969): 179–210, by permission of the University of Illinois Press.

matter of professional storytellers who have spent many years in their youth with a master storyteller and have acquired, by imitation and repetition, an integrated system of creative procedures and artistic conventions. At the same time these materials form a complex of features characterizing the various storytelling genres.[2] Storytellers regard the mastery of these elements as a necessary stage preliminary to any successful practicing of their art in public, for the audience not only expects of them an established manner of interpretation, but also rates them according to the degree of mastery the artists command. For this reason, storytellers do not attempt to exhibit their individuality by overthrowing these principles but by gradual introduction of innovations, based on a command of the professional technique and minute oversteppings of the traditional framework. A careful observation of storytellers practicing their craft may enable us also to discover the rules pertaining to storytelling techniques; they form a fixed and even schematic system, providing no scope for creative originality. In reality, this traditional framework is subject to constant modifications of either a temporary or permanent character. These changes are often limited to details. Yet in the storytelling art it is just these details that make an enormous difference, for the storyteller who presents several roles at the same time, without costume or stage setting, must be able to hold the attention of the listeners by utterly simple, but carefully elaborated, means.

Although professional instruction has its strict principles, there is no hard-and-fast division between the individual storytelling genres one has trained for and what one performs. In the course of their artistic careers, storytellers may, indeed, switch from one genre to another and introduce into the second elements of the art acquired in the first.[3]

In Japan in the history of the development of the storytelling art, two main genres have become established: the narration of long tales, with serious, mostly historical themes (*kodan*)[4] and the relating of short humorous episodes (*rakugo*).[5] The *kodan* and *rakugo* link up historically with the oldest Japanese storytelling traditions. The beginnings of *kodan* go back to the early years of the eighteenth century. This phase was preceded by a period of gradual development and crystallization of the art. Both the *kodan* and the *rakugo* have a rich store of traditional tales, which are still recited today. Besides, new stories arise. The *kodan* was originally the "explanation" of a written text. Therefore these storytellers have a little table in front of them, on which at one time the text was laid. To this day apprentices are given texts to copy by the masters; these they write on sheets of stiff white paper. Master Teijo told me that when he was young he had to copy as many as would make a pile his own height.

The differences between *rakugo* and *kodan* relate not only to content and form, but also to the manner of oral realization. In my essay, I shall direct special attention, within the framework of the general description of the artist's presentation, to those which are the most important from the point of view of genre characteristics.

The traditional setting in which professionally trained storytellers practice their art are the storytelling theaters in Tokyo. In addition, storytellers appear on television and radio programs and occasionally in various places of light entertainment, including night clubs.

Rakugo has undergone considerable development in recent years. The two societies in which the *rakugokas* are associated now number 227 members. More pupils apply for training than the masters are willing to accept. *Kodan*, on the other hand, is struggling to maintain a bare existence. In Tokyo, twenty-two masters[6] of *kodan* are active and have only a few pupils.

Rakugo

The short comic *rakugo* is the backbone of the program of the *yose* theaters, variety halls, of which Tokyo at present has eight.[7] Among the most frequented is the Suzumoto *yose* in the Ueno district, Tokyo's principal shopping and entertainment center. This theater is an interesting combination of modern and traditional elements, as is typical of many other domains of Japanese life. Suzumoto accommodates about three hundred spectators. On the first floor seats are provided. In the gallery, the audience sits in the Japanese manner on cushions thrown on a floor covered with straw mats—*tatami* (see plate 1). Green tea, served to the audience during the performance, was originally sold in tin kettles. Now theatergoers get it in papier-mâché cups from a slot-machine in the corridor. Besides an air-cooling system for the summer months and a microphone on the stage, a modern feature in these traditional centers of entertainment is a television monitor in the manager's office, which enables him to see all that is happening on the stage.

The theater is open all the year round, except for three days before the New Year. Afternoon performances begin at midday and end at 4:30 P.M. Evening sessions last from five o'clock to half-past nine. Besides storytellers, conjurors, jugglers, singers, and other entertainers appear in the *yose* theaters. The program is drawn up so as to leave the best storytellers until last. The theater usually fills up gradually; at midday the audience is still sparse, but by three or four o'clock the theater is usually full.

The stage (*koza*) has a board floor. Before the performance starts, and during the intervals, the stage is concealed by a curtain. The storytellers and other performers enter the stage from the left side, from the dressing room (*gakuya*). On the right-hand side of the stage is a stand (*makifuda*) on which are hung strips of paper inscribed with the names of the performers. An apprentice changes the strip of paper between the individual numbers to show the name, written in large letters in Chinese ink, of the next artist to appear. Also on the right-hand side of the stage are the musicians, behind a partition with an opening covered by a dense wooden lattice. They play on traditional Japanese instruments. In the middle of the stage is an adjustable microphone.

The Japanese storyteller comes onto the *koza* dressed in a *kimono*, girdled with a broad sash (*obi*). The *kimono* is sober in coloring, varying somewhat with the time of the year: in summer it is lighter; in winter, darker. The artist who has completed his storytelling apprenticeship and graduated to the rank of *futatsume* is entitled to wear a *montsuki* (see plate 15)—that is, a *kimono* embroidered with the family crest (*mon*). It is the custom, however, to don it only when the tale the artist tells is of persons of some dignity. If the characters of his tale are common folk—shop assistants, servants, tradesmen— the storyteller appears in a kimono without the family crest. Over the *kimono* he sometimes wears a three-quarter coat, *haori* (plate 20). The *haori* can be regarded as one of the storyteller's props. It adds dignity to the artist's appearance and helps cover up any physical shortcomings, such as too lean a figure, which is considered a deficiency in the Japanese world of the stage, where a robust manliness is the ideal. The storyteller Yanagiya Sansuke told me that he puts on the *haori* to cover up his leanness when he enters the stage, but as soon as he kneels he takes it off. Other storytellers remove the *haori* during the narration. The procedure is related to the content of the tale and its heroes. If the foolish Hachan, one of the typical *rakugo* characters, is talking, the narrator never takes off the *haori* because the flowing movements which accompany this act would not be in keeping with the rhythm of Hachan's often disconnected speech. He does remove it, on the other hand, when playing the role of Inkyo-san, a worthy gentleman in retirement, who is Hachan's willing counselor in matters of ethics and proper behavior. If the storyteller is describing a journey, he cannot take the coat off unless his hero enters a way-side tavern. Nor can he remove the coat when he describes the hero as suffering from the cold, even though the storyteller himself may be suffering from the heat.

The *haori* serves also as a means of communication with those backstage. If the storyteller is not certain whether the next artist has arrived, he takes off the *haori* at a suitable moment before the end of his narration and throws it behind him in the direction of the dressing room. If the apprentice does not pick it up, that means that the dressing room is still empty and the storyteller must prolong his recital until the apprentice, by carrying off the *haori* into the dressing room, gives the sign that the following artist has arrived.

On festive occasions, especially during the New Year season, storytellers wear a ceremonial dress—the *hakama* (plate 22). The only props of the storytellers are the folding fan (*sensu*) and the kerchief (*tenugui*) folded into a square. In professional jargon the fan is called *hakusen* ("ringworm") or *kaze* ("wind"). It is made of stiff white paper and comprised of sixteen to eighteen ribs. The kerchief is called *mandara*—a term taken over by the storytellers from Buddhism.[8]

Upon entering the stage, the storyteller carries the fan in his hand or slipped into his bosom, along with the kerchief. When he kneels, he lays the fan down beside him at his right side and the kerchief on his left side. Some artists, however, take out the kerchief in the course of the recital. The kerchief has a blue-and-white pattern, which, in certain cases, is related to a certain type of narration, so that experienced listeners can tell from it what story the artist intends to relate. Thus for *shibai-banashi* or dramatized narration, a genre related to *rakugo*, the characteristic pattern is the *yamamichi* (plate 21), "mountain path," a delicate white pattern on a blue ground. A white undulating stripe running over the whole kerchief indicates the windings of a mountain path. For *shibai-banashi* there is also a typical "bean pattern" (*mame shibori*)—blue dots on a white ground.

Fan and kerchief are, in Japan, articles of everyday use; in the storytellers' world, however, they are the sacred "tools of the trade" (*shobai no dogu*) and must not be desecrated by the artist using them on the stage as he would in real life—namely, to fan himself when hot or to wipe the perspiration from his brow. Storytellers strictly observe this rule, for professional etiquette regards any sign of personal indisposition, stage fright, or discomfort as a serious offence, as betraying a lack of discipline and so the mark of the storyteller's low artistic standard.

The props of fan and kerchief are employed by a good storyteller without the smallest affectation, as if they were an inseparable part of his body. Fan and kerchief serve in the course of the recital to represent various objects. Let me mention at least some of their uses.

The fan represents, above all, a sword (plate 4). The narrator either draws it from his side (plate 7) or holds it in front of him at arm's length, letting his glance glide over it as if measuring the length of a real sword, from hilt to tip (plates 8 and 9). The storyteller turns the fan into a spear by extending his left hand in front of him and pointing with his index finger at the audience (plate 12). The other end of the weapon is represented by extending his right hand, with the fan, behind him. The artist's glance must always be directed forward toward the tip of the spear.

When the fan is held in the storyteller's right hand, it stands for the three-stringed lute—*samisen*; when he puts it to his lips, it is the ancient pipe—*kiseru* (plate 6). The fan can also change into a pole for carrying a load over the shoulder (plate 10), and, should the storyteller wish to indicate that a second person carries the other end, he looks back over his shoulder when speaking to him.

The kerchief (*mandara*) can represent a book, when the narrator holds it in his left hand and points in it with two fingers of his right hand, or writing paper, on which he writes with the "brush"—the fan (plate 3), or maybe a wallet or a tobacco pouch.

Sanyutei Ensho stresses that everything the storyteller imitates with the fan and kerchief must acquire the essential features of the object in question.[9] The storytelling apprentice observes not only his master's procedure in pouring out the wine on the stage (plate 2), but also the action as performed in real life, so that it may impress itself on his visual memory. Master Ensho mentions the difficulties he had as a nonsmoker in performing the act of smoking on the stage. His master advised him to carry a pouch of tobacco with him in civil life and to smoke now and again. In a similar way Ensho learned to handle a real sword and spear, in order to gauge correctly the weight of these weapons when presenting them with a light fan on the stage.

The stage manner of the storytellers on the platform (*koza*) appears to be as natural and spontaneous as though the artist were telling a story to a circle of friends. The older and more experienced the storyteller is, the more accomplished his art would be in this respect. Regular frequenters of *yose* and lovers of *rakugo* can fully appreciate this art. However, not even the uninitiated spectator fails to note the difference between the less experienced artist and the master, although they differ from each other only in a few details. The apprentice's narration is lacking, as a rule, in plasticity, so that some of the audience chat among themselves and pay little attention to what is happening on the stage. The experienced artist draws the tale in relief, and his figures take shape before the eyes of the audience as creatures of flesh and blood.

The performance of a good *rakugoka* is a well-balanced whole, carefully composed of a multitude of seemingly insignificant details, used to achieve the storyteller's objective. The setting in which this drama of art, discipline, experience, and intuition is played out is very confined. The expressive means at the storyteller's disposal are equally limited. He must, therefore, make use of them with the greatest sensitivity. In Japan, as I have already noted, the storyteller must have several years of professional training before he can practice his craft in public. Training seeks to inculcate in the young novice humility and the consciousness of his personal insignificance and to teach him self-discipline. Then he can absorb unhindered not only the technique of his craft, but also the atmosphere. With these firm foundations, he may then work to develop his individuality and overstep the limits laid down by tradition.

Rakugo are short comic tales or episodes. Their recital lasts from ten to twenty minutes. It is a genre that has its roots in an urban environment, to which its whole character conforms. The audience, among which is a fair proportion of young people, changes every day, so that it is not possible or even advisable, from a business point of view, to present stories in serial form.

The *rakugo* has its traditional structure: introduction (*makura*), literally "the cushion on which the tale lays its head," then the tale itself, which leads to the conclusion, called *sage* or *ochi*. The tale consists almost exclusively of dialogue and only exceptionally does it contain a description in indirect speech, called *ji*.

The *koza*—the platform—is for the artist a hallowed place, the place where he practices his trade, whose honor he must never besmirch. The entry onto the stage, for that reason, is an important part of the performance. The storyteller steps onto the platform through a door connecting with the dressing room. His entry is accompanied by music on the drum and *samisen*. Upon passing through the doorway, he straightens himself up a little and takes several light steps in such a way that his soles "do not stick to the boards" (storytellers wear socks of thick white material without boots) but slip smoothly along.

On approaching the square cushion, the storyteller kneels on both knees and makes a deep bow. His face remains immobile, even when the audience welcomes the artist with clapping or shouts. The artist takes advantage of the moment when he straightens up after his bow, still kneeling, to arrange the fold of his *kimono* below his knees and to take a quick view of the audience. The narrator either introduces himself by name, or he greets the audience with *"konnichiwa"*—good day. He pronounces the first two or three sentences in an ordinary, rather quiet voice. It sometimes happens that they are half-drowned by the talk and shuffling of the audience. The storyteller's introductory words usually refer to the weather, topical events, traditional customs, and so on; for instance: "It is a hot day today! It is very nice of you to take the trouble to come and listen to my story. But, come to think of it, it's not so hot here as at home, where you have no air-conditioning installation as in the *yose*!"

Another storyteller may put his listeners in good humor with the words: "Dear listeners, you have heard, I am sure, about that lover of *rakugo* who became Prime Minister.[10] It is quite possible that you, too, will rise to an equally high position, if you listen attentively to my stories!"

Storyteller Sansuke has this well-tested introduction: "My name is Sansuke—as you see, it isn't worth much. Sansukeee, Sansukeeee—that's what they call every apprentice, so that it is no name of high esteem. But what can I do about it? I've tried to get rid of it several times already, but without success, so there's nothing for it but just to go on using it."

From the opening sentences the storyteller goes on to the *makura*—the introduction—which lasts about five minutes and serves as a transition to the recital of the actual tale. The storyteller still speaks for himself, in the first person, making relatively little use of dialogue form. His presentation continues, very natural and colloquial in tone.

The *makura* has usually some general connection with the tale. Thus, for instance, one of the Tokyo storytellers recites a modern *rakugo* about a visit to a physician and about the advantages and disadvantages of this profession, whereas in the *makura* reference is made to the storytelling profession:

"Who is a *zenza*," you ask? A *zenza* is a storytelling apprentice, the one who turns over the cushion on the stage. And if he learns very well and works very hard, he may reach the degree of *futat-sume*. Some apprentices, however, are such blockheads that you can make nothing of them. And then it is better if such a one gives up storytelling—and the sooner the better—and goes and does useful work, maybe in a factory. There, however, they ask him first of all what he can do in the way of practical work: "Ahem, hem," says he, "turn over the cushion, I could manage that!"

Where most storytellers come to grief is in establishing relations with the audience. In storytelling this is more difficult than in other trades, where the master can win the customer's patronage with a gift, but the storyteller must win the favor of audience by sheer hard work; here gifts do not help!

At this point the storyteller makes a transition to the description of the doctor's profession and so to the tale itself.

The fact that the plot of the *rakugo* unfolds in a miniature setting obliges the narrator to concentrate all his means on expressing what is essential for an understanding of the story and to not lose time with long-winded explanations. The majority of the *rakugo* characters are types, so that the listener recognizes from the first few words who is speaking, whether it is the slow-witted Hachan, the servant Consuke, the Miser, the young Master, or others.

The storyteller's presentation is basically influenced by the Japanese custom of kneeling on a cushion on the floor. The artist remains in this position throughout the whole recital, and this limits the use of broader gestures and movements for the purpose of dramatization. To kneel in such a way as to give a natural and disciplined impression, and so that the contours of the upper part of his body engrave themselves firmly in the listener's memory, requires no mean art. The storyteller's dramatic possibilities are limited to movements of the hands and trunk and to facial mimicry.

The *rakugoka* indicates dialogue by turning his head from right to left. The person of higher rank is always on the right (the stage term is *kami*—"above"), and the person of inferior rank on the left, (*shimo*—"below").

In presenting dialogue by turning his head from one side to the other, the artist must be able to insert a pause halfway between these movements—that is the moment when he looks directly in front of him and so also makes contact with the audience. This look is very important, as the old masters always emphasize.[11] The artist's eyes must be firmly fixed and not shift from point to point, which creates an impression of uncertainty. This firmly fixed gaze is particularly useful when the storyteller is for a moment at a loss how to proceed. As soon as his eyes begin to wander the audience realizes that he is in trouble. Sanyutei Ensho, now sixty-eight years of age, tells that formerly he never had any blind spots. Now, however, his memory occasionally fails him. Then automatically he looks ahead of him and behaves as if it were a normal pause in the narration.

The storyteller also looks straight in front of him when he passes from dialogue to a descriptive passage—*ji*. In *rakugo* this happens relatively rarely, for descriptions of nature and of people must evolve from the dialogue. *Ji* is thus always short and serves as a bridge-passage from one episode to the next, or as a way out of a difficult narrative situation.

The presentation of dialogue is held by storytellers to be the most difficult part of their craft. The narrator represents in it at least two persons of different, often diametrically opposite, character. Thus the storyteller, on turning to the right, must in his posture, facial mimicry, and tone of voice create the impression of an old man, mild and wise; but on turning to the left, he must make a quick transition to the role of an impetuous young man. A natural transition from one role to the other is acquired only by long practice. Young artists often make the mistake of overplaying their parts, so that their attention is often dissipated and the essence of the tale escapes them.

Each of the dramatis personae in the *rakugo* has his characteristic pose. When the storyteller represents a man of the common people, he has his hands laid flat on his knees, his shoulders drawn up, and his trunk slightly bent forward. A *samurai* (plate 14) holds himself erect, with elbows drawn away from his sides to add to his breadth and dignity, his left hand on his knee, his right resting on his "sword." A *ronin* (plate 15), an impoverished *samurai* without a lord, looks more modest, his shoulders in a normal position and both hands on his knees. A feudal lord—*tonosama* (plate 13)—leans his sword against his knee. A woman has sagging shoulders, elbows pressed close to her sides, the knees slightly shifted to one side and hands laid on them, one on the top of the other so as to make them appear smaller. The whole silhouette gives the impression of humility.

Narrators seek models for these poses in the Japanese classical theater (*kabuki*) and also in the art of the dance, which used to be an obligatory part of the storyteller's training. To this day there are storytellers who perform a short dance at the end of their recital.

Every artist has a predilection for a certain type, in the role of which he is most successful with the audience. This naturally affects his choice of repertoire. A change of voice and mode of expression supplements gesture and body pose in identifying the social position of the character. This is especially important in Japan, as the expressive means change according to the social group to which the persons belong. A correct use of language helps the storyteller to characterize more precisely the heroes of the tale.

Although *rakugo* tales are, with few exceptions, without verse interludes, still they must include rhythmic passages. And so storytellers sometimes introduce into their narrative a series of seven- and five-syllable sentences, in order to enliven the intonation of the recital. Formerly pupils learned to recite to the rhythm of fan taps.

The art of the pause is the commonest stumbling block for the inexperienced artist. The pupil imitates the master in every detail and also, of course, in the use of the pause. At first it does not seem to him to be very difficult to control. When, however, he appears before an audience, none of the pauses he has learned comes off properly. And so he must start practicing again. Only after some time does the test of experience gradually bring him back to what he learned from his master.

The pause does not mean merely silence; on the contrary, the flow of the tale must continue during that momentary break in verbal narration. The storyteller, according to need, fills it with a gesture or with a gaze fixed upon the audience, literally pinning them to their seats.

Masters encourage their pupils to learn to beat the drum. This, they say, is one of the ways of acquiring a sense of rhythm in recitation and a proper feeling for the pause.

Storytellers, like actors, must on occasion resort to "artistic lies," as they call them. Thus, when the hero has to say something to his partner that nobody else is intended to hear, he cannot whisper, because the audience would not know what was said. Nevertheless, he must evoke the impression that it is truly a secret that he is imparting. Therefore, the storyteller first looks round him and says in a low voice, "But this is a secret!" This suffices to create the right impression, and the narrator goes on to communicate his "secret" in a normal voice.

In order to impress certain procedures firmly in the minds of his audience, the narrator repeats the same gesture or grimace, whether it be the sagging of the shoulders beneath the "pole" when carrying a heavy burden or the making of a wry face when he bites into something hard. The imitation of eating and drinking, especially the appreciative smacking of lips in the drinking of *sake* (rice wine) and the sucking of noodles from "chop-sticks" (a fan raised high above the mouth) are favorite *rakugo* scenes.

Weeping, anger, and surprise are all aptly expressed by the storyteller and with great economy of means. Raised eyebrows, winking, ducking or bending of the head suffice to express a whole scale of emotions. If the storyteller is "weeping," for instance, he closes his eyes and on his face an expression appears as if tears were running down his cheeks.

Because the storyteller kneels on his cushion for the duration of the recital, he must indicate the passing from one place to another by a pendulous movement of his arms, as in walking. If the hero is riding on a lame horse, the storyteller leans over on one side and carries out jerky movements with his arms.

The most important part of every *rakugo* is the conclusion—*sage*.[12] Experts classify the tales according to which of the twelve established types of *sage* they belong. The narrator's art was evaluated, in the past, in the words: "He's a *rakugoka* with a perfect *sage*." When I asked Yanagiya Sansuke when he, as an artist, would wish most of all, he replied that it was his chief desire to tell stories with a good *sage* —intelligent and inventive. Unfortunately, the level of the present-day audience, mostly little acquainted with storytelling matters, obliges him to relate stories which do not lead to a really good conclusion.

In the opinion of Master Sanyutei Ensho,[13] few storytellers have a true mastery of the *sage*. Many give quite a good performance of "all that goes before," but they come to grief at the conclusion.

An ideal performance is one in which the storyteller carries the story fluently forward, with a smooth and natural transition to the conclusion. For the most part it is not possible to say exactly in what lies the perfection of the *sage* as presented by the great masters, but, perhaps, its most important features are the lightness of touch and the fluidity with which it is handled. It is important that the storyteller, when he reaches the conclusion, should not "funk" it—begin to postpone it with an inflation of words, which would disturb the rhythm of the tale. The *sage* is, to use Sanyutei Ensho's sporting terminology, the finishing tape of the story. As a certain distance in advance of it, the artist must put on his finishing spurt and burst it in with the full strength and with the grace and flourish of a true master.

Although in traditional tales the *sage* remains mostly unchanged, the artist finds here, too, enough room for modifications in keeping with his individuality. Sometimes he need do no more than omit a few words or shift the emphasis and the conclusion sounds different, often wittier than the presentation of another storyteller.

A good *sage* is a simple one. This, however, does not mean that it is not carefully thought out. It must follow naturally from the actions and behavior of the characters, in keeping with their dispositions. The *sage* should be part of the conversation of the dramatis personae, not the storyteller's own pronouncement. In the past, it is true, there existed a school where it was the custom to "announce" the *sage* with the phrase "and now comes the *sage*." This device, however, is no longer used by good storytellers.

It is important, too, that the audience should realize that the tale ends with the last words of the *sage* and react immediately with clapping or acclamation. If the reaction is delayed for any reason, it means catastrophic failure for the narrator. To give the *sage* this final note is not always easy. Sometimes when the storyteller is obliged to break off the tale at an unusual point and is not certain of the effectiveness of his conclusion, he may add, "And this then is the old joke you all know so well!"

Every storyteller has his *sage* technique well thought out. Thus some storytellers, such as Katsura Bunraku and Sanyutei Hyakusho, already make their bow when pronouncing the last words of the *sage*. Sanyutei Ensho, on the contrary, first finishes speaking and then an expression appears on his face as if he were surprised by his own joke and he laughs. Only then does he make his bow and walk off the stage. Hayashiya Shozo makes his final point, turns his eyes upward, and then bows to the audience.

Many listeners used to go to *yose* only to enjoy, with a connoisseur's appreciation, the *sage* of their favorite artists.

Kodan

Besides the short comic tales (*rakugo*) Tokyo storytellers also practice the narration of serial stories—*kodan*. These are performed in a small theater called Honmokutei, in the Ueno quarter, near the Suzumoto *yose*. Both exterior and interior of this theater are in tradi-

1. The *yose* audience

2. Pouring of the sake (rice wine)

3. Writing a letter

4. Drawing a sword

5. Filling a pipe

6. Smoking a pipe

7. Drawing a sword

8. Viewing a sword

9. Viewing a sword—the second phase. Notice the storyteller's glance reaching
the point of the sword.

10. Carrying a load on a pole

11. Carrying a load on the shoulders

12. Holding a spear

13. Feudal lord (*tonosama*)

14. A *samurai*

15. A *ronin*

16. The audience in a *koshakuba* during the performance of a *kodanshi*

17. Same as Plate 16

18. A *kodanshi*

19. A *kodanshi* performing in a *yose*. Reading a letter.

20. A *rakugoka* in a *haori*

21. Master Hayashiya Shozo performing *shibai-banashi*. Notice the kerchief with the *yamamichi* pattern around his neck.

22. A *rakugoka* in a *hakama*

23. *Kodanshi* at the low table—*shokudai*

24. A traditional poster at the entrance of the Honmokutei theater

tional style (plate 24). The performance takes place on the second floor. The hall accommodates at most 150 listeners. The floor is covered with straw mats. Every visitor must remove his shoes at the entrance. The theater is not called a *yose*, but a *koshakuba* or *kodanseki*. Regular performances begin at 12:30 and end at 4:30. In the evening the theater is hired out to storytellers, musicians, or other artists.

On the average thirty persons attend the afternoon performance, most of them older men dressed in working clothes. Many of them are obviously independent tradesmen who have taken time off from their workshops and have come to the theater (plates 16 and 17). Some of them bring a *bento*—a lunch box with cold rice and salted vegetables. At the entrance they buy a little pot of green tea, which they sip during the performance. Those who go to the *koshakuba* performances know each other by sight and exchange greetings. They also have their regular seats. During the performance many of the audience take a snooze (plate 17). They listen stretched out on the floor, for in the *koshakuba* it is not considered an offence against good manners. The atmosphere is more intimate than in the *yose* and the contact between the audience and the storyteller is closer. The smallness of the theater contributes to this relationship. Some listeners lean their elbows on the stage and others even place their lunch boxes upon it.

Listeners have their favorite storytellers. Upon their entry, those who have been dozing wake up and sit so that they can hear well. The "regulars" are, however, also strict critics, and, if they are not satisfied, they do not hesitate to shout out, "Couldn't you recite something that would not disturb us from the sleep?" The last storyteller on the program remains on the stage until all the guests have left, greeting acquaintances and exchanging a friendly word with them. The members of the audience express aloud their impressions of the performance and their views of the storytellers. If they are satisfied, they are not sparing in their praise. Ichiryusai Teiho[14] relates how, not long ago, one old man near the stage said admiringly, "Today it was really splendid!" and placed on the stage a five-hundred-yen banknote wrapped in a piece of newspaper. Another regular guest sends a packet of cheap cakes to the dressing room every day of the year.

In the course of an afternoon performance, three or four *kodanshi*

—*kodan* masters—take their turn. The program of the *koshakuba* is drawn up for a whole month, whereas in the *yose* the program changes every ten days.

The *kodan* is in many respects the opposite of the *rakugo*, in which it is important to be able to express briefly and wittily the substance of the plot and of human character. For the *kodan*, on the other hand, a certain long-windedness is typical. One story is narrated in a series of sessions lasting sometimes the whole month, each session occupying twenty to thirty minutes. What in ordinary conversation is expressed in a single sentence is described by the *kodanshi* in two or three. The language of the *kodan* is flowery and contains many archaic expressions. Some are no longer understood by the audience, but they sound pleasant to the ear and help to establish the atmosphere of the tale.

Another point of difference is that the *kodan* often consists more of descriptive passages than actual dialogue. Dialogue and female roles are held to be the most difficult part of the recital, as noted above in connection with *rakugo*. Thus the apprentices first learn to recite *ikusa no hanashi*—descriptions of battles and wars—in which no women's roles occur. After a year or so the young novitiate goes on to *bugei-mono*—tales about the deeds of famous warriors—in which women's roles and also dialogue begin to appear. It is not easy to give a proper impersonation of a female character in a *kodan*, for the storyteller must not slip into caricature, as he may appropriately do in *rakugo*. The highest grade of difficulty, in respect to technique, is represented by the *sewamono*—domestic dramas. These are tales of everyday life, usually told against a historical background, about loves and passions. As in *kabuki*, an insoluble conflict arises out of the clash between duty and human emotions. Dialogue occupies an important place here. Women also assume greater importance, and, sometimes, are even the principal characters of the tale. *Sewamono* require an experienced artist, and therefore the period of apprenticeship in *kodan* is long, lasting five or more years. This is undoubtedly one of the reasons why this craft has little attraction for young people.

Besides the classical *kodan*, storytellers try to win the favor of their audience by relating topical events (news *kodan*), by describing sporting events (sports *kodan*), or by inserting episodes from modern life into the tales with historical themes. Secondary episodes (*hikigoto*) are an important part of the storytelling technique of the *kodan*. Popular, too, are retellings of translated novels. Ichiryu Teijo, for instance, narrated the plot of *The Count of Monte Cristo* in forty-five installments. All the *kodan* tales have a strong moralizing, feudal coloring, and that is one reason they attract listeners who belong to the older generation.

The storytelling technique of the *kodan* is on a high level. The *kodanshi* have a deep sense of professional honor, although some of them are today no longer capable of earning a living by their trade and must have, in addition, some other source of income. During the recital the *kodanshi*, unlike the *rakugoka*, sits at a small table, *shokudai* (plate 23). In the Honmokutei theater, he speaks without a microphone. In addition to the fan, the *kodanshi* uses, as a second prop, *hariogi*—a bamboo stick wrapped in strong white paper.

The *kodanshi* enters the stage without any musical accompaniment. He kneels behind the table, strikes it simultaneously with fan and *hariogi*, and makes his bow. He pronounces a few introductory sentences of a general kind, but the tale does not have a *makura* introduction, as do *rakugo*. The storyteller takes up his tale from the place where he last left it off, only briefly summarizing what has gone before. The *kodanshi* makes fewer gestures than the *rakugoka*; his recital runs a slower course, some passages being less exciting in the stream of narration. The tapping on the table with the *hariogi* serves to awaken the attention of the listeners. This prop can "speak," and experienced listeners claim that from the first blow they can gauge the measure of the storyteller's art. An early nineteenth-century historical episode about the *kodan* confirms this claim. A storyteller by the name of Torintei Togyoku appeared in the town of Edo. At his first recital the well-known *kodanshi* Kinyosai Tenzan was among the audience. On hearing Togyoku's first tap on the table he said to his companion, "Let's go, I've heard enough. He's a great artist!" And outside he added, "Did you notice how with one blow he was able to attract the attention of the audience? Anyone who can do that is a true master!"[15]

The storyteller makes use of the *hariogi* also when he reaches a turning point in the plot or a point of transition from one milieu to another. Blows of the *hariogi* thus break up the narration into shorter sections. The storyteller also emphasizes the spoken word with a few lighter taps, as, for instance, in describing duels, quarrels, impending danger, and so on.

The fan, though an important prop in the *kodan*, is not used by the storyteller to indicate objects as often as it is in the *rakugo*. During the recital the fan lies on the table, from which the artist picks it up at the moment he needs it. Sometimes, if the hero is suffering from heat, he fans himself with it; at other times, as a sign of relief, he applies it, half spread out, to his forehead (plate 18). Sometimes he holds it closed in his hand, using it to point in front of him, in order to add emphasis to a gesture. In comparison with *rakugo*, the kerchief is little used as a prop in *kodan* recitals.

The *kodan* has no conclusion (*sage*), which would provide such a striking culmination to the story as in the *rakugo*. The *kodan*-stories usually have a happy end. The storyteller's aim is to ensure that the listeners go home satisfied and in good humor, especially if it is a matter of the last installment of a serial. This applies, too, to the teller of horror tales or ghost stories—*kaidan banashi*. In them the narrator adds a few tranquilizing words after the closing scene, or even a joking remark, so that the listener returning home in the dark may not have an unpleasant feeling of fear.

Each installment of the *kodan*, however, has its own conclusion; it is called *kireba*—literally, "end of the session." Before the *kireba*, the narrator must carry forward the plot of the related episode to its culmination—*yama* ("peak")—and finish off in such a way as to whet the appetite of the listener for the next installment.

Occasionally *kodanshi* also give performances in *yose* (plate 19). It is interesting to observe how they adapt their recital to the different environment. Thus the tale of the woodcarver, Hamano Noriyuki—a narration of the *iseki* (one-session) type—lasts thirty minutes in the *koshakuba*. The *kodanshi*, Ichiryu Teijo, cuts it by one half for the *yose* and adds an introduction (*makura*) so as to make it more comprehensible to the *yose* audiences. In this introduction, Teijo relates how one day the director of a lunatic asylum called him and asked him to give a recital for his patients, who, he said, suffered from boredom. Teijo accepted the offer and "this is the story I told those people. I hope that you, too, will enjoy it!"

The burlesque character of the introduction contrasts sharply with the moralizing tale propagating the thesis that strenuous work is always crowned with success. Without the *makura*, the *yose* audience would probably have difficulty digesting the story. Nevertheless I noticed that no sooner did the apprentice bring the little table of the *kodanshi* onto the stage than several spectators left the auditorium. They returned only when the *kodanshi* had finished his recital. The performance, though excellent in every way, received but scant applause.

In conclusion we can say that, in addition to a number of common features deriving from the character of the storyteller's art, there are typical differences between *rakugo* and *kodan* in terms of the oral realization. These differences, together with the common features, form a certain kinetic code without which neither the artist nor audience could properly comprehend the narration. This code is based on a system of artistic principles by which the storyteller is guided in his recital. The identification of these principles is one of the keys to the complete characterization of the two folklore genres. This is, however, no easy task, because the rules of how to tell a story in Japan, as also in China, are handed down orally within the profession and have never been systematically committed to writing. It is therefore necessary to follow carefully the storyteller's performance and also to interview the artists personally. More detailed information can be gained only by repeated questioning, for the storytellers consider many facts about their craft as something so much to be taken for granted that they never discuss them on their own initiative. Fortunately, the memoirs of famous storytellers have become very popular in Japan in recent years. These contain much interesting material that enables us, in combination with experience gained in the field, to penetrate more deeply into this hitherto little-known sphere of oral literature and to throw light upon a number of problems linked with the concept of what constitutes genres in folklore.

Notes

1. For similar experiences relating to Japanese storytellers, see Kata Koji, *Rakugo* (Tokyo: Shakai Shisosha, 1963), p. 112.

2. For a more detailed account, see V. Hrdličková, "Zenza, the Storyteller's

Apprentice," *Transactions of the International Conference of Orientalists in Japan* 13 (1968): 31–41.

3. Thus one of the present-day masters of the *kodan*, whose style is very melodical, was originally a singer of *naniwabushi*, that is, ballads sung to the accompaniment of the three-string lute. Another master of *kodan*, Tanabe Nankaku, was originally a teller of comic tales—*rakugo*—and his presentation contains humorous elements. See Ichiryusai Teiho, *Kodanshi tadaima nijuyonnin* [An introduction to twenty-four *kodan* masters] (Tokyo: Asahi Shimbunsha, 1968), p. 247. I have evidence of the same phenomenon in China.

4. The term is composed of two characters: *ko* ("explain"), *dan* ("talk").

5. The term is composed of two characters: *raku* ("to fall"), *go* ("word"). That means a story which has a point toward which it "falls."

6. In the year after publication of *An Introduction to Twenty-Four Kodan Masters* (see note 3), two of the masters died and so far no others have taken their place.

7. Besides the Tokyo theaters, there are two theaters of similar type in Osaka. In other parts of Japan, the public is acquainted with storytellers from television programs or from tours undertaken by the artists.

8. The Japanese rendering of the term *mandara* means "Buddha's picture" or the depicting of scenes from his life.

9. Sanyutei Ensho, *Yose sodachi* [I grew up in the *yose*] (Tokyo: Seiabo, 1965), p. 300.

10. This is a reference to the postwar prime minister, Yoshida Shigeru. According to my informant, Sakai Shomatsu, an usher in the Suzumoto *yose*, theatergoers include teachers and politicians, for whom the verbal art is important in their profession.

11. See, for example, Ensho, *Yose sodachi*, p. 304.

12. There are twelve types of *sage*. The commonest of them are *kangae-ochi*—the unexpected conclusion; *jiguchi-ochi*—the conclusion based on a play on words; *butsuke-ochi*—the conclusion based on misunderstanding.

13. Ensho, *Yose sodachi*, p. 307.

14. Teiho, *Kodanshi tadaima nijuyonnin*, p. 28.

15. See J. Barth, "Kodan und Rakugo," *Mitteilungen der Deutschen Gesellschaft für Natur- und Volkerkunde Ostasiens* (Tokyo) 22, part D (1928): 12. I noted the same experience in China.

Part Three

The Classification of Folklore Genres

10. The Complex Relations of Simple Forms

ROGER D. ABRAHAMS

Without accepting Northrop Frye's definition of *genre*, one can agree with his dictum on the use of generic criticism: "The purpose of criticism by genres is not so much to classify as to clarify . . . traditions and affinities, thereby bringing out a large number of literary relationships that would not be noticed as long as there were no context established for them."[1] Frye points to the operational basis of this critical approach when he notes that "generic criticism . . . is rhetorical, in the sense that the genre is determined by the conditions established between the poet and his public."[2] But genres are useful not only because they help us focus on the relationship between performer and audience but also because genres give names to traditional attitudes and traditional strategies which may be utilized by the performer in his attempt to communicate with and affect the audience.

Generic criticism is concerned with making a taxonomy of expressive habits and effects; it takes into consideration the content and structure of performances, in addition to the relationship of both creator and audience to the stylized item being performed. We point to genres because by naming certain patterns of expression we are able to talk about the traditional forms and the conventional contents of artistic representation, as well as the patterns of expectation which both the artist and audience carry into the aesthetic transaction. Because of this emphasis on the traditional (or expected) elements in works of art, generic criticism is one area in which the preoccupations of the literary and the folkloristic theorist converge.

But this emphasis on conventions and cues that allow the observer to recognize the forms being used is the very characteristic of genre criticism to which the literary critic often reacts negatively. To stress the conventions of a genre in *belles lettres* is to denigrate, to some de-

NOTE. Reprinted from *Genre* 2, no. 2 (June 1969): 104–128, by permission of the University of Illinois Press.

gree, the originality of the very art object which the critic is in the process of analyzing in terms of its uniqueness. Consequently, there has been little informed commentary concerning the generative literary understandings the author brings to the creative experience and the means by which he elicits the same series of expectations on the part of his reading audience.

The folklorist has no such problems, for he recognizes that he is dealing with conventional objects of art. He knows that if an item of oral literature does not provide very evident cues to this conventionality the traditional performer will be misunderstood by his audience. Just as the narrator or singer must enact an item that conforms to an immediately recognized and accepted type, he must also do so in a manner such that every part of the performance is consonant with the range of expectations of that genre. But he has available to him a range of what some might term clichés, which announce at the beginning and at crucial intervals what type of performance he is presenting. Thus perceptions of genre are of greatest importance in understanding the ceremonial communicative interactions of small groups.

An investigator of expressive culture finds use for generic criticism in two ways. The first of these, used most commonly by ethnographers (especially in recent work), is to investigate what generic typological distinctions are made by the participants in a specific culture.[3] Such analysis provides insights into the ways in which members of that group organize themselves for social and rhetorical purposes and how the social and aesthetic organizations reinforce each other. Such an approach focuses on generic classifications as used by the group as one aspect of their culture.

This approach is of limited use to the comparative folklorist, however, for he is primarily concerned with an analysis of items of traditional expression which appear in the repertoire of different groups. For generic criticism to be useful to him it is necessary to survey expressive types found in a great many groups and in which the same items tend to recur. Unfortunately this approach has tended to be ethnocentric because the investigator often derives the generic typology from the categories of his own language and tradition. Yet, both ethnographers and comparative folklorists must recognize that what is most important for analysis is not the typological system developed but the methodological system by which the genres are discerned and discussed. Though genre criticism is useful in pointing to the conventional elements of form, content, and use, whether found in one community or in many cultures, this is not the major importance of this critical approach. Rather, genre analysis provides a common frame of reference by which such conventions of form and use may be compared and thus permits one genre or group of genres to cast light on others, either within one group or cross-culturally.

If terms for folklore types are to be useful it seems necessary to describe each genre as a member of a class of related items and yet distinct from the other members of the class in specific and discernible ways. In other words, one should not only be able to point to a class of expressions like proverbs and riddles but to demonstrate how they differ from each other—how games differ from rituals and myths from *Märchen*. We can establish a meaningful basis of comparison between the genres by making each genre the member of a class of objects.

I

Folklore is a collective term for those traditional items of knowledge that arise in recurring performances. The concept of folklore is unthinkable without those compositions, for they are the channels of wisdom and entertainment, but for folklore to exist it must be enacted. For folklore to work effectively in a performance there must therefore be a consonance between the situation that has arisen, the item that is called forth, and the enactment. The performer must recognize the situation when it arises, know the appropriate traditions, and be able to perform effectively. Just as in any personal interaction, the enactment must evince understanding of the decorum involved in the social system in which both performer and performance exist.

Such concerns of appropriateness may be regarded as both constraining and liberating. The performer must pick an item that is not only on the appropriate theme and calls for the proper level of diction and has a message which is pertinent, but the item must have internal characteristics that make an appropriate comment on the situation, and this it must do judiciously and economically.

Folklore performance so described may appear to impose upon the speaker delicate and difficult recurrent demands, but in practice this is

not the case. The group's conventions associate certain sets of problems with sets of expressive forms—a genre or genres. In fact, the
situation often *calls for* a definite performance, since such enactments
will encapsulate a problem and propose a solution. This almost reflex-
ive response is apparent in the operations of devices like proverbs and
superstitions. These short traditional statements are directed at obvious problems which have arisen in the course of conversation. But the
culturally conditioned suggestion of appropriateness of occasion is
equally true of larger forms like seasonal rituals and festivals. These
focus on the troubling transitional times of the year, which call for a
traditional setting-aside of occasions for ceremonial performances.

We name most traditional genres through a combination of patterns of form, content, and context. Though the patterns of content
and form are discernible within the items and genres themselves, the
patterns of usage are externally imposed. Custom in a community may
establish a traditional relationship between a specific item and a particular situation, or between a genre and a range of situations. But the
same item or genre may be used in entirely different contexts in another group, or the same situations may be answered by totally different items. However, certain elements of structure or content make the
genres especially useful in particular kinds of recurrent situations.
This results in repeated and similar usage of the same types in different cultures. Even so, the folklorist can never take this cross-cultural
use of specific genres for granted.

The appropriateness of any given genre to a particular situation is
determined by a number of elements. Of these, thematic content is
the most obvious. The subject of a proverb, superstition, or exemplary
story must be pertinent to the problem at hand. Certain content differences are somewhat more subtle, and consequently their particular
use more difficult to discern. For instance, proverbs and taunts are
both overtly ethical in theme, and they attack recurrent problems of
interpersonal behavior with similar economical means of persuasion.
However, they differ considerably in the diction they utilize. Taunts,
direct in their approach, commonly use the pronouns *you* and *I* and
other words of direct personal reference. Proverbs, on the other hand,
are more constrained, using an impersonal approach and an emotionally muted diction. The openly aggressive content of the taunt makes
it inappropriate ("untactful," we say) for most problems in this
range.

If elements of content are the most evident means for assaying appropriateness, structural characteristics such as size or length of the performance item may be equally essential in determining choice. For instance, proverbs and moral tales (such as fables) both attack recurrent interpersonal problems concerned with the common opposition between individual needs and social necessities. Because of the length of the fable, its use is dictated by the amount of time the listeners are willing to give to the performer. Since most such ethical problems are brought to notice through conversation between equals, in many cultures there would be a hesitation to introduce a fable because the decorum of conversation does not often permit allocation of that period of attention to one speaker. Therefore, the brevity of proverbs would increase their utility. In such discourse systems, fables may then be reserved primarily for the use of older people talking to younger, because the older person is permitted both the time and opportunity. Group practice accords the aged more latitude for developing ethical points, and the age-rank hierarchy calls for the use of this kind of educational device.

Another important contextual consideration may be in the effect of the relationships between the component parts of the composition. In this regard, the differences between the riddle and the proverb are instructive.[4] Both are economical descriptions with two or more elements. In proverbs, the elements cohere, creating a clear picture amenable to a specific reading. With riddles, the descriptive elements seem to conflict and therefore to produce confusion, at least until the answer is given. The proverb, therefore, is available in situations calling for clarification, whereas riddles are more useful in contest situations (like riddle sessions), which call for licensed interpersonal aggression. But we do not make the distinction between proverbs and riddles solely on the basis of the different ways in which their elements come together; important differences of content and usage also determine the establishment of genre.

II

It is possible to distinguish three important structural levels in folklore forms: the structure of the materials, dramatic structure, and structure of context. The first involves the interrelationship among the building materials of folklore items—words, actions, tones (wood and stones). At that level we focus both on the physical quality of the material and on the organized relationship among the particular components of each item. Such patterns of repetitions suggest both the expectation and the recognition of different genres. These distinctions are based on stylizations of certain materials. For instance, peoples of many cultures distinguish between verse (i.e., language ordered through imposition of meter, line length, and a sense of balance in the line or between the lines) and prose (relatively spontaneous and casual use of language). Similarly, we distinguish genres that stylize word-sounds (literature), tones (music), movements (dance), colors and two-dimensional shapes (painting), three-dimensional shapes (sculpture), and so on.

A second and equally important level of structure for discernment of genres is *dramatic structure*. This level is important only in those genres in which there is a dramatic involvement—that is, where there is a conflict between characters depicted and a resolution provided for this conflict. There are literary types, for instance, which are differentiated according to the way in which the drama develops—such as comedy (development toward marriage or union of the sexes), tragedy (development toward representative death leading to rebirth of group), and romance (serial conflicts of a hero that lead to his gaining of a source of power). Similarly, we distinguish between hero tales, which establish patterns for emulation, and cautionary tales, which portray actions to be avoided. Though content may establish the requisite tone for distinctions of this sort, commonly a dramatic development (victory of perseverance of hero, defeat of villain, exposure of fool) establishes the point of view and persuasive purpose of the piece.

The third level of structure, and the one of greatest concern in this essay, is the *structure of context*. This is the level of structure where the patterns of relationships between the participants in the aesthetic transaction are considered. That is, on this level the focus is on the way in which actors and audiences interrelate and on how situation or occasion affects this relationship.

Many generic distinctions are primarily based on factors on this level of situational patterns. Some genres, for instance, are named because of the occasion on which they arise—*Christmas* carols, *party* games, and so on. Place determines others—*stage* plays, *bedtime* or *fireside* or *household* stories. But the central focus of the structure of context is on performer-audience relations. It is here, for instance, that we make distinctions among the major folkloristic genres of myth, legend, and folktale, for the difference pointed to in these fictive forms is in the area of belief. This has to do with the way in which the audience apprehends the tone of the performer and interprets his meaning; such interpretation is important because it determines how the members of the group will interpret the actions and distinguish between those motives to be emulated or avoided and those which simply explain, or explain away, or allow for fantasizing.

One of the major conceptual errors committed by folklorists in the past has occurred because, in regard to myths, legends, and folktales, they have not distinguished between structure of context and dramatic structure. To be sure, it is generally agreed that the major differences between these genres lie in the area of belief, but, when compendia of *dramatic* motives were made, these situationally based distinctions were retained. Consequently, there are indexes of types and motifs of folktales, and others of legends, though the dramatic movements are the same or similar, and indeed, the same stories often recur in different situational structures of belief.

III

The structure of context can provide a frame of reference for the comparative examination of traditional genres. There is a significant difference in form and technique between a proverb and a *Märchen*. Their greatest difference (beyond the obvious size of the forms) resides in the distinctive relationship between the proverb sayer or the storyteller and their respective audiences. The proverb generally arises in casual conversation to make a point about the specific situation being discussed.

The proverb sayer appeals, directly or by analogy, to an approved course of action which has been effective in the past. He does so in order to solve an immediate problem and to influence future attitudes or actions. The tale teller, on the other hand, calls into play verbal and instructive techniques and a dimension of aesthetic pleasure ab-

sent from the conversational situation of the proverb. His performance tends toward the highly stylized words and actions requiring a
distinct time and place, in which he can make an imaginary world
with the approval (indeed, encouragement)of his audience. To be
sure, he too is trying to persuade his audience, but his strategy aims at
a less immediate effect. In short then, the narrative involves a psychic
separation of performer and audience not observable in proverb use.

The performance techniques of the proverb and the folktale do not
exhaust the possible relationships of speaker and listener. In fact, the
range of performer-audience relationships, graphically rendered in
Figure 1, runs from the personal interactions of conversation to the
total distance or "removal" of performer from audience, as in the
presentation of objects of art like a folk painting. Between the poles
of interpersonal involvement and total removal are four discernible
segments of a spectrum into which folklore genres tend to group
themselves in terms of describable traits of performance. These are
conversational genres, play genres, fictive genres, and static genres.
The progress from the more interpersonal to the more removed involves a passage from the smaller and more intimate forms invoked
as part of direct and spontaneous discourse to the larger and more
symbolic genres, which rely upon a profound sense of psychic distance
between performer and audience. The shorter forms employ fairly direct strategies that rely on the intensity and color and concision of
manipulated materials to do their convincing. Though all folklore
calls for a sympathetic relation between formal object (the item of
folklore) and audience, the longer genres increasingly draw upon
vicarious, rather than immediate, involvement to induce the sympathetic response.

Conversational Genres

In the conversational genres, one person directs his expression in an
interpersonal fashion to a limited number of others as part of everyday discourse. The speaker does not need to assume any involved
character role to make his point. He, rather, is engaged in a spontaneous communicative relationship in which opportunities to introduce
traditional devices of persuasion commonly arise. Nearly everyone in
a group avails himself of these forms, and fairly often. All the clichés

and commonplace expressions of personal interaction are included in this group.

Two groups of genres are conversational. The first includes the smallest elements of patterned expression common to the group, for example, local naming procedures for people, places, herbs and flowers, birds, and so forth; jargon, slang, colloquialisms, and special languages; intensifying and hyperbolizing description. All of these are used in a conversational context to flavor and intensify speech. Jargon, colloquialisms, slang, special languages (like Pig Latin), and local naming are primarily special in-group vocabularies which serve to define the membership of a group. The intensifiers function adjectivally and are often called "proverbial" because they involve conventional units of composition larger than the single word. However, unlike proverbs, they lack an independent line of reasoning and merely contribute to the strategy of a larger argument. This group includes traditional similes ("as green as grass" and "as slow as molasses in January running uphill sideways") as well as comparisons ("like a bat out of hell" and "in like Flynn"). These exemplify the most common forms of intensification in English; others, more complex in construction ("she's so ugly she'd stop a watch" or "he's so dumb he wouldn't know how to pour piss out of his boot if it had the instructions printed on the heel"), are symbolic extension of these forms.

The second conversational group includes formal conventions of the discourse of address, appeal, and assault. It includes proverbs, superstitions, mnemonics, spells, curses, prayers, taunts, and charms. In the case of proverbs, superstitions, and mnemonics, different kinds of knowledge are communicated. Proverbs contain social wisdom and comment upon man's relation to other men, whereas superstitions (and mnemonics) focus on man's relation to the forces of nature ("red sky in morning, sailors take warning") or to the supernatural ("If you hear a dog bark at night close by, a friend is going to die"). Such expressions help to control the shock value of these forces external to ourselves by formulating a traditional prediction, explanation, or counteraction. On the other hand, curses, spells, and taunts attempt to influence social, natural, and supernatural phenomena through the bare power of the embodied and spoken word.[5]

With such forms as charms and taunts we depart a little from everyday conversation into a special kind of discourse, which is nevertheless based on the model of the conversational back-and-forth and uses the same kind of persuasive devices. Though one does not generally assume any kind of special mask or role in making such an utterance, the occasion for its use is more specialized and therefore is approaching the genres in the play segment of the spectrum. This is even more apparent in the use of a common type of patterned conversation one might term "conversational repartee" of the "See you later, alligator! —After 'while, crocodile!" sort. This is clearly one of the conversational genres because of its performance occasion, but its prepatterned verbal exchange is closer to that of folk drama. Still closer to such "play" forms are longer repartee routines such as: "That's tough. What's tough? Life. What's life? A magazine. Where do you get it? Down at the corner. How much? A dime. Only got a nickel. That's tough. What's tough? . . ."

Play Genres

There are few differences between such traditional repartee and the simplest of the play genres such as riddles or tag games, for they too develop upon the back-and-forth movement of interpersonal communication. Yet riddling arises most commonly in a riddling session, a special occasion for performance somewhat removed from casual conversation and in which an implicit set of rules and boundaries operates. Furthermore, the riddling occasion calls for a donning of certain masks (riddler and riddlee), which are discrete (that is, can be distinguished from each other because of the contest situation and the relative place in the contest taken by a player at a specific time). Those involved in traditional repartee also may be viewed as wearing a temporary mask, but the masks of the two or more speakers can not be readily distinguished from one another. Furthermore, the role played in riddling and other play forms differs more profoundly from those assumed in everyday life than in traditional repartee. The roles played in play genres are as traditional as the pieces performed and therefore as stylized. To make these roles significant and symbolic, and to mark the difference between play and other activities, a stylized play world is created, which is very like the real world but psychologically (and often physically) removed from it in time and space.

The difference between conversational and play genres is perhaps

best describable in terms of the distinction made by sociologists between *particularistic* and *universalistic* roles. When one talks con-
versationally, one assumes a particularistic role, a role determined by
one's social position in relation to those who are listening. Thus it is
a status role that is assumed by the speaker and acknowledged by his
auditors. This is simply saying that the interactants know each other
in terms of a continuing social relationship and that their conversational devices will be in great part determined by this positioning.
On the other hand, as soon as one assumes a role that is named and
therefore can be filled by any number of others, one is playing a more
universalistic role. This is the difference between someone who is "my
father" and someone referred to as "the father," even if they happen
to be the same person. A greater number of rules and conventions of
stylized activity operate in the latter situation.

Play, by definition, arises in an atmosphere that produces the illusion of free and undirected expression while remaining under control.
By effecting a removal from the real world into the stylized one, a
tension is established through the involvement power of sympathetic
identification with the enactment at the same time as a psychic distance is established through the creation of the stylized world and the
mannered presentation. This allows for the cathartic response to the
activity—the simultaneous identification and distancing. We can
identify with even the most anxious situations when they are in the
controlled environment of the play world.

In other words, in this play world the spirit of license reigns, allowing for a "playing out" of motives we don't allow ourselves under
the circumstances of real life. Any place may become the arena for
playing, and any time the occasion, but in the more elaborate play
genres the times and places are often as traditional as the pieces performed in them. Game playing may arise any place, for instance, but
the more complex play activities need a field or stage or consecrated
place with evident boundaries to supplement the rules and conventions of playing.

As with the conversational genres, the play sector divides itself into
the more interactive and the more elaborately removed genres, but
here three subsegments may be discerned. The first subgroup has a
lesser degree of psychic removal and role playing than the others, and
therefore the genres found in it tend to occur more frequently and

spontaneously. Types in this subcategory tend to be more formal in presentation than the other play genres and thus demand more advance preparation. Included in the first subsegment are riddles and joke sessions and other traditional verbal contests, nonprogrammatic folk dances, and most games. In the second are spectator sports and traditional debates and contests like spelling bees. In the third are rituals, folk plays, and those games and dances that have a set progression of movement (such as a story) and traditional role-playing.

The first subgroup, as noted, shares certain attributes of the conversational genres: emphasis on the back-and-forth movement of converse, a near-identification of role and performer, and a not very involved set of those rules, boundaries, and conventions that control the course of play. Yet the total pattern of play *is* predetermined in a riddle session or in a game of tag, though not the direction the play will take. It is this quality of dramatic confrontation without a predetermined resolution that characterizes all of the genres in the first two groups of play forms.

In the more interactive genres of Play I the players are each other's audience, and the activity provides little interest for spectators. Each person is potentially a participant in this play. On the other hand, in the second group of play genres, there is a distinction between players and audience, a distancing movement, which is carried even further in the third group, where the sense of removal is complete. In Play II, interaction is still viewed as interpersonal, but in Play III the personal element is sacrificed to the ensemble effect of the role playing, and the audience therefore focuses primarily on the symbolic motives being reenacted. Whereas in the more interactive play forms there is a sense of removal that, like conversation, is spontaneous and temporary, such a feeling of spontaneity is less in Play II genres with the addition of spectators, and in Play III the degree of formality and conventionality is high. In these last two genres, there is a greater feeling of artificial dramatic involvement, emphasizing that the resolution of the conflict is predetermined.

The distinction between games like tag in Play I and spectator sports in Play II goes further than just this growing sense of removal through the introduction of an audience. In the Play I genres there are commonly only two discrete roles—like "Hare and Hounds," "Cops and Robbers" (i.e., pursuer and pursued), or riddler and riddlee. When spectators take a place in the structure of context, the spectators need a representative to guarantee the maintenance of the rules and the boundaries. Thus in Play II a further discrete role is that of one person on stage or on field who begins and ends the proceedings and who serves to uphold the rules (timekeeper, umpire, scorekeeper, judge). As the sense of removal felt by the audience increases, a greater number of these on-the-spot representatives are called for.

In Play III genres, at least one further discrete role is introduced. It is convenient to view the change as bifurcation of the representative figure and his role in Play II into one figure who introduces and ends the proceedings by direct address to the audience and another figure-type who serves to further or continue the action (blocking character, resuscitator, mediator). Play III forms are thus denominated by commonly having four or more discrete roles.

In the more active genres of Play III, such as folk drama, contact between performers and audience is almost completely severed—this is what is meant by the term "psychic distance." Identification with the conflict occurs vicariously, rather than through participation, as in a game. In a game like "Hide and Seek" the actors would direct their performances to each other, but in the folk play they coordinate their actions for an ensemble effect, which is directed to the spectators viewing from their removed positions. Though the actor may identify with his role and derive ego gain from its performance, he must primarily channel his energies into the total effect of the piece in order for the play to work. The vicarious sympathetic involvement of the audience is an integral part of the technique of all genres on the side of the spectrum consisting of Play III, fictive, and static genres (see Fig. 1) and dictates the organizations and affects the strategies of all items in these genres.

Fictive Genres

The segment of the fictive genres includes those which most folk-lorists would call the major types (and which many would say are the only folklore genres). Here there is a further removal of speaker from spoken-to; all movements and motives are depicted fictively, that is, through suggestive description in words and gestures. As in the play genres, there is symbolic role-playing in a time and place removed from real life, but all dramatic movement must be envisioned by the mind's eye. One performer generally serves as the voice for all the characters, though in certain cases a group performs antiphonally or in concert.

Like other segments, this one tends to divide into the more interpersonal and the more removed. On the more interactive side are those forms in which the audience (or part of it) are drawn into the performance. This group would include all items in the chanter-response, antiphonal pattern and those which have a chorus of added voices. Most work songs and drinking songs qualify for this group. It would also encompass *cante-fables* in which the repeated song is sung by the audience, traditional sermons that call for interspersed responses, and catch tales. The genres in the more removed subsegment are those which have a totally monologue performance. This would include most of the narrative forms: epic, ballad, folktale, myth, legend, anecdote, and most jokes. (Jokes that tell a story are a problem—in a joke-session they are functional equivalents of riddles, insofar as they emphasize the triumph of wit.) This subsegment would also include a number of lyric forms such as laments, love lyrics, and celebratory pieces such as carols when individually performed.

Static Genres

The final group, which I have called static genres, is concerned with those types in which the performer expresses himself in a concrete form that remains after the moment of enactment. Having performed, the artist steps back and lets his creation "speak for itself." He makes something which becomes independent of himself. Like the fictive genres, static pieces rely heavily on the imagination for an understanding of the meanings of their stories. These genres include paintings, carvings, and designs which narrate a story. Other folk-art forms portray an important character from the narratives of the group but do so without reference to a specific story or even scene; such creations are simple celebrations of the abilities or characteristics of the one depicted and in a sense take for granted a knowledge of how these came to be. Folk art of this sort is therefore close to the

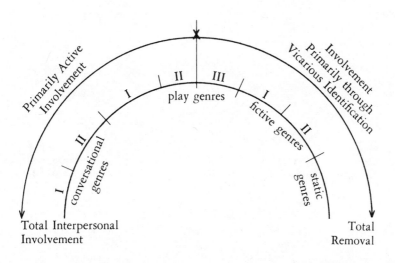

Total Interpersonal
Involvement

Total
Removal

Conversational I	Play I	Fictive I
jargon	riddling	cante fables
slang	joking	catch tales
colloquialism	verbal contest	chanter-response
special languages	nonprogrammatic	songs
intensifiers	games and dances	
naming		*Fictive II*
	Play II	epic
Conversational II	spectator sports	ballad
proverbs	traditional debates	lyric
superstitions	and contests	panegyric
charms		and hymn
curses	*Play III*	legend
spells	festival activities	anecdote
mnemonics	ritual (including	jokes
prayers	various religious	other narrative
taunts	practices)	forms
traditional repartee	folk drama	
		Static
		folk painting
		folk sculpture
		folk design

Fig. 1. Range of level of interaction between performer and audience

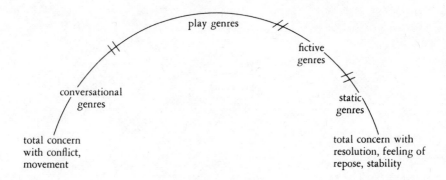

Fig. 2. Range of level of conflict

celebratory fictive genres but differs from the fictive genres in the performer-audience relationship: the performer is completely removed from the performance after the object is made—he has made something which becomes independent of himself.

IV

Elaboration of the genre continuum has permitted an overview of traditional expressions in terms of the range of performer-audience relationships. This spectrum can also cast light on other aspects of traditional aesthetic technique; in this regard, one can see a changing dramatic focus as one traverses the continuum.

By focusing on the relation between performers and audience, the emphasis has been upon genres as sets of performance pieces that performers employ to affect, to *move*, the audience. This affecting is brought about through sympathetic involvement of the members of the audience with the construction of the piece. Each item is performed in an attempt to influence future action by appealing to past usage, but this does not mean that all items are uniform in their focus on the past. Some performers choose items that apply to the present situation in terms of immediate consequences and thus would emphasize the immediate future. Other performers take a longer view, searching the repertoire for illustrative anecdotes that would cast light on the present and, by influencing attitude, also affect actions. Thus, conversational forms emphasize the potentials of the present situation, but as forms grow longer the strategy of persuasion calls more and more for reenactments or descriptions of action already completed.

In all genres there is a strategic articulation of conflict, intended to move the audience sympathetically with the movement of the item. But not all genres emphasize conflict and resolution equally. In fact, as one moves along the continuum from the pole of interpersonal involvement to that of complete removal, the embodiment of movement becomes progressively formal and performer-oriented, more reliant upon symbol, imagination, and vicarious involvement of audience. Moreover, focus is increasingly on the embodiment of dramatic resolution and less and less on the articulation of the conflict. The dramatic focus changes from being almost solely upon conflict in the shorter genres to almost completely upon resolution in the fictive and static types (see Fig. 2). With the Play III and fictive forms, we are concerned with dramatic structure—that is, the articulation of the model of *projected* dramatic conflict and resolution. This model is not available to the conversational genres, however, because there is no such projection in them, nor is it very useful in regard to the static genres.

The conversational genres underline and intensify the conflict inherent in the recurrent situation to which it is addressing itself. But we see no actual resolution, only one which is implied or proposed. Conversational genres attempt to promote an action rather than specifically to produce it. In riddling and other interactive play genres also, conflict is stressed more highly than resolution. In these activities, each component item is built on a small dramatic model, with only small resolutions occurring within the totality of the movement. For instance, each time a person is touched in "Tag" or each time a riddle answer is given there occurs a resolution of the immediately preceding conflict but not one to the entire activity. We have serial conflicts, in other words, without any sense of final and total resolution. Just as there is no real winner in a game of tag, neither is there usually a declaration of the best riddler. Because we see no real resolution, it is impossible to discern dramatic *structure* here, only dramatic focus.

With the more removed kinds of play activities we begin to find a greater emphasis on resolution. This is truer of rituals than festivals, for instance, and truer of folk plays than of most folk dances. Any time narrative movement is concerned, the outcome of the story becomes important in the strategy of the piece—in fact, as important as the original conflict-situation. Traditional stories are generally so well known to the audience and so stereotyped in construction that the resolution is inherent in their performance from the first word or gesture. By the time one reaches the lyric and celebratory pieces in the fictive genres one can see clearly the result of this drift; a lament or a lyric is a relatively static enactment in which any story accompanying a piece is either presented as having happened in the past or the performer takes for granted that the audience knows the events. Action is stopped in favor of a consideration of emotional situation; the scene is generally depicted as occurring after action is completed. Such pieces take for granted some knowledge of the preceding events on the part of the audience. This assumption accounts for the strong retrospective and allusive feeling of such genres. Finally, the static genres present us with a *fait accompli*, an embodied resolution whose dramatic conflicts in many cases we must imagine and reconstruct. As we progress along this segment of the continuum, we become more concerned with the design of the items, less with the situations they are articulating. This focus on style and design commonly produces a feeling of potential repose, perhaps arising from the audience's greater sense of removal from the depiction.

The strategies of all genres are directed toward influencing future action through the appeal of past usage. The conversational genres have a direct appeal, calling for an attitude that leads to action in the near future. Though, for instance, a superstition assumes the past usage and effectiveness of a certain attitude and practice, its rhetorical impact relies and focuses upon the immediacy of the situation and the actions that might be used to answer this problem. The play genres, on the other hand, shift rhetorical emphasis from future action to present reenactment. There is a clear sense of "now-ness" in a game of "Hide and Seek" or even in a hero-combat play like "The Moors and the Christians." To be sure, charter for play comes from past practice and establishes patterns that may be used in the future, but the effectiveness of the activity relies upon its here-and-now quality. Fictive and static genres are both presented by describing or referring to actions that have taken place in the past. In the case of a myth or a *Märchen*, this is made evident by placing the story in the distant past —by starting with "In the beginning . . ." in myth or with "Once upon a time and a very long time . . ." in *Märchen*. Nevertheless, such genres, simply by narrating actions, give more of a renewed sense of the present moment than a lyric or a hymn, even though the story is told in the past tense. The lyric has almost no sense of reenactment at all.

This change of focus and rhetorical technique is observable even in different types of fictional narratives. Most *Märchen*, for instance, are tales of wondrous action in which we hear of startling transformations: Stupid Jack wins the money and the King's daughter; the scullery maid becomes the princess while defeating the forces of her wicked stepmother. On the other hand, in certain narratives like ghost legends focus on the lyrical emotion is much clearer, and the story is told with a much stronger feeling of action re-created retrospectively. These stories, which often explain the origin of specific local phenomena, emphasize the emotional dimension of the present situation (usually a permanent one) and relate the past action in a very brief manner. Such a story is "La Llorona" (The Weeping Woman) told widely in Spanish-speaking communities in North America.[6] The story usually begins with a description of the ghastly sounds and spectral appearance of a woman who, it is then explained, murdered her children (or they were killed through her negligence or merely absence) and who must search for them eternally. Though we are presented here with both a conflict and a resolution, the ending is emphasized so much more strongly because we begin and end at the same place dramatically speaking and because of the permanently indeterminate nature of the resolution.

V

In shifts of narrative orientation such as those described, the relations among the techniques and strategies of different genres and genre groups become clearer. To represent these is reason enough for constructing a hypothetical arrangement. However, it is important to note that this spectrum is not so much a typological formulation as an arbitrary frame of reference that may help the investigator to have a fuller understanding of the range of techniques used in traditional expression. It should permit fuller understanding of what diverse cultures may share and in what ways they are unique.

Thus, the ethnographer might find it useful because it would show him that the groups with which he is most concerned have a predominance of one group of genres over another. Or it may show, as it has for me, that the group with which he is working gravitates toward one sector of the spectrum. In this regard, there is a strong attraction (or *tropism*) on the part of New-World Negro groups toward play genres; both conversational and fictive genres gravitate, in other words, toward the center of the spectrum.

By this is meant that there is a discernible tendency to turn conversations into occasions for traditional repartee, or, even more, into traditional verbal contests like "playing the dozens" among adolescents. On the other hand, it means that folktales and songs are performed with the expectation that the audience will become so totally involved with the performance that they will become a functioning part of it by making audible comments and exclamations to which the performer will react. The most extreme example of this is in some West Indian storytelling communities in which one or more members of the audience will not only sing with the narrator in a *cante-fable* performance, but also will take the part of one of the characters in a scene with dialogue. In contrast to this tropism in Afro-American groups, one can discern the opposite among rural American whites, where the performer in this group commonly creates as great a sense of removal as possible while singing, playing, or telling a story.[7]

The spectrum of genres may also be useful in discerning the operational limits of the central term of the discipline, *folklore*. The hypothetical arrangement has been presented to a number of audiences in the last few years, and it has almost invariably produced a slight sense of malaise as the genres near the pole of complete removal were described. One commentator said that he could accept the scheme completely if I would just eliminate the static segment. The anxiety revealed by such response is similar to that exhibited by most folklorists when they have confronted traditional genres of record, especially those that involve writing. This has been especially evident in folksong scholarship whenever the problem of broadside printings of traditional songs has been encountered; and more recently the same unwillingness to investigate has arisen around the use of the phonograph as a valid tool of folklore study.[8] In terms of the spectrum, however, this kind of phenomenon is easily understood and described—these are fictive items that have been made more removed through techniques of performance which have enlarged the audience; these fictive items have been transmuted into static form.

Perhaps even more troubling in this regard are a number of types of traditional expressions which find their origin and proper form in writing. Numbered among these "peripheral" folklore genres are such expressions as autograph-album rhymes, "latrinalia" and graffiti, chain letters, epitaphs, book inscriptions and warnings, and epigrammatic printed signs (such as those found in barrooms and restaurants). All of these are commonly found in recorded form; yet they are generally transmitted in essentially the same way other folklore genres are, by being carried in the memory of tradition bearers and written down by them for the proper occasions. Since once the performer does the writing he becomes removed from his performance, these might be seen as static genres. In the process of removal they reinstitute an interpersonal approach—they speak to each member of the audience as an individual by using the first-person point of view. This approach becomes especially evident in epitaphs like:

> Remember me as you pass by;
> As you are now so once was I.
> As I am now, so you must be,
> Therefore prepare to follow me.

It is equally evident in autograph-album rhymes; each inscription is ostensibly directed toward the owner of the album, though it will obviously be read by others.

To extend my argument further, there are other expressive genres that have many traditional elements which could also be usefully placed on this spectrum but which no one would want to designate as folklore. This performer-audience continuum, in other words, is really part of a larger spectrum in which all genres of expression, traditional or otherwise, could be placed. The difference between folklore and other expressive phenomena is in the range of relations possible in performance. Essentially, we distinguish between folklore and "popular culture" on the basis of dissemination (performance) methods; folklore, we say, can only exist in face-to-face encounter that leads to purely oral transmission. The same is true, only more so, in the distinction between folklore and high art, or *belles lettres*. These do not differ greatly in expressive capacity, in art, or even in the presence of traditional elements of composition. But with the development of techniques for reproduction of artistic objects (printing, recording, lithography, and so forth), a further removal of performer and audience is made possible, and the opportunity arises for developing popular and high arts distinct from folk arts.

Viewed in this way, *folklore* is meaningful as a term only insofar as it designates artistic expression in which there is a certain degree of personal interrelationship between performer and audience. When a performer loses this interpersonal approach but still attempts to entertain the populace at large (i.e., argues publicly utilizing public values), then we call this performance "popular." And when he restricts his audience and adapts his values to a group of educated initiates, then we enter the realm of high art. But insofar as all forms of expression utilize traditional conventions and genres, all are capable of being usefully compared.

By viewing expressive culture in these terms, it becomes clear that at some arbitrary point in the unarticulated—but obviously unconsciously sensed—spectrum of performer-audience relationships, folklorists decide that there the distance between the performer and his audience is too great to call an enactment folklore. (Just where this "cut-off point" is varies from one folklorist to the next.) A similar, and equally arbitrary, cut-off point is observable in the realm of material folklore. In this case, however, the relationship with which we are concerned is between *maker* and *user*, not performer and audience. At some point in the maker-user–relationship spectrum, the removal between the two becomes so pronounced that we call it a product of technology, not material folklore.

By setting up a continuum of the sort I have, one is able to construct a frame of reference by which the genres of expressive and implemental constructs of culture can be compared. The effect of doing so, however, is to call into some question the hard-and-fast distinction between folklore and devices of the so-called nontraditional cultures. To be sure, it is convenient to distinguish levels of relationship between constructors (performers and makers) and utilizers (members of audience and users), but in doing so it is necessary to remember that one is establishing relative distinctions, not exclusive categories. This point would not be important if investigators of culture—folklorists and others—did not insist on these distinctions as ways of defining their academic disciplines. When terms function so exclusively they often inhibit understanding.

Ultimately, artistic expression, whether traditional or not, arises from the same impulses and shares many of the same functions in any kind of culture. Furthermore, every artist works through conventions to some extent, but artistic activity is determined by the amount of cultural choice the performer feels free to utilize in his performance and by the ability of the artist to capitalize upon this choice. The existence of a tradition or of traditional genres should not blind us to the fact that stylized expression on any level comes to life only through performance. The performer and the tradition are equally essential.

214 Roger D. Abrahams

Notes

I am indebted to many students and colleagues who discussed earlier drafts of this paper with me, suggesting important changes; most notable in this regard are Professors Francis Lee Utley, Richard M. Dorson, Alan Dundes, Linda Dégh, Ed Cray, and Américo Paredes. I am even more in the debt of the editor, Dan Ben-Amos, for suggesting painful wholesale revisions that I feel have made the argument more consistent and more economical. The first draft of this study was written while on a grant from the John Simon Guggenheim Foundation, and was delivered at the 37th Congress of Americanists, Mar del Plata, Argentina, in September 1966.

1. Northrop Frye, *Anatomy of Criticism: Four Essays*, pp. 247–248.

2. Ibid., p. 247.

3. Ethnographers, especially those working in Africa, have done instructive work in this area. Some representative works are Melville J. and Frances S. Herskovits, *Dahomean Narrative: A Cross-Cultural Analysis* (Evanston, Ill.: Northwestern University Press, 1958); D. W. Arnett, "Proverbial Lore and Word-Play of the Fulani," *Africa* 27 (1957): 379–396; John Blacking, "The Social Value of Venda Riddles," *African Studies* 20 (1961): 1–32; Ethel M. Albert, " 'Rhetoric,' 'Logic' and 'Poetics' in Burundi: Culture Patterning of Speech Behavior," *American Anthropologist* 66, no. 6, pt. 2 (1964): 35–54.

4. A fuller development of these differences is contained in my "Introductory Remarks to a Rhetorical Theory of Folklore," *Journal of American Folklore* 81 (1968): 143–158.

5. For a fuller analysis of the persuasive devices of these conversational forms, see my study, "A Rhetoric of Everyday Life: Traditional Conversational Genres," *Southern Folklore Quarterly* 32 (1968): 44–59.

6. For a recent discussion of this story with some versions, see Bess Lomax Hawes, "La Llorona in Juvenile Hall," *Western Folklore* 27 (1968): 153–170.

7. For a discussion of these aesthetic techniques in regard to the Anglo-American tradition, see my "Patterns of Structure and Role Relationships in the Child Ballads in the United States," *Journal of American Folklore* 79 (1966): 448–462. West Indian patterns are described in my "The Shaping of Folklore Traditions in the British West Indies," *Journal of Inter-American Studies* 9 (1967): 456–480, and "Public Drama and Common Values in Two Caribbean Islands," *Trans-Action* 5, no. 8 (July–August 1968): 62–71.

8. A situation often discussed by D. K. Wilgus. See, for instance, his "The Rationalist Approach" in *A Good Tale and A Bonnie Tune*, ed. Wilson Hudson (Dallas, Tex.: SMU Press, 1964), pp. 227–237.

11. Analytical Categories and Ethnic Genres

DAN BEN-AMOS

"Was ist eine *Sage*?" This question, raised by Carl-Herman Tillhagen a few years ago,[1] is equally applicable to other folklore genres. The search for the thematic and structural attributes which distinguish one form from another has continuously occupied folklorists who aspire to establish research in this field on a systematic basis. Thus, Alan Dundes states that "the problem . . . of defining folklore boils down to the task of defining exhaustively all the forms of folklore. Once this has been accomplished, it will be possible to give an enumerative definition of folklore. However, thus far in the illustrious history of the discipline, not so much as one genre has been completely defined."[2]

The blame, however, does not rest so much with the folklorists as with the very incongruity between ethnic genres of oral literature and the analytical categories constructed for their classification. Whereas ethnic genres are cultural modes of communication, analytical categories are models for the organization of texts. Both constitute separate systems which should relate to each other as substantive matter to abstract models. Yet this relationship has not materialized. The basic problem inherent in any analytical scheme for folklore classification is that it must synchronize different folklore communication systems, each with its own internal logical consistency, each based upon distinct sociohistorical experiences and cognitive categories. This is methodologically, if not logically, impossible. Yet, as folklorists, we did not heed this incongruity and, in our zeal for scientific methodology, we abandoned the cultural reality and strove to formulate theoretical analytical systems. We attempted to construct logical concepts which would have potential cross-cultural applications and to design tools which would serve as the basis for scholarly discourse,

NOTE. Reprinted from *Genre* 2, no. 3 (September 1969): 275–301, by permission of the University of Illinois Press.

providing it with defined terms of reference and analysis. In the process, however, we transformed traditional genres from cultural categories of communication into scientific concepts. We approached them as if they were not dependent upon cultural expression and perception but autonomous entities which consisted of exclusive inherent qualities of their own; as if they were not relative divisions in a totality of an oral tradition but absolute forms. In other words, we attempted to change folk-taxonomic systems which are cultural bound and vary according to the speakers' cognitive systems into culture-free, analytical, unified, and objective models of folk literature. The failure, now admitted, almost could have been anticipated.

I

Scholarly attempts to establish folklore studies on scientific grounds have followed four distinct paths: thematic, holistic, archetypal, and functional, all of which were followed in the hope of discovering the formula for methodological definitions of genres at the end of each road. Each of these conducts of inquiry aimed at the construction of a valid, objective order of categories of folk literature. Yet, naturally, the tools, terms, and concepts that emerged were generated by definite theoretics and geared toward distinct sets of problems.

The Thematic Approach

Comparative folklore research concerns itself with the diffusion of themes in different traditions. Consequently, in this framework, genre is a thematic category. The touchstone for such a generic classification of texts is the answer to the question "What is it about?" Legends are about saints, heroes, miracles, and other kinds of supernatural phenomena. *Märchen* are about "humble heroes [who] kill adversaries, succeed to kingdoms and marry princesses."[3] Fables are about plants and·animals, and proverbs encapsulate traditional wisdom. Underlying such an approach to folk literature is the premise that thematic similarity implies universal generic identity. The formal nature of an expression is inherent in its content. Tales about the same themes automatically constitute a single genre. This assumption of direct correlation between subject matter and folkloristic typology does have some significant methodological value. It provides clear clues for the classification of tradition and hence for the comparative examination of texts from different cultures. Yet, at the same time, this premise begets evolutionary and diffusionistic notions about folklore genres which cannot be maintained by the examination of historical and cultural facts. Some examples illustrate this point. The *Märchen* is a European form that flourished in literary circles from the seventeenth through the nineteenth centuries. Simultaneously and during earlier. and later periods, it enjoyed oral circulation among nonliterate rural and urban people of this and other continents. Thematically this genre has its antecedents in oriental and classical literatures; yet to refer to similar subjects in biblical and Greek traditions as examples of the genre *Märchen* is sheer anachronism. Hermann Gunkel's *Das Märchen in Alten Testament* (Religionsgeschichtliche Volksbücher, 2nd Series, Die Religion des Alten Testament, Nos. 23–26 [Tübingen, 1921]) is a milestone in biblical research. In this book Gunkel emphasized the role of oral tradition in the formulation of the Scriptures and proposed to conceive of many biblical tales not as history, as religion dictates, but as poetic narrations which share themes in common with European and Asian nations. Gunkel, like the Grimm brothers before him,[4] defined *Märchen* as poetic narrations, in contrast with legends, which are historical narrations. As far as this definition is concerned, many of his new interpretations of biblical stories as poetry no doubt are valid. But the use of the generic term *Märchen* implies a particular literary form which is absent from the Bible.

The thematic approach for generic definition is even more apparent in Herbert Jennings Rose's discussion of the "*Märchen* in Greece and Italy."[5] He simply used a list of folktale themes compiled by Joseph Jacobs in *Handbook of Folk-lore*[6] and similar subjects singled out from classical literature as examples of ancient Greek and Italian *Märchen*. However, among his examples are such stories as "Cupid and Psyche" and "Beauty and Beast," themes which, although indeed part of the European *Märchen* tradition, in Greece belonged to a completely different genre—the comic romance.[7]

Thus, the a priori assumption of direct correlation between themes and genres has resulted in an anachronistic conception of literary kinds. In other cases, the same premise has suggested genealogical relationships between various forms. For example, historians of literature have outlined the direction of literary development from fable to proverb or, vice versa,[8] from epic[9] and romance[10] to ballad. Among the ancestors of the later genre, ballad, are listed lyrical poetry[11] and metrical religious legends.[12] These relationships are based on the assumptions that no theme can be the subject of two genres simultaneously and that where such thematic similarity does exist it reflects a direct historical relationship. Neither of these assumptions is necessarily true. The story of "The King and the Abbott" is a widely found prose narrative.[13] Antti Aarne and Stith Thompson classify it with romantic tales,[14] in Jewish tradition it is a joke,[15] and in English folklore a ballad.[16] No generic relationship necessarily exists between these forms. Similarly, the theme of the ballad "The Maiden Freed from the Gallows" (Child 95) appears in the West Indies in a *cante-fable*.[17] Although this form provides more background details, which are missing from the abrupt balladic description, it does not imply that one genre evolves out of the other, even though here there are closer formal affinities. Moreover, even within the tradition of a single culture the same theme can appear both in prose and in poetry, as for example, the motif of the "singing bone" that reveals the murderer.[18]

Realization of the lack of correspondence between themes and genres led students of folklore to embrace a kind of Crocean aesthetics and to forego any systematic order of forms in oral tradition. Thompson considered "useless" the "effort devoted to the establishment of exact terms for the various kinds of folktale"[19] and went even as far as making a virtue out of this vagueness, as "it frequently avoids the necessity of making decisions and often of entering into long debates as to the exact narrative *genre* to which a particular story may belong."[20] Ruth Benedict said flatly, "No folktale is generic."[21] This categorical statement reflects Benedict's field research among the Zuni, whose "tales," she found, "fall into no clearly distinguishable categories."[22] Consequently, she adapted Croce's aesthetics to the study of verbal art among nonliterate people and stated, "It is always the tale of one particular people, with one particular livelihood and social organization."[23]

No doubt, thematic classification of folk literature has had pragmatic value in the promotion of comparative studies; yet its basic principle of direct correlation between themes and genres does not stand, as we have just seen, the test of empirical examination. The premise that thematic similarity implies generic identity may be valid in regard to the oral literature of a single culture within a definite period, but it is simply incongruent with the facts of folk literatures of different peoples or of the same society during different historical periods.

However, themes are not necessary standards of order. Any number or combination of attributes can serve as the basis for generic distinctions. Moreover, thematic classification itself involves subjective selection and discrimination, which inevitably biases the system. The choice of some themes as essential and the dismissal of others as irrelevant involves either personal, cultural, or theoretical subjective judgments which defy analytical objectivity. Furthermore, because thematic classification of folklore genres involves selective procedures it can be only an incomplete representation of the literary forms themselves. For example, legends about saints and heroes are often classified as separate genres because they differ in regard to the nature of the protagonist. However, this approach ignores a whole range of narrative and content relationships such as prosody, structure, and performance, which may or may not contribute to the differentiation between these two genres.

The Holistic Approach

According to the holistic conception of folklore genres, tales and songs, riddles and proverbs are not aggregates of episodes or accidental combinations of metaphors. Rather they are formal and thematic entities that have an organic unity of their own. This unity is the intrinsic ontological reality of any folklore form. It is not dependent on any theoretical orientation or conditioned perception, and it does not change with any analytical shift in point of view. Genres, hence, are subject to structural description in the sense that it is theoretically possible to illustrate how the different elements in these forms relate to each other and constitute distinct unified fields of actions. Since the distinctive unity of each folklore genre is the basic premise of the holistic approach, its principal mode of inquiry is that of discovery rather than of systematization, which is characteristic of the comparative school. Students of folklore who pursue research in this direction purport to discover the existing structure of a verbal message, of which the speaker or singer and his addressees are not necessarily aware. Although they may respond intuitively to any violation of the structural principles of such a message, they cannot pinpoint the exact source of their frustration. Only the person who has discovered the formal structure of the genre is able to do so.

Of course, it is possible to describe the particular structural properties of folklore genres as they exist on any linguistic level: phonetic, syntactic, and semantic. It is possible to analyze them in terms of sequences of episodes and actions or to construct abstract models of the relations inherent in the genres.[24] Essentially, the holistic approach affirms the ontology of folklore forms and changes the concept of genre from a nominalistic to a realistic entity. A genre is no longer just a label for a relatively similar corpus of themes but is a real form, which exists regardless of any interpretation or classification. The holistic conception of folklore genres provides, in other words, for the fulfillment of Carl Wilhelm von Sydow's demand to build up a "natural system" of traditional forms.[25] Indeed, Vladímir Propp, one of the pioneers in the application of the holistic approach to folklore genres, emulated the classification methods in natural sciences and regarded his own description as a morphology of the folktales. In analogy with the term *morphology* in botany, he considered it "a description of the tale according to its component parts and the relationship of these components to each other and to the whole."[26]

Inadvertently, the application of the scientific principles of botany to folklore can exceed its heuristic value and lead to conclusions logically and empirically possible in the natural sciences but incompatible with the very nature of oral literature. For example, if structural similarity between forms is regarded as having the same consequences as in botany, the inevitable conclusion would be that there is a genealogical relation between two genres. Propp himself probably would not have objected to that conclusion. After all, one of the main purposes of his research was the formulation of a method which would replace Alexander Veselovskij's thematic discussions of the history of folklore genres with more objective and accurate methods. He himself conceived of the variant versions of a tale as relating to the basic structural model as "*species* to *genus*."[27] Other scholars, in partial criticism of Propp, extended these relations in terms of two distinct genres. Archer Taylor demonstrated that the biographical pattern of the mythic hero, as outlined by J. G. von Hahn, Otto Rank, Lord Raglan, and Joseph Campbell, actually corresponds to the wanderings of the *Märchen* protagonist.[28] Thus, in structural terms, myth and folktale are identical, or at least related to each other genealogically. Claude Lévi-Strauss, who regards the relationship between myth and tales in modalic, not genealogical, terms, phrased it more succinctly: "Les contes sont les mythes en miniature."[29] When it takes this direction, structural analysis no longer serves its original purpose of delineation of folklore forms. Instead, it implies a conception of genres based on approximation rather than differentiation. The genealogy of forms rather than their distinctive attributes may become the central question.

Structural analysis of folklore raised still another problem. The shift from a nominalistic to a realistic conception of folklore genres implied in morphological analysis involves the question of the universality of these forms. Are they only structures of local tradition or are they inherent qualities of human creative imagination? Are they part of an ethnic system of folkloric communication or are they intrinsic to any artistic expression and do they transcend cultural boundaries? Propp himself limited his investigation to Russian folktales, but, since he analyzed only "ordinary tales" (AT 300–749) which are spread widely throughout Europe, it is possible to assume that this structure is common to the European tradition at large. However, Dundes' successful application of the same method and basically the same structural pattern to the oral tradition of the North-American Indians implies the possible universality of this folktale structure.[30] The similarity in narrative forms between cultures as remote as the Slavic and the North-American Indian could have taken place either through historical diffusion, population migration, or independent creation. Any of these possibilities points, at the very minimum, to the universal appeal of these forms.

The Archetypal Approach

For folklore genres to be universal categories there must be a convergence of the structural patterns, thematic content, and social usage of each of these genres. If the legend, for example, is to be considered a cross-cultural category, stories about saintly people must follow the same distinct pattern in all traditions. If such universality does exist it means that folklore genres are ontologically independent of culture and are not subject to variability of social differences. Hence, it is necessary to account for their thematic similarity and formal stability by transcendental, transcultural, universal archetypes. André Jolles's thesis of "einfache Formen" provides, indeed, such a theory of folklore genres.[31] Accordingly, these genres are primary verbal formulations (*Sprachgebärden*) of basic mental concerns (*Geistesbeschäftigung*). He postulates that the human mind is preoccupied with the holy, the family, the essence of the universe, the soluble problem, the accumulated experience. It is occupied with the choice between moral principles, the verbal reproductions of facts, the suspension of immoral reality, and the inadequacies of reality. These are basic mental concerns, and, theoretically, they exist independent of any verbal expression. The *einfache Formen* constitute the elementary, primary linguistic formulations of these attitudes. Thus, the legend, the *Sage*, the myth, the riddle, the proverb, the *Kasus*, the memorabilia, the *Märchen*, and the joke are the respective verbal representations of the above mental attitudes. The folklore genres are not *about* these subjects, but they themselves, in their totality, are the verbal realization of them. Each form constitutes a holistic entity, a field of network interactions which in its entirety is a representation or a verbal formulation of these mental attitudes. These primary forms serve, in turn, as the genealogical model for the secondary forms, the artistic genres, which appear in written literature. In other words, in a Platonic fashion, the genres of oral tradition are an imitation of mental concerns, and the literary forms constitute a secondary development of them.

Kurt Ranke proposed to view the creative process of the primary forms from a different perspective and to conceive of them as verbal representations not of intellectual concerns but of human emotions.[32] Thus for Ranke, they are not imitations of mental attitudes but manifestations of a creative spiritual force, a psychological *enérgeia* which rises to the level of consciousness. For the mental concerns of Jolles, Ranke substitutes a postulation of basic needs of the human soul, which are the "ontological archetypes of various genres."[33] Thus, folktales, legend, myth, and jest are the respective functions of needs

for a sublimated world of mythical perfection, psychological resigna-
tion in the face of human destruction, the religious meditative relations between the present and the next worlds, and the psychological
ability of man to laugh at human things and actions.

Both Jolles and Ranke shift the categorization of oral tradition
from the verbal to the intellectual and psychological level, depending
upon their respective views. Both of them, however, derive their notions about the nature of the ontological archetypes that generate
these genres from the very texts of *Märchen*, legends, jokes, and proverbs themselves. In that way their suggestions involve circularity of
reasoning. First, they reduce the existing genres to either intellectual
or psychological levels, assuming the existence of distinct categories;
then, they proceed to suggest direct causal generative relationships
between the hypothetical system and the folklore forms. Theoretically, the postulation of an existing intellectual or psychological system on the basis of its overt evidence, the verbal expression, is indeed
possible; but the argument that these hypothetical categories are the
models or the source of the texts, from which they were derived to
begin with, involves logical circularity. Jolles and Ranke lack a third
dimension in which the two sets of categories they correlate exist independent of each other. It is necessary to demonstrate that the mental concerns which Jolles postulates and the basic psychological needs
which Ranke surmises do indeed exist independent of folklore genres.

The Functional Approach

The functional approach to the categorization of oral literature actually has focused upon the relationships between forms of verbal art
and existing cultural, psychological, and social needs. Yet the anthropologists who pursued this mode of inquiry were not concerned with
the ontology but the phenomenology of folklore kinds. Their distinction of genre is based not upon any intrinsic qualities of oral literary
forms, but upon the perception and identification of their attributes
by the people themselves. The functional approach is concerned not
with what genres are, but with what the members of the society say
they are. Thus the taxonomy of verbal art has become actually a categorization of cultural experiences, which are represented in the overt
cultural attitudes toward themes and forms. In most cases, these atti-

tudes are represented in the set of relations of belief and nonbelief which has since become the basis for the categorization of formal expressions and for the analytical interpretation of their function in culture. As cultural experiences, such categorizations of oral traditions are unique. No two systems duplicate each other exactly. Hence the construction of a cross-cultural analytical model on the basis of a particular cultural system is a contradiction in terms and amounts to mistaking a deductive model for the real ethnic taxonomies. William Bascom, who proposed a tripartite system of classification for prose narratives,[34] was quite aware of this inherent discrepancy. Hence, he regarded the defined terms *myth*, *legend* and *folktale* only as "analytical concepts which can be meaningfully applied cross culturally even when other systems of 'native categories' are locally recognized."[35] As far as agreement between folklorists is concerned, such an application of clearly defined terms of reference can indeed be meaningful. However, this type of model inevitably falls short of deciphering the ethnic system of folklore categorization whenever it compares an actual cultural experience with an analytical model, a unique phenomenon with a general scheme. When the actual native genres do not agree with the ideal construction, adjustments are necessary. Thus, for example, when some West African societies have a binary rather than tripartite classification of prose narratives, Bascom suggests that "myth and legend apparently *blend* [my italics] into a single category 'myth-legend.'"[36] In making this adjustment Bascom oversteps the limits he himself set for the system he proposed, treating it as if it has a historical-cultural reality and is subject to change. In spite of his constant resort to native terminology, the inherent premise of such a model does not allow for the consideration of the native classification of prose narratives as a complete, complex symbolic system.

II

The frustration felt by comparative folklorists who are struggling to synchronize diversified and incompatible taxonomic systems may often result in statements of desperation such as the declaration by John Greenway that "most pre-literate people are quite indiscriminate about their classification," or that the "primitive mind . . . is [characterized by] unwillingness to abstract."[37] Such pronouncements reflect more the methodological problems of folklore studies than the native powers of perception, distinction, and abstraction. In effect, misconceptions like these arise because of the failure to recognize the differences in function and purpose between analytical and ethnic taxonomies of genres. The former is concerned with the ontology of literary forms. Its ultimate objective is the definition of what a folklore genre is, the description of its literary "mode of existence"[38] in either thematic, morphological, archetypal, or functional terms. Analytical categories of genres have been developed in the context of scholarship and serve its varied research purposes. Native taxonomy, on the other hand, has no external objective. It is a qualitative, subjective system of order. The logical principles that underlie this categorization of oral tradition are those which are meaningful to the members of the group and can guide them in their personal relationships and ritualistic actions. They are reflections of the rules for what can be said, in what situation, in what form, by whom, and to whom. When a person in our society retracts his words by saying, "I was only joking," he actually redirects his words via another genre. Whatever he said violated the rules of regular conversation but is allowed in the genre joke. Hence the incongruity between the analytical and the ethnic systems does not imply that one is more logical, more abstract, or more sophisticated than the other. Any evaluation of that sort is simply irrelevant to ethnic taxonomy. As the grammar of each language is unique and has its own logical consistency, so the native categorization of oral literature is particular and does not need to conform to any analytical delineation of folklore genres.

The ethnic system of genres constitutes a grammar of folklore, a cultural affirmation of the communication rules that govern the expression of complex messages within the cultural context. It is a self-contained system by which society defines its experiences, creative imagination, and social commentary. It consists of distinct forms, each of which has its particular symbolic connotations and scope of applicable social contexts.

Each genre is characterized by a set of relations between its formal features, thematic domains, and potential social usages. For example, alliteration is a formal phonetic feature of redundancy which appears, although not necessarily, in proverbs, riddles, rhymes, and songs,[39] but it is minimal in narratives. When occasionally it does appear in tales and legends it occupies a conspicuous position. On the other hand, prose and poetic narratives can accommodate redundancy on a thematic and structural level. The *Märchen* plot as a story that develops from "villainy or a lack, through intermediary functions to marriage"[40] can appear, with some modification, in epics, but in most European traditions it is rarely a subject for proverbs, as fables and legends often are. The communication of folklore in society operates on the basis of such a system of distinctions and correlations. The native speaker is sensitive to grammatical rules of his own folklore, though not necessarily conscious of them. These the analyst can discover.[41]

From another perspective, it is possible to regard the ethnic system of genres as a cultural metafolklore. Alan Dundes, who first introduced the term, regarded it mainly as oral literary criticism, as "a folkloristic commentary about folklore genres."[42] As examples he cited proverbs about proverbs, jokes about jokes, and the interpretations of expressions by the speakers themselves. However the term *metafolklore* yields itself semantically to a further extension. Metafolklore can be understood to mean the conception a culture has of its own folkloric communication as it is represented in the distinction of forms, the attribution of names to them, and the sense of the social appropriateness of their application in various cultural situations.

The ethnic system of genres is a cognitive correlative of metafolklore, a culturally explicit statement of the conception the speakers have of their expressive forms, formulated in both verbal and behavioral terms. The names of genres are indicative of the attributes people perceive in their verbal art forms. The interpretation of names of genres should not be literal. Such an explanation might point to the etymology of a word but not necessarily to its current meaning. *Märchen* is not simply a short tale, but a complex European narrative form which has a definite thematic domain and stock of characters. The Bini term *umaɾamwen* means literally "a council of animals."[43] Yet in my own work I found only one informant who applied it strictly to animal tales and regarded its contents as purely fictional. Other people understood by *umaɾamwen* a tale without songs.[44]

The behavior of folklore performance also has a defining capacity in terms of genres. The time in which a story is told, for example,

places it in a particular position in the temporal sequence of the social, economical, and political activities of a group. The Marshallese
fairy tale *inoñ* "must be told only at night."[45] Nothing in the term
itself provides any clue to this behavioral pattern, yet the rule is strictly observed, and thus it becomes a component part of the Marshallese concept *inoñ*. Similarly Melville and Frances Herskovits tell us
that the Dahomean

> in his classification of narrative . . . identifies two broad catego-
> ries, the *hwenoho*, literally "time-old-story," which he translates
> variously as history, as traditional history, or as ancient lore; and
> *heho*, the tale. It is a distinction that the youngest story-teller rec-
> ognizes. It has bearing on culturally defined attitudes toward tra-
> ditional lore and improvization, on the one hand, and on priori-
> ties in narration, as governed by seniority rights, professional
> specialization and sexual differentiation of roles, on the other.[46]

In the final analysis each society defines its genres by any number
or combination of terms. Yet the distinctive attributes which speakers
of folklore recognize in their communication can be analytically confined to three levels: prosodic, thematic, and behavioral. The conception of the prosodic nature of an expression is a function of the perception of the relationship between verbal sounds and time; the
formulation of the thematic attributes is dependent upon the relationships between actions, actors, or metaphors; and the recognition
of the behavioral characteristics derives from the potential social composition of the communicative event. An ethnic definition of a genre
may incorporate distinctions made on any or all three levels. A song
can differ from a tale in the prosodic contour of the message, the subject matter, and the occasions the society provides for its performance.

Probably the most commonly recognized attribute of speech is its
prosodic quality. Franz Boas pointed out that "the two fundamental
forms, song and tale, are found among all the people of the world,"
and hence he suggested that "they must be considered the primary
forms of literary activity."[47] For Boas, the notion of primacy, in this
context, refers to the position these two forms have in the development of literary creativity. Rhythmic forms constitute the lowest common denominator of world literatures and hence must be basic to any
verbal expression. However, it is possible to conceive of the primacy

of prose and poetry not in evolutionary but in perceptual terms, in relationship to the immediacy or latency of recognition. The existence or absence of metric substructure in a message is the quality first recognized in any communicative event and hence serves as the primary and most inclusive attribute for the categorization of oral tradition. Consequently, prose and poetry constitute a binary set in which the metric substructure is the crucial attribute that differentiates between these two major divisions. It serves as the definitive feature that polarizes any verbal communication and does not provide any possible intermediary positions. A message is either rhythmic or not. However, within the category of poetry, speakers may be able to perceive several patterns of verbal metrical redundancy which they would recognize as qualitatively different genres. For example, B. W. Andrzejewski and I. M. Lewis note that "the Somali classify their poems into various distinct types, each of which has its own specific name. It seems that their classification is mainly based on two prosodic factors: the type of tune to which the poem is chanted or sung, and the rhythmic pattern of the words."[48]

The very existence or absence of a metric substructure in the verbal message can signify the conception the society has of a particular theme or can provide clues to the narrator's intent. The speaking of prose, for example, associates a message with everyday speech. In spite of the extraordinary events related in a legend, its narration in prose signifies reality and plausibility. However, when the approximation to daily discourse has only an artistic value and the narrator does not seek the credence of his audience, he is likely to preface his tales with cautionary clues such as opening or closing formulae, special vocabulary and phrases inserted into the body of the story, which enable the listeners to grasp the real nature of the message and to not confuse fiction with reality. Thus, among the Marshallese "the fairy tale always begins with the word *kininwante*, which without specific meaning signifies 'this is a fairy tale; it may or may not have happened long ago; it is not to be taken seriously; it is not always supposed to be logical.' "[49] Similarly the Ashanti people open their fictional tales with the formula "we don't really mean to say so; we don't really mean to say so."[50] In current American usage, the phrase "have you heard about . . ." often demarcates the joke from the regular prose speech into which it is inserted.

Similarly, the speaking of poetry signifies the conception the speakers have of their subject matter or of the occasion. The usage of metric prosody can have a wide range of significance, varying from religious sanctions to magical power to mere play, each depending upon the circumstances of delivery. Common to all poetic expression, however, is the deliberate deviation from everyday speech, and with it the departure from the profane, the realistic, or the true. This, of course, does not imply that any information communicated in a poetic form is ontologically false or intended to be imaginary. Most ballads and epics do contain a nucleus of historical truth. Jan Vansina, for example, went so far as to construct a method for the induction of the possible historical truth in African poetic recitations.[51] The ballad "Tom Dooley," popular in the United States a few years ago, was based on a local historical incident.[52] However, the delivery of this story in a metric form indicates an intent to affect the audience emotionally and not merely to transmit factual information to them. As a matter of fact, in prose fiction there is a contradiction between the signification of prose speech and the cultural attitude to the subject matter; hence, such narration often requires special disclaimers of any truth value. In contrast, because poetic forms signify a departure from reality, any intent on the part of the speaker to establish his story as true needs validating statements, such as the opening formulae in broadside ballads which establish the story as a testimony.

In spite of the fact that prose and poetry are mutually exclusive forms of verbal art, the prosodic structure of a single expression, or even of a whole genre, does not have to be metrically uniform. It may include segments of varied prosodic nature. In fact, in Africa, where singing is often an integral part of the storytelling event, some peoples regard the existence or absence of songs interspersed in the prose text as a primary distinctive attribute for the categorization of narratives. Thus Clement Doke informs us that "Lamba folk-lore is classified by the natives in two ways, according to the mode of recitations. First and foremost comes the prose story, called *Icisimikisyo*. The other, which, for want of a better term, is translated as 'Choric Story,' is variously called by the natives . . . *Ulusimi, Icisimi, Akasimi* and *Akalaŵi*. This is a prose story interspersed with songs."[53]

The Gbaya and the Bini peoples also divide their prose narratives in such a way. Among the Gbaya "the main distinguishing feature between the *tô* and the *lizang* is the song [*gima*]."[54] The Bini, who distinguish between songs, *ihuan*, and tales, categorize the latter in terms of the metric composition of the entire narrative: tales with songs are *okha*, and tales without them are *umaramwen*. This kind of classification is by no means universal in cultures where these two modes of storytelling exist. Other societies may ignore the form of recitation as a distinctive attribute between genres and focus upon other characteristics of their narratives.

The basis for the categorization of verbal art into prose and poetry is the concrete, physiological reality of speech. It is an objective, observable, and verifiable process, the attributes of which are not dependent solely upon the subjective perception of the speakers. Metric speech constitutes an ontological system objectively distinct from prose. Although various peoples may draw the demarcation line between the two categories at different points, and boundaries between the two divisions may fluctuate even within a single group, there will always be a substantive distinction between them. In contrast, the ethnic taxonomy of verbal art in terms of its secondary attributes, the thematic and behavioral features, is a phenomenological system. It is a function of the social experience of folkloric communication. Because the speaking of folklore involves a process of exchanging messages that have to be mutually comprehensive to be effective, it must adhere to consistent rules of communication. An ethnic genre must have defining features which signify its potential connotations and clearly distinguish it from other forms of verbal art. This fact of cultural consistency and coherence may permit future discussions of folkloric systems, similar to such studies in other social sciences.

For the time being, any suggestions in this direction must be hypothetical in nature. All the facts required for the deciphering of any given system of verbal art are simply not available since folklorists previously have sought solutions to other types of problems.

Because the folkloric system in any given culture functions in society in both thematic and behavioral terms it seems reasonable to assume, at this preliminary stage of our inquiry, that each genre consists of distinctive attributes on both these levels. Furthermore, because an ethnic genre is a part of a whole folkloric system, it must relate to other forms in the same network of communication. Hence these distinctive attributes are, at the same time, also in contrastive relations to the defining features of other genres. Of course such relations are possible only between attributes that share a dimension of relevance. Thus, it is possible to contrast two types of protagonists, two kinds of social situations, and two different narrative endings.

On the basis of the foregoing assumptions it is possible to consider an ethnic genre as a verbal art form consisting of a cluster of thematic and behavioral attributes and to formulate the relationships between the various elements of the folkloric system in the form of a paradigm.[55] For illustrative purposes it seems best to quote, at some length, a discussion of folklore genres in which there is an attempt to define the nature of each form in a deductive method, in the light of established notions about the nature of "myth," "legend," and "tale," and then to examine the same genres inductively, in the light of the previous argument. William Bascom's description of two prose genres of the Yoruba people of Nigeria will serve that purpose.

> The Yoruba recognize two classes of stories: the folktale (alọ) . . . and the myths, traditions, or "histories" (itan). The folktales are ordinarily told for amusement about the fire on moonlight evenings during the season of harmattan. The myths on the other hand are regarded as historically true, and are quoted by old men to settle a difficult point in a serious discussion of ritual or political matters. Both types, however, are recited under the same conditions by the diviners as part of the Ifa verses.
>
> By and large the myths or histories are distinguished by having deities or legendary figures as characters rather than animals, and by explaining or justifying present-day ritual behavior. But as Boas pointed out, because of the ease of substitution of characters and explanatory elements, these distinctions do not make it possible to classify any plot as either myth or a tale in the generic sense. In some verses the deities Ifa and Eshu appear in the role of trickster instead of Tortoise; but there are many others . . . where the characters are animals, and some in which Tortoise himself is the trickster. And in the Ifa verses, the purpose of both myths and tales is to justify the prediction that is made and to explain to the client why a particular sacrifice is necessary.
>
> It is obvious that these stories are not recited by the diviners simply for the amusement of their clients, and that their function

is not limited to providing entertainment or aesthetic satisfaction. They are not non-utilitarian, but have practical application of a type that can be compared to the use of elaborate costumes, carved masks, or highly decorated paraphernalia in religious ceremonies. It is generally accepted that graphic and plastic art in primitive cultures is seldom pure art; in this instance we have a case of applied art in the field of literature. The verbal incantations, the myths, and the songs used as a part of magical and religious ritual can also be cited as examples of "applied" literary art.

While the full significance of this point may not have been previously recognized, it is implicit in the attempts that have been made to distinguish myths from folktales on the basis of whether or not they are employed as a part of ritual. However since both myths and folktales, according to the Yoruba categories, are associated with the ritual of divination, a distinction between them on this basis is no more satisfactory than one based on the type of characters which appear in the plot. The real basis of the Yoruba categories seems to be whether the accounts are to be regarded as fact or fiction.[56]

Thus Bascom carefully describes the characteristics of each of these genres, weighs the evidence one way or another before he categorizes them, and finally, in conclusion, he reduces the differences between *itan* and *alọ* to the contrast between belief and nonbelief. Yet this very evaluation of narratives as truth or fiction is actually not a primary but a secondary formulation of attitudes toward the thematic and behavioral attributes the speakers perceive in the narratives themselves. There is a whole gamut of distinctions between these two genres, and, although the reduction of their differences to just a single set of contrastive attributes may be analytically convenient, it is ethnographically simplistic.

Yet Bascom's description can serve as a basis for a preliminary formulation of the relations between *itan* and *alọ* as two communicative entities within the Yoruba folkloric system. Accordingly, *itan* is a verbal art form consistently related to ritual or politics, its narrators are either diviners or old men, it revolves around either deities or human heroes, and it is considered as either religious or historical truth. On the other hand, *alǫ* is told for amusement, by any person in the society, its protagonists are often animals, and it is regarded by the Yoruba as fiction. The attributes of *itan* and *alǫ* relate to each other within the framework of several dimensions. Thus in terms of the social situations in which people narrate the two genres, *itan* relates to *alǫ* as ritual or politics to amusement. The singularity of *itan* in Yoruba folklore is analogous to the distinctions diviners and older men have in this society. Thematically, it is possible to consider, for the time being, only the nature of the protagonist, and, in this context, the contrast between the two genres is equivalent to that between deities and heroes on the one hand and animals on the other. In their totality the Yoruba consider *itan* as a true account of historical or religious events, whereas *alǫ* is a narration of fictional matters.

On the basis of the cluster of features that coexist within a single genre and the contrastive attributes on each dimension, it is possible to formulate a paradigm of relations between *itan* and *alǫ* as the Yoruba themselves conceive of them. Thus in the Yoruba grammar of folklore:

itan : *alǫ* :: ritual/politics : amusement :: old men/diviners : any sex/any age :: deities/human heroes : animals :: religious or historical truth : fiction

These relationships are shown in another form in the accompanying table.

Yoruba Paradigm for *itan* and *alǫ*

Dimension	Genre	
	itan	*alǫ*
Situation	ritual/politics	amusement
Narrator's status	old men/diviners	any age/any sex
Protagonist	deities/human heroes	animals
Attitude	truth: religious or historical	fiction

Of course, the more extensive the analytical study of the texts is, and the more detailed the observations of its performance and the inquiry into the attitudes are, the more closely these paradigmatic relations between the distinctive attributes of *alọ* and *itan* will reflect the ethnic conception of these two genres. Such details should include the distinct thematic domains of each genre, their particular formal qualities, and connotative references. The paradigm should point to the entire range of social components that constitute the situations in which they are applicable and any other kinds of relations that can be induced from the formal expressions in the ethnic genre system.

Bascom's description of the Yoruba genres *alọ* and *itan* and the frustrations he encountered in the definitions of the exact distinctions between them illustrate an additional relationship of attributes, that of equivalence. Some generic features are not distinctive, but under certain circumstances they are, borrowing a term from linguistics, in free-variation with each other. That is to say, the substitution of one attribute for another does not produce any significant changes in the symbolic value of the verbal form and has equivalent effect. Attributes in free-variation with each other are culturally determined. Thus, for example, it is no accident that the deity Eshu is substituted for Tortoise in these narratives, for in the Yoruba belief system Eshu is the trickster among the deities,[57] as Tortoise is among the animals; hence under certain circumstances they are found in free-variation with each other without producing any qualitative changes in the genres themselves.

Similarly, the Ifa diviner has a particular conception of Yoruba tradition that deviates from the generally accepted one. Although diviners do quote from and refer to *alọ* as well as *itan* in their divinations, they conceive all narrative traditions as a single category, of which the appropriate usage is in the ritualistic situation. As far as they are concerned all tradition has the same symbolic value and hence the same name, and they "describe all Ifa narratives as *itan*,"[58] ignoring the generally accepted dichotomy between the two prose genres. Consistent with their conception of these narratives, and in spite of the fact that "the diviners are recognized as knowing more folktales than other individuals, . . . they may not use this knowledge for secular purposes." Moreover, "in Ifa it is a professional tabu for diviners to tell folktales (*pa alọ*) for amusement, or even to join in singing the songs in the tales when they are being told by someone else."[59] Thus, what appeared to be an irreconcilable feature of Yoruba genres from an analytical standpoint in an earlier description later turns out to be

consistent with the rules of grammar of folklore as the Yoruba diviner conceives of them.

The set of contrastive attributes represents the structure of relations
between the distinct genres in the system of folklore communication.
They are contrastive only in their cultural context. There is no inherent opposition between amusement and ritual or politics, as there is
no ontological reason for the association of ritual and politics or of
religion and history as equivalent attributes. Similarly, the clusters of
attributes within a single genre have logical consistency within the
cultural context. Animals, for example, might be associated with to-
temism in other societies and would have closer affinity with ritual
and social structure than with amusement and fiction, as is the case in
Yoruba trickster tales. Yet for the Yoruba man who lives in a society
in which divine kingship is the dominant religio-political order, these
contrasts and associations are sound and valid. They are congruent
with the social and religious systematization of his culture. In that
sense the analysis of ethnic genres has a diagnostic value as well.
Since the cultural conception of the folkloric communicative system
is part of the general cultural cognitive reality, it should be methodologically possible to infer from the categorization of folklore some
general principles underlying the taxonomy of the cosmic natural and
social universe.

The summation of thematic and behavioral attributes of a genre
and its position in the folkloric system are best indicated by the terms
people use for their expressive forms. The names of genres often reflect their symbolic value in the network of formal communication
and their position in the cultural cognitive categories. Each name signifies the semantic component of the genre in all its manifestations,
the basic common denominator that unifies all its attributes in the
culture. Thus even expressions which are formally similar have different symbolic meanings in separate ethnic systems of genres. Proverbs,
for example, often deviate from the regular syntactic structure of a
language and thus relate to everyday speech in similar manner in different societies. Yet in each culture they have their particular symbolic connotations and communicative value. The Hausa people of
Northern Nigeria regard a proverb, *karin magana*, in terms of its application in verbal context,[60] whereas the Jabo of Liberia regard it as
"old matter," *da' di kpa*.[61] The proverbs are "first principles" for the

Marshallese,[62] and in biblical Hebrew *mashal*[63] means an exemplary dictum as well as a fable.

Not all cultures have an explicit linguistic taxonomy of verbal art beyond the primary prosodic distinction between prose and poetry. This is so despite the fact that the people are likely to perceive the thematic and behavioral distinctive attributes of the various genres. In such cases the name of the general category points to the primary attribute that unifies all these different forms in the cultural cognition. The Limba people of Sierra Leone, for example, have a single term for their prose expression—*mbɔrɔ*. According to Ruth Finnegan, who recorded their tales, "the Limba themselves do not make any further clear division. In most dialects the same term is used to cover a wide range of formulations, from 'folktales' in the accepted sense of the word to shorter forms such as riddles and proverbs, as well as what we would normally call historical accounts. None of these classes are strictly differentiated by the Limba."[64]

From Finnegan's further discussion it is not quite clear whether the Limba really do not distinguish between the various prose forms or whether the term *mbɔrɔ* is simply a polysemic word with different meanings in different linguistic and social contexts. However, the Limba people seem to differentiate behaviorally, if not overtly verbally, between the various forms of *mbɔrɔ*. The speakers talk the shorter forms, which Finnegan compares with proverbs or analogies, in the context of persuasion, argument, oratory, and joking. On the other hand, storytellers narrate the longer *mbɔrɔ* forms in the relaxed atmosphere before retirement in the evening.[65] Thus the social behavior of the Limba does indicate that the term *mbɔrɔ*, which seems to be all-inclusive, has different meanings and refers to distinct forms on separate occasions.

In any case, although the concept *mbɔrɔ* seems to parallel a somewhat extended notion of the English term *prose narrative*, its connotations are completely different. In their categorization, the Limba people are concerned neither with the prose nor with the narrative qualities of its forms. According to Finnegan,

The concept of *mbɔrɔ* is an integrated one . . . [and has] two main strands. . . . These are first the connexion with age and tradition, and secondly, the idea of analogical expression. . . . In the first place the word *mbɔrɔ* seems to be connected with the root *bɔrɔ*, old. *Mabɔrɔ ma* are the "old times" or "ancient ways," *bebɔrɔ* the "old people," usually referring to the dead ancestors, and *bɔrɔ* commonly occurs in various grammatical forms as the ordinary adjective meaning "old." . . . Moreover, whatever the linguistic facts about the derivation of the word *mbɔrɔ*, the concept does seem to be closely associated in Limba eyes with the idea of age and tradition. . . . The Limba very often are very conscious of the wisdom and presence of "the old people."[66]

In an earlier discussion Finnegan mentioned that "artistic expression and inspiration, whether of singers, storytellers, dancers or drummers, is thought to come from essentially the same source—the dead, 'the old people.' "[67] "The second main connotation of *mbɔrɔ*, apparent in at least the majority of the many usages of the term, is that of a comment or reflection in analogical terms. This is naturally specially clear when *mbɔrɔ* is used to mean metaphor, parable and analogy; but even when *mbɔrɔ* means the more straight-forward stories, it seems to suggest this aspect."[68]

The inquiry into the names for genres must extend beyond the limits of etymological interpretation. Historically and geographically the same names may mean different things in the same language in separate periods and in distinct regional dialects. Conversely, two different words may acquire the same meanings in different periods. Moreover, with usage, the names may develop a complex semantic structure, for which etymology alone would not account. Hence the study of the ethnic system of genres must combine the cognitive, expressive, and behavioral levels of genres in each culture.

Although the significance of ethnic classifications of folklore has long been recognized, in most cases its actual study was frustrated by the discrepancy between the analytical and the ethnic systems. The preceding discussion is merely an exploratory outline which attempts to point to areas of promise rather than to present conclusive theory and method. However, if folklore communication, allusive and complex as it is, is based upon culturally defined rules, then discovery of them is essential. The system of genres is the primary ethnic formulation of such a grammar of folklore.

Notes

In writing this essay I profited from discussions with Kenneth Goldstein and Joel Sherzer. The comments of my wife Paula were indispensable.

1. Carl-Herman Tillhagen, "Was ist eine Sage? Eine Definition und ein Vorschlag für ein europäisches Sagensystem," *Acta Ethnographica* 13 (1964): 9–17.

2. Alan Dundes, "Texture, Text, and Context," *Southern Folklore Quarterly* 28 (1964): 252.

3. Stith Thompson, *The Folktale*, p. 8.

4. Jacob and Wilhelm Grimm, *Deutsche Sagen*, 3d ed. (Berlin, 1891), p. vii [1st ed., 1816].

5. Herbert Jennings Rose, *A Handbook of Greek Mythology Including Its Extension to Rome* (1928; reprint ed., New York: Dutton, 1959), pp. 286–304.

6. Joseph Jacobs, "Some Types of Indo-European Folktales," in *The Handbook of Folk-lore*, ed. Charlotte Sophia Burne, rev. ed. (London: Sidgwick, 1914), pp. 344–355. This is a revised list of "story radicals" which appeared in S. Baring-Gould, "Household Tales," in *Notes on the Folk Lore of Northern Counties of England and the Borders*, ed. William Henderson (London, 1866), pp. 299–311.

7. See Ben Edwin Perry, *The Ancient Romances: A Literary-Historical Account of Their Origins* (Berkeley and Los Angeles: University of California Press, 1967), pp. 236–282.

8. Archer Taylor, *The Proverb*, pp. 27–32.

9. William Paton Ker, *Epic and Romance: Essays on Medieval Literature*, pp. 123–132.

10. William John Courthope, *A History of English Poetry* (New York: Macmillan, 1895), I, 445–468.

11. Louise Pound, *Poetic Origins and the Ballad* (New York: Macmillan, 1921), pp. 28, 45–46.

12. Julie R. Mackey, "Medieval Metrical Saints' Lives and the Origin of the Ballad" (Ph.D. diss., University of Pennsylvania, Philadelphia, 1968).

13. The study of its diffusion is a classic monograph in the historical-geographic school of folklore. See Walter Anderson, *Kaiser und Abt: Die Geschichte eines Schwanks*, Folklore Fellows Communications, no. 42 (Helsinki: Suomalainen Tiedeakatemia, 1923).

14. Antti Aarne and Stith Thompson, *The Types of the Folktale*, 2d rev. ed., Folklore Fellows Communications, no. 184 (Helsinki: Suomalainen Tiedeakatemia, 1961), pp. 320–321.

15. See Haim Schwarzbaum, *Studies in Jewish and World Folklore* (Berlin: Walter de Gruyter, 1968), pp. 115–116, and Dov Noy, *Folktales of Israel* (Chicago: University of Chicago Press, 1963), pp. 94–97.

16. Francis J. Child, *The English and Scottish Popular Ballads* (Boston, 1882–1898), I, 403–414, no. 45.

17. Elsie Clews Parsons, *Folk-Tales of Andros Island, Bahamas*, American Folklore Society Memoir Series, no. 13 (New York: American Folklore Society, 1918), pp. 152–154; and Martha Warren Beckwith, "The English Ballad in Jamaica: A Note upon the Origin of the Ballad Form," *PMLA* 39 (1924): 475–476.

18. For references to both prose and poetic forms, see Aarne and Thompson, *Types of the Folktale*, Type 780 ("The Singing Bone"), p. 269.

19. Thompson, *The Folktale*, p. 7.

20. See "Folktale," in *Funk & Wagnalls Standard Dictionary of Folklore, Mythology and Legend*, ed. Maria Leach and Jerome Fried (New York: Funk & Wagnalls, 1949), I, 408.

21. Ruth Benedict, *Zuni Mythology*, Columbia University Contribution to Anthropology, no. 21 (New York: Columbia University Press, 1935), I, xiii.

22. Ibid., p. xxx.

23. Ibid., p. xiii.

24. For a brief discussion of the "syntagmatic," sequential, and "paradigmatic" types of structural analysis and their application to folklore, see Alan Dundes, "Introduction to the Second Edition," in *Morphology of the Folktale*, ed. Vladímir Propp, pp. xi–xvii. This article includes a short, valuable bibliography about the various approaches to structural analysis in folklore and related texts. Other essays are included in "Recherches sémiologiques: L'Analyse structurale du récit," *Communications*, no. 8 (1966). Also of interest are Anne Retel-Laurentin, "Structure et symbolisme: Essai méthodologique pour l'étude des contes africains," *Cahiers d'études africaines* 8, no. 30 (1968): 206–244; Eugenio Donato, "Of Structuralism and Literature," *Modern Language Notes* 82 (1967): 549–574; Dell Hymes, "The 'Wife' Who 'Goes Out' Like a Man: Reinterpretation of a Clackamas Chinook Myth," *Social Science Information* 7 (1968): 173–199.

25. Carl Wilhelm von Sydow, in *Selected Papers on Folklore*, ed. Laurits Bødker, pp. 127–145.

26. Propp, *Morphology of the Folktale*, p. 19.

27. Ibid., p. 25.

28. Archer Taylor, "The Biographical Pattern in Traditional Narrative," *Journal of the Folklore Institute* 1 (1964): 114–129.

29. Claude Lévi-Strauss, "L'analyse morphologique des contes populaires russes," *International Journal of Slavic Linguistics and Poetics* 3 (1960): 136.

30. Alan Dundes, *The Morphology of North American Indian Folktales*.

31. André Jolles, *Einfache Formen: Legende, Sage, Mythe, Rätsel, Spruch, Kasus, Memorabile, Märchen, Witz*. For discussions of Jolles's theory, see Wolfgang Mohr, "Einfache Formen," in *Reallexikon der deutschen Literaturgeschichte*, ed. Paul Merker and Wolfgang Stammler, 2d ed. revised by Werner Kohlschmidt and Wolfgang Mohr (Berlin: Walter de Gruyter, 1958), I, 321–328; and Walter A. Berendsohn, "Einfache Formen," in *Handwörterbuch des deutschen Märchen*, ed. Johannes Bolte and Lutz Mackensen,

I, 484–498; Robert Petsch, "Die Lehre von den 'Einfache Formen,' " *Deutsche Viereljahrsschrift für Literaturwissenschaft und Geistesgeschichte* 10 (1932): 335–369; Hermann Bausinger, *Formen der "Volkspoesie,"* pp. 51–64.

32. Kurt Ranke, "Einfache Formen," trans. William Templer and Eberhard Alsen, *Journal of the Folklore Institute* 4 (1967): 17–31. First published in German in *Internationaler Kongress der Volkserzählungsforscher in Kiel und Kopenhagen [1959]—Vorträge und Referate*, pp. 1–11.

33. Ibid., p. 27.

34. William R. Bascom, "The Forms of Folklore: Prose Narratives," *Journal of American Folklore* 78 (1965): 3–20.

35. Ibid., p. 5.

36. Ibid., p. 10.

37. John Greenway, *Literature among the Primitives*, p. 35.

38. René Wellek and Austin Warren, *Theory of Literature*, 2d rev. ed. (1956), pp. 129–145.

39. See, for example, S. J. Sackett, "Poetry and Folklore: Some Points of Affinity," *Journal of American Folklore* 77 (1964): 143–153.

40. Propp, *Morphology of the Folktale*, p. 92.

41. The idea that the social usage of folklore in culture follows some principles and regulations is by no means new and was expressed, implicitly and explicitly, in Roman Jakobson and P. Bogatyrev, "Die Folklore als besondere form des Schaffens," in *Donum Natalicium Schrijnen: Verzamenling van opstellen door ond-Leerlingen en bevriende vakgenooten opgedragen ann Mgr. Prof. Dr. Jos. Schrijnen* (Nijmegen-Utrecht: Dekker & van de Vegt, 1929), pp. 900–913; Dell Hymes, "Introduction: Toward Ethnographies of Communication," pp. 1–34, and E. Ojo Arewa and Alan Dundes, "Proverbs and the Ethnography of Speaking Folklore," pp. 70–85, both in *American Anthropologist* 66, no. 6, pt. 2 (Special Publication, *The Ethnography of Communication*, ed. John J. Gumperz and Dell Hymes [1964]); and Dell Hymes, "The Ethnography of Speaking," in *Anthropology and Human Behavior*, ed. Thomas Gladwin and William C. Sturtevant (Washington, D.C.: Anthropological Society of Washington, 1962), pp. 15–53.

42. Alan Dundes, "Metafolklore and Oral Literary Criticism," *The Monist* 50 (1966): 505–516.

43. Hans Melzian, *A Concise Dictionary of the Bini Language of Southern Nigeria* (London: Kegan Paul, Trench, Trübner & Co., 1937), pp. 12, 206.

44. Dan Ben-Amos, "The Modern Local Historian in Africa," forthcoming in *Folklore in the Modern World*, ed. Richard M. Dorson, Proceedings of the IXth International Congress of Anthropological and Ethnological Sciences, Chicago, September 1–8, 1973 (The Hague: Mouton). The examples from Benin interspersed in the present essay are based on my field work in the Benin region, midwestern Nigeria, in 1966.

45. William H. Davenport, "Marshallese Folklore Types," *Journal of American Folklore* 66 (1953): 224.

46. Melville J. and Frances S. Herskovits, *Dahomean Narrative: A Cross-*

Cultural Analysis (Evanston, Ill.: Northwestern University Press, 1958), pp. 14–15.

47. Franz Boas, "Stylistic Aspects of Primitive Literature," *Journal of American Folklore* 38 (1925): 329. This article is reprinted in Boas, *Race, Language and Culture* (New York: Macmillan Co., 1940), pp. 491–502.

48. B. W. Andrzejewski and I. M. Lewis, *Somali Poetry: An Introduction*, Oxford Library of African Literature (Oxford: Clarendon Press, 1964), p. 46.

49. Davenport, "Marshallese Folklore Types," p. 224.

50. R. S. Rattray, *Akan-Ashanti Folk-Tales* (Oxford: Clarendon Press, 1930), p. 8.

51. Jan Vansina, *Oral Tradition: A Study in Historical Methodology*, trans. H. M. Wright (Chicago: Aldine, 1965), pp. 148–151.

52. See *The Frank C. Brown Collection of North Carolina Folklore*, vol. 2, ed. Henry M. Belden and Arthur Palmer Hudson (Durham, N.C., 1952), 703–714; and John F. West, *The Ballad of Tom Dula* (Durham, N.C.: Moore Publishing Co., 1970).

53. Clement Doke, *Lamba Folk-Lore*, American Folklore Society Memoir Series, no. 20 (New York: American Folklore Society, 1927), p. xiv.

54. Philip Noss, "Gbaya Traditional Literature," *Abbia*, nos. 17–18 (1967), p. 38.

55. The notions of "distinctive features" and "contrastive attributes" as used here constitute extensions and modifications of similar concepts developed by Roman Jakobson and his collaborators in regard to language and by Claude Lévi-Strauss in regard to social structure and myth. See Roman Jakobson, Gunnar M. Fant, and Morris Halle, *Preliminaries to Speech Analysis: The Distinctive Features and Their Correlates* (Cambridge, Mass.: M.I.T. Press, 1952); Roman Jakobson and Morris Halle, *Fundamentals of Language* (The Hague: Mouton, 1956); Claude Lévi-Strauss, *Structural Anthropology*, trans. Claire Jacobson and Brooke Grundfest Schoepf (New York: Basic Books, 1963), and *The Savage Mind* (Chicago: University of Chicago Press, 1966).

56. William R. Bascom, "The Relationship of Yoruba Folklore to Divining," *Journal of American Folklore* 56 (1943): 129–130.

57. See E. Bọlaji Idowu, *Olódùmarè God in Yoruba Belief* (New York: Frederick A. Praeger, 1963), pp. 80–85.

58. William R. Bascom, *Ifa Divination: Communication between Gods and Men in West Africa* (Bloomington: Indiana University Press, 1969), p. 130.

59. Ibid., p. 131.

60. G. P. Bargery, *A Hausa-English Dictionary and English-Hausa Vocabulary* (London: Oxford University Press, 1934), p. 569.

61. George C. Herzog and Charles G. Blooah, *Jabo Proverbs from Liberia*, p. 1.

62. Davenport, "Marshallese Folklore Types," p. 231.

63. A. R. Johnson, " משל ," *Vetus Testamentum, Supplement*, 3: 162–169.

64. Ruth Finnegan, *Limba Stories and Story-Telling* (Oxford: Clarendon Press, 1967), p. 28.

65. Ibid., pp. 42–48.

66. Ibid., pp. 46–47.

67. Ibid., p. 25.

68. Ibid., p. 47.

Notes on the Contributors

Roger D. Abrahams is professor of English and anthropology at the University of Texas at Austin. He received his Ph.D. degree in English literature and folklore from the University of Pennsylvania. His field research was conducted in various parts of the United States and the Caribbean. Among his books are *Deep Down in the Jungle* (1964, 1970), *Anglo-American Folksong Style* (with George Foss, 1968), *Jump Rope Rhymes: A Dictionary* (1969), *Positively Black* (1970), *A Singer and Her Songs* (1970), and *Deep the Water, Shallow the Shore* (1974). In addition, he has authored numerous articles and reviews, which have appeared in journals and volumes of essays.

Dan Ben-Amos, associate professor of folklore at the University of Pennsylvania, studied folklore at Indiana University, where he received his Ph.D. degree. He edited *In Praise of the Baal Shem Tov: The Earliest Collection of Legends about the Founder of Hasidism* (with Jerome R. Mintz, 1970), *Thrice Told Tales: Parallel Tales from Three Continents* (with Kenneth S. Goldstein, 1970), and *Folklore: Performance, Communication* (with Kenneth S. Goldstein, 1975) and has written several articles on folklore. He has done field research in Nigeria.

David E. Bynum received his Ph.D. degree from Harvard University, where he continued to teach and research. Currently he is lecturer on oral literature and curator of the Milman Parry Collection of Oral Literature, Harvard University. He has done field work in Yugoslavia, Mali, and Zambia. He has published articles in *Anali Filološkog Fakulteta*, *Filološki Pregled*, *Journal of the Folklore Institute*, and *Publications of the Modern Language Association*, as well as in the *Harvard Literary Bulletin*.

Linda Dégh is the author and editor of over a dozen books in Hungarian on folk narratives. Among her works in English are *Folktales of Hungary* (1965, 1969) and *Folktales and Society: Story-Telling in a Hungarian Peasant Community* (1969). In addition, she has written numerous articles and reviews in both Hungarian and English. Dégh taught at Eötvös Loránd University, Budapest, and currently is professor of folklore at Indiana University. She is the founder and editor of *Indiana Folklore*, associate editor of the *Journal of American Folklore*, and has served as first vice-president of the American Folklore Society (1971–1972). She has done field research in Europe and in the United States. Among her many distinctions is the Giuseppe Pitré folklore prize (1963).

V. Hrdličková received her Ph.D. degree from Charles University, Prague, and is currently assistant professor in the Far Eastern Department of the same institution. She lived in China and Japan for over twelve years, studying storytellers in both countries. Her articles on this subject appeared in *Acta Universitatis Carolinae, Archiv Orientální, Transactions of the Asiatic Society of Japan*, and *Journal of the Folklore Institute*.

Max Lüthi is professor of European folk literature at the University of Zürich, Switzerland. His principal area of interest is the study of prose narratives and Shakespearean dramas, two subjects on which he has written numerous articles and several books. Among them are *Das europäische Volksmärchen: Form und Wesen* (1947; 4th ed., 1974), *Volksmärchen und Volkssage: Zwei Grundformen erzahlender Dichtung* (1961, 1966), *Volksliteratur und Hochliteratur—Thematik, Menschenbild, Formstreben* (1970), *Shakespeares Dramen* (1957, 1966), and, in English, *Once upon a Time: On the Nature of Fairy Tales* (1970).

Harry Oster, professor of English at the University of Iowa, received his Ph.D. degree from Cornell University. His field research extended over a period of five years in Louisiana, during which time he was able to focus on French folklore in Louisiana and on Afro-American folksongs, tales, and music. In addition, his scholarly interests relate to American Jewish literature, the southern novel, and traditional ethnic groups in Iowa. He has produced and edited many records and has published many articles, as well as the book *Living Country Blues* (1969).

Charles T. Scott is professor of English and director of programs in English linguistics at the University of Wisconsin, Madison. He received his Ph.D. degree in linguistics from the University of Texas at Austin. He wrote and edited several books on linguistics, among them *Approaches in Linguistic Methodology* (with I. Rauch, 1967) and *Readings for the History of the English Language* (with J. Erickson, 1968). His main folklore study is *Persian and Arabic Riddles: A Language-Centered Approach to Genre Definition* (1965). In addition he has published many articles on linguistics, on the teaching of English, and on folklore, particularly the riddle.

Peter Seitel, currently with the Division of Performing Arts of the Smithsonian Institution, was an assistant professor in the department of anthropology at Princeton University. He received his Ph.D. degree in folklore from the University of Pennsylvania. His field research was conducted in Tanzania, on the basis of which he wrote several articles forthcoming in various publications.

Barre Toelken lived for several years among the Navahos, including considerable time with the family of Yellowman, the subject of his present essay. Currently he is professor of English at the University of Oregon, from which he also received his Ph.D. degree in English and where he was given several teaching awards. In addition to his interest in Native American folklore, he has written about ballads and folksongs, which he not only studies but also performs. He published many articles in *Western Folklore, Journal of the Folklore Institute*, and other journals and is currently the editor of the *Journal of American Folklore* (1973–).

Francis Lee Utley (1907–1974) was professor of English and director of the Center for Medieval and Renaissance Studies at Ohio State University. He received his doctorate degree from Harvard University and continued with an illustrious career in humanistic scholarship. He was president of the American Folklore Society (1951–

1952), the American Name Society (1966), and the College English Association (1969) and served as a member of the executive council of the Modern Language Association. He wrote numerous articles and reviews; his students and colleagues published *Medieval Literature and Folklore Studies: Essays in Honor of Francis Lee Utley*, ed. Jerome Mandel and Bruce Rosenberg (1970).

Andrew Vázsonyi writes novels, short stories, and essays on literature in Hungarian. He has shifted to English in his more recent writings on folklore, which he has published jointly with his wife Linda Dégh. He is associate chairman and director of publications, Indiana University Research Center for the Language Sciences.

A Selected Bibliography

The bibliography is divided into two sections: "The Concept of Genre in Folklore" and "The Concept of Genre in Literary Criticism." Because the concept of genre is fundamental to folklore research, publication, and instruction and serves as a major organizing principle in this field of study, the first section could have been expanded enormously. To avoid undesirable size, certain limits were set. Text collections, indexes, bibliographies, and dictionary and encyclopedic entries devoted to one folklore genre or another are omitted. Also not included are many important studies that do concentrate on significant aspects of folklore genres—such as their performance, transmission, and function—but not in terms of analyzing their generic properties. To the folklorist, a glaring omission will be that of studies on superstitions. The reason for this lacuna is my view that superstition constitutes a category of belief, not of expression, and hence cannot be conceived on the same level as other folklore genres; any further discussion of this point must await another occasion. The second section, selected works related to the problem of genres in literary criticism, does not include studies of individual genres.

The bibliography lists only English, French, and German publications, though it by no means covers all the relevant publications in these languages. (I hope other students of folklore will prepare similar bibliographies for other languages.) Translated works are entered by English title and date of publication; the date of publication in the original language is in brackets. Also included in brackets are references to reprints and to the availability of further bibliography in a given publication. An asterisk indicates a work available to me only in reprint; bibliographical information on original publication therefore is incomplete.

Dan Ben-Amos

Abbreviations Used in the Bibliography

AEASH	*Acta Ethnographica Academiae Scientiarum Hungaricae*
CA	*Current Anthropology*
Communications	*Communications* (Paris: Ecole Pratique des Hautes Etudes, Centre d'Etudes des Communications de Masse)
EF	*Ethnologie Française*
Fabula	*Fabula: Journal of Folktale Studies*
FFC	Folklore Fellows Communications
HBV	*Hessische Blätter für Volkskunde*
Helicon	*Helicon: Revue internationale des problèmes généraux de la littérature*
Homme	*L'Homme: Revue française d'anthropologie*
HSNPL	*Harvard Studies and Notes in Philology and Literature*
IJAL	*International Journal of American Linguistics*
JAAC	*Journal of Aesthetics and Art Criticism*
JAF	*Journal of American Folklore*
JFI	*Journal of the Folklore Institute*
MF	*Midwest Folklore*
NZV	*Niederdeutsche Zeitschrift für Volkskunde*
Poétique	*Poétique: Revue de théorie et d'analyse littéraires*
Semeia	*Semeia: An Experimental Journal for Biblical Criticism*
Semiotica	*Semiotica: Revue publiée par l'association internationale de sémiotique*
SF*Q*	*Southern Folklore Quarterly*
SG	*Studium Generale*
SS	*Saga och Sed*
Temenos	*Temenos: Studies in Comparative Religion Presented by Scholars in Denmark, Finland, Norway and Sweden*
ZRL	*Zagadienia Rodzajów Literackich (Les problèmes des genres littéraires)*

The Concept of Genre in Folklore

ABRAHAMS, ROGER D.

1962   The Toast: A Neglected Form of Folk Narrative. In Beck, ed., 1962:1–11.

1968   A Rhetoric of Everyday Life: Traditional Conversational Genres. *SFQ* 32:44–59.

1969   The Complex Relations of Simple Forms. *Genre* 2:104–128. [Reprinted in this volume.]

1972   Proverbs and Proverbial Expressions. In Dorson, ed., 1972: 117–127.

1974   Black Talking on the Streets. In Bauman and Sherzer, eds., 1974:240–262.

ABRAHAMS, ROGER D., and ALAN DUNDES

1972   Riddles. In Dorson, ed., 1972:129–143.

ALVER, BRYNJULF

1967   Category and Function. *Fabula* 9:62–69.

ANDRZEJEWSKI, B. W.

1967   The Art of the Miniature in Somali Poetry. *African Language Review* 6:5–16.

AUSTERLITZ, ROBERT

1961   The Identification of Folkloristic Genres (Based on Gilyak Materials). In *Poetics, Poetyka,* Поэтика , edited by K. Wyka, D. Davie, S. Zolkiewski, et al., pp. 505–510. Warsaw: Pantwowe Wydawnictwo.

BABALOLA, ADEBOYE

1973   One Type of Yoruba Folk Narrative Called ÀRÒ. *Fabula* 14:179–193.

BĂRBULESCU, CORNELIU

1964   Les légendes populaires roumaines. In Ortutay, ed., 1964: 75–83.

BARLEY, NIGEL F.

1974   Structural Aspects of the Anglo-Saxon Riddle. *Semiotica* 10:143–175.

BASCOM, WILLIAM R.

1943   The Relationship of Yoruba Folklore to Divining. *JAF* 56: 127–131.

1965   The Forms of Folklore: Prose Narratives. *JAF* 78:3–20.

BAUMAN, H.
1959   Mythos in ethnologischer Sicht. *SG* 12:1–17, 583–597.

BAUMAN, RICHARD
1975   Verbal Art as Performance. *American Anthropologist* 77: 290–311.

BAUMAN, RICHARD, and JOEL SHERZER, eds.
1974   *Explorations in the Ethnography of Speaking.* New York: Cambridge University Press.

BAUSINGER, HERMANN
1958*a*   Schwank und Witz. *SG* 11:699–710.
1958*b*   Strukturen des altäglichen Erzählens. *Fabula* 1:239–254.
1967   Bemerkungen zum Schwank und seiner Formtypen. *Fabula* 9:118–136.
1968*a*   Zum Beispiel. In *Volksüberlieferung: Festschrift für Kurt Ranke zur Vollendung des 60 Lebensjahres*, edited by Fritz Harkort, Karl C. Peeters, and Robert Wildhaber, pp. 9–18. Göttingen: Otto Schwartz.
1968*b*   Exemplum und Beispiel. *HBV* 59:31–43.
1968*c*   *Formen der "Volkspoesie."* Grundlagen der Germanistik 6. Berlin: Erich Schmidt.

BECK, HORACE P., ed.
1962   *Folklore in Action: Essays for Discussion in Honor of Mc-Edward Leach.* American Folklore Society Bibliographical and Special Series, no. 14. Philadelphia: American Folklore Society.

BÉDIER, JOSEPH
1893   *Les fabliaux: Etudes de littérature populaire et d'histoire littéraire du moyen âge.* Paris: E. Bouillon.

BEIT, HEDWIG VON
1965   *Das Märchen: Sein Ort in der geistigen Entwicklung.* Bern and Munich: Francke.

BELDEN, HENRY M.
1911   The Relation of Balladry to Folk-Lore. *JAF* 24:1–13.

BEN-AMOS, DAN
1963   The Situation Structure of the Non-Humorous English Ballad. *MF* 13:163–176.
1968   A Structural and Formal Study of Talmudic-Midrashic Leg-

ends. In *Fourth World Congress of Jewish Studies, Papers*, II, 357–359. Jerusalem: World Union of Jewish Studies. [Hebrew.]

1969   Analytical Categories and Ethnic Genres. *Genre* 2:275–301. [Reprinted in this volume.]

BERENDSOHN, WALTER A.

1921   *Grundformen volkstümlicher Erzähler-Kunst in den Kinder- und Hausmärchen der Brüder Grimm: Ein Stilkritischer Versuch.* Wiesbaden: Martin Sändig. [Reprinted 1968.]

1930–1933   Einfache Formen. In *Handwörterbuch des deutschen Märchen*, edited by Lutz Mackensen and Johannes Bolte, I, 484–498. Berlin: Walter de Gruyter.

BERNHARDT, KARL-HEINZ

1959   *Die Gattungsgeschichteliche Forschung am Alten Testament als exegetische Methode: Ergebnisse und Grenzen.* Aufsätze und Vorträge zur Theologie und Religionswissenschaft, no. 8. Berlin: Evangelische Verlagsanstalt.

BEUCHAT, P. D.

1957   Riddles in Bantu. *African Studies* (Johannesburg) 16:133–149. [Reprinted in Dundes, ed., 1965:182–205.]

BEYSCHLAG, SIEGFRIED

1941   Weltbild der Volkssage. *Dichtung und Volkstum (Euphorion)* 41:186–205. [Reprinted in Petzoldt, ed., 1969:189–216.]

BHAGWAT, DURGA

1965   *The Riddle in Indian Life, Lore and Literature.* Bombay: Popula Prakashan.

BIEBUYCK, DANIEL

1972   The Epic as a Genre in Congo Oral Literature. In *African Folklore*, edited by Richard Dorson, pp. 257–273. Garden City, N.Y.: Doubleday.

BLEHR, OTTO

1973   What is a Proverb? *Fabula* 14:243–246.

BOATRIGHT, MODY C.

1958   The Family Saga as a Form of Folklore. In *The Family Saga and Other Phases of American Folklore*, by Mody C. Boatright, Robert B. Brown, and John T. Flanagan, pp. 1–19.

Urbana: University of Illinois Press.

BØDKER, LAURITS

1965 *Folk Literature (Germanic): International Dictionary of Regional European Ethnology and Folklore, Volume II.* Copenhagen: Rosenkilde and Bagger.

BØDKER, LAURITS, BRYN JULF ALVER, BENGT HOLBECK, and LEEA VIRTANEN

1964 *The Nordic Riddle: Terminology and Bibliography.* Nordisk Institut for Folkedigtning, no. 4. Copenhagen: Rosenkilde and Bagger.

BOOR, HELMUT DE

1966 *Über Fabel und Bispel.* Bayerischen Akademie der Wissenschaften, Philosophisch-Historische Klasse, no. 1. Munich: Bayerischen Akademie der Wissenschaften.

BREITKREUZ, HARTMUT

1973 The Study of Proverbs: A Case-Model of an Integrated Approach. *Fabula* 14:247–252.

BREMOND, CLAUDE

1964 Le message narratif. *Communications* 4:4–32.

1966 La logique des possibles narratifs. *Communications* 8:60–76.

1970 Morphology of the French Folktale. *Semiotica* 2:247–276.

1973 *Logique du récit.* Paris: Editions du Seuil.

BRICKER, VICTORIA R.

1973 Three Genres of Tzotzil Insults. In Edmonson, ed., 1973: 183–203.

1974 The Ethnographic Context of Some Traditional Mayan Speech Genres. In Bauman and Sherzer, eds., 1974:368–388.

BRILL, TONŸ

1967 Der rumänische Sagenkatalog. *Fabula* 9:293–302.

BRUNVAND, JAN HAROLD

1968 *The Study of American Folklore: An Introduction.* New York: Norton. [Especially section 2: "Verbal Folklore," pp. 28–177.]

1972 The Study of Contemporary Folklore: Jokes. *Fabula* 13:1–19.

BUCHAN, DAVID
1972   *The Ballad and the Folk.* London: Routledge & Kegan Paul.

BUCHLER, IRA R., and HENRY A. SELBY
1968   *A Formal Study of Myth.* Center for Intercultural Studies in Folklore and Oral History Monograph Series, no. 1. Austin: University of Texas.

BURDE-SCHNEIDEWIND, GISELA
1964   Zur Katalogisierung Historischer Volkssagen. In Ortutay, ed., 1964:27–41.

BYNUM, DAVID E.
1969   The Generic Nature of Oral Epic Poetry. *Genre* 2:236–258. [Reprinted in this volume.]

CHIŢIMIA, ION C.
1967   Genre et art littéraires surtout dans la création folklorique. *ZRL* 10(1):5–13.
1972   L'évolution de la fable en tant que structure et art littéraires. *ZRL* 15(2):29–35.

CHRISTIANSEN, REIDAR TH.
1955   Myth, Metaphor, and Simile. *JAF* 68:417–427. [Reprinted in Sebeok, ed., 1955:39–49.]

CIRESE, ALBERTO MARIO
1972   *I Proverbi: Struttura delle definizioni.* Documenti di lavoro e prepubblicazioni, no. 12, series D. Urbino: University of Urbino.

ČISTOV, K. V.
1967   Das Problem der Kategorien mündlicher Volksprosa nicht-Märchenhaften Charakters. *Fabula* 9:27–40.
1969a Zur Frage der Klassifikations-prinzipien der Prosa-Volks-dichtung. In *VII⁰ Congrès International de Sciences Anthropologiques et Ethnologiques Moscou 3 août–10 août 1964,* VI, 365–371. Moscow: Nauka. [Reprinted in Petzoldt, ed., 1969:337–347.]
1969b [Tchistov, K. V.], ed. and chairman. Symposium 12: Classification des genres de la poésie orale. In *VII⁰ Congrès International de Sciences Anthropologiques et Ethnologiques Moscou 3 août–10 août 1964,* VI, 391–436. Moscow: Nauka.

COURTES, JOSEPH

1972　De la description à la spécificité du conte populaire merveilleux français. *EF* 2(1–2):9–42.

CROSSAN, JOHN DOMINIC

1974　The Good Samaritan: Towards a Generic Definition of Parable. *Semeia* 2:82–112.

DÉGH, LINDA

1957　Some Questions of the Social Function of Story-Telling.
AEASH 6:91–147.

1965　Processes of Legend Formation. In Megas, ed., 1965:77–87.
[Reprinted in Petzoldt, ed., 1969:374–389.]

1969　*Folktales and Society: Story-Telling in a Hungarian Peasant
Community.* Translated by Emily M. Schossberger. Bloomington: Indiana University Press. [Especially pp. 63–120.
1962.]

1971　The "Belief Legend" in Modern Society: Form, Function
and Relationship to Other Genres. In Hand, ed., 1971a:
55–68.

1972　Folk Narrative. In Dorson, ed., 1972:53–83.

DÉGH, LINDA, and ANDREW VÁZSONYI

1971　Legend and Belief. *Genre* 4:281–304. [Reprinted in this
volume.]

1973　The Dialectics of the Legend. In *Folklore in the Modern
World*, edited by Richard M. Dorson. World Anthropology: Papers and Conference Publications of the IXth International Congress of Anthropological and Ethnological Sciences. The Hague: Mouton, forthcoming.

1974　The Memorate and the Proto-Memorate. *JAF* 87:225–239.

DELEHAYE, HIPPOLYTE PÈRE, S. J.

1921　*Les passions des martyrs et les genres littéraires.* Brussels:
Bureaux de la Société des Bollandistes.

1961　*The Legends of the Saints: An Introduction to Hagiogra-
phy.* Translated by V. M. Crawford. Introduction by Richard J. Schoeck. Notre Dame: University of Notre Dame
Press. [Originally published in London: Longmans, Green
& Co., 1907. Present edition includes updated notes.]

DE VRIES, JAN

1954　*Betrachtungen zum Märchen besonders in seinem Verhält-*

nis zu Heldensage und Mythos. FFC, no. 150, vol. 63. Helsinki: Suomalainen Tiedeakatemia.

1963 *Heroic Song and Heroic Legend.* Translated by B. J. Timmer. London: Oxford University Press. [1959.]

DORSON, RICHARD M.

1970 Esthetic Form in British and American Narrative. In *Medieval Literature and Folklore Studies: Essays in Honor of Francis Lee Utley,* edited by Jerome Mandel and Bruce A. Rosenberg, pp. 305–321. New Brunswick, N.J.: Rutgers University Press.

1972 Ed. *Folklore and Folklife: An Introduction.* Chicago: University of Chicago Press.

DUNDES, ALAN

1964 *The Morphology of North American Indian Folktales.* FFC, no. 195, vol. 81. Helsinki: Suomalainen Tiedeakatemia.

1965 Ed. *The Study of Folklore.* Englewood Cliffs, N.J.: Prentice-Hall. [Especially "Forms in Folklore," pp. 127–215.]

1971*a* Folk Ideas as Units of Worldview. *JAF* 84:93–103. [Reprinted in Paredes and Bauman, eds., 1971:93–103.]

1971*b* On the Psychology of Legend. In Hand, ed., 1971*a*:21–36.

EDMONSON, MUNRO S., ed.

1973 *Meaning in Mayan Languages.* Janua Linguarum, Series Practica, no. 158. The Hague: Mouton.

FAÏK-NZUJI, CLÉMENTINE

1974 Procédés de voilement dans l'énigma luba. *Poétique* 19: 333–339.

FEDERSPIEL, CHRISTA

1968 *Vom Volksmärchen zum Kindermärchen.* Dissertationen der Universität Wien, no. 4. Vienna: Notring.

FIRTH, RAYMOND

1926 Proverbs in Native Life, with Particular Reference to Those of the Maori. *Folk-Lore* 37:134–153, 245–270.

FOWLER, DAVID C.

1968 *A Literary History of the Popular Ballad.* Durham, N.C.: Duke University Press.

FOX, JAMES J.

1974 "Our Ancestors Spoke in Pairs": Rotinese Views of Language, Dialect, and Code. In Bauman and Sherzer, eds., 1974:65–85.

FRENZEL, ELIZABETH

1963   *Stoff-, Motiv- und Symbolforschung.* Stuttgart: J. B. Metzler. [Especially pp. 80–90.]

1966   *Stoff- und Motivgeschichte.* Grundlagen der Germanistik. Berlin: Erich Schmidt. [Especially pp. 106–114.]

GARORIEAU, MARC

1974   Classification des récits chantés. *Poétique* 19:313–332.

GÄŠPARÍKOVA, VIERA

1967   Zusammenhänge und Übergangsstufen in den einzelnen Gattungen der Volksprosa. *Fabula* 9:78–86.

GEORGES, ROBERT A.

1971   The General Concept of Legend: Some Assumptions to be Reexamined and Reassessed. In Hand, ed., 1971a:1–19.

GEORGES, ROBERT A., and ALAN DUNDES

1963   Toward a Structural Definition of the Riddle. *JAF* 76:111–118.

GEROULD, GORDON HALL

1916   *Saints' Legends.* The Types of English Literature. Boston and New York: Houghton Mifflin Company.

1932   *The Ballad of Tradition.* Oxford: Clarendon Press.

GOSSEN, GARY H.

1971   Chamula Genres of Verbal Behavior. *JAF* 84:145–167. [Reprinted in Paredes and Bauman, eds., 1971:145–167.]

1973   Chamula Tzotzil Proverbs: Neither Fish nor Fowl. In Edmonson, ed., 1973:205–234.

1974   To Speak with a Heated Heart: Chamula Canons of Style and Good Performance. In Bauman and Sherzer, eds., 1974: 389–413.

GRANBERG, GUNNAR

1935   Memorat und Sage: Einige methodische Gesichtspunkte. *SS*, pp. 120–127.* [Reprinted in Petzoldt, ed., 1969:90–98.]

GREEN, M. M.

1947–1948   The Unwritten Literature of the Igbo-Speaking People of South-Eastern Nigeria. *Bulletin of the School of Oriental and African Studies* 12:838–846.

GREENWAY, JOHN
1964 *Literature among the Primitives.* Hatboro, Pa.: Folklore Associates. [Especially chapter 2: "The Forms of Literature in the Primitive World," pp. 35–70.]

GREVERUS, INA-MARIA
1964 Bericht zu Veröffentlighungs-und Katalogisierunsplänen aus dem Zentralarchiv der Volkserzählung. In Ortutay, ed., 1964:111–128.

GUMA, S. M.
1967 *The Form, Content and Technique of Traditional Literature in Southern Sotho.* The Hiddingh-Currie Publications of the University of South Africa, no. 8. Pretoria: J. L. Van Schaik.

HAIN, MATHILDE
1937 Volkssage und Sagenlandschaft. *NZV* 15:129–135. [Reprinted in Petzoldt, ed., 1969:99–107.]
1966 *Rätsel.* Stuttgart: J. B. Metzler.

HALPERT, HERBERT
1971 Definition and Variation in Folk Legend. In Hand, ed., 1971*a*:47–54.

HAMNETT, IAN
1967 Ambiguity, Classification and Change: The Function of Riddles. *Man* 2:379–392.

HAND, WAYLAND D.
1964 Stabile Funktion und Variable Dramatis Personae in der Volkssage. In Ortutay, ed., 1964:49–54. [Reprinted in Petzoldt, ed., 1969:319–325.]
1965 Status of European and American Legend Study. *CA* 6: 439–446. [Reprinted in Petzoldt, ed., 1969:402–430.]
1971*a* Ed. *American Folk Legend: A Symposium.* Publications of the UCLA Center for the Study of Comparative Folklore and Mythology, no. 2. Berkeley: University of California Press.
1971*b* The Index of American Folk Legends. In Hand, ed., 1971*a*: 213–221.

HANSEN, WILHELM
1934 Das Volkslied: Wesen und Wandlungen des Volksliedes. In Spamer, ed., 1934:I, 283–297.

HARKORT, FRITZ
1967　Tiervolkserzählungen. *Fabula* 9:87–99.

HARRIS, LYNDON
1971　The Riddle in Africa. *JAF* 84:377–393.

HART, DONN V.
1964　*Riddles in Filipino Folklore: An Anthropological Analysis.* Syracuse: Syracuse University Press.

HAWES, BESS LOMAX
1974　Folksongs and Function: Some Thoughts on the American Lullaby. *JAF* 87:140–148.

HERMANN, FERDINAND
1959　Die Lyrik der Naturvölker. *SG* 12:597–610.

HERZOG, GEORGE C., and CHARLES G. BLOOAH
1936　*Jabo Proverbs from Liberia: Maxims in the Life of a Native Tribe.* London: Oxford University Press.

HOCKETT, CHARLES F.
1972　Jokes. In *Studies in Linguistics in Honor of George L. Trager,* edited by M. Estelle Smith, pp. 153–178. The Hague: Mouton.

HODGART, M. J. C.
1950　*The Ballads.* London: Hutchinson.

HOLBEK, BENGT
1965　On the Classification of Folktales. In Megas, ed., 1965: 158–161.

HONKO, LAURI
1964　Memorates and the Study of Folk Beliefs. *JFI* 1:5–19. [Reprinted in Petzoldt, ed., 1969:287–306.]
1968　Genre Analysis in Folkloristics and Comparative Religion. *Temenos* 3:48–66.
1970　Der Mythos in der Religionswissenschaft. *Temenos* 6:36–67.

HONTI, HANS
1939　Märchenmorphologie und Märchentypologie. *Folk-Liv* 3: 307–318.

HORÁK, JIŘI
1967　Remarks on the Relations between Folk-Tales and Legends. *Fabula* 9:254–258.

HRDLIČKOVÁ, V.

1969 Japanese Professional Storytellers. *Genre* 2:179–210. [Reprinted in the present volume.]

HULTKRANTZ, ÅKE

1960 Religious Aspects of the Wind River Shoshoni Folk Literature. In *Culture in History: Essays in Honor of Paul Radin*, edited by Stanley Diamond, pp. 552–569. New York: Columbia University Press.

HYMES, DELL

1959 Myth and Tale Titles of the Lower Chinook. *JAF* 72:137–145.

1971 The "Wife" Who "Goes Out" Like a Man: Reinterpretation of a Clackamas Chinook Myth. In *Structural Analysis of Oral Tradition*, edited by Pierre and Elli Köngäs Maranda, pp. 49–80. University of Pennsylvania Publications in Folklore and Folklife, no. 3. Philadelphia: University of Pennsylvania Press.

IOANNIDOU-BARBARIGOU, M.

1965 Classification des légendes populaires grecques. In Megas, ed., 1965:179–184.

IRVINE, JUDITH T.

1974 Strategies of Status Manipulation in the Wolof Greeting. In Bauman and Sherzer, eds., 1974:167–191.

JASON, HEDA

1969 A Multidimensional Approach to Oral Literature. *CA* 10:413–426.

1970 The Russian Criticism of the "Finnish School" in Folktale Scholarship. *Norveg: Tidsskrift for Folkelivsgransking* n.s. 14:287–294.

1971 Concerning the "Historical" and the "Local" Legends and Their Relatives. *JAF* 84:134–144. [Reprinted in Paredes and Bauman, eds., 1971:134–144.]

1973 The Genre in Oral Literature: An Attempt at Interpretation. *Temenos* 9:156–160.

JECH, JAROMÍR

1964 Variabilität der Sagen und einige Fragen der Katalogisierung. In Ortutay, ed., 1964:107–110.

1967   Variabilität und Stabilität in den einzelnen Kategorien der Volksprosa. *Fabula* 9:55–62.

JILEK, WOLFGANG G., and LOUISE JILEK-AALL
1974   Meletinsky in the Okanogan: An Attempt to Apply Meletinsky's Analytic Criteria to Canadian Indian Folklore. In Maranda, ed., 1974:143–149.

JOHNSON, A. R.
1955   משל . *Vetus Testamentum* (Quarterly published by the International Organization of Old Testament Scholars), *Supplement* 3:162–169.

JOHNSON, JOHN WILLIAM
1972   The Family of Miniature Genres in Somali Oral Poetry. *Folklore Forum: A Communication for Students of Folklore* 5:79–98.

JOLLES, ANDRÉ
1956   *Einfache Formen: Legende, Sage, Mythe, Rätsel, Spruch, Kasus, Memorabile, Märchen, Witz.* Edited by A. Schossig. 2d ed. Halle (Saale): Max Niemeyer. [1930.]

KAIVOLA-BREGENHÖJ, ANNIKKI
1974   Formula Analysis as a Method of Classifying Riddles. *Studia Fennica: Review of Finnish Linguistics and Ethnology* 17:178–197.

KEENAN, ELINOR O.
1973   A Sliding Sense of Obligatoriness: The Poly-Structure of Malagasy Oratory. *Language in Society* 2:225–243.
1974   Norm-Makers, Norm-Breakers: Uses of Speech by Men and Women in a Malagasy Community. In Bauman and Sherzer, eds., 1974:125–143.

KER, WILLIAM PATON
1897   *Epic and Romance: Essays on Medieval Literature.* London and New York: Macmillan. [2d ed., 1908; reprinted New York: Dover, 1957.]

KIRSHENBLATT-GIMBLETT, BARBARA
1974   The Concept and Varieties of Narrative Performance in East European Jewish Culture. In Bauman and Sherzer, eds., 1974:283–308.

KIREEV, A. N.
1969   On Epical Genres in Bashkir Folk Poetry. In *VIIe Congrès*

International des Sciences Anthropologiques et Ethnologiques Moscou 3 août–10 août 1964, VI, 200–205. Moscow: Nauka.

KLÍMOVÁ, DAGMAR
1967 Versuch einer Klassifikation des lebendigen Sagenerzählens. *Fabula* 9:244–253.

KNAPPERT, JAN
1967 The Epic in Africa. *JFI* 4:171–190.

KOCH, RUTH
1973 Der Kasus und A. Jolles' Theorie von den "Einfachen Formen." *Fabula* 14:194–204.

KÖNGÄS, ELLI-KAIJA, and PIERRE MARANDA
1962 Structural Models in Folklore. *MF* 12:133–192.

KÖNGÄS MARANDA, ELLI
1969 Structure des énigmes. *Homme* 9:5–48.
1971*a* The Logic of Riddles. In *Structural Analysis of Oral Tradition*, edited by Pierre and Elli Köngäs Maranda, pp. 189–232. University of Pennsylvania Publications in Folklore and Folklife, no. 3. Philadelphia: University of Pennsylvania Press.
1971*b* Theory and Practice of Riddle Analysis. *JAF* 84:51–61. [Reprinted in Paredes and Bauman, eds., 1971:51–61.]

KÖNGÄS MARANDA, ELLI, and PIERRE MARANDA
1971 *Structural Models in Folklore and Transformational Essays.* Approaches to Semiotics, no. 10. The Hague: Mouton.

KOSACK, WOLFGANG
1971 Der Gattungsbegriff "Volkserzählung." *Fabula* 12:18–47.

KOVÁCS, ÁGNES
1964 Register der ungarischen Schildbürger-Schwanken-Typen (Rátótiaden) (AATH 1200–1349 MT.). In Ortutay, ed., 1964:55–69.

KRAMER, FRITZ W.
1970 *Literature among the Cuna Indians.* Etnologiska Studier, no. 30. Göteborg: Göteborgs Etnografiska Museum. [Especially pp. 69–108.]

KRAPPE, ALEXANDER HAGGERTY
1930 *The Science of Folklore.* London: Methuen. [Chapters 1–10, in particular. Reprinted 1962.]

KRAUS, CYRIL
  1967   L'Evénement et le héros dans la ballade. *ZRL* 10(1):81–94.
KRZYZANOWSKI, JULIAN
  1961   La poétique de l'énigme. In *Poetics, Poetyka,* Поэтика, edited by K. Wyka, D. Davie, S. Zolkiewski, et al., pp. 519–524. Warsaw: Pantwowe Wydawnictwo.
  1967   Legend in Literature and Folklore. *Fabula* 9:11–17.
LABOV, WILLIAM
  1972   *Language in the Inner City.* Philadelphia: University of Pennsylvania Press. [Especially "Rules for Ritual Insults," pp. 297–353, and "The Transformation of Experience in Narrative Syntax," pp. 354–396.]
LABOV, WILLIAM, and JOSHUA WALETZKY
  1967   Narrative Analysis: Oral Versions of Personal Experience. In *Essays on the Verbal and Visual Arts: Proceedings of the 1966 Annual Spring Meeting of the American Ethnological Society,* edited by June Helm, pp. 12–44. Seattle: University of Washington.
LARIVAILLE, PAUL
  1974   L'analyse (morpho) logique du récit. *Poétique* 19:368–388.
LEHTIPURO, OUTI
  1974   Trends in Finnish Folkloristics. *Studia Fennica: Review of Finnish Linguistics and Ethnology* 18:7–36.
LÉVI-STRAUSS, CLAUDE
  1955   The Structural Study of Myth. *JAF* 68:428–444. [Reprinted in Sebeok, ed., 1955:50–66.]
  1960   L'analyse morphologique des contes populaires russes. *International Journal of Slavic Linguistics and Poetics* 3:122–149.
LEYEN, FRIEDRICH VON DER
  1934   Die Volkssage. In Spamer, ed., 1934:I, 203–215.
LIEBFRIED, ERWIN
  1973   *Fabel.* 2d ed. Stuttgart: J. B. Metzler.
LITTLETON, C. SCOTT
  1965   A Two-Dimensional Scheme for the Classification of Narratives. *JAF* 78:21–27.

LOWIE, ROBERT H.
1959 The Oral Literature of the Crow Indians. *JAF* 72:97–105.

LUOMALA, KATHARINE
1955 Western Polynesian Classification of Prose Forms. *Journal of Oriental Literature* 6(2):16–23.

LÜTHI, MAX
1947 *Das europäische Volksmärchen: Form und Wesen.* Bern and Munich: Francke.
1961 *Volksmärchen und Volkssage: Zwei Grundformen erzahlender Dichtung.* Bern and Munich: Franke.
1962 *Märchen.* Stuttgart: J. B. Metzler.
1967 Urform und Zielform in Sage und Märchen. *Fabula* 9:41–54.
1969 *So leben sie noch heute: Betrachtungen zum Volksmärchen.* Göttingen: Vandenhoeck & Ruprecht.
1970 *Once upon a Time: On the Nature of Fairy Tales.* Translated by Lee Chadeayne and Paul Gottwald. Introduction by Francis Lee Utley. New York: Frederick Ungar. [1962.]
1969 Aspects of the *Märchen* and the Legend. Translated by Barbara Flynn. *Genre* 2:162–178. [Reprinted in this volume.]

MALINOWSKI, BRONISLAW
1926 Myth in Primitive Psychology. London: K. Paul, Trench, Trübner and Co. [Reprinted in Malinowski, *Magic, Science and Religion*, pp. 93–148. Boston: Beacon Press, 1948.]

MARANDA, PIERRE, ed.
1974 *Soviet Structural Folkloristics*, vol. 1. The Hague: Mouton.

MATHIEU, MICHEL
1974 Les acteurs du récit. *Poétique* 19:357–367.

MEGAS, GEORGIOS
1964 Referat über Wesen und Einteilungssystem der griechischen Sagen. In Ortutay, ed., 1964:93–95.
1965 Ed. *IV International Congress for Folk-Narrative Research in Athens (1.9–6.9 1964): Lectures and Reports. Laografia* 22.

MELETINSKY, E. M.
1970 Problème de la morphologie historique du conte populaire. *Semiotica* 2:128–134.

1971   Structural-Typological Study of the Folktale. Translated by Robin Dietrich. *Genre* 4:249–279. Another translation is by Wolfgang G. Jilek and Louise Jilek-Aall in Maranda, ed., 1974:19–51. [1969.]

1974   Marriage: Its Function and Position in the Structure of Folktales. Translated by Wolfgang G. Jilek and Louise Jilek-Aall. In Maranda, ed., 1974:61–72. [1970.]

MELETINSKY, E., S. NEKLUDOV, E. NOVKI, and D. SEGAL

1974   Problems of the Structural Analysis of Fairytales. Translated by Terrel Popoff and Helen Milosevich. In Maranda, ed., 1974:73–139.

MEULI, KARL

1954   Herkunft und Wesen der Fabel. *Schweizerisches Archiv für Volkskunde* 50:65–88.

MICHALSKI, STANILAW F.

1959   Zagadnienia Rodzajow Literackich w. Literaturze Poetyce Indyjskiez [Problems of literary genres in the Indian literature and poetry]. *ZRL* 2(2):69–90. [Polish. Summary in French.]

MILNER, GEORGE B.

1969a   De l'armature des locutions proverbiales: Essai de taxonomie sémantique. *Homme* 9:49–70.

1969b   What Is a Proverb? *New Society*, February 6, pp. 199–202.

MITCHELL, ROGER E.

1968   Genre and Function in Eastern Carolinian. *Asian Folklore Studies* 27(2):1–15.

NATHHORST, BERTEL

1968   Genre, Form and Structure in Oral Tradition. *Temenos* 3: 128–135.

1969   *Formal or Structural Studies of Traditional Tales: The Usefulness of Some Methodological Proposals Advanced by Vladimir Propp, Alan Dundes, Claude Lévi-Strauss and Edmund Leach.* Stockholm Studies in Comparative Religion, no. 9. Stockholm: Almqvist and Wiksell.

NEUMANN, SIEGFRIED

1967   Volksprosa mit komischen Inhalt: Zur Problematik ihres Gehalts und ihrer Differenzierung. *Fabula* 9:137–148.

NYGARD, HOLGER OLOF

1967   Popular Ballad and Medieval Romance. In *Folklore International: Essays in Traditional Literature, Belief and Custom in Honor of Wayland Debs Hand*, edited by D. K. Wilgus and Carol Sommer, pp. 161–173. Hatboro, Pa.: Folklore Associates.

OINAS, FELIX J.

1972   Folk Epic. In Dorson, ed., 1972:99–115.

ORTUTAY, GYULA, ed.

1964   Tagung der Sagenkommission der International Society for Folk-Narrative Research Budapest, 14–16 Oktober 1963. *AEASH* 13:5–131.

OSTER, HARRY

1969   The Blues as a Genre. *Genre* 2:259–274. [Reprinted in this volume.]

PANZER, FRIEDRICH

1934   Das Volksrätsel. In Spamer, ed., 1934:I, 263–282.

PAREDES, AMÉRICO, and RICHARD BAUMAN, eds.

1972   *Toward New Perspectives in Folklore*. American Folklore Society Bibliographical and Special Series, no. 23. Austin: University of Texas Press.

PAULME, DENISE

1972   Morphologie du conte africain. *Cahiers d'Etudes Africaines* 45:131–163.

[PEETERS, K. C., ed.]

1963   *Tagung der "International Society for Folk-Narrative Research" in Antwerp (6.–8. Sept. 1962): Bericht und Referat.* Antwerp: Centrum voor Studie en Documentatie. [Essays on legend classification problems by K. C. Peeters, L. Simonsuuri, C.-H. Tillhagen, L. Bødker, W. D. Hand, J. R. W. Sinninghe, J. Jech, L. Dégh, O. Sirovátka, I.-M. Greverus, and G. Burde-Schneidewind.]

PEETERS, KAREL C.

1964   Kartographische Probleme in Bezug auf die semantischen und onomastischen Begriffe bei der Volkserzählungsforschung. In Ortutay, ed., 1964:43–48.

PENTIKÄINEN, JUHA
1968   Grenzprobleme zwischen Memorat und Sage. *Temenos* 3:
       136–167.
PERRY, BEN EDWIN
1959   Fable. *SG* 12:17–37.
PETERSON, NORMAN R.
1974   On the Notion of Genre in Via's "Parable and Example
       Story: A Literary-Structuralist Approach." *Semeia* 1:134–
       181.
PETSCH, ROBERT
1899   *Neue Beitrage zur Kenntnis des Volksrätsels.* Palaestra 4.
       Berlin: Mayer und Müller.
1917   *Das deutsche Volksrätsel.* Grundriss der deutschen Volks-
       kunde, no. 1. Strassburg: Karl J. Trübner.
1938   *Spruchdichtung des Volkes, von- und frühformen der
       Volksdichtung Ruf, Zauber- und Weisheitsspruch, Rätsel,
       Volks- und Kinderreim.* Halle/Saale: Max Niemeyer.
PETZOLDT, LEANDER, ed.
1969   *Vergleichende Sagenforschung.* Wege der Forschung, no.
       152. Darmstadt: Wissenschaftliche Buchgesellschaft.
PEUCKERT, WILL-ERICH
1938   *Deutsches Volkstum in Märchen und Sage, Schwank und
       Rätsel.* Berlin: Walter de Gruyter.
1965   *Sagen: Geburt und Antwort der mythischen Welt.* Berlin:
       Erich Schmidt.
POP, MIHAI
1967   Aspects actuels des recherches sur la structure des contes.
       Fabula 9:70–77.
1970   La poétique du conte populaire. *Semiotica* 2:117–127.
POUROVÁ, LIBUŠE
1967   Sur les problèmes marginaux de certains genres de récits
       oraux contemporains. *Fabula* 9:149–154.
PRANG, HELMUT
1968   *Formgeschichte der Dichtkunst.* Sprach und Literature, no.
       45. Stuttgart: W. Kohlhammer.
PROPP, VLADÍMIR
1968   *Morphology of the Folktale.* 2d ed. Translated by Laurence
       Scott; revised by Louis A. Wagner. Introductions by Svatava

Pirkova-Jakobson and Alan Dundes. American Folklore Society Bibliographical and Special Series, no. 9; Indiana University Research Center in Anthropology, Folklore, and Linguistics Publication, no. 10. Austin: University of Texas Press. [Originally published 1928; first English edition, 1958.]

1971a Fairy Tale Transformation. In *Readings in Russian Poetics: Formalist and Structuralist Views*, edited by Ladislav Matejka and Krystyna Pomorska, pp. 94–114. Cambridge, Mass.: M.I.T. Press. Another English translation is "Transformations in Fairy Tales" in *Mythology*, edited by Pierre Maranda, pp. 139–150. Baltimore: Penguin Books, 1972. [1928.]

1971b Generic Structures in Russian Folklore. Translated by Maria Zagorska Brooks; edited by Dan Ben-Amos and Philip Tilney. *Genre* 4:213–248. [1964.]

PROVERBIUM

1965– Bulletin d'information sur les recherches parémiologiques. Helsinki: Société de littérature Finnoise.

RANKE, FRIEDRICH

1925 Grundfragen der Volkssagenforschung. *NZV* 3:12–23. [Reprinted in Petzoldt, ed., 1969:1–20.]

1934 Das Märchen. In Spamer, ed., 1934:I, 249–262.

RANKE, KURT

1958 Betrachtungen zum Wesen und zur Funkion des Märchen. *SG* 11:647–664.

1959 Einfache Formen. Translated by William Templer and Eberhard Alsen. *JFI* 4(1967):17–31. [1959.]

1967 Kategorienprobleme der Volksprose. *Fabula* 9:4–12.

REICHARD, GLADYS A.

1921 Literary Types and Dissemination of Myths. *JAF* 34:269–307.

REID, SUSAN

1974 Myth as Metastructure of the Fairytale. In Maranda, ed., 1974:151–172.

RICHARD, PHILIPPE, FRANCIS LÉVY, and MICHEL DE VIRVILLE

1971 Essai de description des contes merveilleux. *EF* 1(3–4):95–120.

RICHMOND, W. EDSON
1972   Narrative Folk Poetry. In Dorson, ed., 1972:85–98.
ROBERTS, JOHN M., and MICHAEL L. FORMAN
1971   Riddles: Expressive Models of Interrogation. *Ethnology* 10: 509–533. [Reprinted in *Directions in Sociolinguistics: The Ethnography of Communication*, edited by John J. Gumperz and Dell Hymes, pp. 180–209. New York: Holt, Rinehart and Winston, 1972.]
ROFÉ, ALEXANDER
1970   The Classification of the Prophetical Stories. *Journal of Biblical Literature* 89:427–440.
RÖHRICH, LUTZ
1956   *Märchen und Wirklichkeit: Eine volkskundliche Untersuchung.* Wiesbaden: Franz Steiner.
1958   Die deutsche Volkssage: Ein methodischer Arbiss. *SG* 11: 664–691. [Reprinted in Petzoldt, ed., 1969:217–286.]
1966   *Sage.* Stuttgart: J. B. Metzler.
1973   Ed. *Probleme der Sagenforschung: Verhandlungen der Tagung veranstaltet von der Kommission für Erzählforschung der Deutschen Gesellschaft für Volkskunde e.V. vom 27 September bis 1. Oktober 1972 in Freiburg im Breisgau.* Freiburg im Breisgau: Deutsche Forschungsgemeinschaft.
ROMANSKA, ZWETANA
1964   Die bulgarischen Volkssagen und Legenden: Zustand ihrer Erforschung, Typen und Motive. In Ortutay, ed., 1964:85–92.
ROSALDO, MICHELLE
1973   I Have Nothing to Hide: The Language of Ilongot Oratory. *Language in Society* 2:193–223.
ROSENBERG, BRUCE A.
1971   The Genre of the Folk Sermon. *Genre* 4:189–211.
ROSENFELD, HELLMUT
1961   *Legende.* Stuttgart: J. B. Metzler.
SALMOND, ANNE
1974   Rituals of Encounter among the Maori: Sociolinguistic Study of a Scene. In Bauman and Sherzer, eds., 1974:192–212.
SCHMIDT, FRIEDRICH-WILHELM
1929   Die Volkssage als Kunstwerk: Eine Untersuchung über

Formgesetze der Volkssage. *NZV* 7:129–143; 30–44. [Reprinted in Petzoldt, ed., 1969:21–65.]

SCHMIDT, LEOPOLD

1963 *Die Volkserzählung: Märchen, Sage, Legende, Schwank.* Berlin: Erich Schmidt.

SCOTT, CHARLES T.

1965 *Persian and Arabic Riddles: A Language-Centered Approach to Genre Definition.* IJAL, vol. 31, no. 4, part 2. Publication 39 of the Indiana University Research Center in Anthropology, Folklore, and Linguistics. Bloomington: Indiana University; The Hague: Mouton.

1969 On Defining the Riddle: The Problem of a Structural Unit. *Genre* 2:129–142. [Reprinted in this volume.]

SEBEOK, THOMAS A.

1955 Ed. *Myth: A Symposium.* American Folklore Society Bibliographical and Special Series, no. 5. Philadelphia: American Folklore Society.

1960 Decoding a Text: Levels and Aspects in a Cheremis Sonnet. In *Style and Language*, edited by Thomas A. Sebeok, pp. 221–235. Cambridge, Mass.: M.I.T. Press.

SEITEL, PETER

1969 Proverbs: A Social Use of Metaphor. *Genre* 2:143–161. [Reprinted in this volume.]

SHERZER, JOEL

1974 *Namakke, Sunmakke, Kormakke*: Three Types of Cuna Speech Event. In Bauman and Sherzer, eds., 1974:263–282.

SHIMKIN, D. B.

1947 Wind River Shoshone Literary Forms: An Introduction. *Journal of the Washington Academy of Sciences* 37:329–352.

SIMINIDES, DOROTA

1971 Volkserzählungsgattungen in der polnischen Folkloristik. *Fabula* 12:77–85.

SIMONSUURI, LAURI

1964 Über die Klassifizierung der finnischen Sagentradition. In Ortutay, ed., 1964:19–26.

SIROVÁTKA, OLDŘICH

1964 Zur Morphologie der Sage und Sagenkatalogisierung. In

Ortutay, ed., 1964:99–106. [Reprinted in Petzoldt, ed., 1969:326–336.]

1967   Stoff und Gattung- Volksballade und Volkserzählung. *Fabula* 9:162–168.

SMITH, PIERRE

1974   Des genres et des hommes. *Poétique* 19:294–312.

SMITH, ROBERT JEROME

1971   The Structure of Esthetic Response. *JAF* 84:68–79. [Reprinted in Paredes and Bauman, eds., 1971:68–79.]

SPAMER, ADOLF, ed.

1934   *Die deutsche Volkskunde.* 2 vols. Leipzig: Bibliographisches Institut.

SPANNER, WERNER

1939   *Das Märchen als Gattung.* Giessener Beiträge zur deutschen Philologie, no. 68. Giessen: Münchowsche Universitäts-Otto Kindt GmbH.

STANOVSKÝ, VLADISLAV

1967   Das formale Prinzip als wichtiger Faktor in der Katalogisierung der Märchenstoffe. *Fabula* 9:105–110.

STEENSTRUP, JOHANNES C. H. R.

1968   *The Medieval Popular Ballad.* Translated by Edward Godfrey Cox. Foreword by David C. Fowler. "A Bibliographical Essay" by Karl-Ivar Hildeman. Seattle and London: University of Washington Press. [Originally published 1891; first English publication 1914.]

STROSS, BRIAN

1971   Serial Order in Nez Percé Myths. *JAF* 84:104–113. [Reprinted in Paredes and Bauman, eds., 1971:104–113.]

1974   Speaking of Speaking: Tenejapa Tzeltal Metalinguistics. In Bauman and Sherzer, eds., 1974:213–239.

SUDHOF, SIEGFRIED

1958   Die Legende: Ein Versuch zu ihrer Bestimmung. *SG* 11: 691–699.

SUPPAN, WOLFGANG

1966   *Volkslied.* Stuttgart: J. B. Metzler.

SUTTON-SMITH, BRIAN

1971   The Expressive Profile. *JAF* 84:80–92. [Reprinted in Paredes and Bauman, eds., 1971:80–92.]

SYDOW, C. W. VON. *See* von Sydow, C[arl] W[ilhelm].

TALLMAN, RICHARD S.
1974 A Generic Approach to the Practical Joke. *SFQ* 38:259–274.

TAYLOR, ARCHER
1931*a* *The Proverb*. Cambridge, Mass.: Harvard University Press. [Reprinted with "An Index to the Proverb," Hatboro, Pa.: Folklore Associates, 1962.]
1931*b* A Theory of Indo-European *Märchen*. *JAF* 44:54–60.
1943 The Riddle. *California Folklore Quarterly* 2:129–147.
1948 *The Literary Riddle before 1600*. Berkeley and Los Angeles: University of California Press.
1953 Riddles in Dialogue. *Proceedings of the American Philosophical Society* 97:61–68.
1962 The Riddle as a Primary Form. In Beck, ed., 1962:200–207.
1970 The Anecdote: A Neglected Genre. In *Medieval Literature and Folklore Studies: Essays in Honor of Francis Lee Utley*, edited by Jerome Mandel and Bruce A. Rosenberg, pp. 223–228. New Brunswick, N.J.: Rutgers University Press.

TCHISTOV, K. V. *See* Čistov, K. V.

TENÈZE, MARIE-LOUISE
1964 Note à l'attention du comité des légendes de l' "International Society for Folk-Narrative Research." In Ortutay, ed., 1964:71–74.
1970 Du conte merveilleux comme genre. *Arts et Traditions Populaires* 18:11–65.
1972 Le conte merveilleux français: Problématique d'une recherche. *EF* 2(1–2):97–106.

THOMPSON, STITH
1946 *The Folktale*. New York: Holt, Rinehart and Winston.
1955 Myths and Folktales. *JAF* 68:482–488. [Reprinted in Sebeok, ed., 1955:104–110.]

THOMSON, J. A. K.
1935 *The Art of the Logos*. London: George Allen & Unwin. [In particular pp. 74–109.]

THURNWALD, RICHARD C.
1936 *Profane Literature of Buin, Solomon Islands*. Yale Univer-

sity Publications in Anthropology, no. 8. New Haven: Yale University Press.

TILLHAGEN, CARL-HERMAN

1964 Was ist eine Sage? Eine Definition und ein Vorschlag für ein europäisches Sagensystem. In Ortutay, ed., 1964:9–17. [Reprinted in Petzoldt, ed., 1969:307–318.]

1967 Die Sage als Dichtung. In *Folklore International: Essays in Traditional Literature, Belief and Custom in Honor of Wayland Debs Hand*, edited by D. K. Wilgus and Carol Sommer, pp. 211–220. Hatboro, Pa.: Folklore Associates.

TODOROV, TZVETAN

1970 Les transformations narratives. *Poétique* 1:322–333.

1973 Analyse du discours: L'Exemple des devinettes. *Journal de Psychologie Normale et Pathologique*, nos. 1–2:135–155.

TOELKEN, BARRE

1969 The "Pretty Languages" of Yellowman: Genre, Mode, and Texture in Navaho Coyote Narratives. *Genre* 2:211–236. [Reprinted in this volume.]

1971 Ma'i Joldloshi: Legendary Styles and Navaho Myth. In Hand, ed., 1971a:203–211.

TUBACH, FREDERIC C.

1962 Exempla in the Decline. *Traditio: Studies in Ancient and Medieval History, Thought and Religion* 18:407–417.

1968 Strukturanalytische Probleme Das mittelalterliche Exemplum. *HBV* 59:25–29.

TUDOROVSKAIA, E. A.

1967 On the Classification of Fairy Tales. *Soviet Anthropology and Archeology* 6:23–31. [1965.]

UPADHYAYA, K. D.

1965 The Classification and Chief Characteristics of Indian (Hindi) Folk-Tales. In Megas, ed., 1965:581–587. [Reprinted in *Fabula* 7(1965):225–229.]

UTLEY, FRANCIS LEE

1969 Oral Genres as a Bridge to Written Literature. *Genre* 2:91–103. [Reprinted in this volume.]

VARNAGNAC, ANDRÉ

1948 *Civilisation traditionnelle et genres de vie*. Paris: Albin Michel.

VIRSALADZÉ, HELENE

1970   Le Problème de la Classification des Oeuvres Lyriques Populaires. *Proceedings VIIIth International Congress of Anthropological and Ethnological Sciences 1968 Tokyo and Kyoto. Vol. 2: Ethnology*, pp. 334–337. Tokyo: Science Council of Japan.

VOIGT, VILMOS

1969   Structural Definition of Oral (Folk) Literature. In *Proceedings of the Vth Congress of the International Comparative Literature Association* (Belgrade, 1967), edited by Nikola Banašević, pp. 461–467. Amsterdam: Université de Belgrade, Swets & Zeitlinger.

1972   Some Problems of Narrative Structure Universals in Folklore. *Linguistica Biblica-Interdisziplinäre Zeitschrift für Theologie und Linguistik* 15/16:78–90. [Reprinted in *AEASH* 21(1972):57–72.]

1973*a*   Position d'un problème: La Hiérarchie des genres dans le folklore. *Semiotica* 7:135–141.

1973*b*   Die strukturell-morphologische Erforschung der Sagen. In Röhrich, ed., 1973:66–85.

VON SYDOW, C[arl] W[ilhelm]

1934   Kategorien der Prosa-Volksdichtung. In *Volkskundliche Gaben John Meier zum sibzigsten Geburstage dargebracht*, edited by Erich Seemann and Harry Schewe, pp. 253–268. Berlin and Leipzig: Walter de Gruyter. [Reprinted in von Sydow 1948:60–85; summary in English, pp. 86–88.]

1937   Folklig dit-tradition: Ett terminologiskt utkast. *Folkminnen och Folktanker* 24:216–232. [Reprinted and translated in von Sydow 1948:106–126.]

1938   Popular Prose Traditions and Their Classification. *SS*, pp. 17–32.* [Reprinted in von Sydow 1948:127–145.]

1940   Das Volksmärchen unter ethnischen Gesichtspunkt. In *Féil-Sgribhin Eóin Mic Néill*, pp. 567–580. Dublin.* [Reprinted in von Sydow 1948:220–240.]

1948   *Selected Papers on Folklore: Published on the Occasion of His 70th Birthday*, edited by Laurits Bødker. Copenhagen: Rosenkilde and Bagger.

VRIES, JAN DE. *See* de Vries, Jan.

WEINREICH, BEATRICE SILVERMAN

1964   Formal Aspects in the Study of Yiddish Proverbs. In *For Max Weinreich on His Seventieth Birthday: Studies in Jewish Languages, Literature and Society*, edited by Lucy S. Dawidowicz, Alexander Erlich, Rachel Erlich, and Joshua A. Fishman, pp. 394–383. The Hague: Mouton. [In Yiddish.]

1965   Genres and Types of Yiddish Folk Tales about the Prophet Elijah. In *The Field of Yiddish: Studies in Language, Folklore, and Literature, Second Collection*, edited by Uriel Weinreich, pp. 202–231. The Hague: Mouton.

WEPMAN, DENNIS, RONALD B. NEWMAN, and MURRAY B. BINDERMAN

1974   Toasts: The Black Urban Folk Poetry. *JAF* 87:208–224.

WESSELSKI, ALBERT

1931   *Versuch einer Theorie des Märchens*. Prager deutsche Studien, no. 45. Reichenberg: F. Kraus.

1934   Die Formen des volkstümlichen Erzählguts. In Spamer, ed., 1934:I, 216–248.

WHITING, B. J.

1931   The Origin of the Proverb. *HSNPL* 13:47–80.

1932   The Nature of the Proverb. *HSNPL* 14:273–307.

WILLIAMS, THOMAS RHYS

1963   The Form and Function of Tambunan Dusun Riddles. *JAF* 76:95–110.

YODER, DON

1971   The Saint's Legend in the Pennsylvania German Folk-Culture. In Hand, ed., 1971*a*:157–183.

ZOLNAI, M. BÉLA

1940   La ballada épique. *Helicon* 2:156–169.

The Concept of Genre in Literary Criticism

ANCESCHI, LUCIANO

1956   A Debate on "Literary Types." *JAAC* 14:324–332.

BEHRENS, IRENE

1940   *Die Lehre von der Einteilung der dichtkunst, vornehmlich vom 16. bis 19 Jahrhundert: Studien zur geschichte der poetischen Gattungen.* Beihefte zur Zeitschrift für Romanische Philologie, no. 92. Halle/Saale: Max Niemeyer. [Bibliography.]

BERTHOFF, WARNER
1970 Fiction, History, Myth: Notes toward the Discrimination of Narrative Forms. In *The Interpretation of Narrative: Theory and Practice,* edited by Morton W. Bloomfield, pp. 263–287. Harvard English Studies, no. 1. Cambridge, Mass.: Harvard University Press.

BROOKS, PETER
1974 Une esthétique de l'étonnement: Le mélodrame. *Poétique* 19:340–356.

BRUNETIÈRE, FERDINAND
1890 *L'Evolution des genres dans l'histoire de la littérature.* Paris: Librairie Hachette.

BURKE, KENNETH
1937 *Attitudes toward History.* New York: The New Republic. [Rev. ed., Los Altos: Hermes Publications, 1959. Especially pp. 34–91.]
1941 *The Philosophy of Literary Form: Studies in Symbolic Action.* Baton Rouge: Lousiana State University Press.

CASTRO, DONALD F.
1974 Tragedy, the Generic Approach: A Metacritical Look. *Genre* 7:250–271.

COHEN, M. GUSTAVE
1940 L'Origine médiévale des genres littéraires modernes. *Helicon* 2:129–135.

COLIE, ROSALIE L.
1973 *The Resources of Kind: Genre-Theory in the Renaissance.* Berkeley and Los Angeles: University of California Press.

CROCE, BENEDETTO
1909 *Aesthetic as Science of Expression and General Linguistics.* Translated by Douglas Ainslie. London: Macmillan. [1902.]

CYSARZ, HERBERT
1940 Die Gattungsmässigen Form-Möglichkeiten der heutigen Prosa. *Helicon* 2:169–180.

DAVIS, ROBERT MURRAY
1969   Defining Genre in Fiction. *Genre* 2:341–353.

DONATO, EUGENIO
1971   The Shape of Fiction: Notes toward a Possible Classification of Narrative Discourses. *Modern Language Notes* 86: 807–822.

DONOHUE, JAMES JOHN
1943–1949   *The Theory of Literary Kinds. I: Ancient Classifications of Literature. II: The Ancient Classes of Poetry.* Dubuque, Iowa: Loras College Press.

DOTY, WILLIAM G.
1972   The Concept of Genre in Literary Analysis. In *Book of Seminar Papers: The Society of Biblical Literature One Hundred Eighth Annual Meeting, Friday–Tuesday, 1–5 September 1972, Los Angeles, California, Vol. 2,* edited by Lane C. McGaughy, pp. 413–448. N.p.: Society of Biblical Literature. [Bibliography with "An Emphasis on 'Form Criticism' in Biblical Scholarship."]

ĎURIŠIN, DIONÝZ
1973   Genre Aspect of Comparative Literature. *ZRL* 16(30):5–17.

EHRENPREIS, IRVIN
1945   *The "Types Approach" to Literature.* New York: King's Crown Press. [Bibliography.]

EICHENBAUM, BORIS
1965   The Theory of the "Formal Method." In *Russian Formalist Criticism: Four Essays,* edited by Lee T. Lemon and Marion J. Reis, pp. 99–139. Lincoln: University of Nebraska Press. [1925.]

FARMER, NORMAN K., JR.
1970   A Theory of Genre for Seventeenth-Century Poetry. *Genre* 3:293–317.

FLEMMING, WILLI
1959   Das Problem von Dichtungsgattung und art. *SG* 12:38–60.

FOWLER, ALASTAIR
1971   The Life and Death of Literary Forms. *New Literary History* 2:199–216.

FRYE, NORTHROP
1957 *Anatomy of Criticism: Four Essays.* Princeton, N.J.: Princeton University Press. [In particular "Rhetorical Criticism: Theory of Genres," pp. 243–337.]

FUBINI, MARIO
1956 *Critica e poesia.* Bari: Laterza. [Especially pp. 143–311.]

GUILLÉN, CLAUDIO
1970 Genere, contro-genere, sistema. In *Critica e Storia letteraria: Studi offerti a Mario Fubini*, I, 153–174. Padua: Liviana.
1971 *Literature as System: Essays toward the Theory of Literary History.* Princeton, N.J.: Princeton University Press. [In particular "On the Uses of Literary Genre," pp. 107–134; "Genre and Countergenre: The Discovery of the Picaresque," pp. 135–158; and "Literature as System," pp. 375–419.]

GUNKEL, HERMANN
1901 *Genesis.* Handkommentar zum Alten Testament, no. 1. Göttingen: Vandenhoeck and Ruprecht. [Especially pp. i–lv.]
1921 *Das Märchen im Alten Testament.* Religionsgeschichteliche Volksbücher für die deutsche christliche Gegenwart. 2d series: Die Religion des Alten Testaments, no. 23/6. Tübingen: Mohr.

HACK, ROY KENNETH
1916 The Doctrine of Literary Forms. *Harvard Studies in Classical Philology* 27:1–65.

HALL, VERNON, JR.
1945 *Renaissance Literary Criticism: A Study of Its Social Content.* New York: Columbia University Press.

HAMBURGER, KÄTE
1973 *The Logic of Literature.* Translated by Marilynn J. Rose. Bloomington: Indiana University Press. [1957.]

HANKISS, M. JEAN
1940 Les genres littéraires et leur base psychologique. *Helicon* 2:117–129.
1958 Les genres littéraires. *ZRL* 1(1):49–64.

HEMPFER, KLAUS W.
1973　*Gattungstheorie: Information und Synthese.* Munich: Wilhelm Fink.

HERNADI, PAUL
1971　Verbal Worlds between Action and Vision. *College English* 33:18–31.
1972　*Beyond Genre: New Directions in Literary Classification.* Ithaca, N.Y.: Cornell University Press. [Bibliography.]

HIGHTOWER, JAMES R.
1957　The *Wen Hsüan* and Genre Theory. *Harvard Journal of Asiatic Studies* 20:512–533. [Reprinted in John L. Bishop, ed., *Studies in Chinese Literature*, pp. 142–165. Harvard-Yenching Institute Studies, no. 21. Cambridge, Mass.: Harvard University Press, 1966.]

HIRSCH, ERIC DONALD
1967　*Validity in Interpretation.* New Haven: Yale University Press. [Particularly pp. 68–126.]

HOCKING, ELTON
1936　*Ferdinand Brunetière: The Evolution of a Critic.* University of Wisconsin Studies in Language and Literature, no. 36. Madison: University of Wisconsin.

HVIŠČ, JOSEF
1972　Die genologische Interpretation der Literatur. *ZRL* 15(1): 5–31.

INGARDEN, ROMAN
1973a　*The Cognition of the Literary Work of Art.* Translated by Ruth Ann Crowley and Kenneth R. Olson. Evanston, Ill.: Northwestern University Press. [1968.]
1973b　*The Literary Work of Art: An Investigation on the Borderlines of Ontology, Logic and Theory of Literature.* Translated by George G. Grabowicz. Evanston, Ill.: Northwestern University Press. [1931.]

JAUSS, HANS-ROBERT
1970　Littérature médiévale et théorie des genres. *Poétique* 1(1): 79–101. [Bibliography.]

KAYSER, WOLFGANG
1951　*Das Sprachliche Kunstwerk: Eine Einführung in die Literaturwissenschaft.* 2d ed. Bern: A. Francke. [Especially pp.

331–388; first edition, 1948.]

KLEINER, JULIUSZ

1959 The Role of Time in Literary Genres. *ZRL* 2(1):5–12.

KOCH, KLAUSE

1969 *The Growth of the Biblical Tradition: The Form-Critical Method*. Translated from the second German edition by S. M. Cupitt. New York: Charles Scribner's Sons. [1964.]

KOHLER, M. PIERRE

1940 Contribution à une philosophie des genres. *Helicon* 2:135–147.

KRAUSS, WERNER

1968 *Essays zur französischen Literatur*. Berlin and Weimar: Aufbau. [Especially pp. 5–43.]

KRIDL, M. MANFRED

1940 Observation sur les genres de la poésie lyrique. *Helicon* 2: 147–156.

LANGER, SUSANNE K.

1953 *Feeling and Form: A Theory of Art Developed from "Philosophy in a New Key."* London: Routledge and Kegan Paul.

MARGOLIN, URI

1973 Historical Literary Genre: The Concept and Its Uses. *Comparative Literature Studies* 10:51–59.

1974 On Three Types of Deductive Models in Genre Theory. *ZRL* 17(1):5–19.

MARIES, JULIAN

1969 Les genres littéraires en philosophie. *Revue Internationale de Philosophie* (Brussels) 23:495–508.

MICHALOWSKA, TERESA

1969 The Beginning of Genological Thinking. *ZRL* 12(1):5–23.

1970 Genological Notions in the Renaissance Theory of Poetry. *ZRL* 12(2):5–20.

1972 The Notion of Lyrics and the Category of Genre in Ancient and Later Theory of Poetry. *ZRL* 15(1):47–69.

MILLS, NICOLAUS

1969 American Fiction and the Genre Critics. *Novel* 2:112–122.

MOORE, ARTHUR K.

1970 Formalist Criticism and Literary Form. *JAAC* 29:21–31.

MÜLLER, LUDOLF
1968   Die literarischen Gattungen und die 'Leistungen der Spruch.'
       In *Festschrift für Klaus Ziegler*, edited by Eckehard Catholy
       and Winifried Hellmann, pp. 427–434. Tübingen: M. Nie-
       meyer.

PEARSON, NORMAN HOLMES
1941   Literary Forms and Types; or, A Defense of Polonius. *Eng-
       lish Institute Annual, 1940*, pp. 61–72. New York: Colum-
       bia University Press.

PETSCH, ROBERT
1925   *Gehalt und Form: Gesammelte Abhandlungen zur Litera-
       turwissenschaft und zur allgemeinen Geistesgeschichte.*
       Hamburgische Texts und Untersuchungen zur deutschen
       Philologie. Dormund: Wilh. Ruhfus.
1942   *Wesen und Formen der Erzählkunst.* Deutsche Vierteljahrs-
       schrift für Literaturwissenschaft und Geistesgeschichte, no.
       20. Halle/Saale: Max Niemeyer.

POMMIER, JEAN
1945   L'idée de genre. In *Conférences*, edited by Franz Cumont
       and Jean Pommier, pp. 45–81. Publications de l'école nor-
       male supérieure, section des lettres II. Paris: E. Droz.

REICHERT, JOHN F.
1968   "Organizing Principles" and Genre Theory. *Genre* 1:1–12.

RIFFATERRE, MICHAEL
1972   Système d'un genre descriptif. *Poétique* 9:15–30.

RUTTKOWSKI, WOLFGANG VICTOR
1968   *Die literarischen Gattungen: Reflexionen über eine modi-
       fizierte Fundamentalpoetik.* Bern and Munich: Francke.

SACKS, SHELDON
1968   The Psychological Implications of Generic Distinctions.
       Genre 1:106–115.

SAN JUAN, E., JR.
1968   Notes toward a Clarification of Organizing Principles and
       Genre Theory. *Genre* 1:257–268.

SCHOLES, ROBERT
1969   Towards a Poetics of Fiction: (4) An Approach through
       Genre. *Novel* 2:101–111.

SCHWARTZ, ELIAS
1971   The Problem of Literary Genres. *Criticism* 13:113–130.

SHUMAKER, WAYNE
1960   *Literature and the Irrational: A Study in Anthropological Backgrounds.* Englewood Cliffs, N.J.: Prentice-Hall. [Especially pp. 155–239. The book includes references to folklore genres as well.]

STAIGER, EMIL
1946   *Grundbegriffe der Poetik.* Zurich: Atlantis.

STROHM, PAUL
1971*a* Some Generic Distinctions in the Canterbury Tales. *Modern Philology* 68:321–328.

1971*b* *Storie, Spelle, Geste, Romaunce, Tragedie*: Generic Distinctions in the Middle English Troy Narratives. *Speculum* 46: 348–359.

STUTTERHEIM, CORNELIUS F. P.
1964   Prolegomena to a Theory of the Literary Genres. *ZRL* 6 (2):5–23.

TODOROV, TZVETAN
1966   Les catégories du récit littéraire. *Communications* 8:125–151.

1973   *The Fantastic: A Structural Approach to a Literary Genre.* Translated by Richard Howard. Cleveland: Press of Case Western Reserve University. [1970.]

TRZYNADLOWSKI, JAN
1961   Information Theory and Literary Genres. *ZRL* 4(1):31–45.

VANGELISTI, PAUL
1970   Semantics of Literary Form. *The University of Southern Florida Language Quarterly* 9(1–2):45–48.

VIËTOR, KARL
1931   Probleme der literarischen Gattungsgeschichte. *Deutsche Vierteljahrschrift für Literaturwissenschaft und Geistegeschichte* 9:425–447. [Reprinted in *Geist und Form Aufsätze zur deutschen Literaturgeschichte*, pp. 292–309. Bern: A. Francke.]

VIVAS, ELISEO
1968   Literary Classes: Some Problems. *Genre* 1:97–105.

WEISSTEIN, ULRICH
  1971   The Study of Literary Genres. In *Comparative Literature: Method and Perspective*, edited by Newton P. Stallknecht and Horst Frenz, pp. 248–274. Rev. ed. Carbondale: Southern Illinois University Press.
  1973   *Comparative Literature and Literary Theory: Survey and Introduction*. Bloomington: Indiana University Press. [In particular "Genre," pp. 99–123. 1968.]
WELLEK, RENÉ
  1967   Genre Theory, the Lyric and *Erlebnis*. In *Festschrift für Richard Alewyn*, edited by Herbert Singer and Benno von Weise, pp. 392–412. Cologne: Böhlau. [Reprinted in R. Wellek, *Discriminations: Further Concepts of Criticism*, pp. 225–252. New Haven: Yale University Press, 1970.]
WELLEK, RENÉ, and AUSTIN WARREN
  1949   *Theory of Literature*. New York: Harcourt, Brace and Company. [In particular "Literary Genres," pp. 235–247; rev. ed. 1956, pp. 215–227.]
WHITMORE, CHARLES E.
  1924   The Validity of Literary Definitions. *Publications of the Modern Language Association* 39:722–736.
ZGORZELSKI, ANDRZEJ
  1968   The Types of a Presented World in Fantastic Literature. *ZRL* 10(2):116–127.

Index

189, 199, 211, 237; Apache, 51;
apprentice of, 179, 186; Breton,
18; Chinese, 171; Japanese, xxxviii,
171–189; of legends, 101–103;
Navaho, 145–165; professional,
171–189; props of, 176
Structural-morphological approach,
xxvi–xxvii, 219–221
Structure, xiii, xv, xx, xxvi, xxvii,
xxix, xxxv, xxxvi, 3, 4, 63–67, 80–
82, 84, 86–88, 90, 146, 156, 157,
160, 161, 193, 196–199, 204, 207,
219, 220, 221, 226; of blues, 63–
67; of contexts, 197, 199, 204;
deep, 84, 86–88, 90; dramatic,
198–199, 207; of riddle, 77–88;
surface, 84, 86–88, 90
Sumatra, 39
Summers, Andrew Rowan, 13
Supernatural, 9, 24, 28–31, 201, 216
Superstitions, 196, 201, 209
Survivals, xxi; theory of, xxiii
Swahili, 137
Swahn, Jan Öjvind, 17
Sweden, 36
Switzerland, 30
Sydow, Carl Wilhelm von, xv, xvi,
xix, xx, 4, 5, 94, 116, 220

Tagmemic theory, 79
Tales, x, xi, xiii, xv, xvii, xxii, xxvii,
xxxix, 4, 6, 14, 17–23, 26, 140,
145–147, 156, 162, 199, 206, 209,
210, 218–231, 236–237; Breton,
17; catch, 206; characters of, 20–
23; composition of, 17; coyote,
145–165; Dahomean, 227; and education, 19; etiological, 147; European, 20; function of, xxiv; Marshallese, 226; Navaho, 145–165;
origin of, 17–18; Russian, 221;
sequence of episodes of, 22; socio-
logical approach to, 19; Swedish,
26; symbolic representations in,
20–21. See also Legends; Märchen;

Structural-morphological approach
Tanzania, 137
Taunts, 196, 201
Taxonomy, 193, 216, 223–225, 230,
236. See also Classification
Taylor, Archer, xxxiii, 29, 30, 79,
221
Teachers College, Columbia Univer-
sity, x
Teiho, Ichiryusai, 185
Teijo, Ichiryu, 173, 187, 188
Tenzan, Kinyosai, 187
Terre Haute, Indiana, 97
Thematic: approach, 216–219; attri-
butes, 227; distinctions, xvi–xvii;
domains, 225–227; similarity, 196,
219, 222
Thomas, Northcote W., 128, 135–
136
Thomas, Willie B., 68–70
Thompson, Stith, xv–xvii, xix, 4, 25,
94, 218
Tillhagen, Carl-Herman, 215
Toelken, Barre, xxxvii, xxxviii
Togyoku, Torintei, 187
Tokyo, 171, 173, 179, 184, 190 n. 7
Tolstoy, L., 53
Tragedy, 7, 8, 10–12, 50, 51, 53, 74,
198
Travnik, Yugoslavia, 36
Troy, 52
Turkey, 35–37, 45, 46
"Two Brothers, The," 3–4
Tylor, Edward B., xx–xxi
Type courses, x
Types, 6, 94; of folklore, 194; of
literature, 198
Tzara, Tristan, 13

Uchendu, Victor Ch., 128
UCLA folklore program, 6
Ueno quarter, Tokyo, 173, 184
"Unquiet Grave, The," 12
Utah, 146, 147, 149